CONFLICT WITHIN THE AFL

CORNELL STUDIES IN INDUSTRIAL AND LABOR RELATIONS: *VOLUME X*

Cornell Studies in Industrial and Labor Relations are research monographs developed by faculty and staff of the New York State School of Industrial and Labor Relations.

IN THIS SERIES

PUBLISHED BY

THE NEW YORK STATE SCHOOL OF INDUSTRIAL AND LABOR RELATIONS

A Unit of the State University of New York at Cornell University

CONFLICT WITHIN THE AFL

A Study of Craft Versus Industrial Unionism, 1901-1938

By JAMES O. MORRIS

*Assistant Professor, New York State School of
Industrial and Labor Relations*

CORNELL UNIVERSITY

Ithaca, New York

PRINTED IN THE UNITED STATES OF AMERICA BY

W. F. HUMPHREY PRESS INC., GENEVA, NEW YORK

Preface

THE history of this study, which was begun five years ago as a doctoral dissertation, is a history of several "readings" and several revisions. The author hopes he has carried the process up to the point of diminishing returns. Certainly both the writer and the study have gained much from the comments and criticisms of others.

There is no one more in whose debt the writer stands than Professor Sidney Fine of the University of Michigan. As chairman of the writer's doctoral committee, Professor Fine devoted his time enthusiastically, and in the most generous portions, to the improvement of the manuscript in both content and form. His infinite patience and his devotion to the highest standards of historical scholarship are qualities which anyone in the profession might properly envy.

More recently, several of the writer's colleagues at the New York State School of Industrial and Labor Relations have contributed importantly toward the further improvement and refinement of the manuscript. Especially helpful in this respect have been Professors Leonard P. Adams, Robert L. Aronson, Alice H. Cook, Robert H. Ferguson, and Maurice F. Neufeld. In his detailed comments on almost all the chapters Professor Ferguson pointed out many inconsistencies and other shortcomings which might otherwise have gone unnoticed and uncorrected. Several persons outside the School also read all or part of the manuscript: Mrs.

Katherine Pollak Ellikson of the AFL-CIO staff, David J. Saposs, Professor Joel Seidman of the University of Chicago, and Mrs. Helen Norton Starr, former member of Brookwood Labor College. Their wise counsel is now incorporated in the study.

The final editing of the manuscript was most capably done by Frances P. Eagan of the NYSSILR. For her many hours of conscientious labor the writer would like to express his deep gratitude. His thanks go also to Mrs. Lucy Straus and Mrs. Joan Johnson at the School for helpful editorial assistance, and for typing and proofreading the index.

Ithaca, New York   J. O. M.
October 1958

Contents

TO NADIE LEE

Introduction

THE purposes of this book are (1) to describe and interpret the organizing policies and campaigns of the American Federation of Labor during the years 1901 through 1938 (with particular reference to the mass-production industries); (2) to describe and interpret the ideological conflict which took place between the craft union majority and the industrial union minority within the AFL during the same period; and (3) to describe and interpret AFL policies as to legislation, political action, and other matters which, like craft unionism, were questioned by the minority bloc within the organization. The emphasis of the study is upon labor organizing and structural controversy.

The treatment of organizing is not intended to be exhaustive in detail. Organizational matters are given only the attention necessary to illustrate the nature of and degree of success or failure of AFL organizing policies and tactics. Moreover, both organizing and structure, as such, are considered to be less important to this study after 1935 when the Committee for Industrial Organization was created and took the initiative in organizing the unorganized. From that time on, until 1938, although organizing and structural questions are not neglected, the writer's attention is focused upon the process of disintegration which led to the establishment of the Congress of Industrial Organizations as a rival federation to the AFL.

This volume does not purport to trace the origins and history of industrial unionism in the United States. To do so, the area of coverage would have to be expanded far beyond the AFL to include, for example, the American Railway Union, the Socialist Trade and Labor Alliance, the Western Labor Union, the American Labor Union, the Industrial Workers of the World, and the

The AFL and the Mass-Production Industries: Early Years

"TO MINGLE highly skilled and lower skilled into one organization is as impractical as endeavoring to mix oil and water, for the oil will persistently seek the higher level."[1] This statement by John P. Frey, a prominent craft union leader, gives in a nutshell the philosophy which made the American Federation of Labor the first successful national federation in this country and also, ironically enough, contributed to its eventual split. The AFL was founded, so far as structure is concerned, on the twin principles of craft unionism and trade autonomy, and respect for these principles built strong unions in the skilled trades. The rise of big manufacturing industries, however, with their scores of lesser skilled workers, demanded a new industrial approach to organizing and created other problems which required policy adjustments in the AFL. Controlled by the leaders of national and international craft unions, the AFL did not respond quickly nor appropriately to changing economic and social conditions and, in the aftermath, experienced a "civil war" in the 1930's. Although the AFL outlived its errors, it paid a price—the Congress of Industrial Organizations. Today, the labor movement is again united, but still carries in the title, AFL-CIO, evidence of past struggle.

[1] John P. Frey, "John L. Lewis—Industrial Unionism, Unsound and Destructive," Ms., Container 5, Frey Papers, Library of Congress.

I

The remark that the AFL was the first successful federation of labor intimates, and correctly so, that there were also unsuccessful ones. In the two decades following the Civil War, American unionists tried six times (including the AFL effort) to form a permanent national federation of labor. The majority of the federations formed lasted but a few years, and in the 1880's only the Knights of Labor (founded in 1878) and the AFL (founded in 1886) were in existence, vying for supremacy. The demise of the AFL's predecessors and of its competitor, the Knights of Labor, is explained partly by their faulty organizational structures and by their pursuit of basically reformistic and politically oriented goals rather than of narrow, economic, trade union programs.

The AFL was formed primarily out of protest against the predominantly anticraft-union structure of the Knights of Labor, that organization's pursuit of policies believed inimical to trade union autonomy, and its lack of concern for the signal importance of the skilled worker. Founders of the AFL, Samuel Gompers and Adolph Strasser of the Cigarmakers' Union, P. J. McGuire of the Carpenters, and Frank K. Foster of the Cincinnati Trades and Labor Assembly, concluded that a successful labor movement could only be built around the superior ability of the craftsman and his sovereign national union.

It is hardly surprising, therefore, that at the very outset there was an abiding faith on the part of the AFL's leaders in the necessity of *autonomous craft* unions. The security of the unions and the welfare of their members were to be furthered by a system of high dues which would provide a "war chest" for use during strikes, boycotts, and lockouts and would also support a program of death, disability, sickness, unemployment, and other benefits. This combination of craft leadership and a strong financial reserve was the cornerstone of the newly established American Federation of Labor. The early membership was firmly rooted in the building and printing trades.

Autonomous national and international unions remained the vital source of AFL strength throughout its existence. They also dominate its successor, the AFL-CIO. Through the method of vote

5

allotment prescribed in the constitution of the AFL, these unions were able to control its convention and, therefore, its policy decisions and election of officers.[2] As early as 1903 over one hundred national and international unions were affiliated with the AFL. When no national unions existed to which they might belong, local trade and federal labor unions were attached directly to the AFL national office. City central organizations and state federations of labor were also part of the AFL's structural framework. Between conventions, which were held annually, the business of the AFL was conducted by an Executive Council, originally composed of five officers: president, two vice-presidents, secretary, and treasurer.

The presidency of the AFL was entrusted in 1886 to the devoted and energetic Samuel Gompers. His office was challenged on several occasions, but, with the exception of a single year, he captained the organization until his death in the closing days of 1924. Short and stubby, sharp of wit and long on bombast, keenly practical, he was ever the nemesis of labor's enemies and a solace to its friends. He remains today perhaps the most revered and, certainly in his prime, among the ablest of all American labor leaders.

By 1900 the AFL had committed itself, through day-to-day experience and struggle, to a program of 'business unionism." The Haymarket bomb and the Pullman strike convinced its leaders of the futility of radicalism and violence. An attempt by the Socialist Labor party to gain entrance into the AFL was repulsed on the ground that a political party had no right to representation in a purely trade union body. After bitter debate socialist ideas were eschewed. The AFL renounced independent political action and declared itself in favor of nonpartisan use of the ballot by labor.

Rejecting any avowed notion of ultimate social or political aims, the AFL evolved an economic program based almost exclusively on the voluntary action of affiliated national unions, which would, it was hoped, achieve higher wages, shorter hours, and better working conditions for their members through direct

[2]National and international unions were allowed one vote for every one hundred members or major fraction thereof. City central bodies and state federations of labor had one vote each regardless of their membership. "Constitution of the American Federation of Labor," Art. IV, Sec. 2, *Official Report of Proceedings of the Second Annual Convention of the American Federation of Labor, 1887*, p. 3.

bargaining with employers. Accordingly, cautious use of the strike and boycott and frequent resort to compromise came to typify the process of contract making. This was "unionism pure and simple." Until the day he died, Gompers remained happily wedded to the belief that trade unionism, to be truly successful, should be motivated almost exclusively by narrow, economic aims.[3]

Justifying its existence mainly as a functional institution in the economic arena, the AFL understandably feared and generally fought government intervention in matters of concern to workers. The state was viewed, on the positive side, as a competitor which, if permitted to extend its aid in the direction of union recognition, collective bargaining, shorter hours, and the like, would by the same token undermine the basis for trade unionism and confuse the loyalty of trade union members. Negatively, the state was an enemy capable of restricting and abusing labor through conspiracy laws and the injunction process. Besides, what the state gave it could also take away. Untiringly suspicious of government, AFL leaders concluded that government intervention would weaken more than it would strengthen unionism and that workers, if paid well enough, could provide for their own security while jobless or after retirement. Greater reliance upon government would also have required more vigorous and more frequent resort to political action, a development AFL leaders disapproved. This is not to say that the AFL had no legislative goals whatever. Indeed, the AFL merits at least partial credit for the passage of such legislation as the labor sections of the Clayton Act, the LaFollette Seamen's Act, and state laws providing accident compensation and placing safeguards around women and children in employment.[4]

In the division of powers between the AFL national office and its affiliates, the former was (and its successor is) distinctly subordinate

[3]Samuel Gompers, *Seventy Years of Life and Labour*, Vol. 1, pp. 70, 286–287.

[4]The AFL did not believe that these state laws compromised its stand against government intervention in industrial relations. Women and children were considered incapable of protecting themselves, and the working men covered by accident legislation were usually employed in hazardous industries and, therefore, subject to dangers beyond their power to control. Not until the 1930's and then only reluctantly, did the AFL admit the necessity of government intervention in the affairs of adult male laborers. The AFL's objective in supporting the Clayton Act, and later the Norris-LaGuardia Act, was to remove the use of the injunction in labor disputes and thus limit the restrictive influence of government upon labor.

in the paramount field of strict trade union activity. Except in organizational matters, the AFL did not possess the right to exercise trade union functions. The strike burden, contract negotiation, qualifications of union members and their officers were matters reserved exclusively to each national union and its locals. William Green, who followed Gompers as president of the AFL, explained that the voluntary nature of the AFL meant that "the organization has no power to compel any union or person to do anything."[5] The voice of AFL headquarters, when raised, was advisory or suggestive. The authority to suspend or expel an affiliated union did exist, however, although this was somewhat vaguely phrased and seldom exercised against the larger unions. In a large sense the AFL served rather than guided the labor movement.

From the very beginning, nevertheless, the Executive Council was recognized as a central organizing agency of the labor movement.[6] Perhaps the major preoccupation of Gompers and his associates during the first fifteen to twenty years of the AFL's existence was organizing the unorganized and securing the affiliation of unions already formed. Indeed, Gompers boasted that AFL organizers were "the pioneers of most of our organizations."[7]

The kind of laissez faire craft unionism championed by the AFL was surely appropriate for the building and printing trades and for other areas where skilled, highly paid workers predominated and where business establishments were relatively small. Just as surely, time and the CIO have demonstrated the success of industrial unionism in those manufacturing or other basic industries which employ predominantly unskilled and semiskilled workers—industries which arose entirely or enjoyed tremendous expansion only after the AFL had been founded. This is not to say that, except for its craft unions which sometimes claimed the skilled workers in these industries, the AFL ignored the new or expanded segments

[5]William Green, "A Great American Institution," *American Teacher*, Vol. 20, November–December 1935, p. 4.

[6]The constitution adopted in 1886 proclaimed that the first objective of the AFL was to encourage and form local and national trade unions. The Executive Council was specifically delegated to execute this obligation. "Constitution of the American Federation of Labor," Art. II, Secs. 1 and 2, Art. VI, Sec. 2, AFL, *Proceedings, 1886*, pp. 3–4.

[7]*Ibid., 1903*, p. 74, *1898*, p. 21.

of the economy. On the contrary, very early in its history the AFL chartered a number of industrial unions and, until the formulation of the Scranton declaration in 1901, did not have, for reasons to be clarified later, a written policy on union structure. After 1901 some of the industrial unions were beleaguered by the crafts who contested their right to organize the skilled workers. Partly as a consequence of this situation, the industrial unions in question did not enjoy a robust membership health and in a few cases were destroyed. In some new industries there were no national unions at all—either craft or industrial.

A statistical analysis of AFL membership with regard to the growth of the organizable labor force during 1910–1930 and the industrial location of this membership will indicate the real magnitude of the organizing challenge posed by the manufacturing industries and the extent to which organized labor was able to meet this challenge. After this information is presented, an analysis will also be made of the Scranton declaration, pertinent jurisdictional disputes between craft and industrial unions, and the manner and the results of the application of the Scranton policy in specific organizing situations. This should convey some notion of the degree to which labor leadership, quite apart from other very important factors which must also be considered, was responsible for the poor showing unionism made in manufacturing industries in the pre-New Deal era and will also set the stage for an account, in Chapter II, of the oppositionary forces which developed within the AFL at an early date.

II

Between 1910 and 1930 the number of organizable workers[8] increased from 20,709,232 to 30,246,719, but during this same

[8]For the purposes of this study the organizable labor force is defined as the total labor force minus professional, supervisory, and self-employed persons and agricultural workers. The relevant complexities and perils of this definition are ably discussed in Leo Wolman, *Ebb and Flow in Trade Unionism*, pp. 110–114. The year 1910 is used as the base year because it is the earliest one for which Wolman supplies comprehensive data relating union membership to the industrial and occupational classifications of the decennial census. Comparable data for 1900 would permit a somewhat more meaningful analysis but would not alter the basic conclusions to be drawn therefrom. The statistics presented in the following pages are either taken or derived from the Wolman study.

period the percent of the organizable labor force actually organized into AFL unions increased only from 7.7 to 9 percent. When the membership of independent unions is added, the total percent of unionization remains low and increases even less—from 9.9 in 1910 to 10.2 in 1930.[9] Thus the overwhelming bulk of the organizable labor force remained untouched by unionism in the pre-New Deal era.

While these total figures and percentages do indicate that, in general, AFL unions did little more than hold their own during 1910–1930, nevertheless, they conceal much more than they reveal. Thus in 1910, as also in 1930, most of the AFL's members came from unions (largely of the exclusive craft type) in building construction, the printing trades, and transportation and communication, and also from the United Mine Workers. In 1910, 59.5 percent of the AFL's 1,586,600 members were so located, and in 1930, 63 percent of the organization's 2,745,300 members were so located. Moreover, since the UMW while remaining one of the largest AFL unions actually lost members during this period, it is readily apparent that most of the AFL's numerical gain was accounted for by the unions in building construction, the printing trades, and transportation and communication: the AFL grew by 1,158,700 members between 1910 and 1930 and these unions contributed 793,000 members to this increase. It was largely because these unions were extraordinarily successful that the AFL was able to hold its own, on a percentage basis, relative to the increase in the total number of organizable workers. The success of the building and printing unions is evident not only in their numerical membership increase but also in their increasing share of the number of potential unionists in their jurisdictions. The building trades' unions, for example, claimed roughly 28 percent of all building tradesmen in 1910 but increased that percentage to roughly 40 percent by 1930. Likewise, the printing trades' unions claimed about 35 percent of all printing tradesmen in 1910 but about 45 percent in 1930. The building and printing trades' unions alone, whose potential membership amounted to but 8.5 percent

[9]Compiled from data in *ibid.*, Table 27, p. 116, Table 35, pp. 138–139.

of the total organizable labor force in 1930, in the same year accounted for 38.6 percent of the AFL's membership.[10]

The hint contained in these statistics is that in a large sector of the organizable labor force, unionism was at a very low ebb during the years under discussion. As a matter of fact, the influence of unionism in the manufacturing industries, which contained about one third of all organizable employees (in 1910 and also in 1930), was not only weak in 1910 but by 1930 actually declined both in numbers and percent. In 1910 unions in manufacturing industries (exclusive of printing and clothing[11]) claimed but 430,000 members, and this figure dropped to 380,000 by 1930.[12] Expressed as a percentage of all organizable employees in manufacturing (7,143,-433 in 1910 and 10,088,565 in 1930), unionism in the area declined from 6 percent in 1910 to 3.8 percent in 1930. Emphasis should be placed, however, not upon the decline in membership but upon the extremely low level of membership in manufacturing.[13]

A general comparison of the total membership of AFL unions with total potential union membership, therefore, conceals both the exceedingly low numerical level of unionism in the populous manufacturing industries and the fact that the solid, dependable foundation of the house of labor rested narrowly on the building

[10]Compiled from data in *ibid.,* Table 35, pp. 138–139, Appendix, Table I, pp. 172–193, Appendix, Table III, pp. 200–211.

[11]The printing unions, which could be placed in the category of manufacturing, have been excluded because their degree of success in organizing would tend to distort the status of unionism in the newer, mass-production industries. The clothing unions have been excluded for the same reason, as well as for the fact that the largest of these unions, the Amalgamated Clothing Workers, was independent of, and in fact opposed by, the AFL until 1933.

[12]Because a particular union's membership cannot be neatly and precisely related to a particular industry, these figures must be considered as only rough approximations of union strength in manufacturing as defined above. In fact, they probably exaggerate the real strength of unionism in manufacturing, since a number of the metal trades' unions included in the compilation drew much of their membership from the railway shops—e.g., the Blacksmiths, International Association of Machinists, Railway Carmen, and Boilermakers. The latter indeterminable portion of their membership should properly be credited to the transportation industry. At least partially offsetting this distortion on the other hand, is the fact that several building trades' unions, such as the Carpenters and Painters, which are not included in the compilation, did have some members in manufacturing. See Wolman, *Ebb and Flow in Trade Unionism,* pp. 85–86, 89–90.

[13]Compiled from data in *ibid.,* Appendix, Table I, pp. 172–193, Table III, pp. 200–211.

and printing trades. Disagreement between the craft and industrial unionists as to the most efficient way of filling the organizing vacuum in the manufacturing industries led eventually to the formation of the CIO. Of course, once the CIO became an avowed rival of the AFL, the competition for members between the two federations carried far beyond the manufacturing industries and involved practically every industrial grouping. Nevertheless, prior to that time, the organizing problem was spoken of almost exclusively in reference to the manufacturing industries and particularly in reference to the "large-scale," "mass-production" industries.

Before proceeding, it should be pointed out that the membership figures presented for the terminal dates 1910 and 1930 do not reveal the fact that AFL unions, in manufacturing and elsewhere, grew by leaps and bounds during World War I. The growth, an artificial, hothouse phenomenon, was largely due to the temporary increase in employment in strictly war industry and to a policy (adopted by the federal government at the AFL's behest) of encouraging labor's right to organize and bargain collectively during the war. After the war, union membership fell off about as rapidly as it had increased, although some of the gain was held. Thus, total AFL membership spurted from 1,968,300 in 1915 to 4,093,000 in 1920, but fell to 2,918,900 in 1923 and remained at approximately this level throughout the 1920's.[14]

Some of the more important manufacturing industries which grew rapidly and remained almost entirely outside the union pale in the pre-New Deal era are listed, along with their employment, in the table. A nonmanufacturing industry which also enjoyed tremendous expansion during this period was oil and gas production. Its employment increased from 25,562 in 1910 to 105,224 in 1930. If employment figures for oil refining and "gas works" (manufacturing industries whose employment is included in the category of "chemical and allied industries" in the table) are added, then total employment in the oil and gas industry increased from 60,797 in 1910 to 214,107 in 1930.[15]

The importance of several of these industries to the American

[14]*Ibid.*, pp. 29–31, Table 35, p. 138.
[15]*Ibid.*, Appendix, Table III, pp. 203–205.

12

Table. SELECTED MANUFACTURING INDUSTRIES AND THEIR EMPLOYMENT, 1910 AND 1930.*

	1910	1930	Increase
Chemical and allied industries...........	120,761	269,385	148,624
Food and allied industries, total..........	237,658	379,302	141,644
(Factory bakeries)...................	(13,448)	(40,263)	(26,820)
(Fruit and vegetable canning)........	(9,960)	(38,292)	(28,332)
(Slaughter and packing houses)......	(59,800)	(96,104)	(36,304)
Iron and steel, machinery and vehicle industries, total...........................	851,981	1,313,529	461,548
(Automobile factories)...............	(36,874)	(319,012)	(282,138)
(Blast furnaces, tinplate and steel rolling mills).......................	(272,665)	(342,390)	(69,725)
(Other factories, including iron foundries)...........................	(292,779)	(420,725)	(127,946)
Textile industries......................	776,699	937,903	161,204
Miscellaneous manufacturing industries, total..............................	471,546	1,011,956	540,410
(Electric light and power plants).....	(17,056)	(84,934)	(67,878)
(Electrical machinery and supply factories)..........................	(36,111)	(154,212)	(118,101)
(Rubber factories).................	(45,139)	(109,958)	(64,819)
Total employment.....................	2,458,645	3,912,075	
Total increase........................			1,453,430

*The information in this table is excerpted from Wolman, *Ebb and Flow in Trade Unionism*, Appendix, Table III, pp. 200–211.

economy can also be demonstrated by examining their annual product value. Automobiles, standing eighth in value of product among our leading industries in 1914, zoomed to the very top by 1929. Both industrial and home use of electric power caused the manufacture of electrical machinery and appliances to skyrocket in importance. Not even listed among the first fifteen industries in 1914, this industry achieved sixth ranking in 1929. As a separate category, radio manufacture also developed phenomenally. The value of its product increased from $10,648,000 in 1921 to $411,-637,000 in 1929. Other leading industries in product value in 1929 were wholesale meat packing, iron and steel, foundry and machine-shop products, and petroleum refining.[16]

III

Why organized labor failed to penetrate the manufacturing industries seems to be primarily a story of employer hostility to unionism. To a lesser extent, however, it is also a story of faulty

[16]Harold Underwood Faulkner, *American Economic History*, pp. 405, 613.

labor policies, real wage advances which took the nub off the union appeal in unorganized areas, legal obstacles, geographical mobility of some industries, and yet other matters. All of them merit some discussion, but it is with labor policies that this study is primarily concerned.

During its early years the AFL chartered a number of metal trades' unions which relied very heavily on the manufacturing industries for members. Among the more prominent of these unions were the International Association of Machinists, Molders, Boilermakers, Metal Polishers, Blacksmiths, and Pattern Makers. In 1910 these five unions alone accounted for more than one third of all unionists in manufacturing. It is also true that some of the building trades' unions, the Carpenters and the Painters, for instance, while drawing most of their members from the construction industry, also claimed members in the growing manufacturing industries. Although most unionists in manufacturing were members of these exclusive craft-type unions, a goodly number of them were members of unions which laid claim to all workers in particular industries. Thus, between 1886 and the turn of the century, the AFL chartered the Amalgamated Association of Iron, Steel and Tin Workers, Brewery Workers, United Garment Workers, Carriage and Wagon Workers, Amalgamated Wood Workers, United Textile Workers, Quarry Workers, International Ladies' Garment Workers' Union, and the Rubber Workers' Amalgamated Union. In the mining industry, the AFL chartered the United Mine Workers and the International Brotherhood of Oil and Gas Well Workers. This is not intended as a comprehensive list of all unions with broad membership bases chartered in the manufacturing and mining industries. Moreover, it is possible to identify a few unions of this type in yet other industries—such, for example, as the Amalgamated Assocation of Street and Electric Railway Employees in the field of transportation.

The unions in the industrial category which were in existence prior to the turn of the century created no problem because they were very small (e.g., in 1897 the UMW claimed only 9,700 members) and because some of them, while claiming workers of all skills, actually enrolled few unskilled members (e.g., the Amal-

14

gamated Association of Iron, Steel and Tin Workers, Carriage and Wagon Workers, United Textile Workers). The craft unions, therefore, sensed in them no important threat to their own expansion. The craft unions themselves were not so large as they were shortly to become, and there were so many unorganized workers everywhere that jurisdictional boundaries seemed of little consequence. A few industrial unions, however, and a host of craft organizations were added to the AFL roster between 1898 and 1904, an era of growth during which the number of AFL unions nearly doubled and AFL membership more than quintupled.[17] What is more, during these years the United Mine Workers became far and away the largest of the AFL's affiliates and, with the exception of the Carpenters, contained more than four times as many members as its nearest rival. The United Garment Workers, Brewery Workers, and Amalgamated Wood Workers also came to be ranked among the top fifteen AFL unions.[18]

The unparalleled success of the UMW, the membership growth of other industrial unions, and the increase in the number of industrial unions were developments which the crafts did not contemplate with pleasure. They controlled the AFL and wanted to retain control; they were making handsome additions to their own domains and wanted to continue making them. Drawing their members from select occupations regardless of industrial location, they could suffer only an increasing abridgment of their own growth potential as a consequence of the chartering of more and more industrial unions. Gompers, voicing the fears harbored by the craft leaders on this score, declared in 1903 that "industrial organization is perversive of the history of the labor movement, runs counter to the best conceptions of the toilers' interest now, and is sure to lead to the confusion which precedes dissolution and

[17]The number of national and international unions affiliated with the AFL increased from 67 to 120 during these years and the AFL's membership grew from 311,500 to 1,618,800. Wolman, *Ebb and Flow in Trade Unionism*, Table 6, p. 18, Table 35, p. 138.

[18]Thus, in 1903 the UMW claimed 247,000 members, the Carpenters 167,200, and the Painters, which was the third largest union, 53,600 members. In that year the UGW was the sixth ranking union with 45,700 members, the Brewery Workers twelfth with 30,000, and the Amalgamated Wood Workers fifteenth with 27,300 members. *Ibid.*, Appendix, Table I, pp. 172–193.

15

disruption." "It is time," he resolved, "for our fellow-unionists. . . to help stem the tide of expansion madness lest either by their indifference or encouragement their organizations will be drawn into the vortex that will engulf them to their possible dismemberment and destruction."[19]

When Gompers made this statement he was articulating a policy of union structure which had been made by the AFL at its Scranton convention in 1901. That pronouncement on the subject of craft and industrial unionism was made primarily in response to certain jurisdictional disputes which had arisen between a number of craft unions and the UMW and Brewery Workers and also in response to an industrial union resolution presented to the convention for its consideration.[20] Between 1896 and 1900 the Brewery Workers' right (granted the union in 1887 by the AFL) to organize all workers employed in breweries was contested by the Coopers, Stationary Engineers, Stationary Firemen, and the Teamsters who demanded that the union release all coopers, engineers, firemen, and beer truck drivers. A decision of the 1900 AFL convention, which upheld the Brewery Workers' jurisdiction over all disputed members except the coopers, was not accepted by the losing craft unions. Also the Brewery Workers refused to unhand its coopers, and thus the matter stood when the Scranton convention assembled.

The United Mine Workers was chartered in 1890 with a jurisdictional grant which covered all workers employed "in and around" the coal mines. Despite this grant to the UMW, in 1899 the AFL also chartered the Coal Hoisting Engineers. Encouraged perhaps by the latter event, the Blacksmiths and Stationary Firemen disputed the UMW's right to organize members of their trades who were attached to the mining industry. Getting no satisfaction from the UMW, they brought the matter before the 1900 AFL

[19]AFL, *Proceedings, 1903*, pp. 18–19.

[20]Only the matter of jurisdictional disputes will be detailed at this point. The introducer of the industrial-union resolution, the first to be brought before an AFL convention, was a delegate from a small city central body. The resolution had no direct bearing on the jurisdictional disputes which seem to have been the major stimuli to the genesis of the Scranton declaration. The early industrial-union movement, which was really an effort to amend the Scranton declaration, will be discussed in Chapter II.

16

convention asking that body to settle once and for all the question of whether or not a craft union, in accordance with the principle of trade autonomy, had the right to enroll all members of its craft irrespective of the industry in which they were employed. The convention ruled that because of "the necessity for solidarity among the laborers employed in and about the mines" the UMW should retain jurisdiction over all blacksmiths and firemen in the coal industry.[21]

Had the decisions in these two cases become firmly established as precedent for the adjudication of all future disputes between craft and industrial unions, the situation would certainly have augured ill for the notion of unrestricted trade autonomy. Sensing a need for an early limitation of the concept of industrial unionism, craft leaders took command at Scranton and, upon a motion put by James Duncan, first vice-president of the AFL and president of the Granite Cutters, secured the appointment of a special committee to study and report on the general subject of trade autonomy. The committee brought forth a unanimous report which, without debate or a roll-call vote, received the approval of the convention. The report declared that the magnificent membership growth of the AFL was due to the policy of organizing along "trade lines" and that it was, therefore, not expedient "to make any radical departure from this fundamental principle." Organizing by trades should in fact be adhered to as closely "as the recent great changes in methods of production and employment make possible." With respect, however, to a few industries which were isolated from thickly populated centers and in which there were few workers over whom "separate organizations" claimed jurisdiction, all workers in these industries should be enrolled in "the paramount organization."[22]

The terms "isolated industry" and "paramount organization"

[21]AFL, *Proceedings, 1900*, pp. 19, 89–90, 152.

[22]Even this minor exception to the principle of unrestricted trade autonomy was not necessarily to be considered permanent, for, in the language of the report, the paramount organization was to have jurisdiction over all workers in an isolated industry "at least until the development of organization of each branch [of the industry] has reached a stage wherein...[its skilled workers] may be placed, without material injury to all parties in interest, in affiliation with their national trade unions." *Ibid., 1901*, pp. 150, 240.

were obvious references to coal mining and to the UMW. Although the Scranton declaration was later interpreted to justify the granting of full industrial status to the Western Federation of Miners,[23] it was meant in 1901 to cover unionism in the coal industry. Tending to support this conclusion is the fact that when the Blacksmiths and Stationary Engineers (joined by the Coal Hoisting Engineers) continued after 1901 to question the UMW's jurisdiction, UMW President John Mitchell declared that since coal mining was "an isolated industry," he would be glad to have the AFL Executive Council settle the matter in accordance with the Scranton declaration. The Council affirmed the UMW's right to unrestricted industrial jurisdiction and, logically enough, revoked the charter of the Coal Hoisting Engineers.[24] Craft unions made no serious effort to invade the miners' ranks again until 1935.[25]

More pointed evidence that the UMW was probably the only "paramount organization" the framers of the Scranton declaration had in mind derives from certain discussions which took place at the Atlanta convention in 1911. At that convention the Committee on Adjustment submitted a policy recommendation dealing with that type of intercraft membership dispute which involved the principle of regularity. When the committee asked the convention to declare that henceforth the AFL would not tolerate the existence of "two organizations of the one craft," a delegate put the question as to whether such a statement could not be construed "as being in more or less opposition" to the Scranton declaration, which, he said, recognized the right of unionists "in some instances...to contain within their organization all the people who are engaged in the industry." James O'Connell, chairman of the committee and an AFL vice-president, answered that the new pronouncement "does not interfere in any way with the

[23]See below, p. 25.
[24]AFL, *Proceedings, 1903*, pp. 87, 223–224, 251, *1904*, p. 68.
[25]It is a matter of record, however, that in 1913 the UMW and the Carpenters agreed that all carpenters employed permanently in the coal mining industry should belong to the UMW and that those employed temporarily to build new breakers, tipples, washers, houses, or other buildings should belong to the Carpenters. Also, in 1917 the Boilermakers contested the UMW's enrollment of workers "doing any work on or making any repairs whatsoever to steam boilers." The controversy was evidently settled with no difficulty at a postconvention conference. AFL, *Proceedings, 1913*, p. 327, *1917*, p. 370.

decision and declaration of the Scranton convention. *It recognizes fully the rights of the miners as they are now organized.*" He added that the committee had the delegate's question in mind when it drafted the policy recommendation and that no one proposed the latter as an amendment to the Scranton declaration. Samuel Gompers seconded O'Connell's view.[26]

Assuming the accuracy of the above analysis of the Scranton declaration, three significant conclusions can be drawn. In the first place, the craft unions suffered a loss of jurisdictional rights in the coal industry. Had the UMW not been the biggest union in the AFL, however, it is doubtful that the crafts would at that time have sanctioned this amendment to the principle of trade autonomy. Secondly, all industrial-type unions, with the exception of the UMW, could now be ordered to transfer their skilled workers to claimant craft unions. If the latter chose to exploit thoroughly the Scranton declaration, a full industrial union could not legally exist in any unisolated industry. Finally, the Scranton declaration was testimony to the relatively low priority the AFL's controlling leaders assigned to the organization of the lesser skilled workers, who of course knew no "trade," in the technical sense of the term. To be sure, organization "by trades" rather than by industries did not mean that as of 1901 the AFL wished to prevent or was opposed in principle to the further organization and chartering of unions of lesser skilled workers, as will shortly be made evident. Nevertheless, it is logical to infer that organization by trades was a principle adopted primarily with the skilled worker in mind. It also seems true that, as a practical matter, the lesser skilled (segregated from and, therefore, without the leadership of the skilled) did find it more difficult to organize "by trades" than did the craftsmen and

---

[26]*Ibid., 1911*, pp. 333–334, italics added. O'Connell went on to explain the new declaration in some detail. He said that it applied only to craft unions and that it meant that "in the machinists' craft, for instance, or the printing craft, or any other trade recognized as a trade, there is not room in this country for two organizations. That is what it means." He added that it also meant that "if a faction of a trade breaks away or the organization splits, the portion that goes on the outside may know at the very start that there can be no recognition of two divisions of that organization in this Federation, nor can some faction of a craft not yet affiliated with the organization that is affiliated here, some independent portion of a trade on the outside, hold out with the hope that in the future it is possible for that portion of that craft to be chartered by the American Federation of Labor."

that the AFL's great concern over the years after 1901 was for the welfare of skilled workers. The application and consequences of the Scranton declaration, particularly as to jurisdictional disputes and organizing matters, will now be discussed at some length.

Beginning in 1902, the craft unions invoked the Scranton declaration and the principle of trade autonomy in an effort to detach skilled members from some of the existing industrial-type unions. This is not to say, however, that the target unions displayed a consistent willingness to abide by the awards handed down by the Executive Council and the AFL convention. Indeed some of the disputes became institutions, were "decided" almost annually, and the industrial unions involved eventually joined or helped erect the CIO. The stubbornness of the industrial unions resulted in other cases in their suspension, expulsion, or voluntary withdrawal from the AFL; some of the industrial unions reluctantly surrendered skilled workers to the crafts that claimed them.

The Brewery Workers, for example, victor against three of its four foes in 1900, was in 1902 and 1906 judged the loser to all four parties. Defying the high court of labor, the union was expelled in 1907 but was reinstated the following year. In 1913 the Executive Council reversed the judgment in the case of the teamsters, awarding them to the Brewery Workers partly on the ground that they did not always work as teamsters but often performed duties inside the breweries. The Teamsters never accepted the reversal and always pointed to the 1902 and 1906 decisions to justify its claims to beer truck drivers. Arguing the brewery dispute many years later, Teamsters' President Daniel Tobin asserted that the AFL had both the right to create and the right to destroy and had exercised both rights against the Brewery Workers. Chartering the latter as an industrial union, the AFL had later told the Brewery Workers "on two different occasions... that they could not remain an industrial union, and that jurisdiction over all the crafts within an institution belonged to the several craft unions."[27]

[27]"Proceedings of the Executive Council of the American Federation of Labor in the Matter of Charges Filed by the Metal Trades Department against the Committee for Industrial Organization and the National and International Unions Holding Membership Therein, Washington, D. C., August 3, 1936," CIO File, Reel #1, Microfilm, AFL-CIO Archives.

When prohibition darkened the brewing industry in 1919 the disputes in that area ceased. To compensate for its legal calamity, the Brewery Workers asked for and was granted by the AFL an extension of its jurisdiction to cover the flour and cereal industry. Its officers agreed in advance that "all legitimate claims of jurisdiction [in the flour and cereal industry] on the part of existing national and international unions would be satisfactorily adjusted."[28]

Among the other industrial unions which became involved in jurisdictional disputes after the adoption of the Scranton declaration was the American Brotherhood of Cement Workers. This union joined the AFL in 1903, claiming cement workers in the construction industry and also those employed in the manufacture of cement. After years of controversy, the union agreed in 1915 to disband and to surrender its skilled cement finishers to the Plasterers and its unskilled construction workers to the Hod Carriers.[29] There was then no union in the field with any serious desire to organize the growing cement manufacturing industry.

With the approval of the Carpenters, the Amalgamated Wood Workers secured entrée into the AFL in 1890.[30] The union organized workers of all skills in planing mills (suppliers of building trim and fixtures formerly handmade by journeymen carpenters), furniture factories, and other woodworking establishments. The Carpenters came to regret its approval of the AWW charter and a long and bitter struggle ensued, the Carpenters refusing to handle AWW-labeled products and seeking, beginning in 1902, a favorable decision from the AFL. Ignoring an adverse ruling by an impartial umpire,[31] the Carpenters persisted and finally

[28]AFL, *Proceedings, 1919,* p. 157.

[29]*Ibid., 1906,* p. 217, *1907,* pp. 309–310, *1908,* p. 244, *1915,* p. 166. The Cement Workers claimed a peak membership of 9,000 during 1909–1913. It had only 2,900 members when it disbanded.

[30]This union was actually chartered as the "International Union of Machine Wood Workers." It merged in 1895 with the International Furniture Workers' Union and the title "Amalgamated Wood Workers" was then adopted.

[31]The 1902 convention of the AFL was reluctant to decide the AWW-Carpenters dispute and called in an impartial umpire who rendered a decision in favor of the AWW. Why the AFL itself chose not to handle the case, and, indeed, why it did not promptly declare in favor of the Carpenters, are questions to which there are as yet no definitive answers. The AFL's hesitancy may have been due to the influence

forced the destruction of the AWW. Ordered to amalgamate with the Carpenters in 1911 the AWW, worn to a frazzle, did so. Despite its victory, the Carpenters had no intention at that time of stepping with both feet into the AWW's former jurisdiction. It did not want to organize the woodworking industry but to "police" it—that is, to organize only those planing mills whose output was used in and had an effect upon the construction industry. Even in these mills, the Carpenters evidently employed a selective admissions policy, taking in primarily the machine carpenters (and excluding, for example, shipping clerks and boiler-room personnel). The union did not want to organize all woodworkers because it opposed industrial unionism and feared that "by their very numbers woodworkers might swamp the carpenters in their own union."[32] Although the Carpenters, therefore, did not want and did not enroll the bulk of the woodworkers,[33] the union kept a tight fist on its claim to the entire woodworking industry.

Another instance in which the policy of the Scranton declaration was probably of some importance in the difficulties unionism experienced in a mass-production industry involved the Carriage and Wagon Workers. The membership of this union dropped from 5,500 members in 1902 to 1,100 members in 1910. Although the bulk of this membership reduction can probably be traced to the decline of the carriage and wagon manufacturing industry, some of it was doubtless also due to the consistent claims made

---

the AWW wielded in the Executive Council through its general secretary, Thomas I. Kidd, who was the AFL's fifth vice-president. Perhaps a majority of the Council members believed that machine carpenters were not within the Carpenters' jurisdiction but did not wish to alienate that powerful union by telling it so. At any rate, after Kidd resigned from the Council in 1905 and after the AWW's membership began to dwindle, the AFL, which had endorsed the award of the impartial umpire, began to back the Carpenters.

[32] Robert A. Christie, *Empire in Wood*, p. 196. The Carpenters authorized auxiliary locals for those woodworkers it did take in who were "difficult to handle." Such locals were allowed no voice or vote in the regular locals or in the national convention. *Ibid.*, pp. 195–197.

[33] According to Christie, there is no way of knowing precisely how many woodworkers the Carpenters did organize in the years after 1914. He points out, however, that while in 1935 the census listed 179,000 furniture and planing mill workers (who constituted only a small fraction of all persons employed in the woodworking industry), the Carpenters' total membership was but 200,000. *Ibid.*, 197 n.

during these years by craft unions on the CWW's skilled workers.[34]

Eager to change its fortune, the CWW in 1910 petitioned the AFL to grant it jurisdiction over all workers in the automobile industry. The Upholsterers, Blacksmiths, and Painters intervened, and although the Painters refused any compromise settlement, the other two crafts agreed to the novel arrangement of allowing the automobile blacksmiths and upholsterers themselves to choose between craft and industrial representation. Thereupon, the CWW's title was changed to read "Carriage, Wagon and Automobile Workers." The agreement enjoyed only a brief trial. Discovering that the skilled workers in whom they were interested preferred to join the CWAW, the crafts repudiated the pact and reasserted their autonomous rights.[35]

The Blacksmiths and the Upholsterers were shortly joined by seven additional crafts in a demand, affirmed by the 1913 convention of the AFL, that the CWAW cease organizing their men and release all those it had already organized. The nine unions, acting through the AFL's Metal Trades Department,[36] then launched a joint organizing campaign in the automobile industry. Presumably, they had decided that, like railroad repair shops, automobile factories could be organized almost to a man on a craft basis and that the CWAW had little justification for existence. The campaign lasted from January to June 1914 and was a failure. Explaining that the "dull season" and unemployment in Detroit had slowed down the drive, the MTD confidently reported, nevertheless, that by a second effort "we shall organize the automobile industry beyond doubt."[37]

[34]The craft claimants were the Painters, Metal Polishers, Upholsterers, and Blacksmiths. AFL, *Proceedings, 1902,* pp. 70, 190, *1903,* pp. 224, 227, 238, *1904,* pp. 209, 219, *1905,* pp. 207, 211, *1906,* p. 216, *1907,* pp. 243–244, *1908,* pp. 198–199.

[35]*Ibid., 1910,* pp. 278–279, *1911,* pp. 126–127, *1912,* pp. 320–321. The Blacksmiths justified its repudiation of the agreement by charging that the CWAW was levying initiation fees of less than one third the uniform fee ($3.00) which the agreement stipulated each signatory union should charge. *Ibid., 1912,* pp. 320–321. The CWAW's membership increased from 1,100 to 1910 to 2,700 in 1912.

[36]The Metal Trades Department was set up in 1908 to coordinate various activities of the metal trades' unions.

[37]AFL, *Proceedings, 1913,* pp. 240, 341, *1914,* p. 182. The participating craft unions, other than the two already identified, were the International Association of Machinists, Metal Polishers, Molders, Pattern Makers, Sheet Metal Workers, Carpenters, and Painters.

The CWAW contended, on the other hand, that its own growth despite the dull season (the union paid per capita tax on six hundred more members in 1914 than it did in 1913) proved that automobile workers preferred industrial unionism; the AFL ought, therefore, to give the union the right to organize on an unrestricted industrial basis. The AFL reasserted autonomy by trades and again asked the CWAW to refrain from organizing workers belonging to the several crafts, to strike the word "Automobile" from its title, and to forward its charter so that the word might also be stricken from it. The CWAW put the matter to a referendum vote and reported that only six members cast ballots in favor of deletion. The union then notified the AFL that its members, most of whom were automobile workers, believed that to eliminate "Automobile" would be to vote themselves out of their union, a fate which they did not wish to suffer. The AFL finally ordered the CWAW to comply by April 1, 1918 or be suspended. Believing that suspension was the lesser of the two penalties, the CWAW remained defiant and was therefore dropped from the AFL on the appointed date.[38]

The union immediately merged with the United Automobile, Aircraft and Vehicle Workers, an independent industrial union. The UAAVW grew very handsomely during World War I and claimed a respectable total of 45,400 members in 1920.[39] Nevertheless, the union appears to have been destroyed by the open-shop and company-union movements of the 1920's. As for the AFL's interested craft unions, they began a second joint campaign in the automobile industry in 1926 and that one, to be discussed in detail in Chapter III, also failed. What is more, by 1926, the crafts came to realize that with the universal use of the moving assembly line and the intensification of mechanical production methods there were large numbers of unskilled and semiskilled automobile workers whom they did not want to accept into their own unions.

The small International Brotherhood of Oil and Gas Well Workers which the AFL chartered in 1899 disbanded six years later,

---

[38]*Ibid., 1914,* pp. 409–411, *1915,* pp. 138, 423–424, *1916,* pp. 321–323, *1917,* pp. 369–370, *1918,* p. 129.

[39]Wolman, *Ebb and Flow in Trade Unionism,* Appendix, Table I, pp. 174–175.

and unionism did not revive in the oil industry until World War I. At that time, thousands of oil workers joined the AFL's federal labor unions. Requesting that they be permitted to form a new national union, the oil workers faced an array of craft claims, and agreeing to respect the principle of trade autonomy, they received a charter as the Oil Field, Gas Well and Refinery Workers. At an early date, several craft unions charged the Oil Workers' Union with violating its chartered jurisdiction,[40] and eventually the Oil Workers, in order to gain protection and support for its belief in industrial unionism, helped create the Committee for Industrial Organization.

In one instance the AFL, amid the objections of eight craft unions and after the UMW threatened to secede, applied the "isolated industry" provision of the Scranton declaration to justify the chartering of a union with a virtually unrestricted industrial jurisdiction—the Western Federation of Miners in 1911. With but one minor exception, the WFM was granted a jurisdiction "on the basis of the jurisdiction of the United Mine Workers of America."[41] Endeavoring to secure a reversal of the grant and to establish unrestricted trade autonomy in metal mining, the rebuffed crafts disputed with the WFM (renamed in 1916 the "Mine, Mill and Smelter Workers") through the year 1919.[42] The drastic decline of the union in the 1920's left the matter in temporary abeyance, but in the next decade, when its fortunes showed a decided upturn, the disputes recurred and finally the Mine, Mill and Smelter Workers also helped create the CIO.

The Amalgamated Rubber Workers, chartered in 1903 with a claim to all workers employed in the manufacture of rubber products, including tires, disbanded two years later. The rubber

[40]AFL, *Proceedings, 1918,* p. 151, *1919,* p. 385, *1921,* pp. 446–447.

[41]The WFM conceded that "members of machinists' locals now existing in mining camps are not to be required to join the Western Federation of Miners." This exception did not grant the IAM jurisdiction over all machinists in metal mining but protected only a few locals the IAM had already established in Butte, Anaconda, and Great Falls. It was specifically declared that the exception made for the IAM "did not relatively apply to other trades." *Ibid., 1910,* pp. 90–96, 293–295, 320–323, 331–333, *1911,* p. 125, *1935,* pp. 625–626.

[42]*Ibid., 1916,* p. 331, *1917,* pp. 130, 370, *1918,* pp. 269–270, *1919,* pp. 154–155, 310–311.

industry, therefore, grew up virtually untouched by unionism.[43] A federal labor union of rubber workers asked the AFL in 1923 to take steps toward organizing the rubber workers in Akron, and the AFL agreed with the understanding that the "rights, claims and autonomy" of craft unions would be recognized.[44] No drive appears to have been launched, however. Because the International Union of Timber Workers failed to make progress in the organization of the lumber industry, the AFL in 1916 revoked its jurisdiction over sawmills and logging camps. The union disbanded in 1922, leaving the lumber industry without a claimant union.[45]

The Amalgamated Meat Cutters and Butcher Workmen in 1904 proved itself an exception to the general rule that AFL craft unions shunned the unskilled when it tried to organize the "Big Six" Chicago packing companies. The union had been setting up craft locals in Chicago since 1900, but later declared itself in favor of a uniform contract for all workers regardless of skill. The companies opposed the move, a strike resulted in 1904, and the Meat Cutters were shortly driven out of the packing industry.[46] In 1915 the union asked the AFL to assign it one full-time organizer to help organize workers employed by the "meat trust," and the AFL consented to render such aid, again, however, with the stipulation that recruits "shall be assigned to their respective organizations."[47] With the aid of the federal government, the union established effec-

[43]Theodore W. Glocker believed that the ARW was "an unnatural combination of workers having no interest in common" and that this explained its downfall. Glocker, "Amalgamation of Related Trades in American Unions," in John R. Commons, ed., *Trade Unionism and Labor Problems*, p. 379. There is an element of truth in this judgment, but, nevertheless, the present United Rubber Workers, while drawing the core of its membership from the rubber tire industry, also organizes in a variety of rubber products' industries.

[44]AFL, *Proceedings, 1923*, pp. 343–344.

[45]Selig Perlman and Philip Taft, *History of Labor in the United States*, Vol. 4, pp. 392–393. Until 1914 this union was titled the "International Union of Shingle Weavers, Sawmill Workers and Woodsmen." Glocker intimates that in 1912 the AFL granted the union unrestricted jurisdiction over all workers in the lumber industry. Glocker, "Amalgamation of Related Trades in American Unions," p. 365.

[46]The Meat Cutters respected the claims of other unions in the packing industry and the members of two such unions (the Stationary Engineers and Stationary Firemen) remained at work during the 1904 strike. The Meat Cutters believed the strike would have been won had these members joined the walkout. Glocker, "Amalgamation of Related Trades in American Unions," pp. 365–366, 377–378. See also Perlman and Taft, *History of Labor in the United States*, Vol. 4, pp. 117–123.

[47]AFL, *Proceedings, 1915*, p. 469.

tive organization in the industry during World War I, but after the war it was again driven out by employer opposition. At this point the Meat Cutters returned to the AFL for assistance. The AFL agreed to cooperate with the union in devising a plan for reorganizing the packing industry but nothing substantial seems to have come of the agreement.[48]

The steel industry was not organized in the pre-New Deal period. The difficulty here, so far as labor leadership is concerned, was primarily in the policies of the Amalgamated Association of Iron, Steel and Tin Workers. The Amalgamated had the misfortune of being founded too early—1876, a time when skilled workers still figured very prominently in iron and steel production. For a number of years thereafter the union claimed none but the skilled workers and their helpers, and although this claim was eventually expanded to include "all men working in and around" the mills and factories of the iron, steel, and tin industries,[49] most of the union's local lodges did not admit unskilled workers.[50] Consequently, the Amalgamated remained primarily a skilled organization throughout its existence and until it was superseded in 1936 by the Steel Workers' Organizing Committee (CIO).

Being exclusive became a progressively less realistic policy as the steel industry grew and waves of technical improvements made possible the substitution of a greater proportion of unskilled labor for skilled workmen.[51] These developments, and the Amalga-

[48]*Ibid., 1923,* pp. 217–218.

[49]In 1889 the Amalgamated enlarged its jurisdiction to include all workers except "laborers"; in 1911 the latter limitation was also removed. Jesse S. Robinson, *The Amalgamated Association of Iron, Steel and Tin Workers,* pp. 43–44, 49–50.

[50]*Ibid.,* pp. 39, 45, 56; Henry E. Hoagland, "Trade Unionism in the Iron Industry: A Decadent Organization," *Quarterly Journal of Economics,* Vol. 31, August 1917, pp. 681–682, 685, 688. With reference to iron mills, Hoagland declared that "some employers frankly admit that they consider an agreement with the Amalgamated Association, covering a relatively small percentage of their employees, and these the most indispensable, as a sort of insurance against a more democratic union which might force terms for all men in the mills."

[51]It should be indicated that when the Amalgamated was formed it drew nearly all of its members from the iron industry. Relative to the latter, the steel industry did not become important until the 1880's and 1890's, and the Amalgamated never became as strong in steel as it was in iron because the policy of exclusivism was more realistic in iron and also because the firms in iron remained small in their holdings. Writing in 1917, Hoagland explained that skilled workers were still very important in iron mills because "no inventions have as yet been found practicable

mated's inflexibility, not only made the union less and less of a representative body but also denied it the wholehearted support of the growing masses of unskilled in its early, pivotal disputes with the steel magnates. The situation also provoked, at an early date, a minority demand within the Amalgamated for industrial unionism.[52] This demand, reasserted in the 1930's, was destined to split the union asunder. It should be added, however, that while the narrow admissions' policy of Amalgamated lodges was an expression of the lodges' own aristocratic leanings, steel employers also opposed the organizing of the unskilled and "made their contracts with the union contingent on the Amalgamated Association's not pressing the issue."[53] In its origins, however, the Amalgamated was a skilled organization and its lodges did not wish to make sacrifices for unskilled steel workers.

Until 1901 the Amalgamated also agreed to the signing of contracts which covered only part of the mills of a steel company and which obligated the Amalgamated not to attempt to organize its remaining mills. This practice too became less tenable, and also more difficult to break, as the merger movement gathered force in the 1890's and was climaxed in 1901 by the formation of United States Steel. By the simple process of transferring work to its non-union mills, a company so inclined could easily kill unionism within its bounds. Realizing the folly of its past acquiescence in the policy and hoping to ensconce itself in the steel industry before U.S. Steel became firmly established, the Amalgamated insisted in 1901 that its contracts with U.S. Steel cover all mills. Since U.S. Steel had from the start privately vowed to prevent the growth of unionism in the steel industry, the Amalgamated's demand led to a test of strength.

The strike, a disastrous loss from the labor standpoint, has been ably analyzed recently, the gist of the analysis being that the strike probably should not have been called in the first instance and that

---

to do for iron what has been done for steel in making the latter primarily a machine product." Hoagland, "Trade Unionism in the Iron Industry: A Decadent Organization," *Quarterly Journal of Economics,* Vol. 31, August 1917, pp. 675, 681–682.

[52]*Ibid.,* pp. 683–685; Robinson, *Amalgamated Association of Iron, Steel and Tin Workers,* pp. 53–55, 159–160.

[53]Lewis L. Lorwin, *The American Federation of Labor,* p. 180.

the strike actions and judgments of T. J. Shaffer, president of the Amalgamated, were often liabilities rather than assets to the union cause.[54] The present writer would add that even had the strike been successful, it is unlikely that the steel industry would at that time have been thoroughly organized, for the Amalgamated was still an exclusive organization from the standpoint of membership. It has long been known, of course, that the U.S. Steel victory in 1901 set "an anti-union pattern of conduct" which spread "to most of the other heavy industries which were then getting into their stride."[55]

Currently, there is no evidence to suggest that the 1901 strike was a joint endeavor from which craft unions hoped to derive a membership reward. The Amalgamated did recognize, in the years before 1901, the claims of two or three small craft unions in the iron and steel industry,[56] but in 1901 the union evidently was not yet ready to invite the crafts on a wholesale basis into the industry as the price of obtaining their full support. It should be remembered, too, that the 1901 strike was called, fought, and lost before the adoption of the Scranton declaration in December. It is interesting to note that in the post-Scranton steel campaigns the crafts did participate on a share-the-membership basis.

The Amalgamated Association of Iron, Steel and Tin Workers retained a hold on only a few U.S. Steel mills after the 1901 strike and in 1909 was notified that henceforth these mills would also be operated under open-shop conditions. The anemic Amalgamated had no choice but to strike again. In recognition of its hour of peril and perhaps also in deference to the fact that trade autonomy was now a matter of legal guarantee, the union proposed the launching of a joint organizing campaign in steel. Gompers called a conference for this purpose and nearly fifty unions attended. It was agreed that the nationals and AFL headquarters should supply organizers and that recruits should be divided among

[54]Philip Taft, *The A. F. of L. in the Time of Gompers*, pp. 237–242. See also Marguerite Green, *The National Civic Federation and the American Labor Movement, 1900–1925*, pp. 24–36.

[55]Perlman and Taft, *History of Labor in the United States*, Vol. 4, pp. 107–109, 635–636.

[56]Robinson, *Amalgamated Association of Iron, Steel and Tin Workers*, p. 43 n.

the interested organizations. The Amalgamated's president has asserted, however, that the number of organizers who took the field "was so small that the plans mapped out had to be abandoned."[57] Nevertheless, a campaign of sorts continued well into 1910, and at one point, when the unorganized employees of the Bethlehem Steel Company staged a spontaneous strike, AFL organizers moved in and placed 3,500 recruits in twelve unions, about one tenth of them going to the Amalgamated.[58]

The campaign was uneven all the way and at its conclusion unionism was all but obliterated in the steel industry. The Amalgamated had no steel mills under contract and the bulk of its membership (4,355 in 1911) was located in the iron mills of the West.[59]

Compared with some of the other mass-production industries the steel industry employs sizeable groups of skilled workers; this may help to explain why the AFL made a second and more serious attempt to organize steel during 1918–1920. The effort again came to naught. The campaign pointed to some weaknesses in craft unionism as a method for organizing large-scale industry and also revealed a feeling on the part of some AFL leaders that big industry could not be unionized through militant tactics. The latter point is especially interesting in view of the AFL's refusal, on doctrinaire grounds, to seek government aid in the form of a law supporting the right to organize.

The AFL hoped to organize the steel industry during, and before the termination of, World War I. With employers and the government desirous of maintaining uninterrupted production, with labor in short supply, and with the government committed temporarily to a policy of encouraging collective bargaining, the time seemed ripe indeed. Early in 1918 the AFL therefore agreed to direct a coordinated organizing campaign in the industry and set up a National Committee for Organizing Iron and Steel Workers. In accordance with the spirit and the letter of the Scranton declara-

[57]Amalgamated Association of Iron, Steel and Tin Workers, *Proceedings, 1910,* pp. 8931–8932.
[58]*Ibid.,* p. 8860; Perlman and Taft, *History of Labor in the United States,* Vol. 4, p. 143.
[59]Robinson, *Amalgamated Association of Iron, Steel and Tin Workers,* pp. 9, 20–21.

tion, twenty-four international unions were represented on the National Committee, and each of them sought to establish its own steel locals.

The steel workers, who were at the time eager for unionism, responded immediately and enthusiastically. The Armistice in November, however, removed the other favorable conditions which labor sought to exploit and made success immensely more difficult to achieve.

Rebuffed by Elbert H. Gary, head of United States Steel, in its efforts to negotiate a settlement in the summer of 1919, the National Committee began early in September to encourage President Woodrow Wilson in his efforts to bring about a general postwar conference between labor and industry. Committee members apparently felt that through such a conference organized labor might be able to put sufficient pressure on U.S. Steel to cause the company to accept unionism and collective bargaining. Learning, however, that Wilson had not enlisted Gary's cooperation and, therefore, that a conference was not yet assured, the committee, on September 9, scheduled a strike to begin in the steel industry on September 22. A few days after September 9, however, the President's Industrial Conference was arranged to begin on October 6 and Wilson, for this reason, appealed to Gompers to secure a postponement of the strike. Gompers knew, he wrote in his autobiography, "that the strike would fail" and besides he agreed with Wilson that a background of conflict in steel would endanger the success of the forthcoming conference.[60] He therefore asked the internationals to rescind the strike call.

As a consequence of Gompers' request, eight internationals announced their opposition to the strike when the National Committee assembled on September 17 to reconsider its decision.[61] The committee resolved, nevertheless, to go ahead with the original strike plan and the walkout therefore began on the appointed day.

When the President's Industrial Conference brushed aside a labor-sponsored resolution calling for the selection of a tripartite

[60]Gompers, *Seventy Years of Life and Labour*, Vol. 2, pp. 516–517.
[61]Commission of Inquiry, Interchurch World Movement, *Report on the Steel Strike of 1919*, p. 175.

committee to settle the strike and also rejected labor's proposal that employers voluntarily recognize the right of workers to organize and bargain collectively,[62] it was clear that the strike had to run its course. The strike was lost and the National Committee officially surrendered on January 8, 1920. Although the cooperating unions had enrolled a total of about 250,000 steel workers (70,000 to 90,000 of whom joined the Amalgamated), by the time the dust of battle had settled the open-shop and company unions claimed them all.[63]

That twenty-four unions were able to enroll so many thousands of steel workers has encouraged one writer to conclude that the feat "contradicts the notion that workers could not be organized except through an industrial union" and that the craft organizing technique was not a factor in bringing on the strike defeat.[64] As a short-run view this conclusion accurately describes the experience of the 1919 steel strike, for thousands were indeed organized by craft methods and the campaign's loss is attributable almost entirely to the active opposition of U.S. Steel. Nevertheless, one can wonder whether the steel workers who rushed into craft unions in 1919 would have stayed in these organizations had the strike been successful and bargaining relationships been established in the steel industry. Surely labor's successful experience since the 1930's in organizing in the basic industries indicates that, over the long run, workers have preferred industrial unionism and that industrial unionism has made possible an efficient and effective bargaining structure in these industries. Thus, the fact that the steel workers joined the crafts in 1919 was not, it seems, a decisive test of their thinking on the issue of craft versus industrial unionism. What is more, the events of 1919 offered no test at all of the workability of craft unions as instruments of collective bargaining in mass-production industries.

It would be fair to say that the steel strike did test and prove two things: (1) the strong and uncompromising opposition of U.S. Steel to the unionization of its employees, and (2) the overwhelm-

[62]Department of Labor, *Proceedings of the First Industrial Conference, Called by the President, October 6 to 23, 1919*, pp. 5, 58–59, 79–83, 187.
[63]Commission of Inquiry, *Steel Strike of 1919*, pp. 175, 194.
[64]Taft, *A. F. of L. in the Time of Gompers*, pp. 390, 393–394.

ing sentiment for unionism among these employees—in 1919 they probably would have joined, for a time at least, almost any type of union. In the latter regard, one is reminded of the mid-1880's and the fact that at that time literally hundreds of thousands of working men and women flocked into the local assemblies of the Knights of Labor and then abruptly abandoned the organization partly because they discovered that trade unions are more effective than geographical unions in collective bargaining.

Despite the fact that 1919 offered no decisive test of union structure, one cannot entirely ignore the findings of the Interchurch World Movement to the effect that even in that year some of the rank and file preferred to look upon themselves as "steel workers" rather than as men of different skills and that they preferred industrial unionism. Some of them were actually placed in shop and plant unions by local leaders, but the internationals quickly stopped this practice. The craft approach also led to jurisdictional disputes among the cooperating unions. The Steam Shovelmen and the Stationary Engineers, for example, fought over crane operators: the Amalgamated and the Hod Carriers both claimed the common laborers.[65] Nor is it at all beside the point to indicate that eight of the twenty-four unions barred Negroes from membership,[66] for in the years after World War I Negroes were of increasing numerical importance in the big industries of the North. In view of these considerations, it would perhaps not be unrealistic to speculate that even more than 250,000 workers would probably have been organized in 1919 had there been but one industrial union for them to join.

Another effort to organize the steel industry got under way in June 1923, without AFL aid, but it fizzled out when United States Steel voluntarily granted the eight-hour day to its employees. The following year the Amalgamated Association of Iron, Steel and Tin Workers made an unsuccessful bid at the AFL convention to get

[65]Commission of Inquiry, *Steel Strike of 1919*, pp. 160, 169.
[66]Compare information in *ibid.*, pp. 145–146, with other information in Sterling Spero and Abram L. Harris, *The Black Worker*, pp. 57–70. Among the eight unions were such important ones as the International Association of Machinists, International Brotherhood of Electrical Workers, Boilermakers, and the Structural Iron Workers.

other unions to relinquish their claims of jurisdiction over steel workers.[67] Although the AFL did make large concessions to industrial unionism in the rubber and automobile industries in 1935, it continued even after that date to regard the steel industry as the bailiwick of the craft unions. It remained for the CIO to bring industrial unionism to the steel workers.

To recapitulate, by the 1920's there were fewer unions and fewer unionists in the big industries than there had been at the turn of the century. Unions in the automobile, rubber, lumber, cement, and woodworking industries had gone out of existence. No unions had yet been organized in the electrical manufacturing, aluminum, and aircraft industries. There was no unionism in the meat packing industry. There were unions in the oil, steel, textile, brewery, clothing, coal, and metal mining industries, but with the exception of the coal and clothing unions, their membership strength was inconsequential. Jurisdictional disputes between craft and industrial unions and emphasis upon the organization of skilled workers help, along with other factors related below, to explain this situation.

To the extent that the policies of the AFL help to explain the low level of union membership in the mass-production industries in the pre-New Deal period, what can be said in defense of the policies? In the first place, organization by trades and emphasis upon the skilled worker made the AFL the first really successful labor federation in the United States. The Scranton declaration espoused a policy the effectiveness of which had already been demonstrated in the building and printing trades and in certain other areas where skilled workers predominated, craft lines were distinguishable, and the workers were ripe for organization. Had there been no success with this policy in these areas, there would probably not have been an AFL in the first instance.

Moreover, the dramatic failure of the Knights of Labor, with its emphasis upon the lesser skilled, was still, at the turn of the century, a relatively current event, and the Knights' fate had probably convinced more than one trade union leader that the lesser

---

[67]Metal Trades Department of the AFL, *Proceedings, 1923*, pp. 56–57; AFL, *Proceedings, 1923*, pp. 149–150, 221.

skilled did not make good union material. The Socialist Trade and Labor Alliance (1895), the American Labor Union (1902), and the Industrial Workers of the World (1905), each of which also appealed to the unskilled, had far less success than did the Knights of Labor.

In defense of the controlling leaders of the AFL, one can also say that many mass-production industries were not so clearly defined nor their future importance so predictable in 1901 as in later years. A related matter is that the lesser skilled seem not to have been sharply identified with particular industries in the early years but were looker upon as a large amorphous mass outside the bounds of established unionism. Perhaps this explains why there was an organization in existence in 1902, the Laborers' International Protective Union, which proposed to organize all of the millions of unskilled laborers in the country.[68] (Of course, however, the method of separating men into crafts also encouraged the notion of placing the unskilled leftovers in a general union.) Even John Mitchell, president of the UMW, lumped the unskilled together and described them as a huge untrained mass of "poor wretches," "professional idlers," and "worn-out factory children grown up," some of whom were "permanently. . . below the level of trade unionism."[69]

One cannot contend, therefore, that AFL leaders should from the start have put their main trust in the lesser skilled and launched big and expensive organizing campaigns on their behalf.

Looking back, however, over the long span of large-scale industrial development in this country and the rise and success of the CIO, it is easy to see that the Scranton declaration went too far in protecting craft autonomy and also that it discouraged the effective organization of lesser skilled workers. Had the craft leaders, who controlled the AFL, permitted and encouraged industrial unions to function in the automobile, rubber, and other industries before they grew so spectacularly and became so resolutely antiunion, it is possible that the seeds of unionism might have

[68]See AFL, *Proceedings, 1902,* pp. 67, 115, 143, 220, *1903,* p. 171, *1905,* pp. 22, 142–143. For a few remarks on the weaknesses of this union see Glocker, "Amalgamation of Related Trades in American Unions," p. 382.
[69]John Mitchell, *Organized Labor,* p. 169.

been successfully sown and that they might have flowered just as the industries did. In some instances, a craft union occupying a "paramount" position in an industry (e.g., the Carpenters in woodworking and lumber, the International Brotherhood of Electrical Workers in electrical manufacturing) might also have opened its doors to the lesser skilled. At any rate, as the years passed and the industries defined their own importance, it became ever more necessary to amend the Scranton declaration if the industries were to be unionized.

Why then did the craftsmen support and enforce the philosophy of the Scranton declaration until internal conflict exploded into dualism? For one thing, they did not wish to endanger positions of authority and prestige in their own unions, a possible consequence had their unions enrolled large numbers of lesser skilled workers. Craft pride was also a factor which made some craft leaders ignore these workers. Years of independent organization and association with men of similar skill developed among craftsmen a feeling of superiority over the less fortunately situated workingman. At the same time, craftsmen did not wish to surrender to industrial unions their own potential skilled recruits and did not favor flooding the AFL with new unions of the lesser skilled—to lose control within the AFL family might have resulted in the amendment or repudiation of the Scranton declaration. This may have influenced the AFL in its refusal to charter the Laborer's International Protective Union, although it is very doubtful that this shapeless union would have succeeded even with AFL support. Finally, in the short run at least, the skilled had little to gain from the organization of the unskilled and, therefore, had little incentive to fight battles on their behalf. As Glocker pointedly remarked in 1915, "the keynote of the dominant unionism has been self-interest."[70] These points are illustrated in detail in later chapters.

IV

Changes in the economy not only presented problems of organizing and organizing methods, however, but affected other aspects of AFL policy as well. For example, the antistate position of the AFL

[70]Glocker, "Amalgamation of Related Trades in American Unions," p. 382.

became less realistic once manufacturing employers became powerful and evidenced a determination to fight organized labor to the finish rather than permit their employees to join unions. At that juncture, the AFL's own weakness and its obligation to extend unionism to areas made virtually "unorganizable" by employer opposition were compelling reasons why the organization should have begun to work toward securing government enforcement of labor's right to organize and bargain collectively. Yet the AFL did not seem to understand the need for such legislation as an aid to the extension of unionism. Leaders of the organization did not want government "interference" in industrial relations and argued, moreover, that the right to organize and bargain collectively was already guaranteed by the common law and the Thirteenth Amendment. A statutory law on the subject would amount to "class legislation," and the AFL, its officials insisted, did not contend for special privileges or immunities.[71]

During the President's Industrial Conference in 1919 the program submitted by the labor group called only upon industry and not the government to recognize the right of labor to organize and bargain collectively. The single service requested of the federal government was provision of "adequate information and advice" through the Department of Labor.[72] Although the Industrial Conference did not bring results favorable to labor, the AFL declined in December 1919 to endorse a bill "to provide for collective bargaining between employers and employees in all industries engaged in interstate commerce," which was introduced into the House of Representatives by M. Clyde Kelly of Pennsylvania.[73] The bill died for lack of support before committee hearings could

[71]Lorwin, *American Federation of Labor*, pp. 400–401, 456.

[72]Department of Labor, *Proceedings of the First Industrial Conference*, pp. 58–59. Matthew Woll, speaking for the AFL, analyzed the labor proposal as follows:

"Let us read this report here and see what we ask, and let us endeavor to interpret it in the light of reason, and not by prejudice.

"First, the right of the wage earners to organize is recognized. That is one clear declaration. Are we to have that right or not? I say that we have it in law. We want it recognized by this industrial conference *as a right of industry*.

"We say it is the wage earner's right to bargain collectively. Are we to be denied that? The law again gives us that right. We ask that this industrial conference recognize that right to bargain collectively." *Ibid.*, p. 187, italics added.

[73]*Congressional Record*, 66 Cong., 2 Sess., pp. 4, 26.

37

be held to discuss it. In justifying its attitude toward this bill, the AFL contended that "such a principle [collective bargaining] can only be established through the economic power of the trade unions. In the demand for collective bargaining labor has never asked that it be gained by law. It must come through...evolution in the minds of the employers, who will be induced to accept it because of its advantages."[74] Throughout the twenties the AFL, as will be detailed in Chapter III, attempted to persuade employers that they should invite unionism into their plants. The events of the years from 1901 to the mid-1930's demonstrated, however, that something more than this was needed to bring unionism to the mass-production industries. Without the Wagner Act, which guaranteed organizing and bargaining rights to labor, some large plants could probably not have been organized or at least could not have been organized as early as proved to be the case.

It clearly should not be assumed, however, that a law like the Wagner Act could have been had merely for the asking at any time prior to the 1930's; indeed, in all likelihood, the AFL could not have won such legislation even with the most vigorous lobby. The point to be made and stressed is that a change in the AFL's attitude toward a law of this kind appears to have been in order prior to the 1930's. Government enforcement of the right to organize was needed as a realistic way of extending the benefits of unionism to the unorganized.

The tremendous increase in the number of lesser skilled, lower paid workers with the development of giant manufacturing industries also gave rise to the matter of a government-sponsored social insurance program. Unions in these industries, unlike craft unions, could not expect to develop benefit features for their members based upon a system of high dues. Unemployment, illness, disability, old age, and similar interruptions of earning power therefore became increasingly severe social problems in a rapidly expanding, wage-earning economy. The AFL's answer to the old-age pension problem, so far as federal legislation is concerned, was a scheme to create an Old Age Home Guard as a branch of the United States Army. Under this plan, all pensioners, who were to

[74]AFL, *Proceedings, 1920*, p. 115.

38

draw annual salaries, were to be furnished arms and ammunition at the discretion of the Secretary of War and were to submit to the Secretary of War an annual report on "the conditions of military and patriotic sentiment" in their communities. It goes without saying that this plan, drafted in 1909, was not intended to provide a comprehensive pension program. The AFL looked upon a government pension as income for "the poor and needy" and also realized, it said, "the danger of a further extension of authority over the conditions affecting individuals in the several States, by the Federal Government."[75] The convention proceedings of the years before the 1930's leave the impression that the AFL really did not want legislation on this subject either by the federal or state governments, however. At any rate, when two state pension laws were declared unconstitutional by the courts in the early 1920's, the Executive Council was readily convinced that constitutional barriers were prohibitive and that unions ought to study the old-age pension offerings of the private insurance companies and also the possibilities of their doing more in this area through the benefit programs of their own organizations.[76]

The AFL declined to support federal unemployment and health insurance bills introduced into the Congress during World War I, and although the Executive Council later studied health insurance for two years, it was "unable to reach a unanimous agreement upon the subject of voluntary health insurance and trade union health insurance on the one hand as against compulsory state or industrial health insurance on the other," and the matter was soon forgotten.[77] Gompers explained that the AFL opposed unemployment compensation because to do otherwise would be "to accept the principle that it could not be eliminated."[78] In reality, during his last years Gompers' antistate position became "a veritable

[75]The federal bill was introduced into the Congress in 1909 and was reintroduced in 1911 and 1922. *Ibid., 1909,* pp. 97–101, 330–331, *1912,* pp. 52, 347, *1922,* pp. 141–144, 360.

[76]*Ibid., 1924,* pp. 53–54, 251.

[77]*Ibid., 1916,* pp. 144–145, *1918,* pp. 94, 116, 282–283, *1919,* pp. 144–145, 378–379, *1920,* pp. 176, 387.

[78]Gompers to Robert Fechner (a vice-president of the International Association of Machinists), Jan. 18, 1923, National Union File #6 (IAM), Microfilm, AFL-CIO Archives.

obsession...a sort of governmental nihilism."[79] Since the AFL opposed any shift toward greater reliance upon government for the achievement of its goals, it had no reason to assign any higher priority to its nonpartisan political party activities.

V

Although the leadership and policies of the general labor movement were probably not without their effect on the movement's poor showing in the manufacturing industries before the 1930's, it is already evident that employer antagonism posed perhaps the major obstacle to union growth. At the turn of the century this antagonism was of grave importance in only a few older and bigger industries such as steel and meat packing. As already suggested, it is possible to speculate that despite labor's strategic defeat in steel in 1901, unionism might have been securely established in nascent and weaker industries such as automobiles, rubber, and electrical manufacturing had the leadership sensed the future importance of these industries and used different organizing techniques. As the industries grew in size and power, however, employer hostility took on added significance and by the 1920's a closed-door policy toward unionism ruled virtually without exception in industries which had become the bellwethers of the economy.

In the 1920's, moreover, antiunion employers went beyond the negative refusal to recognize and bargain with bona fide unions and erected positive barriers to any attempted union advance. Schemes of "welfare capitalism," surely not unknown before the 1920's, were promoted on a grand scale in that decade partly for the purpose of staving off trade unionism. Capped by the employee-representation plan, or company union, these welfare capitalism programs also included a variety of bonus plans, employee stock ownership, many plant conveniences, and beneficial, insurance, and recreational features. The number of company unionists in 1919 is estimated at 403,765, but more than a million members had been added to company unions by 1928, when a peak enrollment

[79]Louis S. Reed, *The Labor Philosophy of Samuel Gompers*, p. 47.

for the 1920's of 1,547,766 was reached.[80] In terms of industries, the heaviest concentration of company unionists was in iron and steel, electrical manufacturing, railroads, and public utilities.[81] Eventually claiming a membership equal to more than half the total enrollment of the AFL, company unions stood in the 1920's as a tremendous barrier to any efforts that organized labor might make to tap new areas.

The problem of organizing became progressively more difficult for yet other reasons. In the period from 1915 to the Great Depression wage earners in the manufacturing industries enjoyed probably their greatest advance in purchasing power in the entire history of our country up to that time. Real wages in manufacturing, fluctuating around a constant level from 1889 to 1915, surged upward after 1915, and by 1926 had advanced about 30 percent.[82] Since the increase in real wages was a result of increased productivity and lower farm prices rather than the bargaining of union officials,[83] it greatly weakened one of the most compelling reasons for joining trade unions. Apathy toward unionism among the unorganized themselves must therefore be reckoned with in any analysis of the AFL's record in manufacturing industries.[84]

Also, throughout the first three decades of the twentieth century state and federal courts alike were often unfriendly to organized labor and, in many instances, went out of their way to discourage the extension of trade unionism.[85] Their invalidation of anti-yellow-dog contract laws was an especially sharp and conspicuous blow to the progress of organized labor. Extensive use of injunctions, permitted by such laws as the Sherman and Clayton Acts, also

[80]Company union membership was estimated by the National Industrial Conference Board in *Collective Bargaining through Employee Representation*, Table I, p. 16.

[81]Robert W. Dunn, *The Americanization of Labor*, pp. 129–130; Lorwin, *American Federation of Labor*, pp. 238–239.

[82]Paul H. Douglas, *Real Wages in the United States, 1890–1926*, pp. 246–247. The rise of 30 percent in manufacturing compares with an average rise of 26 percent for wage earners in all industry as a whole.

[83]*Ibid.*, pp. 557–564.

[84]See Selig Perlman, *A Theory of the Labor Movement*, pp. 212–213; Lyle W. Cooper, "American Labor Movement in Prosperity and Depression," *American Economic Review*, Vol. 22, December 1932, pp. 642–643; Perlman and Taft, *History of Labor in the United States*, Vol. 4, p. 581.

[85]Charles O. Gregory, *Labor and the Law*, p. 174.

sapped the strength and broke the spirit of the union movement.[86] As previously mentioned, the prohibition amendment and the Volstead Act practically destroyed the brewing industry and the Brewery Workers. Changes such as the rapid shift in the 1920's of textile and coal production to the nonunion South posed great problems for the unions concerned. Similarly, the development of new materials and fuels and changes in consumption habits placed labor immediately on the defensive in industries that declined as a result of such developments.[87]

For a variety of reasons, therefore, the problem of organizing the unorganized became vastly more complicated and more difficult with the passage of time, and indeed by the 1920's government aid was needed to establish unionism in some areas. The opposition of the business community was a hurdle which labor could not take in stride. This fact tended to cloud the importance of the structural question in the pre-New Deal era and not until the 1930's, when the right to organize was guaranteed by law, did craft versus industrial unionism emerge as a great and crucial debate within the AFL.

[86]Lorwin, *American Federation of Labor,* pp. 210–213.

[87]Examples of these industries are textiles and clothing, coal and metal mining, and lumbering. *Ibid.,* p. 235; President's Research Committee, *Recent Social Trends,* Vol. 2, pp. 833–834.

CHAPTER II

Solidarity

ALMOST from its hour of birth there was opposition within the AFL to some of its policies. Until the 1920's, however, this opposition sprang very largely from Socialists whose ideas on union structure and functions were doctrinaire and rigid. Interpreting history in class-struggle terms, they were committed a priori to policies which would in their theory best promote "labor solidarity," strengthen "the toilers" against "the bosses," and speed the advent of the millenium. While their criticism was truly aimed at the AFL's weak spots, their specific remedies were nevertheless often impractical. To be sure, even in the 1920's and 1930's there were many Socialists among the AFL's critics. Yet, by the 1920's the Socialist party had demonstrated an inability to grow in American soil, and the Socialists themselves had become less doctrinaire in outlook. In fact, by the 1920's the Socialists in the labor movement had clearly become trade unionists first and Socialists second.

In the first decade of the AFL's history, the Socialist opposition-ary effort consisted almost entirely of moves to commit the AFL to independent political action and to the espousal of government ownership and operation of the means of production. The failure of these moves caused Daniel De Leon, head of the orthodox-Marxist Socialist Labor party, to bolt the AFL and erect in 1895 the dual Socialist Trade and Labor Alliance. The STLA never attracted a large membership, and in 1905 it merged with the Industrial Workers of the World, a radical organization which fared little better.

With the founding in 1901 of the revisionist Socialist party and its adoption of a policy of "boring from within" AFL unions, the internal opposition to AFL policies revived, reached an early crest in 1902 and 1903, and thereafter fluctuated in accordance with the fortunes of the Socialist party itself, attaining considerable strength in the years immediately preceding, and also in those immediately following, World War I. Although not all of the AFL's critics between 1901 and the 1920's were members of the Socialist party, the socialists did supply the drive behind the oppositionary forces of this period. Their primary interests were to wean the AFL away from its procapitalist position and to have it adopt instead the socialist economic program, to transform the AFL's nonpartisan political policy into third-party action, and to amend the Scranton declaration in favor of a policy of industrial unionism. They also fought against the National Civic Federation[1] influence in the labor movement and became increasingly interested in federal social insurance measures such as old-age pensions and sickness and unemployment insurance.[2]

The strength and also the doctrinaire orientation of the opposition during this earlier period are revealed by a study of the industrial union proposals brought before the AFL conventions. Beginning in 1901 and extending to 1923, twenty-one industrial union resolutions were introduced into fifteen AFL conventions.[3] Eight of the resolutions were sponsored by city central bodies, five by state federations of labor, four by single delegates from national union delegations, three by entire national union delegations, and one by a federal labor union. Four of the six resolutions introduced before

[1]The National Civic Federation was a tripartite organization formed in 1900 to promote, through the conciliation of industrial disputes and the growth of collective bargaining, more harmonious relations between unions and employers. A number of prominent labor leaders supported the organization, and Samuel Gompers served as its first vice-chairman, a position which he retained until his death.

[2]Information on all of these matters, with the exception of industrial unionism which is discussed in this chapter, can be found in Perlman and Taft, *History of Labor in the United States*, Vol. 4, pp. 150–151; Lorwin, *American Federation of Labor*, pp. 30–31, 73–75, 112–116, 126–127, 147–153; Green, *National Civic Federation*, pp. 133–189; AFL, *Proceedings, 1904*, pp. 204–205, *1905*, pp. 179, 181–182, *1906*, p. 235, *1907*, pp. 218–219, 340, *1910*, p. 251, *1911*, pp. 217–258, 268–269, 357–358, *1916*, p. 335, *1918*, pp. 282–283, *1919*, p. 288, *1921*, pp. 330–333, *1923*, pp. 293–294.

[3]Except for one year, the subject of industrial unionism was not brought before AFL conventions between 1923 and 1933.

1911 were sponsored by the well-known Socialist, Victor L. Berger.[4]

These figures do not indicate, however, the real strength of industrial unionism in the years just before and just after World War I. To illustrate, in 1912 the United Mine Workers brought an industrial union resolution to the AFL convention and, after a day-long debate, it won 5,929 votes of a total of 16,863 votes. Those who favored industrial unionism thus garnered 35 percent of the vote, just a little less than the proportion that was to be won in 1935 at the climactic Atlantic City convention. An analysis of the losing vote reveals that industrial unionism was supported by eleven national unions, nine state federations of labor, and thirteen city centrals and federal labor unions. Also, part of the vote of seven additional national unions was cast for the industrial policy.[5] The total losing vote exaggerated the sentiment for industrial unionism, however, because several of the voters were craft leaders who had either espoused socialism and, therefore, probably did not reflect the majority sentiment in their unions on the structural issue or who were really not voting for industrial unionism as it came to be understood in the 1920's; this point is clarified below.

In this group of craft leaders were, for example, delegates from the Painters, Carpenters, International Association of Machinists, and International Typographical Union. The prominent industrial unions that voted to amend the Scranton declaration (the UMW, Brewery Workers, and the WFM) were also officered by Socialists.[6] The fact that these leaders were Socialists is not in itself significant. It does, however, help one understand the peculiar brand of industrial unionism they, and the Socialists in

[4]For these resolutions and their disposition, see AFL, *Proceedings, 1901,* pp. 92, 152, *1903,* pp. 160–161, *1904,* pp. 175–176, *1905,* p. 180, *1906,* pp. 148–149, 176, *1907,* p. 317, *1911,* p. 353, *1912,* pp. 265, 309–312, *1913,* p. 377, *1915,* pp. 295–299, *1919,* pp. 348–349, *1921,* pp. 391–392, *1922,* pp. 190–191, 204, 264–265, *1923,* pp. 265–268.

[5]The 11 national unions that voted solidly for industrial unionism were the UMW, Bakery Workers, Brewery Workers, Carriage, Wagon and Automobile Workers, United Cloth Hat and Cap Makers, Amalgamated Association of Iron, Steel and Tin Workers, WFM, Printing Pressmen, Brotherhood of Railway Carmen, Brotherhood of Timber Workers, and the Journeymen Tailors. The 7 nationals that cast part of their votes for industrial unionism were the Painters, Carpenters, IAM, ILGWU, Cigar Makers, ITU, and the Quarry Workers. *Ibid., 1912,* pp. 311–312.

[6]See David J. Saposs, *Left Wing Unionism,* pp. 33–34.

45

general, promoted. As already indicated, this matter will be discussed shortly.

A veritable movement for industrial unionism occurred during the four years following World War I. Fifteen state federations of labor and twelve national unions (with the notable exception of the UMW, then captained by John L. Lewis) endorsed the policy.[7] William Z. Foster, who was the movement's organizing genius, formed the Trade Union Educational League in 1920 to coordinate the sentiment for industrial unionism (and for a labor party). The sudden collapse of the movement for industrial unionism in 1923 is partly attributable to Foster's leadership. His interest was to further the aims of the Workers' (Communist) party, of which he was a leader, rather than to advance the cause of labor. When the industrial unionists discovered that the TUEL was a branch of the Workers' party and not the independent organization Foster had led them to believe it to be, they abandoned the organization.[8] Other sources of discouragement to these unionists, however, were the continuing resolute opposition of the AFL to their proposals and the loss of many of their rank-and-file supporters as a result of the precipitous drop in union membership between 1920 and 1923.[9] After the critics of the AFL forsook the Foster organization they turned to the youthful workers' education movement through which they sought to effect a more gradual reform of AFL policies. Their activity for the balance of the 1920's is discussed in Chapters IV and V.

Before the mid-1920's, the proponents of structural change set no limits at all to the area of application of industrial unionism.

[7]The national unions were the Brewery Workers, ITU, Bakers, IAM, Bookbinders, Fire Fighters, Molders, United Textile Workers, Maintenance-of-Way Employees, Lithographers, Meat Cutters and Butcher Workmen, and the Railway Clerks. Edward B. Mittelman, "Basis for American Federation of Labor Opposition to Amalgamation and Politics at Portland," *Journal of Political Economy*, Vol. 32, February 1924, p. 90.

[8]David J. Saposs, "The Line-Up at Cincinnati," *Labor Age*, Vol. 11, September 1922, pp. 18–20; Phil E. Ziegler, "Why Amalgamation?" *Ibid.*, Vol. 12, August 1923, pp. 2–3; "Leader's Mistake," *New Republic*, Vol. 38, March 12, 1924, pp. 60–61; J. B. S. Hardman, "Communism in America," *New Republic*, Vol. 64, Sept. 3, 1930, pp. 63–65; J. B. S. Hardman, ed., *American Labor Dynamics*, pp. 14–20, 22; Theodore Draper, *The Roots of American Communism*, pp. 314–315, 320–322, 370–372.

[9]Total AFL membership fell from 4,093,000 members in 1920 to 2,918,000 members in 1923. Wolman, *Ebb and Flow in Trade Unionism*, Table 35, p. 138.

Unlike the progressives who were to gather at Brookwood Labor College and elsewhere in the 1920's, they did not think of industrial unionism narrowly and practically as a technique for the thorough organization of the unorganized in select mass-production industries. To them, industrial unionism was a broad magic formula for the complete reconstruction of the labor movement all along the line. They spoke of industrial unionism exclusively in terms of the immediate and compulsory amalgamation, along industry lines, of all existing craft unions rather than in terms of the erection of entirely new unions in whose formation craft unions would not have to participate. Their approach, therefore, envisaged a radical transformation of the AFL from a federation primarily of craft unions to one entirely of industrial unions. Of course the amalgamationists recognized that this approach would not disturb the UMW and the Mine, Mill and Smelter Workers and that it would implicitly guarantee an unrestricted industrial jurisdiction to other existing unions, such as the Brewery Workers, who were continually beset by craft claims on their memberships. Nevertheless, they were so preoccupied with the crafts and so consistently framed their resolutions in terms of amalgamation that at one point the Committee on Resolutions declared, with righteous wrath, that the whole idea of amalgamation erroneously assumed that there were only craft unions in the AFL and that the AFL opposed "any organization that resembles or approximates an industrial form."[10]

The very notion that the craft unions could be neatly classified according to industrial location and then merged to form one union for each industry was a misconception. The essence of many craft unions, especially those in the metal trades, is that they are not restricted to single industries but draw their members from whatever industries employ them. A decision to amalgamate the crafts by industries would, therefore, have been impossible to execute in any consistently logical way and would have been a source of chaos and confusion. Also, the idea of abolishing all the crafts was an unwarranted denial of the fact that the principle of craft unionism had a secure and deserved place in the labor move-

[10] AFL, *Proceedings, 1923,* pp. 266–267.

ment, and at any rate, it was hardly to be expected that the crafts, which controlled the AFL, would plunge the dagger into their own backs. Another weakness in amalgamation was that the crafts had very few or no members at all in many industries and there was little or nothing to amalgamate. How, for example, could amalgamation have brought unionism to the rubber tire industry or to the automobile industry? By definition, amalgamation had to conform to the existing pattern of organization and was, therefore, no answer to the problem of organizing the unorganized. It is true that from this membership standpoint amalgamation would have been somewhat more practical during World War I when enrollment burgeoned in the metal trades' unions. This dubious advantage for amalgamation was lost in a flash, however, because the unions concerned failed to retain their membership gains and once again held only paper jurisdictions in most manufacturing industries.[11]

Moreover, an amalgamation of exclusive, craft unions, even if they could and ought to have been grouped by industries, would not necessarily have created industrial unions in the membership sense of the term unless the new unions accepted unskilled and semiskilled workers into membership. The fact that amalgamation permitted the continued exclusion of the lesser skilled was an important loophole which made it possible for certain of the larger craft unions (not all of which had Socialist leaders) to support the doctrine. Thus, although they could never get together on the matter at the same time, the ITU, Printing Pressmen, and Bookbinders endorsed industrial unionism, and what they had in mind was the amalgamation of the skilled printing trades' unions.[12] Likewise, the IAM, Molders, and Metal Polishers favored industrial unionism, and their objective was to merge the skilled metal trades' unions, an act which would hardly have produced an industrial union.[13] It is very revealing to note that once trade union progressives began to advocate industrial unionism in terms

[11]David J. Saposs, "Industrial Unionism," *Journal of Political Economy*, Vol. 43, February 1935, pp. 81–82.
[12]ITU, *Proceedings, 1921*, p. 77.
[13]MTD, *Proceedings, 1919*, pp. 93–97, *1921*, pp. 67–71; Albert T. Helbing, *The Departments of the American Federation of Labor*, p. 63.

of the creation of new unions in the mass-production industries, most of these craft unions no longer supported it and, in fact, became its bitterest enemies.[14] Their attitude changed because they no longer stood to benefit by the policy. Indeed, new and inclusive industrial unions would, from their standpoint, not only bring "undesirables" into the labor movement but they would also be "dual" to the crafts and would thus take potential members from them.

One can understand, therefore, that amalgamation was an unrealistic doctrine and that the industrial plans sketched in some of the resolutions were rather strange. It should be noted, however, that most of the resolutions were formulated in very vague terms and contained no definite suggestions as to precisely how amalgamation was to be effected and what the results would be. In only a few instances were positive suggestions made. One plan, for example, called for the amalgamation of the crafts in such a way as to produce a "Mason Group, Iron Group, Pipe Trades Group, Building Finishing and Wood Working Group, Printing Trades Group, Tobacco Industry Group, Leather Industry Group, etc."[15] Another proposal was to form a single union in the metal trades by amalgamating such unions as the IAM, Molders, Pattern Makers, Blacksmiths, and Buffers; to form one union for the "woodworking trades" which would include the "Carpenters, Joiners, Millworkers, Cabinet Makers, firemen in mills, engineers in mills, piano makers, upholsterers"; and to recognize single unions also for railroad workers, brewery workers, mine workers, and iron and steel workers.[16] In yet another plan, industrial unionism would be produced by amalgamating all crafts "bound with others by the use of the same machinery, by contact in the same productive process, or, by working for a common employer, or, for the same group of organized employers."[17] Finally, a suggestion was also made that "industrial or plant unions" should be formed from the crafts and that plant, district, and state delegate bodies should be reared, presumably in an ascending order of authority and under

[14]Of the six unions named above, only the Printing Pressmen voted for industrial unionism at the Atlantic City convention of the AFL in 1935.

[15]AFL, *Proceedings, 1915*, pp. 295–299.

[16]*Ibid., 1901*, p. 92.   [17]*Ibid., 1906*, pp. 148–149.

the supreme control of the national office of the AFL.[18] That proposal, if adopted, would have remade the AFL largely in the image of the Knights of Labor.

The doctrinaire impulse which lay behind the industrial union sentiment of this period is evidenced not only in the method by which industrial unionism was to be accomplished but also in the arguments advanced in support of industrial unionism. The amalgamationists justified their proposals not so much in terms of a need for organizing the unorganized but as means of avoiding jurisdictional disputes and craft jealousies and of assuring to the labor movement greater strength in its struggles with powerful employers. To be sure these points were well taken and were to reappear in the arguments of later industrial unionists, but standing virtually alone they exuded the socialist spirit of labor solidarity and the psychology of class struggle and shed little light on the problems of organizing and collective bargaining in the mass-production industries.

As to jurisdictional disputes, the amalgamationists were concerned not only with those between craft and industrial unions but with those among the craft unions themselves. In chartering the latter during the early years, the AFL had given "only casual consideration to possible future jurisdictional conflicts" among them,[19] and, in addition, technological changes constantly disrupted jurisdictional patterns. As a result, intercraft disputes began to plague the AFL at the turn of the century. Gompers himself deplored the "unseemly scramble,"[20] and the harried Committee on Grievances cried out in exasperation that if "half the energy displayed in these inter-union disputes [were] applied to the betterment of the condition of the disputants, the effect would be more profitable and redound to the greater credit and prestige of the trade union movement."[21]

The Socialist element in the AFL took the extreme position that these jurisdictional disputes proved that technological changes had eliminated craft lines of demarcation everywhere and that there was thus no longer need for any craft unions whatsoever.

[18]*Ibid., 1919,* pp. 348–349.
[19]Lorwin, *American Federation of Labor,* p. 67.
[20]AFL, *Proceedings, 1901,* p. 19.
[21]*Ibid., 1900,* pp. 146–147.

They added that trade autonomy was nothing more than the application to the labor movement of the "outworn" principle of individualism and that it put labor at a serious disadvantage opposite big employers who stood united in the National Association of Manufacturers and other organizations. What was required, therefore, was the thorough amalgamation of the crafts by industry "so as to present a solid front and increase the solidity of all workmen irrespective of trades"; or, as it was put in another resolution, amalgamation would provide "a modern alignment of the United working class against the growing rapacity of manufacturers' and citizens' alliance organizations."[22]

Compulsory amalgamation, as understood by true industrial unionists and not the self-seeking craft leaders, was a doctrine whose currency in this period can perhaps be explained by other factors as well as the outlook, predominantly socialist, of its proponents. In defense of these doctrinaires it can be said that the giant mass-production industries were not the strikingly obvious targets for organization at the beginning of this period that they were at its end. Also, the number of industrial unions already in existence was larger at the beginning than at the end of the period, and for this reason amalgamation was less impractical at the earlier date if only because it would have involved a smaller area of the economy had it been adopted. Nevertheless, it was not until after the Socialist party sun had passed its zenith and many of its "left-wing" members had joined the Workers' party that trade union progressives began to think of industrial unionism in terms of new unions for specific mass-production industries and, primarily, of the need for organizing the unorganized.

In turning down the various amalgamation proposals, the AFL majority frequently reasserted the Scranton declaration and indicated that that declaration properly set forth labor's position on the structural question.[23] On occasion, Samuel Gompers himself spoke out on the subject of amalgamation. He was keenly aware that it was an amorphous doctrine, for he declared in 1912 that "no comprehensive definition has as yet been found to prescribe its bound-

---

[22]*Ibid., 1901,* pp. 92, 152, *1906,* pp. 148–149.
[23]For example, see *ibid., 1905,* p. 180, *1912,* pp. 265–266, *1923,* pp. 265–268.

ary lines or to classify the elements to be contained therein."[24] From time to time Gompers reminded the amalgamationists that the AFL had always encouraged craft unions in related trades to amalgamate voluntarily and that many such natural amalgamations had been effected. Suddenly to force the destruction of all craft unions in accordance with a preconceived and ill-conceived blueprint was, however, "not only foolhardy, but it is ruinous, aye, almost criminal."[25] Gompers, and the Executive Council as well, also contended that industrial unionism had been proved wrong as a general all-embracing principle by the failure of the Knights of Labor, which they erroneously believed had followed a policy of industrial unionism,[26] and by the fact that the ITU had voluntarily broken up into five separate organizations.[27]

In retrospect it would seem that the craft majority was justified in blocking the amalgamationist variety of industrial unionism. It was calculated to do little good and would actually have done much harm if adopted, in so far as it posited the dissolution of craft unions which had a legitimate claim to existence in areas, for the most part, outside the big mass-production industries. Unfortunately, the whole structural controversy in this early period was rationalized by both sides as a head-on clash between two absolute rights; the parties believed their differences had to be resolved in favor either of unrestricted trade autonomy (except for "isolated" industries) or unrestricted industrial unionism. The trade autonomists made the mistake of reacting too extremely to the all-

[24]"Industrial Unionism," Gompers to A. Rosebury, April 2, 1912, *American Federationist*, Vol. 19, May 1912, p. 374.

[25]AFL, *Proceedings, 1907*, p. 20. See also *ibid., 1903*, pp. 18–19, *1906*, pp. 13–14.

[26]The "mixed" local assemblies of the Knights of Labor can be considered to have been industrial organizations only in a membership sense. All workers, regardless of skill, could join. Nevertheless, these assemblies were not related to particular industries; they claimed membership on a geographic basis.

[27]Between 1889 and 1902 four craft groups withdrew from the ITU and set up their own national unions. These unions were the Printing Pressmen, Bookbinders, Photo-Engravers, and Stereotypers and Electrotypers. Glocker, "Amalgamation of Related Trades in American Unions," p. 362. As already indicated, there was recurring sentiment among some of these unions for a reunion with the ITU, but no amalgamations actually occurred. It should be mentioned that even before 1889 the ITU was not an industrial union, as the AFL seemed to intimate it was, because it claimed only skilled printing tradesmen. For the statements of Gompers and the Executive Council as to the Knights of Labor and the ITU, see AFL, *Proceedings, 1906*, pp. 13–14, *1907*, p. 20, *1923*, pp. 37–39.

inclusive, geographic structure of the Knights of Labor, and the class-conscious Socialists erred in assuming that craft unionism was, in the absolute sense, "wrong," while industrial unionism was, in the same sense, "right." Equally unfortunate is the fact that when, in the 1920's, trade union progressives ceased claiming the lives of the craft unions and demanded only new industrial unions for the big industries, AFL conservatives clung doggedly to trade autonomy. A compromise would obviously have cost them members, but a compromise was needed and could alone have prevented disruption of the labor movement.

It must be emphasized that the AFL's insistence upon the preservation of trade autonomy did not, as Gompers pointed out, mean that the AFL was tolerant only of "pure" craft unions— those which united men engaged in work requiring identical skill and training. On the contrary, partly to minimize the scourge of jurisdictional disputes, the AFL advised unions in related or allied trades to merge.[28] What is more, the combination of trades was a natural development which began, for a variety of reasons, almost from the moment national unions first appeared in the United States.[29] While the pure craft may at one time have been the dominant form among national unions, there were by 1915, as a result of the process of combination, only 28 simple craft unions in a total of 133 nationals. The overwhelming bulk, 100 unions, were amalgamations of related trades.[30] Thus the controversy which

---

[28]AFL, *Proceedings*, 1901, p. 240; Lorwin, *American Federation of Labor*, pp. 67–68, 340, 343, Appendix A, pp. 489–491.

[29]Glocker, "Amalgamation of Related Trades in American Unions," pp. 363–371.

[30]*Ibid.*, p. 362, 365, 376–377. Glocker classified the remaining 5 nationals as industrial unions. He identified 4 of these as the UMW, WFM, Brewery Workers, and Quarry Workers. His fifth industrial union was probably the Timber Workers. The classifying of national unions necessarily involves arbitrary decisions, often the result of how one chooses to define an industry, of one's distinction or failure to distinguish between what a union claims and what it has been legally granted, and of one's taking into account whether a union chooses to exercise the jurisdiction it claims or has been granted. Depending on one's handling of these matters, one could either expand or cut down the Glocker list of industrial unions. For example, one might wish to strike out the Brewery Workers, in so far as the AFL did not recognize it as an unrestricted industrial union. On the other hand, taking a broader point of view, one could accept the Glocker list and add such unions as the ILGWU, ACW, and UTW. For further information on union structural types, see Robert F. Hoxie, *Trade Unionism in the United States*, pp. 38, 41–42; Ben Stephansky, "The Structure of the American Labor Movement," in Industrial Relations Research Association,

reared the CIO was never one of industrial unionism versus craft unionism narrowly conceived.

Related to this matter is the fact that between 1908 and 1911 the AFL created three autonomous departments. Allied crafts in the metal trades, building trades, and railroad industry were urged to join their respective departments voluntarily in an effort to reduce interunion friction, to improve their collective bargaining power, and to cooperate on other matters of mutual interest.[31] Although some historians have chosen to regard this departmental structure as "a perfect substitute" for, or as "fairly equivalent" to, industrial unionism,[32] the departments actually established can also be regarded as devices for maintaining the integrity and supremacy of craft unions.[33] In support of the latter point of view, it can be added that the departments being but loose federations of completely sovereign unions did not resemble industrial unionism any more than the AFL itself did. This was especially true of the all-important Metal Trades Department, which did not pretend to unite unions in the same industry and which provided no solution whatever to the problem of organizing lesser skilled workers. Indeed, it was the MTD and its constituent unions which came to spearhead the die-hard opposition to industrial unionism in the 1930's.

Interpreting the Labor Movement, pp. 43–44, 46; Lorwin, American Federation of Labor, pp. 305–306; David J. Saposs and Sol Davison, Structure of AFL Unions, Research Memorandum No. 8, National Labor Relations Board, May 15, 1936; Florence Peterson, American Labor Unions, pp. 57–71.

[31]For a full discussion of the departments see Helbing, Departments of the American Federation of Labor. The Building Trades and Metal Trades Departments were chartered in 1908 and the Railway Employees Department in 1909. A Union Label Trades Department was also set up in 1909, but its sole concern was promotion of the sale of union-made products. A Mining Department was added in 1911, but it was never operative and was abolished in 1922. Samuel Gompers anticipated the need for departments of this type as early as 1888. A provision of the Scranton declaration not previously mentioned also encouraged crafts in related trades to create district and national trade councils to which jurisdictional disputes could be referred. AFL, Proceedings, 1888, pp. 14, 24, 1901, p. 240.

[32]See John R. Commons, "Tendencies in Trade Union Development in the United States," International Labor Review, Vol. 5, June 1922, p. 867; Perlman and Taft, History of Labor in the United States, pp. 365–373. See also Christie, Empire in Wood, pp. 136n., 167.

[33]Helbing, Departments of the American Federation of Labor, pp. 121–124, 134. The Mining Department, in which the UMW and WFM were the ruling members, must be excepted from this conclusion.

CHAPTER III

A Strategy of Defense

FULLY aware of the nonstructural obstacles which stood in the way of union growth in the mass-production industries and correctly believing that these obstacles could not, at the time, be surmounted by militant tactics, the American Federation of Labor in the 1920's developed a twofold strategy of defense. The organization sought (1) to promote organizing through union-management cooperation and (2) to convince businessmen, politicians, Legionnaires, other groups, and the public in general that organized labor was a "respectable," "patriotic," and "American" institution. That the two objectives were not unrelated is obvious. If they had been successfully prosecuted, union membership would have been increased handsomely despite the apathy toward unionism of workers who were already enjoying higher take-home pay than ever before and despite the absence of a federal law guaranteeing the right to organize and bargain collectively. In essence, workers would have been placed in unions after labor leaders, having created a favorable public opinion, had also persuaded employers to abandon their traditional hostilities and to accept unionism as a tonic for increasing production efficiency.

In its logic, this strategy was a praiseworthy response to all the major obstacles with which the AFL was faced in the 1920's—with the salient exception of the craft versus industrial union question. In the mass-production industries, the AFL national office conceived of union-management cooperation as providing

55

a free entry ticket for the existing craft unions. Even had the AFL authorized the creation of new industrial unions in the 1920's, how-ever, this change would not have made its strategy of defense a successful one. The purpose of this chapter is not, therefore, to argue that the mass-production industries could have been organ-ized in the 1920's had the AFL promoted industrial unionism. It provides rather the immediate background of AFL policy and leadership against which the progressive labor movement of the 1920's (Chapters IV and V) took shape. A reading of this chapter will also, it is hoped, further one's understanding of the CIO movement of the 1930's.

I

The brand of union-management cooperation popularized by the AFL in the 1920's was really a prounion revision of the originally antiunion system of scientific management which Frederick W. Taylor began to develop in the 1880's.[1] Union-management cooperation was presumably intended by its promoters ("scientific managers" as well as union leaders) to accomplish the same objec-tives as the original Taylor system, in the absence, however, of a "scientific" preordained formula. Measures to promote greater efficiency in production and thus to make possible increases in profits and wages were simply to be determined through the mutual give-and-take of bargaining between industrial and labor statesmen. For the AFL leadership, the first attraction of cooperation was not that it would provide organized labor with some voice in matters of production, however, but that it would, through the employers' voluntary grant of union recognition and collective bargaining, permit the easy organization of the unorganized. In fact, the promise of greater efficiency was all labor could offer in exchange for the uncontested right to organize. From the AFL standpoint, therefore, cooperation was a kind of "if you can't lick 'em, join 'em" philosophy; but unfortunately for the AFL most employers did not want to be "joined."

For ten years after World War I the AFL, through the writings

[1] For background information on this subject and an explanation of the meta-morphosis of scientific management, see Milton J. Nadworny, *Scientific Management and the Unions*, pp. 1–121.

56

and speeches of its leaders, endeavored to sell the industrial world
on the merits of union-management cooperation.[2] In addition to
this type of general propagandizing, the AFL also conducted its
organizing campaigns in the automobile (1926–1929) and textile
(1929–1931) industries along cooperative lines. While the cooperative aspects of the textile campaign have already been admirably
recounted,[3] the full story of the AFL's efforts at cooperation in the
automobile industry has not heretofore been told.

As originally discussed in the Metal Trades Department in 1925,
the automobile campaign was not, however, visualized as a venture
in union-management cooperation. MTD President James O'Connell even proposed that such a campaign be conducted along semi-
industrial union lines. In his report to the 1925 MTD convention,
O'Connell submitted that he had for many months been endeavoring to create some plan which would bring unionism to all auto
workers. Since the industry was "so highly and scientifically specialized as to produce a jumble of jurisdictional claims and disputes
that would be almost impossible of unraveling" if the crafts were
to attempt a division of the workers, he was convinced that a
semi-industrial form of organization would have to be used. There
was, O'Connell said, "a tremendous number of occupations in the
automobile industry which could well be combined and put under
the jurisdiction of one organization to be chartered by the American Federation of Labor." He pointed out, however, that this new
organization need not enroll the thousands of skilled tradesmen
who were eligible to membership in existing craft unions. The
committee on organization of the MTD expressed hearty accord
with O'Connell's views and recommended that the Department's
executive council devise ways and means of organizing the auto
workers along industrial lines. Objections to this plan, however,
were raised on the floor of the convention, and upon a motion put
by John P. Frey, who was to become secretary-treasurer and later
president of the MTD, the convention struck out all reference to
the form of organization to be followed and simply advised the
calling of a conference of metal trades unions "for the purpose of

[2]See, for example, *ibid.*, pp. 122–141. See also AFL, *Proceedings, 1920*, pp. 64, 67–
68, 86–88, *1921*, pp. 56–62, *1923*, pp. 31–34.

[3]See Jean Trepp McKelvey, *AFL Attitudes Toward Production: 1900–1932*, pp.
99–113.

adopting ways and means and a policy for organizing the automobile industry." Frey told the delegates that craft procedure "might make very slow progress" in the automobile industry but that if industrial unionism were demanded by the convention the crafts would not spend their money on the campaign and, therefore, nothing could be accomplished.[4]

In accordance with the direction of their convention, officials of the MTD met early in 1926 but were unable to reach agreement on the proposed campaign. Since they believed that several unions outside the MTD might wish to participate in a drive to organize automobile workers, the officials decided to divest themselves of sole responsibility in this matter and to refer it to the 1926 convention of the AFL.[5]

William Green recognized from the start that an automobile campaign conducted along the traditional militant lines could not be successful. In advance of the 1926 AFL convention, therefore, he wrote to Max S. Hayes, a long-time member of the International Typographical Union and editor of the socialist *Cleveland Citizen,* and put these most interesting questions to him with regard to the Ford Motor Company and union-management cooperation:

Could you secure information regarding the attitude of the Ford Company toward the American Federation of Labor and its policy? Could you learn if it would be possible for the American Federation of Labor to establish contractual relations with the Ford Motor Company along cooperative lines and through the recognition of the principle embodied in the Baltimore & Ohio and the Canadian National plans? Could you find out if it might be possible to arrange a conference to be composed of responsible representatives of the American Federation of Labor and of the Ford Motor Company where a frank, full, and free discussion might take place?

Green wanted Hayes to explore these matters and then come to the AFL's Detroit convention in November 1926 prepared to discuss them.[6] What direct or indirect connections Hayes may have had with the Ford Motor Company is indeed an intriguing question, an answer to which the author has not found.

[4]MTD, *Proceedings, 1925*, pp. 22–23, 55.   [5]*Ibid., 1926*, pp. 13–14, 46.
[6]Green to Hayes, Sept. 10, 1926, President's Copy Book #2, Book 366, New York State School of Industrial and Labor Relations Library.

Meeting in Detroit, the nerve center of automobile production, the AFL in November 1926 decided without argument or fanfare to try to organize the automobile workers. Then, hardly before the convention hall was emptied, Green announced that the AFL had not met in Detroit "to make war on industry." At the same time, he issued a "challenge to Henry Ford" in which he declared that labor had long said to management, "We have brains as well as brawn, give us a chance to mobilize the creative ability of workers and cooperate with management." Green invited Ford to become a "manager of men, cooperating with them in a quest for better methods and better results."[7] Apparently Hayes, if he made an investigation at all, carried an encouraging report to Green on the subject of AFL-Ford Motor Company cooperation.

When the Executive Council met in January 1927, Green reported that, according to his information, General Motors also was willing to permit the AFL to organize some of its key automobile plants as the initial step of an experiment in union-management cooperation—provided, however, that there be no jurisdictional fights in these plants. Green therefore recommended to the Council that the ultimate purpose of the participating national unions ought to be "to organize works committees representative of all the organizations having jurisdiction within the industry." The recommendation was approved by the Council and accepted later by the interested national unions.[8]

Green and the craft leaders also reached agreement on the jurisdictional allotment of potential automobile unionists. Their plan required that all workers engaged in "the construction and maintenance of plants, equipment, parts or tools" be placed in existing national and international unions. These unions would suspend jurisdiction over all assembly-line workers who would be enrolled in federal labor unions. Suspension of jurisdiction was, however, to be temporary, the AFL's "definite aim and avowed purpose" being to transfer production workers to craft unions "as

[7]*American Federationist,* Vol. 33, November 1926, pp. 1305–1307.

[8]"Extract from AFL Executive Council Minutes, Jan. 11–19, 1927," Convention File # 11, Microfilm, AFL-CIO Archives; "Adopted by Conference of National and International Union Representatives—March 24, 1927, Tentative Plan for Organizing Automobile Production Workers," Convention File #11, *ibid.*

speedily as possible."[9] Even though the suspension of claims to production workers was viewed by the craftsmen as a temporary expedient, it was the most significant modification of craft autonomy they had ever made in preparation for a campaign in a mass-production industry.

Nothing came of the alleged General Motor's offer, however, nor of Green's offer to Henry Ford. In May, therefore, Green told the Council that he would again "try to get to the heads of the General Motors Company in an effort to see if they would not look on the labor movement a little more favorably."[10] Still, there was no favorable reaction from GM. Green and nine, or perhaps fewer, of seventeen unions which had originally indicated an interest in enrolling automobile workers finally went ahead with their organizing plans in late June 1927. The regular two dollar initiation fee and one dollar monthly dues charged by the federal labor unions were raised to five dollars and two dollars, respectively, in order to help defray the costs of the campaign. There was to be no guarantee of payment of strike benefits, however. Green assigned Paul J. Smith from the AFL staff to direct the drive, and the nationals contributed an undisclosed number of organizers to work under him. Headquarters was set up in Detroit.[11]

Scarcely a month had passed, however, before Smith wrote to Green that no progress had been made and that some of the organizers had become disconsolate. They could not induce the automobile workers to join the unions, Smith said, because unemployment in Detroit made it impossible for some workers to pay initiation fees and because employed workers were afraid "of doing something that would cause them to lose their jobs." The only alternative, as Smith saw it, was to persuade automobile employers "to try collective bargaining." He supposed that Henry Ford was the best prospect for such a deal because Ford was in a bad way competitively and would "do most anything to produce the

[9]The jurisdictional agreement can be found in International Association of Machinists, *Proceedings, 1928,* pp. 71–72 and in International Molders' Union of North America, *Proceedings, 1928,* pp. 6–7.

[10]"Extract from AFL Executive Council Minutes, May 10–17, 1927," Convention File # 11, AFL-CIO Archives.

[11]*Ibid.,* Green to Smith, June 24, 1927, PCB #3, Book 377, NYSSILR Library.

greatest sensation." As a matter of fact, Smith proudly informed Green that he had already seen Ford's attorney, Earl Davis, and that Davis had indicated Ford would be willing to confer with the AFL president in about thirty days. Smith thought it unwise to approach GM until the Ford conference materialized. He proposed that in the meanwhile the best thing to do would be "to keep quiet in Michigan" and move on to the Nash and Studebaker plants in Chicago, Kenosha, and Racine. He was convinced, though, that if no organizing results could be obtained in Chicago, where conditions were more favorable than in Detroit, then it would be impossible to do anything anywhere in the industry except on the basis of union-management cooperation, "at least until there is a change in the condition of the automobile industry."[12]

Green promptly responded that Smith's plan had his "full approval".[13] In the August issue of the *American Federationist* Green again released the "challenge" of the AFL to Henry Ford, adding this time that Ford needed organization among his workers "in order that they may tell him the things he does not know about his production force."[14] No meeting between Green and Ford appears to have materialized in 1927, and in February 1928 Smith was also reporting that his automobile organizing had achieved nothing. Green consolingly answered that he hoped "that at some future time, when conditions seem to be more favorable, we may be permitted to take up again this work of organizing automobile workers."[15] Smith later did return to automobile organizing in Kenosha and Milwaukee, but again his labor went for naught. Green, who had become impatient, addressed a couple of scolding letters to him in 1929 and finally, when the textile campaign got under way late that year, sent him into the South.[16]

Also in 1929 Green attended, at the invitation of Henry and Edsel Ford, the Edison Golden Jubilee celebration at Dearborn,

[12]Smith to Green, July 27, 1927, Convention File #11, AFL-CIO Archives.
[13]Green to Smith, July 29, 1927, PCB #3, Book 378, NYSSILR Library.
[14]*American Federationist*, Vol. 34, August 1927, pp. 914–915.
[15]Green to Smith, March 19, 1928, PCB #4, Book 386, NYSSILR Library.
[16]Green to Smith, May 11, June 17, Dec. 12, 1929, PCB #6, Books 400–402, 409, *ibid.*

Michigan.[17] Perhaps encouraged by this invitation, Green negotiated between September and December 1929 for a personal
meeting with Ford. Although he was promised an appointment,
there is no evidence that he did in fact see Ford, nor does available
correspondence reveal whether Green's purpose was still to sell him
on the merits of union-management cooperation.[18] Perhaps the
final echo of the AFL's vain effort to organize the automobile
industry along cooperative lines is to be found in a letter from
Green to Ford in August 1930, in which Green, with incredible
naiveté, wrote that he had always been under the impression that
Ford "conceded the right of a worker to belong to a Trade-Union
if he so desired and to enjoy this right without discrimination on
the part of the employers of labor."[19] Thus ended the AFL's first
attempt in the 1920's to organize a specific industry by primary
reliance upon selling employers on the virtue of union-management cooperation, rather than upon selling workers on the merits
of unionism. Two years later, the textile campaign, conducted on
the same principle, met the same ignominious fate.

Before leaving the subject of AFL organizing, however, it is
pertinent to note that some of the craft leaders, who vowed
speedily to transfer automobile assembly-line workers from the
federal labor unions to national craft unions, had in reality no

[17]Green to Henry Ford, Oct. 23, 1929, Accession 285, Box 958, Ford Motor Company Archives; Green to Henry and Edsel Ford, October 1929, PCB #6, Book
406, NYSSILR Library. Green later told Ernest G. Liebold, Henry Ford's secretary,
that he regarded his attendance at the Edison Golden Jubilee Celebration "as an
outstanding event in my life" and "as a rare event filled with deep significance."
Green to Liebold, July 24, 1936, PCB #21, Book 562, NYSSILR Library.

[18]See Liebold to Peter J. Brady (president of the Federation Bank and Trust
Company), Sept. 10, 1929; Green to Liebold, Oct. 23, 1929; Liebold to Green, Nov.
25, Dec. 6, 1929; and Green to Liebold, Dec. 8(?), 1929: Accession 285, Box 931, Ford
Motor Company Archives.

[19]Green made this statement after he had received news alleging that Ford dealers
in Seattle, Washington, had refused to deal with an AFL local union of automobile
mechanics and its individual members. Green hoped that Henry Ford would adjust
the situation in the AFL's favor, but he was informed that the Ford Motor Company
did not tamper with the labor policies of its dealer organizations. See Green to
Ford, Aug. 5, 1930; Liebold to Green, Aug. 14, 1930; James A. Duncan (business
representative of Auto Mechanics' Local Union No. 289) to Arthur O. Wharton
(president of the IAM), Sept. 10, 1930; Green to Liebold, Oct. 1, 1930; W. C. Asen
(chief clerk of the Seattle district agency of the Ford Motor Company) to Liebold,
Dec. 2, 1930; Liebold to Green, Dec. 12, 1930; Green to Liebold, Dec. 16, 1930:
Accession 285, Box 1085, *ibid.*

intention to do so. They did not want unskilled and semiskilled workers in their unions and believed, as other craft unionists had believed in earlier years, that such workers would not "stick" with the unions even if they were accepted as members. This attitude is illustrated in the following statement of the grand lodge officers of the IAM: "Our opinion [they reported to the 1928 convention of the IAM] regarding the automobile production plant is that *we cannot expect to secure or hold* any large number of the workers in these plants other than the toolmakers, equipment, maintenance and construction men."[20] Yet, of course, these leaders did not surrender their claims of jurisdiction over the lesser skilled workers. John P. Frey, a staunch defender of craft organizing, privately admitted in 1935 that he had felt for many years "that the policy of some International Unions gave some cause for the criticism that they would not take into their organizations semi-skilled [and unskilled] workmen, while on the other hand, they refused to permit these groups to secure charters from the A. F. of L."[21] This paradox helped propel insurgency within the American Federation of Labor.

On the other hand, William Green, although obliged as AFL president to execute the policy decisions of the controlling craft bloc, personally would have preferred an industrial union drive in the automobile industry. In January 1927 he began to write in the *American Federationist* of the extreme difficulty of organizing large-scale industries along craft lines, suggesting that new national and international unions be created in those industries.[22]

II

In addition to the AFL's organizing campaigns in specific industries, the Metal Trades Department attempted between 1928 and 1931 to establish unionism in many large-scale industries at once through a general conference with employers. The mastermind of this effort was John P. Frey. Frey had gained a brilliant reputation

[20]IAM, *Proceedings, 1928*, p. 72, italics added.
[21]Frey to Thomas J. Donnelly, Nov. 16, 1935, Container 8, Frey papers.
[22]See the *American Federationist*, Vol. 34, January 1927, p. 18; Vol. 34, March 1927, p. 277; Vol. 34, May 1927, p. 536; Vol. 35, June 1928, pp. 661–662; Vol. 35, December 1928, pp. 1426, 1428.

in trade union circles as editor of the *Molders' Journal* and became secretary-treasurer of the MTD in 1927. His proposed conference has not heretofore been a matter of public record; it will therefore be described in some detail.

In December 1927 at a meeting of the American Economic Association in Washington, Frey was won over to the notion that open-shop and company-union employers could be induced by gentle means to accept trade unionism. On that occasion Frey was introduced to a personal friend of Magnus W. Alexander (president of the National Industrial Conference Board) who informed him, Frey later revealed, of a "growing conviction on the part of Mr. Alexander and the leaders of his group, that present policies toward the trade union movement, which are carried out by many large employers, are unsound; that neither finance and management on the one hand or labor on the other is competent to work out long time, satisfactory adjustments between employer and employee; that what is required is a coming together around a conference table in an entirely different manner from what takes place in company unions." Frey warmed to the idea, and upon invitation, he conferred with some of the men who held this view. Subsequently, Frey and Alexander tried, in an undisclosed manner, to bring representatives of labor and industry together in a national conference, but their efforts were futile.[23] Thereupon Frey broke his contact with the Alexander group, but his interest in an industrial conference was sharpened rather than dulled by his experience.

In the hope that he might persuade President Hoover to aid in effecting the kind of a conference he had in mind, Frey secured an audience with him in April 1929. He confided to the President that an industrial conference would have to be secret and without direct government sponsorship in order to permit conferees "to frankly lay their cards on the table in an attempt to reach a common understanding." Since Hoover favored "something in the nature of a commission," which Frey could not approve, the

[23]Frey to Walter A. Draper, Dec. 30, 1927, Container 8, Frey Papers; Frey to George L. Berry, April 1, 1929, Container 13, *ibid*. For Alexander's connection with the NICB, see Alexander to Edsel B. Ford, May 13, 1929, Accession 6, Box 114, Ford Motor Company Archives.

meeting brought little satisfaction to Frey. He continued, however, to discuss the matter with persons close to the President "whenever the opportunity presented itself."[24]

Several months after his talk with Hoover, Frey conferred with Assistant Secretary of Commerce Julius Klein. Frankly admitting that the policy of militant unionism had failed to establish collective bargaining in the mass-production industries, Frey suggested that the AFL could adopt either of two alternative policies as regards these industries: it could seek government intervention in industrial relations or it could attempt to persuade big employers to accept collective bargaining voluntarily. His mind was clear of doubt as to the better course. Collective bargaining, he said, "is immeasurably more advantageous as well as practical, than . . . the enactment of legislation which, history teaches, cannot be either successful or enforcible [sic]."[25]

At a later meeting with Klein, Frey proposed that a nationwide labor-management conference be arranged.[26] When informed of this idea, Secretary of Commerce Robert P. Lamont was favorably impressed and, after sounding out several prominent industrialists as to their attitude, resolved to try to bring representatives of labor and industry together.[27] He and Frey agreed that the conference should begin, if possible, sometime in February 1930 in New York City.[28] Frey intended that, on the labor side, the conference would initially involve only the Metal Trades Department as represented by himself, James O'Connell (president of the MTD), James Wilson (president of the Pattern Makers), and Arthur O. Wharton (president of the International Association of Machinists). If success seemed likely, however, Frey planned to call in William Green and John Coefield (president of the Plumbers and a member of the AFL Executive Council) to represent the AFL and to help

[24]Frey described his conversation with Hoover in a letter to James Wilson, president of the Pattern Makers. Frey to Wilson, Jan. 28, 1930, Container 7, Frey Papers.

[25]Frey to Klein, Aug. 15, 1929, Container 7, ibid. The typewritten letter is actually dated 1928, but this must be a typographical error, since Klein did not become Assistant Secretary of Commerce until 1929.

[26]Frey to Klein, Dec. 9, 1929, Container 7, ibid.

[27]Frey to O'Connell, Jan. 10, 1930, Container 7, ibid.

[28]Lamont to Frey, Jan. 8, 1930; Frey to O'Connell, Jan. 10, 1930, Container 7, ibid.

negotiate a more general agreement.[29] Industrialists whom Frey named as willing to participate in the proposed conference were Walter Teagle (chief representative of Standard Oil), Alfred P. Sloan (president of General Motors), Myron C. Taylor (president of United States Steel), Gerard Swope (president of General Electric), Owen D. Young (chairman of the board of directors of General Electric), A. W. Robertson (chairman of the Westinghouse board of directors), Henry M. Robinson (banker and chairman of the board of the Newport News Dry Dock and Shipbuilding Company), Alexander Legge (president of International Harvester), and Robert P. Lamont.[30]

The first portent of failure was Lamont's difficulty in obtaining the cooperation of the industrialists, some of whom chose to cold-shoulder the plan. According to Frey, word of their resistance reached President Hoover "with the result the President let certain gentlemen know that he favored the conference, and desired their participation."[31] Whatever may have been the nature of Hoover's intervention, Frey believed that the President had whipped the industrialists into line and, therefore, that the conference, which finally had been arranged to open on February 12, 1930, would materialize. In fact, Frey seemed confident that the conference would bring results of far-reaching consequence to the labor movement and especially to the metal trades' unions. "Time alone will tell what will result," Frey wrote to Wilson on January 28, 1930, "but I feel that it is the greatest opportunity which has come to us since the war. If we can put our thoughts across, as I am certain we can, we will open doors which have been closed to us for many years." A few days later he told Wilson that the conference "should be the beginning...of a relationship which should permit us to once more do business with the big corporations employing metal trades workers....As a matter of fact, before we get through it may go a little farther."[32]

[29]Frey to O'Connell, Jan. 10, 1930, Container 7, *ibid.* Later Joseph A. Franklin, president of the Boilermakers, was named to replace O'Connell.

[30]Typewritten list of prospective conference representatives, Container 7, *ibid.* Frey also mentioned most of these men as representatives of industry for the conference in the course of his correspondence with the labor representatives.

[31]Frey to Wilson, Jan. 28, 1930, Container 7, *ibid.*

[32]Frey to Wilson, Jan. 28, 31, 1930, Container 7, *ibid.*

Frey's high hopes for an industrial conference were abruptly dashed, however, on February 10, when Lamont informed him that some important industrialists would be unable to attend the conference.[33] Frey and Lamont made further unsuccessful attempts to hold an industrial conference in April and in June 1930 and in August 1931. The second and third attempts, like the first, failed because of difficulties with spokesmen for industry. To Frey's chagrin, the fourth and last effort, which seemed at one point near victory, came to naught because of opposition from the union side[34] —and another setback was recorded for the AFL's policy of attempting peacefully to persuade employers to abandon their hostility toward unions.

Some AFL leaders in the 1920's also tried to inject new life into the National Civic Federation, an organization which had been of little value to organized labor for many years, although at one time it had tried to spread collective bargaining and settle industrial disputes. They visualized the NCF as a convenient forum in which to air labor's views and through which to develop rewarding contacts with the organization's employer and public representatives. Among the labor leaders who took an active part in NCF affairs in the 1920's were Samuel Gompers, Matthew Woll (an Executive Council member and president of the Photo-Engravers' Union), Hugh Frayne (an AFL national representative), and Frank Morrison (secretary of the AFL).[35] Some of the employer and public representatives who met with labor in the NCF were Elihu Root, Owen D. Young, Nicholas F. Brady (president of the New York Edison Company), Ralph M. Easely (founder of the NCF and chairman of its executive council), Samuel Insull (president of Commonwealth Edison Company), Nathan L. Miller (general counsel for United States Steel), E. K. Hall (vice-president of American Telephone and Telegraph), Robert P. Lamont (president of American Steel Foundries), and the banker Otto H.

[33]Frey to Wilson, Feb. 10, 1930, Container 7, *ibid.*

[34]Lamont to Frey, April 7, June 3, 17, 1930; June 19, 1931; Frey to Wharton, Aug. 21, 28, 1931; Wharton to Frey, Aug. 21, 31, 1931; Franklin to Frey, Aug. 24, 31, 1931; Frey to Franklin, Aug. 28, 1931; Wilson to Frey, Aug. 25, 31, 1931; Frey to Wilson, Aug. 28, 1931; Owen D. Young to Frey, Aug. 31, 1931; Frey to Young, Sept. 1, 1931; Green to Frey, Sept. 2, 1931: Container 7, *ibid.*

[35]Green, *National Civic Federation,* p. 429.

67

Kahn.[36] Many in the employer group, including Young, Brady, Insull, Miller, and Hall, were representatives of open-shop or company-union industries. Woll was elected to an NCF vice-presidency in January 1926 and became acting-president in June of that year upon the death of Judge Alton B. Parker, who had served as president for many years.[37]

Perhaps the most significant policy development in the NCF in the 1920's was the attempt of some of its leaders, including Matthew Woll, to establish a *modus vivendi* between organized labor and nonunion employers. It is particularly the NCF activities with regard to this policy which justify a suspicion that some AFL leaders were willing to discuss a compromise with company unionism in order to organize the unorganized. Thus, in a pamphlet mailed to businessmen in 1924, Easely built up the case for an industrial relations department in the NCF by first declaring that the labor movement of every industrial country except the United States was in the hands of Communists or radical Socialists who were "harassing their governments." In contrast, at its El Paso convention, the AFL had discussed a working arrangement with the Citizens' Military Training Camps,[38] had voted overwhelmingly against the diplomatic recognition of Soviet Russia by the United States and against the formation of a labor political party, and had reaffirmed its traditional opposition to government "interference in industry." "In the light of such a record...," Easely queried, "Why should any good American be opposed to the trade union movement?"

Easely noted, however, that a number of employers did not appreciate the AFL's "worthy record" and were in fact intensely antiunion in outlook. The situation was anomalous and raised the question of whether something could be done "to allay this bitterness between two forces which, logically, should be working together against common foes whose philosophy spells the taking over of all their property and the government as well? In other words: Can a *modus vivendi* be established?"

[36]*Ibid.; New Leader*, Jan. 19, 26, 1929; *New York Times*, Dec. 14, 1925, Feb. 6, 1928.
[37]*New York Times*, Jan. 30, July 5, 1926.
[38]Discussed further below, pp. 74–78.

Although he listed a number of obstacles to the achievement of harmony in industry, Easely believed that an effort should be made along this line and that the NCF should set up a department on industrial relations the purpose of which would be "to seek a common ground for the two great forces, capital and labor, reducing to a minimum the existing friction and misunderstanding." In fact, Easely announced that Judge Parker had already appointed a committee to organize such a department. He listed Woll, Frayne, and the presidents of two railroad brotherhoods as the labor representatives on the committee.[39]

The department was set up and, in April 1925, held its first round-table discussion in New York City. Speakers at the meeting included Herbert Hoover, William Green, and Gerard Swope.[40]

About two years later Easely acknowledged, in a letter to Matthew Woll, that the NCF had held talks on the subject of a trade-union company-union compromise and that additional talks were in the offing:

In my last Labor Day address [Easely informed Woll], after reciting the fine achievements of the trade unions and the vicious attacks being made upon them by certain anti-union employers' organizations, there was proposed the holding of a conference with a view to finding a *modus vivendi* between the bona fide unions and the so-called "Right Wing" employers who, while maintaining company unions in their plants, do appreciate the splendid stand taken by the American labor leaders in contrast with that of the leaders of the English Labor Party.

Growing out of that article, as you know, there have been held three important conferences which you have attended, two executive and the other public, and which will, we hope, go far toward eventually achieving the aim sought. The public conference, as you will recall, was held to discuss the so-called B & O Labor Plan. . . . The committee appointed by you to study a method for promoting the cooperative principles of that plan has already begun its work.[41]

Perhaps the latter committee was the one the noted educator John Dewey had in mind when in 1929 he charged that Woll

[39]Easely, *Proposed Industrial Relations Department, the National Civic Federation,* pp. 1–2.
[40]Alton B. Parker to Edsel Ford, May 14, 1925, Accession 6, Box 69, Ford Motor Company Archives.
[41]Easely to Woll, March 3, 1927, printed in the *New Leader,* Jan. 26, 1929.

69

was still chairman of an NCF committee whose avowed purpose was "to find a *modus vivendi* between employers having company unions and the regular labor unions.[42]

Both William Green and John P. Frey also seem to have been willing at least to discuss the possibility of a compromise between company unionism and trade unionism. Both of these men tried to arrange a private meeting with Owen D. Young of General Electric, a company-union concern, to ascertain how far GE might be willing to go toward establishing a cooperative relationship with organized labor. Green used the Industrial Relations Department of the NCF as the channel through which he hoped to effect such a meeting.[43] Frey, at least, was successful in his endeavor and, after meeting Young, he reported to Green that he (Frey) was

rather surprised at the frankness with which Mr. Young discussed his attitude toward company unions. Referring to the one in the General Electric, he said it was his hope that a way would be found through which the employees of the GE, *in addition to the company union,* would be members of the trade union of their respective crafts and occupations. That a way would be found through which trade union activities and responsibilities could be carried on without conflicting with the beneficial features. . . and the purchasing of homes which the GE had established.[44]

To be sure, Frey did not say that he agreed with Young, but neither did he say that he disagreed, and one might even interpret the spirit or tone of his letter as one of approval of Young's views.

Throughout the 1920's and into the following decade the AFL sold advertising space in the *American Federationist* to concerns which at that time had company unions or operated on the open-shop principle. Among these concerns were General Electric, Westinghouse, American Telephone and Telegraph, Standard Oil, Procter and Gamble, General Motors, Chrysler Corporation, and the Botany Worsted Mills of Passaic, New Jersey.[45] Officially the

[42]Dewey, "Labor Politics and Labor Education," *New Republic,* Vol. 57, Jan. 9, 1929, p. 212.

[43]See Green to Easely, Sept. 14, 1926, Feb. 16, March 9, 1927, PCB #2, 3, Books 366, 372; Green to Robert Fechner (vice-president of the Machinists), Dec. 15, 1927, PCB #4, Book 382, NYSSILR Library.

[44]Frey to Green, Aug. 20, 1931, Container 7, Frey Papers, italics added.

[45]Examine almost any issue of the *American Federationist* published during 1920–1934. See also, Robert W. Bruere, "Resolution No. 68; the A. F. of L. Goes in for Research," *Survey,* Vol. 57, Dec. 15, 1926, p. 375.

practice was justified on financial grounds,[46] but one suspects that it was also designed as evidence to businessmen that organized labor could be and wanted to be of some service in promoting the sale of their products. It was stopped in 1935 when the AFL convention adopted a resolution on the subject proposed by John L. Lewis.[47]

It should be stated, however, that in its official pronouncements in the 1920's, the AFL took a firm stand against company unions and considered union-management cooperation to be the substitute for (and not to be complementary to) company unions.[48] Also, Green assured a rank-and-file unionist, who had become disturbed about Woll's NCF activities, that he (Green) was "satisfied that Vice-President Woll is not engaged in trying to bring about cooperation between company unions and organized labor."[49]

III

Pertinent to the AFL's desire that it be known and accepted as a loyal, patriotic, and American organization are the contacts and alignments its leaders developed with military institutions and personnel. From 1919 and until his death in 1924, Samuel Gompers lectured annually at the Army War College in Washington and the Naval War College in Newport.[50] For many years after 1924 Frey was also a frequent lecturer at the Army War College and the Army Industrial College.[51] William Green was often asked to address the Army War College in the 1920's, and accepting the invitation in 1925, he fervently assured his listeners that labor "is intensely patriotic and conscientiously devoted to American ideals, to American institutions and to the American form of government. . . . I can say with certainty [he concluded] . . . that . . . labor . . . will

[46]Bruere, "Resolution No. 68," *Survey*, Vol. 57, Dec. 15, 1926, p. 375.
[47]AFL, *Proceedings, 1935*, pp. 793–794.
[48]*Ibid., 1925*, pp. 33–34, 230, *1926*, pp. 7–8, 45–46, 169–170, 286–293, *1927*, pp. 42–43, 318, *1928*, pp. 37, 115, 256.
[49]Green to E. F. Stout, Jan. 18, 1929, PCB #5, Book 396, NYSSILR Library.
[50]Gompers, *Seventy Years of Life and Labour*, Vol. 1, p. 440. Concerned that this activity might be interpreted improperly by other labor leaders, Gompers assured unionists that in his lectures he never toned down the philosophy of the labor movement or "uttered in a minor key" the workers' struggle for justice and freedom.
[51]War Department communication to Frey dated June 3, 1930; Frey to Major Donald Armstrong, May 25, 1931; "Biographical Notes on Frey"; and other papers and letters in Container 2, Frey Papers. Frey lectured at the colleges noted above until at least 1945.

offer itself, when the Republic is assailed, in defense of the Home-land, our Glorious Flag and the United States of America."[52] The following year Matthew Woll substituted for Green, and his speech pleased the Commandant of the College who declared it a fine presentation of the "sound and patriotic" views of the AFL.[53]

A more important manifestation of the AFL's policy in this area was the "alliance" formed with the American Legion. Founded in 1919 the Legion, nationally speaking, was officially neutral toward organized labor. From their inception, however, a number of the Legion's local posts engaged in antilabor activities, such as strike-breaking, or became otherwise involved in controversies with organized labor. As a consequence, the Legion came to be regarded by some working people as an antilabor organization, and several labor bodies barred Legionnaires from membership. Partly as a result of this action, the Legion suffered a decline in membership. The circumstances set the stage for an AFL-Legion "alliance."[54]

In November 1920 Samuel Gompers and Frederic W. Galbraith, Jr., the Legion's National Commander, began an exchange of correspondence which looked toward the establishment of a coop-erative and fraternal relationship between the AFL and the Legion.[55] The Legion commander sent a personal representative to the AFL convention in Denver in 1921 to tell the "representa-tives of the laboring people of America that the heart of the Legion beats for them."[56] The AFL was receptive to the Legion's appeal and decided, therefore, to send a representative to the next annual convention of the Legion "to convey to that organization greetings from the American Federation of Labor, to the end that the relations between these two great organizations now so happily established may be the more closely cemented and made perma-nent, to the advantage of all the members of each of these patriotic

[52]Copy of the address delivered by Green before the Army War College in Wash-ington, D. C., Dec. 10, 1925, PCB #4, Book 383, NYSSILR Library.

[53]Major-General H. E. Ely to Green, Dec. 24, 1926, PCB #3, Book 370, *ibid.*

[54]Richard Seelye Jones, *A History of the American Legion,* pp. 192–197; Justin Gray, *The Inside Story of the Legion,* pp. 134–138; Perlman and Taft, *History of Labor in the United States,* pp. 427–429.

[55]Jones, *History of the American Legion,* p. 196.

[56]From the address of Colonel Alvin M. Owsley, director-general of the American Legion, delivered to the AFL convention, AFL, *Proceedings, 1921,* p. 278.

societies."[57] The Executive Council delegated George L. Berry, who was president of the Printing Pressmen's Union and who claimed to have been one of the founders of the Legion,[58] to speak to the Legionnaires.

Berry carried out his assignment with consummate skill, and the Council was able to inform the AFL delegates in 1922 that Berry had been elected Senior Vice-Commander of the American Legion and that he had concluded important talks with Legion spokesmen. The Council maintained that the contacts with the Legion had revealed that the two organizations had common views with respect to certain legislative matters and that meetings of this sort were "very helpful in preventing interference with the normal activities of labor." For these reasons the Council recommended that such conferences should be continued and be spread to "every city in which there are Legion posts established." Such action would remove "any misunderstanding that might arise" and would "tend to cement the friendly relations existing between the two organizations."[59]

Explaining the "soldier-labor alliance" to the delegates to the AFL convention of 1922, Berry claimed that a community of interest existed between the veterans and trade unionists which placed them in complete agreement on such fundamental matters as public education and the furtherance of Americanism.[60] Gompers also made conspicuous mention of the AFL's new friendship. "I may say now," he declared, "that there is no question of the absolute cordial relations existing between the American Legion and the American organized labor movement. . . . I could not now recount the services which the American Legion has rendered to the cause of labor. . . in the past year or two, and we

[57]*Ibid.*, p. 404.
[58]*Ibid., 1923*, p. 314.
[59]*Ibid., 1922*, pp. 137–138. The AFL and the Legion cooperated in 1921 and 1922 in the observance of National Education Week. In hundreds of communities representatives of the two organizations jointly appointed the committees which carried out the education week programs. *Ibid., 1923*, p. 63; *American Federationist*, Vol. 29, November 1922, p. 847.
[60]Berry, "The Legion and Labor," *American Federationist*, Vol. 29, September 1922, pp. 680–681.

have been of some assistance in spreading the cause of the American Legion."[61]

Gompers himself went to the Legion convention in 1922 and 1923 to address the Legionnaires, and Green, upon succeeding to the AFL stewardship, accepted the Legion's invitation in 1928 and 1930 personally to deliver his organization's greetings to the annual gathering of World War I veterans. The Legion, after 1921, was also usually represented at the AFL convention by its national commander.[62]

The relationship which the AFL established with the American Legion in the 1920's proved to be a lasting one, and it is carried on today by the AFL-CIO. Today, however, the relationship does not fit into any general strategy of defense on the part of the AFL-CIO, as it did on the part of the AFL in the 1920's. Both the spirit and the purpose of labor's cooperation with the Legion have in recent years changed in some degree. The AFL-CIO's cooperation with the Legion is based not so much upon a desire to remove barriers to union activity (or to demonstrate labor's "Americanism") as upon the desire to promote labor's own firm convictions in the area of foreign policy.[63]

The AFL also attempted to promote its reputation as a loyal, patriotic organization by endorsing in 1926 the Citizens' Military Training Camps, which had been set up as a result of the postwar National Defense Act.[64] The principals in securing AFL endorse-

[61]AFL, *Proceedings, 1922,* pp. 278–279.

[62]*Ibid., 1922,* pp. 285–288, 360, *1923,* pp. 63, 314–317, *1924,* pp. 63, 193–196, *1928,* pp. 135–138, *1929,* pp. 233–236, *1930,* pp. 216–221. It was not until the closing months of 1922, after Gompers had gone to the Legion convention in New Orleans, that the nation's press began to speculate on the meaning of the "soldier-labor alliance." Editorial opinion, as reported in the *Literary Digest,* indicated unamimous disapproval of the development, especially in its political significance, the fear being that the Legion might become the tail to labor's political kite. "A Soldier-Labor Alliance," *Literary Digest,* Vol. 75, Nov. 4, 1922, pp. 12–13.

[63]In a recent letter to the writer, Peter Henle, secretary of the AFL-CIO Veterans Affairs Committee, said that the views of the AFL-CIO and the Legion roughly coincide in the area of foreign policy, although even here "there would be some differences on specific programs." On many vital issues of economic and domestic policy, on the other hand, the AFL-CIO and the Legion do not, he said, agree. Henle to the writer, Dec. 20, 1957. For further evidence of the present almost exclusive foreign policy focus of AFL-CIO-Legion relations, see *AFL-CIO News,* Sept. 21, Dec. 14, 1957.

[64]The National Defense Act became law in 1920, and in 1921 the first Citizens' Military Training Camps were established. By 1926 there were 47 camps. Military

ment of CMTC appear to have been Lieutenant Colonel Clarence B. Ross and John P. Frey, both of whom, according to Frey, had been named after the war by General Charles P. Summerall, Chief of Staff, as "liaison officers" between the War Department and the AFL.[65] In 1922 Ross, a career military man who had been ordered to duty with the Organized Reserves, began to recruit candidates for CMTC and, believing that he ought to enlist the cooperation of organizations unfriendly to the War Department, turned first to the AFL. He was familiar, he said, with the fact that the AFL had condemned compulsory military training in 1921, and he knew that there was in the army "a considerable prejudice against organized labor"; but, apparently with the full support and encouragement of Summerall, he felt that it was his duty to foster a better understanding between the two organizations.

As the first step in this direction, Ross began to sound out AFL officials with regard to their possible endorsement of the Citizens' Military Training Camps. During 1924 Ross conversed with Gompers on this subject, and he also attended the third quarterly meeting of the AFL's Executive Council to oppose a resolution placed before that body which condemned the first "Defense Test" the General Staff was planning. Owing partly to Ross's intervention, the resolution did not pass. Ross also took occasion, at that time, to ascertain the views of Executive Council members with regard to CMTC. The results were apparently greatly encouraging to him because in November 1924 he appeared at the El Paso convention of the AFL with a resolution on CMTC in his pocket.[66] The resolution called not only for endorsement of CMTC but also for the appointment by the Council of three aides to the Secretary of War and one aide in every state who would cooperate with the government in the recruitment of young men for the camps.

The convention's Resolutions Committee reported unfavorably upon Ross's proposition, and the convention therefore referred it

---

Training Camps Association, *The Military Training Camps Association of the United States,* pp. 3–4; *New York Times,* May 8, 1926.

[65]Lectures delivered by Frey at the Army Industrial College and the Army War College in 1924 and 1934, Container 2, Frey Papers.

[66]This account of Ross's activity is taken from a "Memo for John P. Frey" written by Ross in 1930, Container 13, *ibid.*

75

to the Executive Council with the stipulation that before such a project could be approved the AFL had to assure itself that the camps were operated "for the upbuilding of the mind and body of our young men," and not conducted in a militaristic spirit.[67] Acknowledging that he had helped Ross at the convention, Frey confessed that his own organization, the Molders' Union, "wondered whether something had happened to me because I was one of the first signers of the resolution."[68]

Ross was undismayed by the initial setback, and when he visited with the Executive Council in the spring of 1925 he extended to its members an invitation from Secretary of War Dwight F. Davis to inspect one of the training camps. Although the Council declined the invitation, Ross renewed it a year later, and this time the Council accepted. After the Council had decided to visit the training camp located at Plattsburg, New York, Ross remarked that "this would be a very enjoyable outing, having at least the charm of novelty for the majority of the members" of the Council.[69] AFL officials journeyed to Plattsburg in August 1926 for a three-day inspection tour of the camp. They were regaled by local Elks and Rotary clubs during their stay, and after winding up their visit with "a colorful review of the 1,600 infantrymen," they announced approval of what they had seen. Green, for example, was convinced that there was "a wrong impression in some quarters as to the work, training, purposes and objectives of the military training camps."[70]

The Executive Council reported to the October 1926 convention of the AFL that military training "occupied the smallest part of the day" at the Plattsburg camp and that athletic events took up most of the trainees' time. "This kind of training," the Council continued, "is building up the mind and body of the American youth. It stimulates the patriotic spirit of the youth. He is taught citizenship...we believe it would be advantageous to all of the

[67]AFL, *Proceedings, 1924,* pp. 295–296.
[68]Lecture delivered by Frey at the Army Industrial College in 1924, p. 9, Container 2, Frey Papers.
[69]Excerpt from the minutes of the meeting of the Executive Council of the AFL, Cincinnati, Ohio, June 25–30, 1926, included in a letter Green to Ross, July 21, 1926, PCB #2, Book 365, NYSSILR Library.
[70]*New York Times,* Aug. 19, 21, 1926.

boys of our country to take advantage of the opportunity afforded to them in these camps."[71]

The Cloth Hat, Cap and Millinery Workers' International Union, the International Ladies' Garment Workers' Union, and the Pennsylvania Federation of Labor roundly attacked the Council's bid for endorsement of CMTC, contending that the camps not only encouraged the cult of militarism but also that the Military Training Camps Association, the directing agency of the camps, derived its chief support from open-shop employers who were bent upon inculcating antiunionism among the trainees and turning out scabs and strikebreakers.[72] There is inconclusive evidence which partially supports the latter charge. Thus in 1926 "several of the larger manufacturing and financial institutions" of Detroit, at that time a citadel of the open shop, permitted a number of their employees to attend the Citizens' Military Training Camp at Camp Custer without loss of pay. They did this because they realized that the training would increase their workers' "loyalty, efficiency, obedience, and power for leadership."[73] The Ford Motor Company contributed small sums in support of CMTC in 1923 and 1924.[74]

Matthew Woll, speaking as secretary of the Resolutions Committee, emphatically denied the imputation that the AFL wished to encourage militarism, but on the other hand, he submitted that the organization had never opposed the building up of "strong bodies, healthy minds and patriotic souls." The convention voted to concur in the Council's report, and as a consequence, the AFL endorsed the Citizens' Military Training Camps.[75]

In 1927 Green became a civilian aide for CMTC in the District of Columbia, a position which he held until at least 1934, and in

[71]AFL, *Proceedings, 1926,* p. 56.

[72]*Ibid., 1925,* pp. 303–304, *1926,* pp. 235–236. The Amalgamated Clothing Workers, though not affiliated with the AFL at that time, also vigorously condemned CMTC. Amalgamated Clothing Workers of America, *Proceedings, 1926,* pp. 342–243.

[73]Wade Millis (a CMTC official) to Henry Ford, May 7, 1926, Accession 285, Box 531, Ford Motor Company Archives.

[74]George F. James (a CMTC official) to Edsel B. Ford, Feb. 28, 1924; A. J. Lepine (secretary to Edsel B. Ford) to George F. James, March 5, 1924, Accession 6, Box 59, *ibid.*

[75]AFL, *Proceedings, 1926,* pp. 236–237.

this capacity he collected funds for the support of the camps.[76] The AFL also lobbied for increased congressional appropriations for CMTC.[77]

Green and members of the Executive Council reviewed the cadets on parade at West Point in 1929 and considered the trip "one of the most delightful experiences in all our personal and official life."[78] Green joined the United States Flag Association and the National Security League.[79]

In view of these persistent efforts of AFL leaders during the 1920's to cultivate a reputation for loyalty and patriotism—the speeches to the War Colleges, the alliance with the American Legion, the endorsement of the Citizens' Military Training Camps, etc.—it is perhaps not surprising that at least one army officer came to believe that the AFL had a "Military Sub-Section"![80]

It must not be forgotten, however, that AFL leaders hoped and expected that their strategy in these matters would result in some tangible benefits to organized labor. Thus, since the AFL had demonstrated its willingness to further some of the aims of the Department of War, Ross and Frey, with the initial assistance of George L. Berry, began to make overtures to that Department in the hope of obtaining certain concessions in return. Very probably the program which these men desired was outlined by Ross in a memorandum which he submitted in May 1929 to Assistant Secretary of War Patrick J. Hurley. Ross sought to impress upon Hurley the fact that there was a basic difference between the American Federation of Labor and the radical wing of the labor movement which was "definitely militant" and "definitely pacifistic," whereas the AFL was

[76]Green to the Secretary of War, June 7, 1927, PCB #3, Book 376; Green to Major General Paul B. Malone, Jan. 15, 1934, PCB #14, Book 480, NYSSILR Library. Green did not collect funds for CMTC after 1930, although he did retain the position of civilian aide. See Green to J. Monroe Stick (executive secretary of Military Training Camps Association), Sept. 11, 1931, PCB #12, Book 464, ibid.

[77]Green to Charles Pike (president of the Military Training Camps Association), Jan. 21, 1929, PCB #5, Book 396, ibid.

[78]Green to Colonel Irving Phillipson, June 6, 1929; Green to General Charles P. Summerall, June 11, 1929, PCB #6, Book 403, ibid.

[79]Green to Colonel James L. Moss (president-general of the United States Flag Association), April 15, 1929; Green to General R. L. Bullard (president of the National Security League), Nov. 12, 1928, PCB #5, Books 394, 399, ibid.

[80]Green to Lieutenant-Colonel C. H. White, Jan. 12, 1934, PCB #14, Book 481, ibid.

"conservative" and "essentially patriotic." The AFL would not only support the country during war, but it would also "favor and advocate" measures strengthening the national defense during eras of peace so long as these measures were not taken at the expense of workers. In view of these considerations, Ross recommended that the War Department set up a Wage Board of Review, upon which the AFL would be represented, similar to the board already functioning in the Navy Department; that wages in "arsenals, manufacturing and repair plants and similar establishments" under War Department control conform, henceforth, as nearly as possible to the local prevailing wage standards; that a board on wages be established in each Army Procurement District; that "all restrictions regarding the methods by which employees in the arsenals and other similar establishments of the War Department shall select their representatives to confer with the management...be removed;" that the Baltimore and Ohio Cooperative Plan, based upon the right of employees to organize and bargain collectively, be given a one-year trial "in all arsenals and similar establishments;" and that the War Department establish a permanent fact-finding board, upon which the AFL would again be represented, "to consider and make recommendations to the Assistant Secretary of War on labor disputes" not otherwise settled and not involving terms of employment.[81]

Berry was apparently the first to solicit War Department support for a program of this nature; his efforts began at least as early as 1928. In a letter to Berry, Frey expressed gratification for the work Berry had done in 1928 which had been so successful "in opening doors in the War Department, and establishing a point of view which made it possible for me to follow up."[82]

Frey conferred with Secretary of Labor James Davis, Ross, and Mr. E. E. Hunt in March 1929, and he subsequently told Berry that these men advised "that what was accomplished last year should be laid before President Hoover." If Hoover knew of the "national services which the AFL was endeavoring to give," he

[81]Memorandum titled "Cooperation of Labor in National Defense," dated May 4, 1929, and submitted by Ross to the Assistant Secretary of War, Container 13, Frey Papers.
[82]Frey to Berry, April 1, 1929, Container 13, *ibid.*

might express to the War Department "the thought that we were working along sound and patriotic lines," and such intercession would greatly strengthen the AFL's standing with that Department.[83] Although Frey saw Hoover in April 1929, he does not refer in his correspondence to any remarks he may have made at the time about the AFL and the Department of War. Be that as it may, the War Department refused to go along with the Ross-Frey-Berry notions, despite the fact that these men continued to press for some favorable response through the year 1930.

The persistent rebuffs left Ross in a rather melancholy state of mind. "Why the army is unwilling to cooperate is a mystery too deep for my powers of comprehension," he complained. "So far from accomplishing my purpose of developing this mutual friendliness, I seem to have reached the point where I am accomplishing nothing except the losing of what little popularity I had with my military superiors. This is growing more marked since the retirement of General Summerall withdrew his support."[84] On another occasion, Ross appraised in greater detail the difficulties involved in his vain efforts to coordinate the views of the War Department and the AFL:

In this work I have had the active and wholehearted support of Generals Bullard, Summerall, Hagood, and Drum, but I have had to contend with the equally active hostility of other officers of high rank and the total indifference of the vast majority of the others....I have spent about nine years of time...in the attempt to demonstrate to labor and to the army the justice and advantage to our country and its people of working together for the common good. If I had attained the same result with the army that I have attained with labor I should be quite content. The greater part of labor's misunderstanding has been cleared away. I fear greatly that the greater part of the army's misunderstanding still remains.[85]

Ross was ordered to duty in the Philippines early in 1932, but when the Democratic party won the presidential election in November of that year, Frey's interest in negotiating with the War

[83]Frey to Berry, April 8, 1929, Container 13, *ibid*. See also Berry to Frey, April 4, 1929, Container 13, *ibid*.
[84]Ross to Frey, Dec. 29, 1930, Container 13, *ibid*.
[85]Memo for John P. Frey" written by Ross in 1930, Container 13, *ibid*.

Department revived, and he tried to get Ross to return to the United States to assist him. Ross, however, had no hope that he could accomplish at that time any more than he had accomplished during former years, and, as a result of his indifference, Frey dropped his AFL-War Department plan of cooperation.[86] Thus, the AFL's cooperative policy of this era proved as fruitless in winning benefits from the War Department as from private industry.

IV

The isolationist foreign policy followed by the AFL in the 1920's can also be interpreted as a part of its larger strategy of defense. In 1921 the AFL refused to affiliate with the new International Federation of Trade Unions, contending in part that it could not lend support to a revolutionary socialist organization. Yet the European labor movements had always had a predominantly socialist orientation and the AFL had, until 1921, found it possible to cooperate with them in the IFTU.[87] Also, although Samuel Gompers was instrumental in founding the International Labor Organization after World War I, and although the 1920 convention of the AFL declared that it was of the utmost importance for Americal labor to be represented in the ILO, the AFL rapidly lost interest in that international body.[88] A basic feature of the ILO program was the recommendation to member nations of uniform labor laws on such subjects as maximum hours, night work, and the employment of women and children—laws which, in some instances at least, the AFL had advocated for many years. Nevertheless, AFL leaders pointed to the legislative program of the ILO in justifying their changed attitude toward the organization. Matthew Woll, for example, stamped the ILO program as socialistic and "a menace to a free citizenry." "If only," Woll exclaimed, "we could impose upon that foundation the philosophy of freedom, instead of the philosophy of exalting the State without regard to its control or to the desirable limits of its function!"[89] While

[86]Frey to Ross, Dec. 12, 19, 1932; Ross to Frey, Jan. 21, 1933, Container 13, *ibid.*
[87]Taft, *A. F. of L. in the Time of Gompers,* pp. 433–437.
[88]AFL, *Proceedings, 1920,* pp. 168–171, *1929,* pp. 367–370.
[89]Woll, "The International Labor Office: A Criticism," *Current History,* Vol. 31, January 1930, pp. 683–689. In a confidential report to Green on the International

some of the laws advocated by the ILO may have been contrary to traditional AFL policy, it nevertheless seems that AFL leaders stepped somewhat out of character in generally condemning the ILO program. Alignments with the socialist IFTU and the "statist" ILO were probably considered as liabilities by labor leaders who wanted to show businessmen and the community in general that their brand of unionism was conservative and that they could be accepted as reliable partners in the self-regulation of industry.

In his prolonged efforts to promote the acceptance of unions by employers, Matthew Woll engaged in activities which tended unofficially to commit the AFL to policies of tariff protectionism and the freeing of big business from state regulation. Woll did not win any general support within the AFL for these policies, however. On the contrary, because of his activities he incurred the wrath of several laborites. Officially, therefore, the AFL continued in the 1920's to maintain a policy of neutrality with regard to the tariff (supporting both increases and decreases in duties in accordance with the desires of individual unions) and to hold to the conviction that government should have regulatory power over the abuses and evils of monopoly.[90]

V

While one cannot quarrel with—in fact can only praise—the logic of the greater part of AFL strategy in the 1920's, one can question whether the results, in practice, were ever so encouraging as to justify adherence to the strategy for so long. Actually, the AFL high command not only held to the strategy, but often told the AFL annual convention that its policies were rapidly gaining new

---

Economic Conference held at Geneva, Switzerland, in 1927, Frey outlined views with regard to the ILO which were similar to those held by Woll. Frey to Green, June 15, 1927, Container 10, Frey Papers. Furuseth also opposed any encouragement of the ILO Program. Green, on the other hand, favored the ILO and felt that Gompers also wanted the AFL to participate in its activities. AFL, *Proceedings, 1929*, pp. 369–370.

[90]As a small sample of the literature upon which this paragraph is based, see Lyle W. Cooper, "The Tariff and Organized Labor," *American Economic Review*, Vol. 20, June 1930, pp. 210–217; Cooper, "Organized Labor and the Trust," *Journal of Political Economy*, Vol. 36, December 1928, pp. 720–725, 734–736; Matthew Woll, "Labor and the Tariff," *Boilermakers' Journal*, Vol. 41, August 1929, pp. 321–324; Woll, "Organized Labor's Volteface on the Trusts," *Current History*, Vol. 25, October 1926, p. 71.

friends for labor in industry. In 1928 the Executive Council's imagination ran wild. "At no time in its history," the Council commented, "has the trade union had greater influence in industrial circles. The constructive policies which we advocate and follow challenge the attention and respect of employers in this country and abroad...those who look to the trade union movement for leadership are increasing."[91]

The AFL was whistling in the dark, and there were critics of this self-deception even within the organization's inner councils. Andrew Furuseth, president of the Seamen's Union, said that he "felt like getting up and protesting" in 1927 when the Executive Council "reported that there is a tendency to understanding and friendly relations between the employers of this country and the unions."[92] O'Connell admonished the delegates who attended the 1931 convention of the Metal Trades Department that they should not permit themselves "to be deceived by surface indications or to be misled into believing" that the willingness of the labor movement to cooperate with industry was sufficient to win the cooperation of very many employers. "We must keep in mind," O'Connell continued, "all of the experiences our movement has passed through, including the steady, determined and aggressive methods which have been applied by many employers in their effort to make trade union organization among their employees impossible."[93]

These comments seem to point to a lack of united and forthright leadership at the AFL's helm during this time. This is also evident in the aforementioned political repercussions in the AFL produced by Matthew Woll's activities in support of tariff protectionism. In fact, Woll's activities in this respect eventually caused John P. Frey candidly to deplore the ineffective leadership of William Green. During the congressional elections of 1932, Woll endorsed the re-election of Senators Reed Smoot of Utah and James

[91]AFL, *Proceedings, 1920*, p. 115, *1924*, p. 32, *1927*, p. 35, *1928*, pp. 50–51.
[92]*Ibid., 1927*, p. 291.
[93]MTD, *Proceedings, 1931*, p. 4. O'Connell's attitude toward union-management cooperation may also help to explain his defection, earlier, from the labor group which was waiting on the development of Frey's industrial conference and his replacement in that group by Franklin.

E. Watson of Indiana because of their high-tariff convictions. The AFL, on the other hand, looked with disapproval upon the re-election of these two men because they had voted in the Senate against measures of interest to organized labor. With this anomalous situation in mind, Frey confided to his close friend Lieutenant Colonel Ross that if "it were not for the injury being done to the trade union movement by some of these tactics, I would not be concerned, but as it is *I recognize more than ever the absence of a dominating A. F. of L. policy and that type of executive control* which would prevent such a spectacle as the A. F. of L. justly condemning a Senator for his labor record, and a group within the A. F. of L publicly supporting such a Senator because of his vote on the tariff."[94]

It would seem reasonable to conclude that the policies AFL leaders pursued to meet labor's dilemma in the prosperity decade failed totally to achieve their ultimate objective—membership expansion with the consent of employers. Moreover, the AFL devised no alternative policies but relied upon union-management cooperation and ingratiating alignments and contacts through years of consistent disappointment. Toward the close of the 1920's a situation of drifting leadership appears to have compounded the AFL's predicament.

The alternatives were admittedly few and not overly encouraging. Most assuredly the AFL could not have evoked response among its affiliated unions for a policy of militant organizing. They had neither finances nor interest adequate for such a venture. But even if the labor movement had undertaken such a campaign, it would have proved a suicidal action because of the generally resolute anti-union pattern in big industry, the lack of union sentiment among the rank and file, and the absence of a legal guarantee of organizing and bargaining rights. Perhaps, however, it would have been wise had the AFL at some point shelved its cooperation policy, accepted as a primary legislative goal a guarantee of the right to organize and

[94]Frey to Ross, Oct. 12, 1932, Container 13, Frey Papers, italics added. In his answer to Frey, Ross suggested that Frey ought to make himself a candidate for the AFL presidency. Ross recognized that the UMW would oppose such a move but felt that if Frey could enlist the support of the Teamsters, Carpenters, and a few others "that don't like the Miners any too well anyway" that he would have a better than even chance to becomes president. Ross to Frey, Nov. 16, 1932, Container 13, *ibid.*

bargain collectively, and readied itself psychologically to spring into action when conditions for successful organizing ripened. As it was, AFL leaders preached cooperation and their own conservatism so much that their attitude was still a liability when, in 1933, the opportunity for militant organizing opportunities arrived.

It must be acknowledged that in one respect the AFL strategy of the 1920's paid off. That is, some unbelievers were convinced that the AFL was patriotic and American. As John Dewey remarked in 1929, the AFL "is no longer cursed as revolutionary and subversive, but is blessed as a constructive, safe, and patriotic organization."[95] Dewey said so disdainfully, and what bothered him was that in establishing this reputation for itself the AFL had also become harmless. With unusual candor even John P. Frey privately confessed in 1932 that "we [AFL leaders] have been so 'good' that we have almost become no good, and unless we begin to insist upon being heard in the nation's councils, and particularly in the industrial world, we might as well fold up our tent and continue to receive with thanks what industry may be willing to give us."[96]

[95]Dewey, "Labor Politics and Labor Education," *New Republic*, Vol. 57, Jan. 9, 1929, pp. 212–213.
[96]Frey to Ross, Dec. 12, 1932, Container 13, Frey Papers.

→ CHAPTER IV ←

The Self-Styled
Labor "Progressives"

EVEN before the collapse of the postwar amalgamation movement in 1923, a new opposition to AFL leadership had begun to develop among self-styled labor "progressives." These people, many of them representatives of left-wing philosophies (especially socialism), came to express their reform sentiment through such workers' education enterprises as the Workers' Education Bureau and Brookwood Labor College and also through the Labor Publication Society and the Conference for Progressive Labor Action. The opposition generated from these sources in the 1920's involved individuals primarily rather than unions and is thus to be distinguished both from the earlier (1901–1923) and the later (1930's) oppositions. The progressives gained no significant strength in the 1920's, and their ranks were eventually weakened as a result of the AFL-Brookwood split (discussed in Chapter V) and by the Great Depression.

While the progressives of the 1920's were fewer by far than the critics who preceded and followed them, they were in some respects more articulate than both the other groups and by the mid-1920's were advocating a more realistic brand of industrial unionism than their predecessors had. For these reasons, and also because so little has heretofore been written concerning the progressives, an extended account of their role in the AFL's internal conflict seems justified.

86

I

Had the American Federation of Labor not gained control of the Workers' Education Bureau, that organization might have become a center of progressive labor opposition to the AFL. The Workers' Education Bureau of America was formed in New York City in April 1921 by a few trade unionists and labor educators to coordinate the educational work being carried on by organized labor and to stimulate the further development of the young workers' education movement. The founding convention of the WEB elected an executive committee of nine members to determine the Bureau's policies and to administer them. James H. Maurer, a top leader in the conservative wing of the Socialist party and president of the Pennsylvania Federation of Labor, was elected chairman of the committee. The other members were John Brophy, president of District No. 2 of the UMW; Fannia M. Cohn, secretary of the education department and a vice-president of the ILGWU; J. B. S. Hardman (then known as J. B. Salutsky), educational director of the ACW; W. F. Kehoe, secretary of the Central Trades and Labor Council of Greater New York; Harry Russell of the Metal Trades Council of Springfield, Massachusetts; Harry W. L. Dana of the Boston Trade Union College; Frieda Miller of the Trade Union College of Philadelphia; and Spencer Miller, Jr., a labor educator.[1]

The founders of the WEB conceived of workers' education in part as a means of reforming the leadership and policies of organized labor. They wanted, for example, to popularize among trade unionists the need, as they saw it, for industrial unionism (amalgamation), a labor party, and greater militancy in the labor movement and to spread the idea that unions "must go on," after achieving higher wages and shorter hours, toward more ultimate aims if they were to satisfy the demands of the workers. They believed, furthermore, that the workers' education movement should train labor leaders with "ideals," men and women who would "take hold of things" and who would be guided in their

[1]*Workers Education in the United States, Report of Proceedings, First National Conference on Workers Education in the United States, 1921*, p. 6.

leadership by "social thinking" rather than by the "business psychology" of typical laborites.[2]

Membership in the WEB was opened to national and international unions, state federations of labor, city centrals, local unions, cooperative associations, and workers' study classes conducted under trade union auspices. Since each organization was allowed but one vote in the annual convention of the WEB, control of the Bureau's business rested with the more numerous local and state organizations rather than with the national and international unions.[3]

The AFL immediately became interested in the WEB and, in 1921, Matthew Woll, acting as chairman of the AFL's permanent Committee on Education, effected a temporary agreement with the WEB providing for cooperation between his committee and the Bureau. Samuel Gompers and Woll attended the 1922 convention of the WEB and proposed a more permanent agreement which would accord the AFL "appropriate" representation in the WEB. Woll assured the WEB delegates that the AFL did not wish "to control the affairs of the Workers' Education Bureau" but did, on the other hand, want representation in the WEB sufficient "to guarantee to all the wage earners of the American Labor Movement *that the true philosophy of the American Federation of Labor and this movement would be faithfully carried out*" by the WEB.[4]

Some WEB leaders were not enthusiastic about such a concord. Hardman doubted that the philosophy of the AFL was acceptable to WEB members and feared that the AFL might "swallow" the WEB and that WEB publications might be "worded differently" were the AFL given a voice in Bureau affairs. Nevertheless, he believed these risks had to be taken in order to gain the financial support of the AFL. Maurer said he did not know "what we W.E.B. delegates want to think of...the Federation or how proud we may be of it," but, he concluded, it "is after all here and we have got

[2]*Ibid.*, pp. 64, 72–73, 76, 82, 88–89, 108, 124–125. See also AFL, *Proceedings, 1923,* p. 161; James H. Maurer, "Autobiography of a Labor Leader," *Atlantic,* Vol. 181, June 1923, p. 750.

[3]"Constitution of the Workers Education Bureau of America," WEB, *Proceedings, 1921,* p. 142, *1922,* pp. 135, 153.

[4]*Ibid., 1922,* pp. 10, 133–134, 141, italics added.

to recognize it...if we are going to get anywhere." Consequently, the 1922 convention of the WEB authorized negotiations "to develop a working plan of cooperation with the American Federation of Labor."[5]

During conferences in May and July 1922, WEB and AFL negotiators reached an agreement. According to its terms, all members of the WEB executive committee were to be unionists, and three of them were to be appointed by the president of the AFL. Matthew Woll, John P. Frey, and George W. Perkins of the Cigarmakers were duly appointed to serve as the AFL's representatives. Woll was elected chairman of the executive committee, and Maurer became president of the Bureau. Only those workers' study classes "doing bona fide educational work" were declared eligible to membership in the Bureau, thus eliminating the Rand School of Social Science, the Workers' (Communist) School, and the Work People's College (IWW); all dual and seceding (non-AFL) unions were also declared ineligible for Bureau membership, thus removing the Amalgamated Clothing Workers from the Bureau.[6]

With this agreement as an entering wedge, the AFL and its national unions gradually assumed control of the Workers' Education Bureau. By 1929 state and local bodies and workers' educational enterprises, which originally controlled the Bureau, had virtually no voice in WEB decisions and the WEB had become a close supporter of the traditional policies of the American Federation of Labor.[7] In effecting the latter result, the AFL had assumed censorship control over WEB publications and had, as Hardman predicted, deleted from several books published under WEB auspices passages which did not square with AFL principles and policies.[8] The AFL also secured assurances from the WEB conven-

---

[5]*Ibid.*, pp. 141–142, 145–146, 148, 151–152.

[6]*Ibid., 1923*, pp. 33–36, 47. See also AFL, *Proceedings, 1923*, p. 60.

[7]WEB, *Proceedings, 1925*, pp. 62–79; *Outline of the Major Actions Taken by the 6th Annual Convention of the Workers Education Bureau, 1929*, Appendix A, "Constitution," pp. 1, 2, 4.

[8]The AFL's attention was directed by Victor Olander in March 1926 to alleged pro-Communist, antiunion and antireligious material in a few books of the WEB's Workers' Bookshelf series, namely Alfred D. Sheffield, *Joining in Public Discussion;* Walton Hamilton and Stacy May, *The Control of Wages;* James H. Robinson, *The Humanizing of Knowledge;* and Mary Beard, *A Short History of the American Labor*

89

tion in 1927 that the Bureau would not concern itself in any way with trade union policies but would function strictly as an educational and research organization.[9]

John P. Frey, writing to William Green in 1927, acknowledged that the AFL had taken over the WEB in order "to eliminate those conditions which we thought were unsound, and to build up the W.E.B. so that it could carry on the work which the A.F. of L. desired." "We could not expect to work a revolution in a day," Frey continued, and "neither could we expect to throw out of the Workers' Education Bureau a number of educators and other men and women who had taken a very profound interest in the work which the Bureau was attempting to do."[10]

II

Although a few labor progressives clung to important posts in the WEB throughout the 1920's, most of them came to center their activities at Brookwood Labor College, in the Labor Publication Society, and, after the AFL-Brookwood split, in the Conference for Progressive Labor Action. Plans for the establishment of Brookwood Labor College, the first resident school for workers in the United States, were laid at a conference held near Katonah,

---

Movement. Passages to which Olander objected criticized the craft form of organization and recommended amalgamation, approved the formation of a labor party, referred to signs of rebellion in the AFL and to conditions within unions which encouraged labor racketeering, praised some of Nicholai Lenin's views, and advocated evolution, the nationalization of industry, and "some form of workers' control." In 1927 John J. Manning, secretary-treasurer of the Union Label Trades Department, submitted a similar report on the Workers' Bookshelf to William Green. Green subsequently wrote to the AFL representatives in the WEB, Woll, Frey, and Perkins, and told them he had examined the books in question and had found the designated portions "highly objectionable from a Trade-Union point of view." He urged them, therefore, to eliminate immediately "all objectionable articles and printed matter which is not in accord with the principles, policies and philosophy of the American Federation of Labor." Such a revision was begun forthwith, and AFL leaders took steps in 1927 to prevent the future publication by the WEB of ideas with which they disagreed. See Olander to Frey, March 1, 1926, Container 15, Frey Papers; John J. Manning, "Report on [the 1927] Convention of Workers' Education Bureau," Container 15, *ibid.;* Green to Frey, July 18, 1927, Container 15, *ibid.;* AFL *Proceedings, 1927,* p. 404.

[9]Green to the Delegates to the Fifth Convention of the Workers' Education Bureau of America, April 21, 1927, PCB #3, Book 374, NYSSILR Library; AFL *Proceedings, 1927,* p. 67.

[10]Frey to Green, July 25, 1927, Container 15, Frey Papers.

New York, on March 31 and April 1, 1921. Present at that conference were James Maurer; John Brophy; John Fitzpatrick,
president of the Illinois Federation of Labor; Rose Schneiderman,
president of the Women's Trade Union League; Joseph Schlossberg, secretary-treasurer of the ACW; Jay G. Brown, president
of the International Timber Workers' Union; Abraham J. Muste,
executive secretary of the Amalgamated Textile Workers of America (independent of the AFL); Abraham Lefkowitz, vice-president
of the American Federation of Teachers and an officer in the
important Central Trades and Labor Council of Greater New
York; and Charles Kutz, who was a business agent in the International Association of Machinists, "ran" a labor paper in Pennsylvania, and in 1927 was president of System Federation No. 90 of
the Pennsylvania System Lines at Harrisburg.[11]

The founders of Brookwood released the following statement of
purpose which they expected the college to serve:

After two days conference we, laboring men and women and labor
educators, would speak what we have in mind in the founding of. . .
Brookwood. . . . It was decided to unite with the American labor union
movement a force of education that will serve American labor with
trained, responsible liberally educated men and women from the ranks
of the workers. The new college is not intended to act as a propagandist
institution. Thoroughly in sympathy with the aims and aspirations of
labor as a whole, the college will closely cooperate with the national
and international labor groups, also with the various local colleges and
schools that send to it working men and women who show promise and
need further education in order best to serve the labor movement and
through it society.[12]

[11]William Fincke and Toscan Bennett were nonunionists present at the conference. Fincke donated fifty-three acres of land and a fine old farmhouse near
Katonah as the campus for the proposed labor college. Bennett agreed to help
finance the school. William Z. Foster was also present, but he took no further part
in the establishment of Brookwood. William Green to Charles Kutz, Dec. 21, 1927,
PCB #4, Book 383, NYSSILR Library; Matthew Josephson, *Sidney Hilman*, p.
105; Israel Mufson, "Machinists, Weeds and Brookwood Labor Colege," *Machinists'
Monthly Journal*, Vol. 38, May 1926, p. 203; *New York Times*, April 2, 1921; "A Resident Labor College at Katonah, N. Y.," *School and Society*, Vol. 13, April 9, 1921, p.
436; "Who is this A. J. Muste?", *World Tomorrow*, Vol. 12, June 1929, p. 253.

[12]Quoted in "Resident Labor College at Katonah, N. Y.," *School and Society*, Vol.
13, April 9, 1921, pp. 436–437.

Located at Katonah, some forty miles from New York City, Brookwood opened its doors to students in October 1921. The college featured a two-year course in the social sciences which, according to the college prospectus, was intended to "train workers to work in the workers' movements."[13]

In the early 1920's spokesmen for Brookwood elaborated upon the original statement of the institution's purpose and its point of view. A. J. Muste, who served as chairman of the faculty throughout the 1920's, explained in 1923 that:

Brookwood believes in what has been called the "factual approach." We would have the organized workers confront every situation not with prejudices, superstitions, mere notions or feelings, personal animus, but with the willingness to seek out the facts and to base judgment and action on the facts. If we negotiate with employers, let us not go with opinions or "hot air" but armed with facts. When a town is to be organized, let us proceed not by guesswork but with careful knowledge about the place, its workers, their conditions.

At the same time, Muste indicated that Brookwood did not intend to ignore internal union politics and policies but rather intended to face these matters in the same factual spirit in which it faced organizing and bargaining problems. "Too often," Muste complained,

. . . differences between so-called "rights" and "lefts" degenerate into mere personal squabbles, to the destruction of trade unions and the delight of our common foe. There are facts, economic, social, psychological, to account for varying points of view. Let us get at the facts and act on the basis of them. The man with "right" tendencies who goes out of Brookwood thinking that every "left" is necessarily a destructive fool, or the man with "left" tendencies who goes out thinking a "right" is merely a yellow coward, has utterly failed to get the Brookwood point of view.[14]

In the bylaws adopted by the college it was also stated that

teachers are to be accorded the fullest possible freedom to investigate and set forth the truth, since it is clearly undesirable that a school

[13]Quoted in *American Labor Year Book, 1921–1922*, p. 204.
[14]Muste, "The Brookwood Point of View," *Workers' Education*, Vol. 1, July–August 1923, pp. 5–6. *Workers' Education* was published by the Workers' Education Bureau.

carried on under the auspices of the labor movement and serving that movement should fall into the same error of suppressing freedom of thought and expression which both the labor movement and intelligent educationalists deplore in the case of other institutions of learning."[15]

While the above quotations show that Brookwood considered workers' education to be a practical trade union tool and a means of getting at "the truth," the college also regarded workers' education as having as its ultimate goal emancipation of the working class and establishment of a new social order. This facet of the Brookwood point of view was perhaps best described by James Maurer, a devoted supporter of Brookwood who in 1925 became president of its Board of Directors. According to Maurer, it was the desire for a better social order that motivated the founders of the workers' education movement in the United States, and this desire, he said, "must remain its treasured inheritance. Labor education aims at the ultimate liberation of the working masses.... Unless it is education which looks toward a new order of society, with more wisdom and justice than is found in our present order, its right to existence is questionable."[16] The professed goal of abolishing capitalism did not figure very importantly in the education program at Brookwood, however, any more than it did in the program of the Socialist party itself in the 1920's.[17] Brookwood was a school with a trade union emphasis.

The chief policy-making body at Brookwood until 1925 was a Labor Cooperating Committee of ten trade unionists whose announced objective was to keep Brookwood "close to the heart and purpose of the American labor movement and to enable it to serve...its best interests."[18] Serving on this committee were Maurer, Brophy, Lefkowitz, Fitzpatrick, Schneiderman, Kutz, Brown, Cohn, Phil E. Ziegler, editor of the *Railway Clerk,* official journal of the Brotherhood of Railway Clerks, and Thomas

[15]Quoted in Marius Hansome, *World Workers' Educational Movements,* p. 205.

[16]WEB, *Proceedings, 1927,* p. 12. For similar statements, see Muste, "The Brookwood Point of View," *Workers' Education,* Vol. 1, July–August 1923, pp. 5–6; Hansome, *World Workers' Educational Movements,* pp. 24, 43, 200–201.

[17]David A. Shannon discusses at some length the nature of socialist thinking and the Socialist party program in the 1920's. See Shannon, *The Socialist Party of America,* pp. 168–204.

[18]Quoted in *American Labor Year Book, 1923–1924,* p. 219.

Van Lear of the International Association of Machinists. In 1925 Brookwood was incorporated and the Labor Cooperating Committee became the Board of Directors. The following year Robert Fechner, a vice-president of the IAM, who became director of the Civilian Conservation Corps in 1933, and Gustav Geiges, president of the Full-Fashioned Hosiery Workers (an affiliate of the United Textile Workers), replaced Brown and Van Lear as board members.[19]

Within a few years after its establishment Brookwood was officially endorsed, and in most cases financially supported, by thirteen national and international unions. These were the UTW, Hosiery Workers, AFT, IAM, Brewery Workers, Coopers, Maintenance-of-Way Employees, Railroad Clerks, Railway Carmen, Painters, Hat and Cap Makers, ILGWU, and the ACW.[20] Financial

[19]In addition to the ten nonfaculty, trade union members, eight other persons, who represented the faculty (four), students (two), and alumni (two), also sat on the board in 1926; the faculty representatives were Muste, Saposs, Arthur W. Calhoun, and Josephine Colby. *Ibid., 1923–1924*, p. 219, *1926*, p. 308, *1927*, p. 162; "Brookwood Directors Review Year's Work," *Machinists' Monthly Journal*, Vol. 38, June 1926, pp. 259–260; Albert H. Jenkins, "Machinist Makes Good in Man-Sized Job," *Machinists' Monthly Journal*, Vol. 47, February 1935, p. 74; *New York Times*, May 2, 1926. Nonfaculty, trade union members of the Board of Directors had tenure for life or until such time as they severed their connections with the labor movement. Maurer was elected president of the board. Maurer, Cohn, Lefkowitz, Brophy, and Ziegler remained on the board until at least July 1936, just a year before Brookwood closed its doors. Julius Hochman, a graduate of Brookwood and a vice-president of the ILGWU, joined the board in 1935 and became its chairman shortly thereafter. Emil Rieve, until recently head of the Textile Workers' Union of America, also joined the board in 1935. *Brookwood Review*, Vol. 14, January 1936, p. 2, Vol. 14, July 1936, p. 2; "Academic Labor," *Time*, Vol. 30, Nov. 29, 1937, pp. 66–67.

[20]United Textile Workers of America, *Proceedings, 1921*, p. 108, *1924*, pp. 484–485; American Federation of Full Fashioned Hosiery Workers, *Proceedings, 1924*, p. 18, *1926*, p. 27; International Association of Machinists, *Proceedings, 1924*, pp. 151–154, *1928*, pp. 80–81; International Union of United Brewery, Flour, Cereal and Soft Drink Workers of America, *Proceedings, 1923*, pp. 70–71; Brotherhood of Maintenance of Way Employes, *Proceedings, 1925*, pp. 58–59, 150, 153; Brotherhood of Railway and Steamship Clerks, Freight Handlers, Express and Station Employes, *Proceedings, 1922*, p. 269, *1928*, pp. 479–482; Brotherhood of Railway Carmen of America, *Proceedings, 1925*, pp. 509–510; Brotherhood of Painters, Decorators and Paperhangers of America, *Proceedings, 1925*, p. 175; Cloth Hat, Cap and Millinery Workers' International Union, *Proceedings, 1925*, pp. 72, 102, *1927*, pp. 220, 275; International Ladies' Garment Workers' Union, *Proceedings, 1922*, pp. 148–149, *1924*, p. 122, *1925*, p. 166, *1928*, p. 303; Amalgamated Clothing Workers of America, *Proceedings, 1926*, pp. 349, 370–371; American Federation of Teachers, *Semi-Monthly Bulletin*, Sept. 20, 1923, p. 7; *Headgear Worker*, Vol. 9, Feb. 22, 1924, p. 1; *Brookwood Review*, Vol. 2, Dec. 1, 1923, p. 2, Vol. 3, Dec. 15, 1924, p. 8, Vol. 4, December 1925, p. 1, Vol. 4, May–June 1926, p. 1.

assistance was usually tendered by a union in the form of scholarships which made it possible for one or more of its members to enroll at Brookwood every year. In addition to the thirteen unions just listed, four others (the Telegraphers, IBEW, Boilermakers, and Upholsterers), although they did not endorse the college at their conventions, spoke well of its aims or its activities. The editor of the *Journal of Electrical Workers and Operators,* for example, said of Brookwood in March 1926:

If you are discouraged about labor's future, if you have about lost hope, pay a visit to Brookwood Labor College. . . . You will be surprised. You will be thrilled. . . . It's a big place, a live place. It's not "red." It's not reactionary. It teaches facts—not theories; conditions—not propaganda. . . . Yes, it's quite refreshing. Brookwood means real progress. It provides real encouragement. It is the most promising, the most hopeful spot in the American Labor World today.[21]

Districts 1, 2, and 9 of the UMW endorsed and helped finance Brookwood as did the state federations of New York, Pennsylvania, Ohio, Virginia, Illinois, Michigan, Maryland, Utah, Kansas, and Oregon, and a number of local and city central labor bodies.[22] Robert Fechner suggested to William Green in January 1927 that the AFL might want to endorse Brookwood, but Green believed that if the AFL were to do so "we would open the way for similar requests and find ourselves involved in the problem of making decisions which properly belong to the Workers' Education Bureau."[23]

Because these unions endorsed and helped finance Brookwood, it must not be assumed that all of them were aware of and approved

[21]*Journal of Electrical Workers and Operators,* Vol. 25, March 1926, p. 106. See also *Boilermakers' Journal,* Vol. 37, July 1925, pp. 297–298; Order of Railroad Telegraphers, *Proceedings, 1927,* p. 416; Upholsterers' International Union of North America, *Proceedings, 1927,* p. 51.

[22]*Brookwood Review,* Vol. 2, Dec. 1, 1923, pp. 1–2; Vol. 3, Dec. 15, 1924, pp. 3, 8; Vol. 4, May–June, 1926, p. 1. Forty-five city central and local unions had endorsed Brookwood by December 1923. *Ibid.,* Vol. 2, Dec. 1, 1923, pp. 1–2. See also Brookwood Labor College, *The Only Resident Trade Union Educational Institution in the United States,* 1927 (leaflet).

[23]Green to Fechner, Jan. 11, 1927, PCB #3, Book 370, NYSSILR Library. Actually, Green did not mention Brookwood by name, and this writer was unable to locate Fechner's letter. Since Fechner was a member of the Brookwood board, it is assumed he wrote to Green on behalf of Brookwood.

the growing criticism of AFL policies which came to emanate from Brookwood. On the contrary, as will shortly be explained, when some of them did become aware of this criticism, they withdrew their support.

Nor is it to be assumed that Brookwood obtained all of its financial support from its students and the trade unions. This may have been true during the first two years of the school's operation but by 1924 the Garland Fund was matching student and union income with an equal amount not to exceed $10,000 annually. Shortly thereafter the Fund evidently made a new and more favorable arrangement with Brookwood, for in 1926 the college was able to loan the ILGWU $100,000 (which it had received from the Fund) to help defray the expenses of the New York Cloakmakers' strike.[24]

Some of the more able members of the faculty at Brookwood were A. J. Muste, David Saposs, Tom Tippett, and Mark Starr. Muste, an ordained minister, was probably the leading spirit in the progressives' activities of the 1920's, and, in fact, he directed what was in no small sense a one-man show. He was elected a vice-president of the AFT in 1923 and became a member of the WEB executive committee in 1927.[25] David Saposs was a contributor to the ten-volume *Documentary History of American Industrial Society,* edited by John R. Commons, and to the two volume *History of Labour in the United States,* also edited by Commons, and was elected to the executive committee of the WEB in 1925. Tom Tippett, before he came to Brookwood in 1928, was director of education for Subdistrict 5 of District 12 of the UMW. Mark Starr came to Brookwood from the National Council of

---

[24]*Brookwood Review,* Vol. 2, Jan. 1, 1924, p. 2; ILGWU, *Proceedngs, 1928,* p. 68. The Garland Fund was set up in 1922 by the young millionnaire Charles Garland with a capital of $900,000. The capital increased to almost $2,500,000 by 1928. The Fund went out of existence in 1941. The board of directors of the Fund was made up predominantly of "left wingers" who allocated Fund monies to communist as well as to socialist and other leftist causes. See Benjamin Stolberg, "Muddled Millions," *Saturday Evening Post,* Vol. 213, Feb. 15, 1941, pp. 9–10, 88–90, 92; "Radicals; Mr. Garland's Million," *Time,* Vol. 37, June 30, 1941, p. 17.

[25]"Who is This A. J. Muste?", *World Tomorrow,* Vol. 12, June 1929, pp. 250–254; *American Teacher,* Vol. 17, October 1932, p. 6; WEB, *Proceedings, 1927,* pp. 122–123.

Labor Colleges of England and is at present director of education for the ILGWU.[26]

All members of the Brookwood faculty were members of Local 189 of the AFT, which in turn was affiliated with the Central Trades and Labor Council of Greater New York and the New York State Federation of Labor. The college was also an affiliate of the Workers' Education Bureau.[27]

In order to establish as broad a contact with the labor movement as possible, Brookwood used a quota system in its selection of students which brought to the college persons of different religions, representatives of various industrial areas, and conservative trade unionists as well as radicals and progressives.[28] Its initial policy required prospective students to have been union members for at least a year but this was amended in the latter 1920's and a considerable number of students were selected from the unorganized mass-production industries. Throughout the 1920's, however, the vast majority of Brookwood students were trade unionists, and they came particularly from the needle trades' and coal miners' unions.[29] Although most Brookwood students were not Communists, there were generally in the left-wing group a not insignificant number of Communists.[30] The Brookwood student body annually celebrated May Day.[31] By 1928 Brookwood had graduated 111 students.[32]

There is some evidence to indicate that at first a spirit of equal

[26]Theresa Wolfson, "Schools the Miners Keep," *Survey*, Vol. 56, June 1, 1926, pp. 308–310, 332; "ILGWU Builds Body and Brain," *American Teacher*, Vol. 20, September–October 1935, p. 23; *American Labor Year Book, 1925*, pp. 208–209, *1927*, p. 162, *1929*, p. 213; WEB, *Proceedings, 1925*, pp. 83–84.

[27]*American Labor Year Book, 1923–1924*, p. 220; Brookwood Labor College, *Brookwood, 1927* (leaflet).

[28]Interview by the writer with Saposs on June 24, 1953. See also A. J. Muste, "Brookwood—Labor's Training Camp," *Amalgamated Illustrated Almanac, 1924*, p. 153.

[29]*American Labor Year Book, 1925*, p. 208; Helen Norton, "Brookwood in its First Decade," *Labor Age*, Vol. 20, May 1931, pp. 18–19.

[30]Jean A. Flexner, "Brookwood," *New Republic*, Vol. 43, Aug. 5, 1925, pp. 287–289; interview by the writer with Saposs, June 24, 1953.

[31]See "International Import of Labor Symbolized," *Brookwood Review*, Vol. 4, May–June 1926, p. 3.

[32]*Ibid.*, Vol. 2, Dec. 1, 1923, p. 1; Vol. 3, Dec. 15, 1924, p. 8; Vol. 4, October 1925, p. 12; Vol. 4, May–June 1926, p. 1; Vol. 5, June–July 1927, p. 1; Vol. 6, April–May 1928, p. 25.

respect for both the "right" and "left" points of view did indeed prevail in the Brookwood classrooms. A student debate in 1923 on craft versus industrial unionism in a course titled "Labor Problems" was reported as follows:

If we advocate a change in the form or structure of trade unions, it is up to us as the affirmative in the debate to prove our case. Has a change in structure from craft form to industrial proved a help or a detriment? The proponent of amalgamation says Yes; the opponent says No. Either may be right, or they may both be wrong. Off hand we don't know. What unions in the movement have made the change, and what were the results? Assuming that we are still cool-headed about it we will form our judgment on the basis of those results. Therein lies the value of a course in Labor Problems.[33]

Note that in 1923 industrial unionism was discussed at Brookwood in terms of amalgamation.

How long this spirit of debate prevailed at Brookwood is a question which cannot be answered precisely, but by the latter 1920's at least, and probably much earlier, Brookwood had developed a leftist or progressive line clearly critical of conservative trade union policies. As an illustrative instance, in 1927 Tom Tippett cautioned a group of labor educators against eliminating from classroom discussion such matters as union structure, organizing the unorganized, and labor political action. These topics drew "fire inside the family," but Tippett would prefer to abandon workers' education entirely rather than weaken it to avoid antagonizing conservative labor leaders.[34] That a change in classroom spirit took place on the structural question seems rather definite, judging from these excerpts from notes used by David Saposs in 1929 in a course titled "Trade Union Organization Work":

The great problem of American unions is organizing the unorganized. . . . The labor movement has permitted itself to be deceived and cowed by the psychology of welfare capitalism. In the large this is merely a myth, and concerted and aggressive organizing work with

---

[33]"Studies in Curriculum," *ibid.*, Vol. 1, April 15, 1923, p. 2. See also Rebecca Holland, "A Brookwood Class in Action," *ibid.*, Vol. 2, April 15, 1924, p. 6.

[34]Tippett, "Education Versus Propaganda—The Standpoint of Union Policy," *Fourth Annual Conference of Teachers in Workers' Education, 1927*, pp. 83–84. Beginning in 1924, Brookwood became host to an annual conference of teachers in workers' education.

evangelical methods and an emotional appeal will undoubtedly turn the tables and the workers will come into the unions. . . . Only industrial unions with central control can successfully cope with the present problems. . . . Since conditions are ripe for industrial unions what prevents their realization?. . .Leaders are old and fixed in ideas; are unadaptive and accustomed to conditions a generation ago. . . . Trade unions will not bother with unskilled and others who are difficult to organize. Industrial unions can only be organized when a new spirit of idealism permeates the labor movement.[35]

Why did the Brookwood point of view undergo this change (if indeed there ever was any really equal emphasis upon the thinking of both the "right" and the "left")? A relatively simple explanation is that there were no persons with craft union sympathies on the teaching staff and that few of the students came from the old-line craft unions. Under these circumstances, it was probably difficult to stimulate genuine debate or to convert anyone to a different view of union policies and practices. Practically everyone had the "progressive" outlook from the start.

The contribution made by Brookwood, so far as classroom training is concerned, was not therefore that the college increased the number of progressives in the labor movement, but rather that it brought together promising members of the ILGWU, UTW, Hat and Cap Workers, and other organizations and equipped them for better union service. Incidentally, several Brookwood people became lower-echelon leaders in the CIO movement of the 1930's.

While the classroom training of working men and women at Brookwood had consequences pertinent to labor's internal conflict, Brookwood also held a series of summer institutes in the 1920's, some of which brought together labor progressives and provided them a forum for the exchange of their opinions and experiences. These institutes and the writings of the progressives in *Labor Age,* matters which will now be discussed in turn, were probably as important in causing the AFL to repudiate Brookwood in 1928 as was the nature of classroom instruction.

Between 1924 and 1928 Brookwood held twelve summer institutes which dealt with the textile, "giant power," and railroad

[35]Saposs' notes on "Trade Union Organization Work," Brookwood Labor College, 1929–1930. Typed copy in the writer's possession.

industries, women's trade union auxiliaries, and general problems of interest to the labor movement. The four general labor institutes attracted the progressives; most of the others served the needs of craft groups. In 1924 there was only one two-week general institute; such topics as labor's responsibility in production, the meaning of "new methods of collective bargaining," the labor press, and the amalgamation movement were discussed. Details of the institute were not reported.[36]

The interest created among trade unionists by the initial institute experiment encouraged Brookwood to set aside a three-week period in the summer of 1925 for a railroad institute and a general labor institute. The latter was arranged by a committee representing such unions as the ILGWU, Hat and Cap Makers, Lithographers, Furriers, Upholsterers, Printing Pressmen, and the Women's Trade Union League.[37] The participants summarized the trend of trade unionism since World War I and, although they decided that the loss of union membership after the war was not too great, they expressed the belief that the loss could and should be made up by the organization of the mass-production workers. They also suggested the need for a broader program of union activities than existed at that time in the labor movement:

Labor has a big problem [they concluded] in the trustified industries, in the organization of the unskilled and particularly in the metal trades where on account of invention it is hardest to maintain stable standards....Mature unionism tends to take on...a complete range of activities covering the whole economic and political field. It is impossible to draw an arbitrary line and say that any particular type of activity is in itself inconsistent with sound unionism. We should rather stress the necessity of judgment and efficiency in what we undertake, together with constant vigilance to guard against pitfalls that may damage the effectiveness of unions in the battle of labor.[38]

During the following summer Brookwood held textile, giant

[36]"Brookwood Trade Union Summer School," *School and Society*, Vol. 19, June 21, 1924, p. 727; "Labor Summer School," *Brookwood Review*, Vol. 2, April 15, 1924, p. 8.

[37]A. J. Muste, "From Dawn to Dusk at Katonah," *Labor Age*, Vol. 14, October 1925, p. 3.

[38]Quoted by A. J. Muste in "Brookwood Labor Institute," *American Federationist*, Vol. 32, October 1925, p. 940.

power, and railroad institutes which were well attended by national and local trade union officials, and in the summer of 1927 it scheduled a second textile institute, the first institute for women's trade union auxiliaries ever held in the United States, and a general labor institute. The subjects which aroused the greatest interest among those participating in the general labor institute, which lasted for two weeks (August 1–13), were organizing the unorganized, craft versus industrial unionism, and labor political action. The consensus of opinion at the conference with regard to union structure and organization was that craft unionism would have to be abandoned in the mass-production industries if company unions were to be challenged effectively and if the unskilled and semiskilled workers were to be given the opportunity to become trade union members. The progressives declared it their duty to persuade craft union leaders to aid in organizing the unorganized into industrial unions. If these leaders continued to withhold their support, however, then the steel, automobile, and other mass-production workers would pretty largely have to organize themselves, "precisely as all new groups coming into industry have had to organize themselves, as for example,. . .the hod carriers and asbestos workers." In this eventuality the progressives should "clear the way" so that new unions of these workers would be welcomed into the AFL. Furthermore, there was a need, in the opinion of those who attended the institute, for improving morale and stirring enthusiasm in the labor movement, for organizing women workers and the wives of workers, and for "more effective" workers' education. As to political action, the consensus was that organized labor ought to consider the establishment of a third party or "should at any rate throw itself much more earnestly into electing its friends and defeating its enemies."[39]

[39]A. J. Muste, "Organizing and the Organizer," *Brookwood Review*, Vol. 6, September 1927, pp. 3–4. See also "How Can We Organize the Big Industries?" *ibid.*, Vol. 6, September 1927, pp. 1, 5; and Helen Norton, "Brookwood's Summer Institutes," *Survey*, Vol. 59, Oct. 15, 1927, p. 95. Brookwood also sponsored a "Symposium on the Negro in Industry and in the Labor Movement" during the summer of 1927. The National Association for the Advancement of Colored People, the National Urban League, and the Atlanta School of Social Work, as well as trade unions, sent representatives. They agreed that organizing the Negro was complicated by racial discrimination in some unions but that even so the problem was "not essentially different from that of organizing any [other] group of unskilled or semi-skilled

The summer institutes of 1928 were similar to those of the preceding year. Special significance again was attached to the general institute and particularly to the two-day (August 4–5) discussion of union-management cooperation. Participants contended that organized labor had failed to come to grips with the antiunion challenge posed by employers' welfare capitalism programs and that union-management cooperation was not a "50–50" proposition but merely a "rationalization" by organized labor "for conditions forced upon. . . [it] by organized employers."[40]

In addition to its institute program, Brookwood also arranged two conferences on "Youth and the Labor Movement," one in December 1927, the other in May 1928. Members of twenty-two unions attended the first conference, and they did not differ in regarding the organizing of youth as largely a part of the "whole great problem of organizing the unorganized." They repudiated the notion that young people were interested only in jazz and automobiles and had no desire to join unions. The eleven million young workers were almost entirely unorganized, they charged, because the craft unions, by restricting their membership to skilled workers and charging high dues and initiation fees, denied young men and women union status. More important, in the view of the conference, as an obstacle to the organization of the great number of young workers was the fact that the crafts would not abandon their claims of jurisdiction over the workers in mass-production industries, where most young persons were employed. Hinting, therefore, that industrial unionism would be the most effective remedy, the conference also concluded that the craft unions themselves could contribute to a more complete organization of young workers by lowering their dues and initiation fees, appealing to the "imagination" and "ideals" of young workers as well as to their desire for higher wages, devoting more time to apprentices, establishing work-schools, and "activizing" the leadership potential of

workers." Negroes might look for help from white unions, but "in the last analysis" they would have to organize themselves and then "affiliate with the main body of the American labor movement." Helen Norton, "Considering the Negro," *Labor Age*, Vol. 16, August 1927, p. 11. See also "Negroes Can Organize is Conference Feature," *Brookwood Review*, Vol. 5, June–July, 1927, pp. 1, 3.

[40]" 'Welfare Capitalism' Conference Subject," *Brookwood Review*, Vol. 6, June–August 1928, pp. 1, 4; *American Labor Year Book, 1929*, p. 213.

their younger members.[41] The second conference on "Youth and the Labor Movement" appears to have resulted in similar conclusions.[42]

In 1928, owing partly to Brookwood influence, the labor colleges of Philadelphia and Baltimore began to sponsor conferences on current labor problems. Philadelphia Labor College was founded in 1920 by a group of union machinists, and by 1925 it was financially supported by forty-six local unions and district-union councils. The college was affiliated with the education department of the Pennsylvania Federation of Labor and with the WEB. It specialized in "shop economics" to train union officers and members "in the best methods of organizing the unorganized," to inculcate among unionists a group rather than an individualistic point of view, and to teach the most effective methods of contract negotiation.[43]

Apparently at the suggestion of Muste, Israel Mufson, a Brookwood graduate who became secretary of Philadelphia Labor College, scheduled a conference for January 28–29, 1928 dealing with the question of "How to Organize the Unorganized."[44] The leaders of the conference were Muste; Maurer; Cohn; Thomas Kennedy, Secretary-treasurer of the UMW; Joseph Ritchie, the AFL representative in Philadelphia; James Maloney, president of the Glass Bottle Blowers' Association; H. H. Broach, a vice-president of the International Brotherhood of Electrical Workers; William McHugh, a vice-president of the Printing Pressmen; Edward L. Rogers, representative of Typographical Union No. 2; Adolph Hirschberg, president of the Philadelphia Central Labor Union; Dr. Harrison Harley, professor of Psychology at Simmons College; Professor Rexford G. Tugwell of Columbia University; and Louis F. Budenz, editor of *Labor Age*.[45] An average of two hundred and

[41]"Brookwood's 'Youth' Institute," *Labor Age*, Vol. 16, December 1927, p. 11; Eva Shafran, "A Good Beginning—What Next?", *ibid.*, Vol. 17, March 1928, pp. 4–5; " 'Youth' Conference Covers Much Ground," *Brookwood Review*, Vol. 6, December–January 1927–1928, pp. 1, 2.

[42]Helen Norton, "Young Labor Speaks Up," *Survey*, Vol. 60, June 15, 1928, p. 346.

[43]E. J. Lever, "Labor College of Philadelphia," *Machinists' Monthly Journal*, Vol. 37, April 1925, p. 203; Lever, "Shop Economics," *ibid.*, Vol. 37, December 1925, pp. 662, 687.

[44]Muste, "Who's Your Organizer?", *Labor Age*, Vol. 16, October 1927, p. 10; " 'How to Organize' Conference," *ibid.*, Vol. 16, November 1927, p. 10.

[45]"Last Call for the 'How to Organize Conference,' " *ibid.*, Vol. 17, January 1928, p. 5. Budenz did not become a member of the Communist party until August 1935;

fifty persons attended the conference sessions, and for the final session some five hundred persons reportedly crowded the conference room. Craft and industrial unionists, Socialists, Communists, and young workers all were represented. Despite the divergent experiences of conference delegates, the "surprising feature of the whole conference was the absence of bitter wrangling over differences of opinion." The delegates agreed that organizing the unorganized was the major problem facing the labor movement and that its solution required four basic policy changes. In the first place, "craft unionism must be modified or entirely eliminated if the basic, large scale industries are to be made safe for the trade union movement." This course of action was necessary, they said, because the machine was "increasingly obliterating skill differences" and because modern factory production required a collective, rather than an individualistic, labor effort. The American Federation of Labor was not founded in response to the "increasing means for communication and widening markets. It was a union for skilled artisans and not for factory workers."[46] Therefore, they concluded, in order to organize "Coal, Steel, Oil and other big industries, a great move is required. It is—INDUSTRIAL UNIONISM."[47]

In the second place, the delegates believed that in organizing the unorganized, a great deal more attention had to be given to working women, who were rapidly increasing in numbers, and to young workers, the opinion of the conference being that the old-guard leaders of the labor movement expressed "too much resentment of the characteristically critical attitude of young people to make them interested in labor organizations." This attitude would have to be changed before there could be "any success in drawing these young workers into the movement and in keeping them there once they are in."

Finally, the conferees concluded that not only the nature but the spirit of organizing had to be altered. Rather than stress the old slogans of higher wages and shorter hours, the labor movement

Budenz, *Men Without Faces,* p. ix. In the 1920's Budenz was a free-lance labor organizer and a follower of La Follette progressivism. Justus Ebert, "What Have the Progressives Done?", *Labor Age,* Vol. 18, July 1929, p. 8.
[46]Mufson, "Organizing the Unorganized," *Survey,* Vol. 59, March 15, 1928, p. 757.
[47]"Speed Industrial Unionism!", *Labor Age,* Vol. 17, March 1928, p. 24.

104

should present itself to the unorganized as a "crusade for human rights and human values." The imagination of these workers could be captured and their loyalty won if they could be convinced that organized labor was "a champion leading the masses all through history in the fight for recognition and expression."[48]

On July 28–29, 1928 Philadelphia Labor College sponsored a conference on the "Five-Day Week and Unemployment Insurance" in which one hundred and fifty people representing thirty unions took part. The conference declared in favor of a national system of unemployment insurance as the only adequate way to handle the relief problem of the jobless.[49]

William Ross, another Brookwood graduate and secretary of Baltimore Labor College, acted as chairman of a two-day conference on unemployment arranged by Baltimore Labor College in April 1928. Among the speakers at the conference were: Professor Broadus Mitchell of Johns Hopkins University; Theodore G. Risley, Solicitor General of the United States Department of Labor; C. W. Galloway, vice-president of the Baltimore and Ohio Railroad; Professor Irving Fisher of Yale; and Professor Sumner Slichter. Recommendations made by the conferees for relieving unemployment ranged from "the six-hour day, five-day week, to unemployment insurance, federal employment agencies, labor pools, city, state and [federal?] government public work."[50]

It should be mentioned that Brookwood graduates helped to found or gained influential positions in a total of six labor colleges in the East. In addition to those in Baltimore and Philadelphia, the other four were located in Salem (Massachusetts), Wilkes-Barre, Pittsburgh, and Shenandoah.[51] There is evidence, meager to be

[48]Mufson, "Organizing the Unorganized," Survey, Vol. 59, March 15, 1928, pp. 757–758.
[49]Mufson, "Conference on Hours of Work and Unemployment," American Federationist, Vol. 35, September 1928, pp. 1109–1110; Mufson, "American Supremacy Tested," Labor Age, Vol. 17, September 1928, p. 20.
[50]Andrew T. McNamara, "The Baltimore Conference on Unemployment," Machinists' Monthly Journal, Vol. 40, June 1928, pp. 354–355.
[51]"Bring School to Workers," Labor Age, Vol. 17, October 1928, p. 11; "The Brookwood Alumni Protest," ibid., Vol. 18, March 1929, p. 32; and Leonard Craig, "Workers' Education in Pennsylvania," Machinists' Monthly Journal, Vol. 40, October 1928, p. 667. In 1928 John Brophy was secretary of Pittsburgh Labor College. See William Green to Spencer Miller, April 4, 1928, PCB #4, Book 387, NYSSILR Library.

sure, that some unionists considered these and other labor colleges to be "subsidiaries of the Brookwood College."[52]

III

As Brookwood Labor College was an "action" center of trade union opposition to the AFL in the 1920's, the Labor Publication Society, many of whose members also served Brookwood, was a "literary" center of opposition. The Labor Publication Society was formed in 1921; its monthly journal, *Labor Age,* appeared for the first time in November of that year. Many of the original members of the society had been on the editorial staff of the *Socialist Review,* which had been founded in 1919 to present "the extremes of socialist thought and aspiration." The *Socialist Review* was discontinued in 1921 in favor of *Labor Age,* and a new policy declaration indicated that "while the more narrowly socialist problems should not be ignored, far more attention should be given to the problems of labor unionism—problems of increasing importance with every passing day."[53] Nevertheless, many of the original members of the Labor Publication Society were nonunionists and socialist, rather than trade union, aims seemed to dominate a good deal of their thinking.[54] Gradually, however, trade unionists gained control of the LPS, and *Labor Age* became an outlet for the public expression of the thoughts and activities of labor progressives.

In 1926 the officers of the LPS were James Maurer, president; Thomas Kennedy, vice-president; Philip Umstadter (president of Printing Pressmen's Union No. 51), vice-president; and Louis F. Budenz, managing editor and secretary. On the board of directors were J. F. Anderson, a vice-president of the IAM; Abraham Baroff, secretary-treasurer of the ILGWU; H. H. Broach; John Brophy; J. M. Budish, editor of the *Headgear Worker* (official journal of the Hat and Cap Makers); Fannia Cohn; Thomas J.

[52]From a letter sent by P. J. McGrath (secretary of the Central Labor Union of Pittsburgh) to Frank Morrison, Sept. 12, 1928, PCB No. 5, Book 394, NYSSILR Library. McGrath attributed the above-quoted view to other Pittsburgh unionists besides himself.

[53]Harry W. Laidler, "The Future of the Review," *Socialist Review,* Vol. 10, April–May 1921, pp. 33–35.

[54]"Labor Publication Society," *Labor Age,* Vol. 10, November 1921, p. ii; "A Composite Picture of What American Labor is Thinking and Doing," *ibid.,* Vol. 10, November 1921, p. ii.

Curtis, vice-president of the New York Federation of Labor; Max D. Danish, editor of *Justice* (official journal of the ILGWU); Chris J. Golden, president of District 9 of the UMW; Clinton S. Golden, recruiter and fund raiser for Brookwood; Timothy Healy, president of the Firemen and Oilers; William Kohn, president of the Upholsterers; A. J. Kennedy, secretary of the Lithographers; Abraham Lefkowitz; Henry R. Linville, vice-president of the AFT; A. J. Muste; Philip Zausner, a district secretary of the Painters; H. W. Laidler of the League for Industrial Democracy; Prince Hopkins, educator; Joshua Lieberman, secretary of Pioneer Youth; and Anna S. Walling, publicist and wife of William English Walling, the famous Socialist.[55] Once again the reader is to be warned that not all of the LPS board members of 1926 lent their full support to the anti-AFL tone *Labor Age* articles were to take in succeeding years. When the AFL-Brookwood showdown came in 1928, about half of the members left the board, although some of them probably still favored the progressive cause. The leading articles in *Labor Age* were contributed by A. J. Muste.

The ILGWU in 1922 warmly endorsed *Labor Age,* declaring that the intolerance of opinion "even within the labor movement" made "such a medium of impartial and genuinely solid information" valuable and desirable. In 1924 the union contributed toward the financial support of the journal, and in 1928 the ILGWU's general executive board praised *Labor Age* as "a monthly publication devoted to the interests of organized labor." "Issued by a group of men and women active in the Labor Movement," the board continued, "it devotes its columns to every phase and interest of the American Labor Movement. . . . Our international in general and the Educational Department in particular is helping the development of this publication." The Hat and Cap Makers also endorsed *Labor Age.*[56]

[55]*Ibid.*, Vol. 15, April 1926, p. ii. A. J. Muste replaced Umstadter as a vice-president of the society in 1929. *Ibid.*, Vol. 18, February 1929, p. ii. The Labor Publication Society established its offices in the ILGWU building in New York City. In the spring of 1925 the publication of *Labor Age* was transferred to the headquarters of the Pennsylvania Federation of Labor in Harrisburg, the editorial office remaining, however, in New York City. *Ibid.*, Vol. 14, March 1925, p. ii.

[56]ILGWU, *Proceedings, 1922,* pp. 126–127, *1924,* pp. 250–251, *1928,* p. 305; United Cloth Hat and Cap Makers of North America, *Proceedings, 1923,* p. 109, *1927,* p. 275. The title of the latter union was by 1927 changed to the "Cloth Hat, Cap and Millinery Workers' International Union."

The Labor Publication Society did not begin regularly to question the policies of organized labor until 1926. Thereafter, however, the articles in *Labor Age* indicated dissatisfaction on the part of the progressives with a number of these policies.[57] Considerable space was devoted to problems of organizing and union structure, and one can see that the progressives had, during 1926–1928, abandoned amalgamation in favor of the type of industrial unionism later championed by the CIO. As well as campaigning for the organization of the mass-production industries, *Labor Age* waged publicity battles for the organization of women, Negro, and young workers, for more adequate training of organizers and more enlightened organizing methods, and against the company union and the open shop.[58]

In defense of their concern for the organization of mass-production industries and industrial unionism, the progressives developed arguments which were not in any substantial way improved upon by the labor insurgents of the 1930's. They alleged that only 12 percent of the employed labor force in the United States was organized and that in every other major industrial nation the percentage was much higher, ranging from about 35 percent in Sweden, Great Britain, and Germany to over 40 percent in Austria and over 50 percent in Australia. Furthermore, they pointed out that the absolute strength of unionism had steadily waned in the

[57]In addition to organizing the unorganized, these articles dealt, for example, with workers' education, labor political action, union-management cooperation, and old-age pensions. See Fannia Cohn, "Company Unions and Workers' Education," *Labor Age*, Vol. 15, October 1926, pp. 2–4; A. J. Muste, "Back Up Labor Education!", *ibid.*, Vol. 17, July 1928, pp. 5–6; Abraham Lefkowitz, "A.F. of L's Demands Spurned," *ibid.*, Vol. 17, August 1928, p. 12; Israel Mufson, "What of Union Management Cooperation?", *ibid.*, Vol. 15, October 1926, pp. 8–10; Muste, "Peace or Pep?", *ibid.*, Vol. 17, January 1928, pp. 6–7; J. M. Budish, "Breaking the Vicious Circle," *ibid.*, Vol. 17, May 1928, pp. 2–3; Abraham Epstein, "Pensions for Aged Workers," *ibid.*, Vol. 16, December 1927, p. 20.

[58]Fannia Cohn, "Are Women Organizable?", *ibid.*, Vol. 16, March 1927, pp. 18–19; Geneva M. Marsh, "Can Women be Organized?", *ibid.*, Vol. 17, March 1928, pp. 5–7; Thomas L. Dabney, "Negro Workers at the Crossroads," *ibid.*, Vol. 16, February 1927, pp. 8–10; "Our Negro Brothers," *ibid.*, Vol. 16, June 1927, p. 22; Muste, "Appeal to Youth," *ibid.*, Vol. 16, July 1927, pp. 2–4; Muste, "Who's Your Organizer?", *ibid.*, Vol. 16, October 1927, pp. 9–10; Muste, "Getting the Most Out of Your Organizer," *ibid.*, Vol. 16, November 1927, pp. 15–17; Robert W. Dunn, "Company Union in Oil," *ibid.*, Vol. 15, April 1926, pp. 15–18; Louis F. Budenz, "Industrial Unionism vs. Company Unionism?", *ibid.*, Vol. 15, October 1926, pp. 5–7.

United States since 1920, and they concluded that it was the duty of the labor movement to do something about the situation. Since 80 percent of all nonunion workers were employed in the basic industries, these industries were the obvious source for the recruitment of union members. Lack of organization in these sectors of the economy tended, through competition, to reduce union standards, create unemployment, and diminish union membership elsewhere. Moreover, unionism had to be established in the basic industries were working men and women ever to gain "full control of their destiny." In answer to the charge, which they attributed to conservative labor leaders, that mass-production workers were unorganizable, the progressives contended that millions of these workers had accepted union cards during and shortly after World War I. As for high wages constituting a barrier to the extension of unionism, the progressives argued that unions had their inception in the United States among the skilled workers and that an appeal to the "labor consciousness, labor idealism, [and] spiritual energy" of the unorganized was perhaps more important to the initial success of a campaign than a promise of higher wages.[59]

New industrial unions were necessary in the mass-production industries, said the progressives, because the assembly-line technique of modern production had broken down craft distinctions and produced a large group of unskilled and semiskilled workers. Existing craft unions either had no really clear jurisdiction over these workers or their claims were so hopelessly confused that the only solution seemed to be to create new industrial unions. Moreover, although craft unions asserted claims to mass-production workers, they did not exercise these claims and did not wish to. The craftsmen's experience with lesser skilled workers, whom they enrolled during World War I, convinced them that if they improved working conditions for the lesser skilled they would, by the same token, place limits on the concessions they could win for themselves. Equally important, mass-production workers were

[59]"The Challenge to Progressives," *ibid.*, Vol. 18, February 1929, p. 3; Margaret Hutchinson, "Organize the Unorganized," *ibid.*, Vol. 17, February 1928, pp. 4–5; Louis F. Budenz, "Why Industral Unionism?", *ibid.*, Vol. 16, June 1927, p. 23; J. M. Budish, "Selling Unionism—To Whom?", *ibid.*, Vol. 18, April 1929, pp. 17–18; Muste, "Nothing to Offer?", *ibid.*, Vol. 17, March 1928, pp. 2–4.

opposed to being separated into a number of unions and, at any rate, had little faith that craft unions were effective collective bargaining agencies. Industrial unionism, the progressive argument ran, would virtually eliminate intercraft jealousies, race prejudice, and jurisdictional disputes, would make organized labor stronger in its relations with big employers, and would enhance the power and prestige of the labor movement in general. Finally, it was declared, industrial unions had always been successful, in one way or another, whether they functioned within or outside the AFL.[60]

The tendency of Muste and others was to become increasingly outspoken and biting in their criticism of AFL leadership. For example, in April 1927, Muste declared that the mass-production industries would never be organized by the kind of unionism that considered assembly-line workers unorganizable or expected the "bosses" to do the organizing; rather than try to sell unionism to management, Muste advised, labor leaders should sell it to the workers. Neither would the mass-production industries be organized by a labor movement concerned with proving to itelf and to its enemies that it was "respectable," by a labor movement which was "wedded to an arbitrary idea of craft unionism," or by a labor movement which feared, or considered itself superior to, the workers' education movement.[61]

[60]Hutchinson, "Organize the Unorganized," *ibid.*, Vol. 17, February 1928, p. 5; J. M. Budish, "Whose Business?", *ibid.*, Vol. 17, June 1928, p. 7; Muste, "Appeal to Youth!", *ibid.*, Vol. 16, July 1927, p. 2; E. J. Lever, "What of the Metal Trades?", *ibid.*, Vol. 15, August 1926, pp. 11–13; Louis F. Budenz, "Industrial Unionism vs. Company Unionism?", *ibid.*, Vol. 15, October 1926, p. 6; Thomas Kennedy, "Industrial Unionism? Miners' Experience Approves It," *ibid.*, Vol. 15, September 1926, pp. 2–3; Budenz, "Why Industrial Unionism?", *ibid.*, Vol. 16, June 1927, p. 23; Muste, "Whose Job?", *ibid.*, Vol. 17, February 1928, p. 6.
[61]Muste, "The Kind of Unionism That Will Not Organize the Basic Industries," *ibid.*, Vol. 16, April 1927, pp. 2–4.

CHAPTER V

The AFL Split With the Progressives

BROOKWOOD Labor College was by 1928 one of the most out-standing of some forty workers' educational enterprises affiliated with the Workers' Education Bureau and through its classroom training, institute and conference programs, and its dominating influence in the Labor Publication Society had become a source of opposition to AFL leadership and policies. At the same time, the AFL leadership had become a formidable source of opposition to Brookwood, for reasons detailed below. The result was a split, directed by the AFL, which was, in turn, followed by the progressives' founding of the Conference for Progressive Labor Action.

I

As early as 1926 the AFL cast a critical eye in the direction of the Katonah College. At William Green's request, Ralph M. Easely forwarded to him in May 1926 confidential information concerning Arthur W. Calhoun, a Brookwood faculty member who was to figure prominently in the AFL-Brookwood split.[1] The following spring Green delegated Spencer Miller, Jr., secretary of the WEB, to inquire into the celebration of May Day at Brookwood, and somewhat tardily, Miller sent Green a report on this subject.[2]

[1]Green acknowledged receipt of this information on May 7. Green to Easely, May 17, 1926, PCB #2, Book 362, NYSSILR Library.
[2]Green to Miller, Jan. 27, 1928, PCB #4, Book 384, *ibid.*

After adjournment of the 1927 convention of the WEB, Miller reported at length to Green upon the general subject of Brookwood, its programs, and personnel. He told Green that representatives and former students of the college had been present at the WEB convention in "goodly numbers." This was not bad in itself, Miller explained, but Brookwood taught radical doctrines and, at the behest of the Garland Fund directors, accepted "a certain number of radical students." Although A. J. Muste always seemed eager to point up trade unionism at Brookwood, he never took a definite stand against the radicals. Miller felt that Calhoun was "a most destructive influence" at Brookwood. Perhaps Miller's greatest apprehension was over the growing importance Brookwood was assuming in the field of workers' education. "Not only is Brookwood getting a control by its students who become leaders in workers education," he told Green, "but by the fact that . . . nationals and internationals find the Brookwood plant a convenient environment and allow the development of the Institute program to drift into Brookwood control." This meant that "Mr. Muste" controlled the whole institute program "without seeking W.E.B. cooperation." Miller suggested that the WEB could counteract Brookwood's growing influence by holding institutes itself and by "securing the cooperation of state universities."[3]

At the May 1927 meeting of the AFL Executive Council in Indianapolis Martin F. Ryan, president of the Brotherhood of Railway Carmen, handed Green a letter, critical of Brookwood, which he had received from "Mr. Rattigan," a Canadian official of the Carmen. According to Green the letter contained "much inside information regarding certain activities being carried on at Brookwood College," and although he had "rather suspected that the atmosphere at Brookwood was sort of surcharged with radical tendencies," he had not thought, he told Ryan, that the situation was "quite as bad as reported by your friend, Mr. Rattigan."[4] By August 1927 anti-Brookwood rumors had spread among trade unionists to the extent that the International Brotherhood of

[3]"Report on the 1927 WEB Convention" in a letter, Miller to Green, April 26, 1927, Convention File #11, AFL-CIO Archives.
[4]Green to Ryan, June 3, 1927, PCB #3, Book 376, NYSSILR Library.

Electrical Workers' committee on resolutions, in response to three requests that the union endorse Brookwood, decided to refer the matter to the union's international officers; the committee explained that there had been "various objections to the manner of [teaching] and subjects taught" at Brookwood.[5]

It was a disturbance within the Brookwood student body itself in April 1928, however, which precipitated an official AFL investigation of the college—a move which led immediately to an open break between the two organizations. At a student body meeting on April 17, five students (R. M. Ware and Hector Daoust of the Railway Carmen; William Absolon of the Painters; P. E. Powers, a machinist; and James Boyd, a coal miner) resolved that Brookwood should no longer celebrate May 1 as a labor holiday because, they contended, such an activity placed the school "in an unfavorable light" within the "responsible labor movement." The resolution was defeated, whereupon Ware promptly communicated its content and the names of its signers to William Green. The AFL president complimented Ware and his associates on the stand they had taken and suggested that he would appreciate further information "in connection with this matter."[6] On May 3 Ware obliged Green with a report describing the manner in which May Day had been celebrated. He later forwarded to AFL headquarters a copy of a more general report on the spirit of Brookwood which he and Daoust had already prepared for the officers of their own union.[7]

Because Green regarded the information he had received from Ware and Daoust as "proof of the situation at Brookwood which we had occasion to suspect," he asked Matthew Woll, as chairman of the WEB's executive committee, to investigate Brookwood and report the facts as soon as possible.[8] Woll, who later said that the subject of Brookwood Labor College was "one in which I have held myself in restraint for some time,"[9] secretly inquired into the

[5]IBEW, *Proceedings, 1927*, pp. 155–157.
[6]Green to Ware, April 20, 1928, PCB #4, Book 387, NYSSILR Library; AFL, *Proceedings, 1928*, p. 321.
[7]Green to Ware, May 12, 20, 1928, PCB #4, Book 388, NYSSILR Library.
[8]Green to Woll, May 31, 1928, PCB #4, Book 389, *ibid.*
[9]AFL, *Proceedings, 1928*, p. 318.

113

nature of classroom instruction at Brookwood and into the activities of the college faculty and student body.

On August 7, 1928 the AFL Executive Council announced that it intended to advise all of the AFL's affiliated unions to withdraw their support from Brookwood Labor College. A report made by Matthew Woll revealed, the Council said, that anti-AFL and antireligious doctrines were being taught at Brookwood and that "pro-Soviet demonstrations had occurred there."[10] On October 29 the Council so advised its affiliates, and the action of the Council was approved by the 1928 AFL convention. On January 18, 1929 the executive council of the Workers' Education Bureau disaffiliated Brookwood from the Bureau and declared Muste's position on the council vacant.[11]

In the course of these events the Carmen, Machinists, Painters, and some other, unidentified, unions severed their connections with Brookwood. The UMW decried the fact that some of its members had "absorbed the fallacious doctrines" taught at the college and commented that many people had always wondered "why any labor union would embrace Brookwood." Since state and city central bodies were under direct AFL control, all of those that had endorsed Brookwood probably withdrew their support. John Fitzpatrick, head of the Illinois Federation of Labor, reluctantly resigned from the Brookwood Board of Directors.[12]

[10]*New York Times*, Aug. 8, 1928.

[11]*Ibid.*, Oct. 31, 1928; AFL, *Proceedings, 1928*, pp. 314–325, 327, 338–339; A. J. Muste, "Who Closed Door on Negotiations?", *Brookwood Review*, Vol. 7, February-April 1929, p. 2.

[12]The IAM, upon the recommendation of its officers, who were influenced not only by the AFL Executive Council's announcement but also by anti-Brookwood material gathered by the IAM's New York City district body, withdrew all support from the college in September 1928; the step was taken over the opposition of Fred Hewitt, Robert Fechner, Charles Kutz, and the membership of the union's committee on education. The Painters and the Carmen had taken similar action by the time the AFL convention met in late November 1928. *Report of Grand Lodge Officers to the Eighteenth Convention of the International Association of Machinists,* pp. 16–17; IAM, *Proceedings, 1928,* pp. 80–81, 365–375; "Synopsis of Proceedings, Sixteenth Convention," *Railway Carmen's Journal*, Vol. 34, October 1929, p. 410; AFL, *Proceedings, 1928,* p. 317; "Labor Places Ban on Brookwood College and Asks Trade Unions to Sever all Connections with It," *United Mine Workers' Journal*, Vol. 39, Sept. 1, 1928, p. 11. Upon resigning from the Brookwood Board, Fitzpatrick told Green that he was "deeply grieved on account of the way in which this matter was handled." Green, in turn, was deeply impressed by Fitzpatrick's attitude, and evidently not sure that the AFL had acted fairly, he sent Fitzpatrick some of Woll's

On the other hand, some two hundred individuals and several union bodies came to the defense of Brookwood, many of them protesting the secrecy of Woll's investigation, declaring the AFL's action an unjust interference with academic freedom, and asking that Brookwood be granted a hearing on the charges. Among the protesting individuals were union officers and members, educators and editors, social workers and reformers, and ministers.[13] Among the unions were the AFT, UTW, Hosiery Workers, Railway Clerks, and Lithographers.[14]

Matthew Woll's report on Brookwood was never made public in its entirety, but at the November convention of the AFL considerable detail was added to the cryptic statement which had been released by the Council the preceding August. At the convention Woll and Green summarized or quoted from statements which had been made by six Brookwood students and from documents they had received or had compiled from other sources. Most of the evidence they presented to the convention, however, had been supplied to them by three students, Ware, Daoust, and Absolon.[15]

The portions of evidence cited by Woll and Green indicated that all Brookwood faculty members were "left-wing," that during the academic year 1927–1928 three of them (Calhoun, Saposs, and an unidentified member) had served on the Board of Advisers of the Workers' (Communist) School in New York City, two of them

---

reports on Brookwood and asked him if in the light of this information he believed "the action of the Council was justifiable? I will thank you very much if you will write me promptly giving me your opinion on this matter." There is no evidence that Fitzpatrick answered. Green to Fitzpatrick, Dec. 13, 1928, PCB #5, Book 395, NYSSILR Library.

[13]For a sample of the protesting letters addressed to William Green, see PCB #5, Book 391, Document Numbers 544–552, 556–558, 560–563, 565, 705, 722, 723–733, NYSSILR Library.

[14]American Federation of Full Fashioned Hosiery Workers, *Proceedings, 1928,* pp. 77–78, 252–253; UTW, *Proceedings, 1928,* pp. 113–114; "Friends Rally to Brookwood," *Labor Age,* Vol. 17, October 1928, p. 21.

[15]Green himself, at the suggestion of "a friend," wrote to Absolon on August 3 and told him that the AFL was "very anxious to know something about the work of Brookwood College, the attitude of the faculty and officers of this college toward the philosophy and policies of the trade union movement, and the course of study that students follow while in attendance at Brookwood." Absolon's reply, dated August 6, very likely was not considered by the Council before it made the August 7 announcement. See Green to Absolon, Aug. 3, 14, 1928, PCB #5, Book 391, NYSSILR Library.

(Calhoun and Saposs) had been lecturers there, and one (Muste) had been a discussion leader at that school. Calhoun was labeled "an avowed Communist," and it was alleged that Muste favored communism and that it was "under that guidance that the institution [Brookwood] is being conducted."

As to the nature and quality of instruction at Brookwood, the charge was made that "radical doctrines" were taught in every class. Sociology was taught by Calhoun from an anarchistic and anti-religious (that is, proevolutionary) point of view. The economics instructor, Tom Tippett, contended that it was the purpose of workers' education to analyze and discuss trade union policies. Foreign Labor History, "while of an impartial character, . . dealt almost wholly with the activities of radical elements in the labor history of Europe." Social Economics was a "partly helpful" course but was concerned largely with "abstract theories" which had no application to the labor movement. The course in Social Psychology dealt mainly with "sex impulses, sex behavior, and kindred subjects." The purpose of Labor Journalism was to spread radical propaganda. Public Speaking was taught by an anarchist who used "all kinds of guttery language" in his lectures. David Saposs, who gave the course in Trade Unionism, was extremely biased in favor of radical doctrines and against the principles for which the AFL stood.

It was also announced that Brookwood observed May Day "with ceremonies" and with pictures of Charles E. Ruthenberg, Marx, Lenin, Trotsky, and Gompers draped with red bunting and celebrated the victory of the Soviet October Revolution using "every resource and every appeal. . . to laud Communism and Communists . . . on that day." Brookwood gave scant attention to the International Federation of Trade Unions but praised the Third International "as the great institution that will save labor and the workers the world over." Finally, it was charged that five Brookwood students had participated in 1928 in the "Save-the-Union" movement, the purpose of which was to erect a "dual organization to the United Mine Workers"; they had done so with "the silent, if not the direct acquiescence and permission of the faculty."[16]

[16]AFL, *Proceedings, 1928,* pp. 315–323.

II

Who was right and who was wrong in the AFL-Brookwood controversy? How many of the AFL charges were true? What significance is to be attached to these charges? What motivated AFL leaders to move against Brookwood? Should the AFL have granted Brookwood a hearing? Can unions be expected to stand squarely behind academic freedom in a college they help to support? Not all of these questions can be answered satisfactorily, but there is some light to be shed on the AFL-Brookwood controversy.

Perhaps the severest charge against Brookwood was the one which associated it with communism. It is true that Muste and Saposs lectured occasionally at the Workers' School, but neither of them was a Communist.[17] Calhoun was a teacher at the Workers' School, he voted the Communist ticket in the elections of 1924 and 1928, and although he denied membership in the Workers' party, the Brookwood Board of Directors eventually released him from the staff because he contended, according to the Board, that the college "should adopt a policy of Communism."[18]

As already stated a sizable minority of Brookwood students were Communists. (In 1928 Brookwood stopped admitting Communists.[19]) Although the written evidence presently available does not show that Brookwood students celebrated the Soviet October Revolution, it is not unlikely that the Communist students did so. As for May Day, it has seldom been celebrated by the main body of American trade unionists, but it is celebrated by the workers in most industrial countries—non-Communist as well as Communist.

[17]Interview by the writer with Saposs, June 24, 1953. See also Muste, "Kind of Unionism That Will Organize the Basic Industries," *Labor Age,* Vol. 16, May 1927, p. 8. In this article Muste stated: "I have never been a Communist, and...I am on record in previous issues of *Labor Age* and in plenty of other places as critical of Communist or Left Wing methods."

[18]Quoted in *American Labor Year Book, 1930,* p. 185. See also *ibid., 1927,* p. 164; "Green's 'Irrefutable Changes' Answered," *Brookwood Review,* Vol. 7, December-January 1928–1929, pp. 1, 4; Arthur W. Calhoun, "Mr. Calhoun and Brookwood," *Brookwood Review,* Vol. 7, December-January 1928–1929, pp. 1, 4; Arthur W. Calhoun, "Mr. Calhoun and Brookwood," *New Republic,* Vol. 60, Aug. 21, 1929, p. 20; *Daily Worker,* Aug. 8, 1928; *New York Times,* June 4, 1929.

[19]Notes on Brookwood supplied the writer by Helen Norton Starr, a former member of the Brookwood staff.

Although Brookwood was not, therefore, entirely free of Communist influence, the college was probably neither dominated nor controlled by Communists. The acid test came in 1928 when Brookwood remained loyal to the AFL after the Workers' party abandoned the policy of "boring from within" AFL unions and began to sponsor the formation of dual unions.[20]

The reactions of official Workers' party spokesmen to the AFL report on and action against Brookwood tend to support the conclusion that, over-all, Brookwood was not a Communist institution. The *Daily Worker* greeted the Council's August announcement by declaring:

There are no Communists on the staff of the school. Its teachings are known [to be] those primarily of class collaboration. The fact seems to be that the A. F. of L. has made up its "mind" not to contribute to the Endowment Fund which Brookwood has been seeking to raise. It has no use for the liberals and individualists who dominate its policies. The labor misleaders prefer to control their "educational" propaganda through the Workers' Education Bureau, endowed by the Carnegie Foundation.

A few days later, a *Daily Worker* columnist reported the incident with derision:

Few will be sorry that the executive council of the A. F. of L. hurled a well-directed shot of garbage at the Brookwood Labor College.... That the A. F. of L. charges are unfounded does not affect the chuckle which goes up from this department. Matthew Woll, the chief heressy [sic] hunter of the executive council, learned that Brookwood was a nest of atheism and Soviet propaganda. The fact is that it is neither fish, flesh nor good frog jelly. The writer never knew or heard of any graduate of Katonah that was fit for anything better than lecturing before the left wing of the National Womans' [sic] Party. Its directorate catered to the bureaucrats of the A. F. of L. for the sake of dough and respectability. Its fate at the hands of the executive council is one

[20]For an account of the switch in Communist policy, see Louis Stanley, "Communist Dual Unionism," *Labor Age*, Vol. 18, October 1929, p. 9. For Muste's reaction to this switch, see Muste, "Mother Throws Out the Baby," *ibid.*, Vol. 17, October 1928, pp. 20–21. None of the following accounts of Communist activities in the United States mentions Brookwood or any of the persons associated with the college: Benjamin Gitlow, *I Confess;* William Z. Foster, *History of the Communist Party of the United States;* and James Oneal and G. A. Werner, *American Communism.*

118

more demonstration that those who stand neither with the right nor with the left get the bricks from both extremes.

The young Workers' (Communist) League revealed its conviction that Brookwood had always played the game of "the corrupt and reactionary labor bureaucracy" in its attitude toward young workers and that the League would continue, therefore, to struggle against Brookwood and "to make every effort to destroy whatever influence it may have among working youth."[21]

As regards the AFL charge that Brookwood was antireligious, Calhoun did teach evolution. The college did not directly attack religion, however. On the contrary, persons of all faiths were accepted as students and transportation was furnished to those who wished to attend church at Katonah, a few miles from the campus.[22]

The lack of direct evidence makes it impossible to determine exactly what went on inside the Brookwood classrooms. In contrast to the appraisal of Brookwood courses made by the three dissatisfied students, however, are the comments of twenty-one former Brookwood students who individually wrote to Green during late 1928 and protested the course of action taken by the AFL. They contended that Brookwood did not teach "isms" of any kind, that their Brookwood experience had made them neither Communists nor atheists, that contrarily their training at Katonah had prepared them to serve more effectively the cause of trade unionism, and that they felt deeply indebted to the college.[23] In February 1929 thirty-five Brookwood alumni signed an open letter

[21]*Daily Worker,* Aug. 8, 12, 1928. For additional anti-Brookwood statements in the *Daily Worker,* see *ibid.,* Nov. 29, 30, Dec. 1, 1928. The Brookwood building and endowment fund campaign mentioned by the *Daily Worker* was launched in June 1926. Its goal was two million dollars with which Brookwood hoped to expand its facilities so as to make possible the accommodation of one hundred students. Although a long list of persons of public reputation, such for example as Jane Addams, John R. Commons, and Robert M. La Follette, Jr., supported the campaign, it had raised only a little more than $50,000 by March 1928. "Two Millions for Brookwood is Aim," *Brookwood Review,* Vol. 4, May-June 1926, p. 1; "Endowment Campaign Generously Endorsed," *ibid.,* Vol. 5, October-November 1926, p. 1; "As Other See Us," *ibid.,* Vol. 5, December-January 1926–1927, p. 2; "Establish Scholarship to Honor Jim Maurer," *ibid.,* Vol. 5, February-March 1927, p. 1; "$50,-050 for Building and Endowment Fund in Sight," *ibid.,* Vol. 6, February-March 1928, p. 1.

[22]A. J. Muste, "Brookwood—Labor's Training Camp," *Amalgamated Illustrated Almanac, 1924,* p. 153; interview by the writer with Saposs, June 24, 1953.

[23]These letters are in PCB #5, Book 391, NYSSILR Library.

to Green declaring that "Brookwood Labor College has given us such an understanding of organized labor as to make it utterly impossible for us to be otherwise than loyal to it."[24] The difference between the dissident students (two railway carmen, a painter, a machinist, and a coal miner) and the loyalists, with regard to Brookwood training, appears essentially to have been the difference between the "pure and simple" craft unionist and the more sophisticated, politically oriented needle trades' worker.

The "Save-the-Union" movement, begun in 1926 under the leadership of John Brophy, a Brookwood director, was intended as its name implies to function as a reform opposition within, rather than as a rival to, the UMW. The dissident miners who supported the movement wanted to wrest control of the UMW from John L. Lewis, organize the unorganized miners, and restore autonomy to the UMW's district bodies.[25] Some coal miners who had graduated from Brookwood supported Brophy from the very beginning of his movement, and in April 1928 five Brookwood students did attend a Pittsburgh conference of the movement called and chaired by Brophy.[26]

After the conference, and also after Brophy had resigned as the leader of the "Save-the-Union" movement, Communist elements gained control of the movement, redirected its purpose, and erected the dual National Miners' Union. This was not done, however, until September 1928, a month after Woll had completed his investigation of Brookwood and the Council had decided to take action against the college.[27]

Nevertheless, one should not conclude from the above that, on the UMW issue, Brookwood did not imprudently expose itself to criticism. Teaching and politicking in internal union affairs is an explosive combination, especially when the institution involved has labor support and wants more of it.

[24]Quoted in *New York Times*, Feb. 14, 1929. See also "The Brookwood Alumni Protest," *Labor Age*, Vol. 18, March 1929, p. 32.

[25]Interview by the writer with Brophy, July 3, 1953; David Saposs, "Labor," *American Journal of Sociology*, Vol. 34, May 1929, pp. 1013–1014.

[26]A. J. Muste, "The Crisis in the Miners' Union," *Labor Age*, Vol. 19, March 1930, p. 6; Green to Muste, Dec. 14, 1928, PCB #5, Book 395, NYSSILR Library.

[27]Interview by the writer with Brophy, July 3, 1953; David Saposs, "Labor," *American Journal of Sociology*, Vol. 34, May 1929, pp. 1013–1014.

It need scarcely be affirmed that Brookwood was, as the charge ran, openly critical of the conservative principles and policies of the AFL. This charge raised perhaps the most significant issue of the whole controversy—academic freedom versus union control of policy-making. The way the issue was resolved was to have consequences of far-reaching importance in the future development of workers' education in this country and the new direction the progressives were forced to take in their role as critics of AFL policies.

It must be remembered that from the start Brookwood announced its intention to discuss and analyze the internal policies of trade unions, and that some of the pioneer labor educators in the United States conceived of workers' education as a leavening force which would permit the gradual reform of union policies and lead ultimately to the establishment of a new and better social order. Obviously, these goals were at variance (1) with the traditional belief in the labor movement that the unions themselves had exclusive control of union policies and (2) with the job-conscious philosophy of the majority element in the AFL. Pertinent to the first point are these remarks made in 1928 by the AFL's permanent Committee on Education:

In the development of workers' education a number of facts have become clear. The first of these is the importance of restricting interference with the trade union's final and absolute right to determine its own policy. This principle is inherent in the philosophy of the American trade union movement; it is the basis of its insistence on voluntarism and local autonomy.[28]

So long as labor educators clung to their original aims, a showdown with AFL leaders was bound to come. Brookwood and other labor colleges could not expect to get and keep the endorsement and financial support of conservative unions and, at the same time, cast doubt upon and advocate changes in the basic principles of these unions. Under these circumstances the doctrine of academic freedom would not appear to have been relevant. Nor is it likely that a public investigation or hearing would have changed the predicament in which Brookwood found itself.

[28]AFL, *Proceedings, 1928*, p. 86.

Conservative labor leaders, therefore, were understandably suspicious of workers' education in the 1920's. They were perhaps even more suspicious of the "intellectuals" within the labor movement than of those outside it.[29] Those outside could be ignored; those inside could not. Trade union intellectuals not only raised and discussed "touchy" questions of union policy within the movement but they were also able in some instances in the 1920's to advance to official positions of importance in local and national unions. John H. Walker, chairman of the AFL's temporary Committee on Education, declared that the faculty and students of all workers' education schools seemed "to have formed themselves into an organization for office-seeking purposes to place their men in every job in the labor movement."[30]

In the private papers of William Green and John J. Manning (a member of the United Garment Workers who was also secretary-treasurer of the Union Label Trades Department) one finds evidence that top labor officials also distinguished a fundamental personality difference between the ordinary trade unionist and the labor educator. As Green said,

a Workers' Education Convention cannot be measured by the same standard as that found in a Trade Union convention or in a convention of the American Federation of Labor. An "Education" convention is made up of different types of people than those who attend a Trade Union convention. Many of those who attend an Education convention look at matters from a theoretical and academic point of view while those who attend Trade Union Conventions are practical men and women dealing with Trade Union problems in a practical way. We cannot help but draw the line of distinction between those who are drawn to an educational conference and those who represent trade unions in a trade union convention.[31]

After attending the 1927 WEB convention, Manning reported that "the general atmosphere of the Convention was such that many

[29]For an account of the AFL's attitude in the 1920's toward intellectuals outside the labor movement, see Lyle W. Cooper, "The American Federation of Labor and the Intellectuals," *Political Science Quarterly*, Vol. 43, September 1928, pp. 388–407.

[30]AFL, *Proceedings, 1928*, pp. 319, 322.

[31]Green to Frey, July 18, 1927, Container 15, Frey Papers.

trade unionists with whom we [Garment Workers' delegates] talked said they felt out of place."[32]

It was probably, however, the basic policy-making conflict between unionism and workers' education which caused AFL leaders (1) to censor WEB publications, (2) to secure from the WEB a commitment not to discuss trade union policies, and (3) to repudiate Brookwood Labor College. As a logical conclusion to this chain of events, the WEB convention in April 1929 declared in favor of the extension departments of state universities, rather than labor colleges, as the future source for workers' education.[33] The AFL Executive Council directed the Bureau to make the policy statement.[34] This did not interfere, of course, with an individual union's traditional right to have its own internal educational program. What it meant was that for the broader or "cultural" type of workers' education, the AFL had put its stamp of approval upon the public universities. It also meant, therefore, the inevitable decline of the labor colleges.[35]

Also at the 1929 convention of the WEB, the executive council of the organization, chaired by Woll, asked for and secured the final changes in vote allotment which gave the AFL and its national unions firm control of the Workers' Education Bureau and provided for the abolition of a regularly scheduled, biennial convention.[36] The WEB did not meet again for more than four years.

By the close of the 1920's, therefore, the AFL had taken the necessary steps to throttle that type of workers' education which

[32]"Report on Convention of Workers Education Bureau" by John J. Manning, Container 15, *ibid.*

[33]AFL, *Proceedings, 1929,* p. 121.

[34]*Ibid.,* 1928, p. 86.

[35]John R. Commons and John Dewey, although they recognized that public universities could contribute a great deal to the education of working people, believed that organized labor needed its own colleges to train men and women for positions of leadership. Commons, "Workers Education and the Universities," *American Federationist,* Vol. 34, April 1927, pp. 424–426; Dewey, "Freedom in Workers Education," *American Teacher,* Vol. 13, January 1929, p. 3.

[36]WEB, *Outline of the Major Actions Taken by the 6th Annual Convention, 1929,* Appendix A, "Constitution," p. 3. As a result of these decisions, James Maurer resigned from the presidency of the Bureau feeling that the AFL had demoralized the workers' education movement and had violated the original pledge that it did not seek to control the WEB. " 'Jim' Maurer's Warning," *Labor Age,* Vol. 13, May 1929, pp. 3–4.

had been critical of fundamental AFL policies. So far as its position in the general labor movement is concerned, workers' education was thereafter recognized and treated, more than ever before, as a staff operation under the strict control of union officers. Progressives could no longer hope peacefully to reform the labor movement through its educational arm.

The progressives of the 1920's, unlike the Committee for Industrial Organization, did not have the union support to back up the strong critical line they were taking. The UMW was split internally and in a steep membership decline. The ILGWU was seriously weakened for a time by Communist infiltration of its New York locals. The ACW was still an independent union. These three unions provided the core of the CIO movement in the 1930's. Also, the progressives of the twenties did not seem to realize that at that time there was really no strong sentiment for unionism in the big industries. They were barking up the right tree, but alone and in the wrong season.

Quite apart from the advanced reform tendencies of Brookwood as a factor in stimulating AFL leaders to action, these leaders were probably also genuinely concerned about Brookwood radicalism. They did not wish to be connected, even remotely, with a leftist institution supported in part by the leftist Garland Fund. To have been found guilty of radicalism, even by association, would have thwarted their desire to be respected as "sound" and "American" citizens. The militant tenor of the entire Brookwood-LPS program (even excepting May Day, etc.) was at variance with the union-management cooperation line being followed by the AFL.

One can conclude that AFL leaders desired (1) to arrest the progress the college was making as a source of opposition to AFL policies, (2) to "expose" Brookwood as a left-wing organization, and also (3) to limit the college's growth as an educational institution. On the latter score, it is to be recalled that Spencer Miller thought that Brookwood was taking the education spotlight from the WEB.

III

Student enrollment at Brookwood Labor College did not begin to decline until 1932, when many unions were no longer able, due to the deepening depression, to finance the education of their members. For lack of funds, Brookwood finally closed its doors in 1937. Yet the college had long since been superseded as a center of opposition to AFL leadership when, in May 1929, the Conference for Progressive Labor Action was formed.

An important link in the chain of events leading to the formation of the CPLA in May was the issuance by the "Musteites" in February of a ringing, sixteen-point challenge "to all honest, militant, progressive elements—to all those who are in accord neither with Communist tactics nor with reactionary elements . . . —a challenge to clarify their thinking, define their purposes, and organize their efforts." The major plank of the progressives, and the most important task facing the labor movement, the statement declared, was the organization of the unorganized into industrial unions. The first slogan should be "Organize, Organize, Organize!" Also, the labor movement represented a struggle between employers and employees rather than a situation of congeniality, and for this reason progressives should fight union-management cooperation and the "National Civic Federation influence over the labor movement and its policies." Progressives should seek to end the denial of trade union membership to anyone for racial, political, social, economic, or religious reasons, and they were urged to stand unreservedly for the right of a minority opposition to exist in the labor movement. The elimination of injunctions and yellow-dog contracts was recommended, and genuine cooperative enterprises, the various types of social insurance, a "dependable year-round income" for workers, the five-day week, higher wages, shorter hours, and better working conditions were declared to be among the primary objectives of progressives. Other goals set forth in the challenge were a labor party, workers' education with a "union label," and the recognition of Soviet Russia by the United States. Finally, the progressives indicated a need for a "definitely anti-imperialistic" and anti-militaristic" labor movement and one which would become international in both spirit and action by encouraging "a closer union of all the workers of the world."[37]

[37]"The Challenge to Progressives, An Editorial Statement," *Labor Age*, Vol. 18, February 1929, pp. 3–7. It might appear that some of the points in this challenge,

Later on in the month of February, at the annual conference of teachers in workers' education which met at Brookwood, a handful of labor progressives took stock of trade union developments in the 1920's and discussed their future course as critics of the labor movement. Their choice, they believed, was between adopting a conciliatory attitude toward organized labor or "going ahead and doing as much as possible." Although they recognized that the latter course would involve "outrunning the labor movement" and although there was some concern over assuming a role which might not properly belong to them, those present at this meeting were almost unanimous in their support of the bolder action. Declaring that a fight was on and that it would be fatal to halt in the middle of the battle, Muste vowed to see "this thing through." J. M. Budish was equally willing. "Brookwood must go over the heads of the leaders," he said, for the leadership "will not change except under pressure." To Israel Mufson, the course was self-evident: Brookwood had to "go out and organize the progressives" or perish. Abraham Epstein favored organizing "a fighting group throughout the country, even if in our fight we have to hit individuals. . . . A group led by Brookwood can build up something which will revitalize the labor movement." Jack Lever, a Brookwood graduate, wanted a "line of communications across the country for progressives." David Saposs added that the task of the progressives was "to permeate the labor movement." On the other hand, Fannia Cohn advised that there was no cause for alarm, and she cautioned the progressives against reading themselves out of the labor movement.[38]

---

for example the recognition of Russia and a labor party, had no important basis in trade union sentiment. However, the UTW, Cloth Hat and Cap Makers, ILGWU, and the ACW all demanded in the 1920's and early 1930's the diplomatic recognition of Russia by the United States, and with the exception of the UTW the same unions endorsed, in the 1920's, a national labor party. As was indicated in Chapter III, the latter three unions also opposed the AFL's endorsement of the Citizens' Military Training Camps. UTW, *Proceedings, 1922,* p. 421; "Resolutions and Disposition of Same," *Textile Worker,* Vol. 20, October 1932, pp. 221–222; Cloth Hat, Cap, and Millinery Workers' International Union, *Proceedings, 1923,* pp. 94–95, 137, *1925,* pp. 139, 144, *1927,* pp. 313–314, 323–324; ACW, *Proceedings, 1924,* pp. 278–279, *1926,* pp. 337, 352; ILGWU, *Proceedings, 1922,* p. 129, *1924,* pp. 237–238, 245–246, *1925,* pp. 202–203, 224–225, *1928,* pp. 90–91, 153, *1929,* p. 93, *1932,* pp. 193–196, 231.

[38]*Sixth Annual Conference of Teachers in Workers' Education, 1929,* pp. 18–29.

Many of the more prominent directors of the Labor Publication Society apparently agreed with her that the time was not appropriate for a direct, frontal assault upon the leaders and policies of the AFL. Between December 1928 and March 1929, eleven of these directors, namely Miss Cohn, Thomas Kennedy, Philip Umstadter, William Kohn, Abraham Baroff, Max Danish, H. H. Broach, Thomas J. Curtis, Gustav Geiges, Chris J. Golden, and Abraham Shiplacoff, resigned from, or declined to seek reelection to, the *Labor Age* board.[39]

Despite this alienation of important support, the Musteites scheduled a meeting of labor progressives for May 25–26 at the Labor Temple in New York City, and at that time one hundred and fifty-one persons gathered to organize the first body whose basic and avowed purpose was to reform the American Federation of Labor from within. About two thirds of those present were reported to be active trade unionists, the others were representatives of the Socialist party and "friends" of organized labor. They came from thirty-one cities in eighteen states, were associated with twelve educational classes or institutions, and were members of, although they did not represent, thirty-three unions, the vast majority of them AFL affiliates.[40]

In his welcoming address to the meeting Muste, who presided over the two-day session, declared that the progressives, as compared with AFL spokesmen, reflected new and different thinking on labor matters but that they would not follow the Communists out of the AFL.[41] They should resolve, however, "to create a new movement, to infuse the rank and file of the A. F. of L. with courage and determination to cope with the new problems of industry

[39]*Labor Age,* Vol. 17, December 1928, p. i; Vol. 18, January 1929, p. i; Vol. 18, March 1929, p. i. Shiplacoff, manager of the Pocket Book Workers, had joined the board in January 1928.

[40]*New York Times,* May 26, 27, 1929; Leonard Bright, "C.P.L.A. Organizes," *Labor Age,* Vol. 18, June 1929, pp. 3–4. Of the 129 persons who attended the first day's meeting, 82 were described as active trade unionists, 11 as representatives of the Socialist party, and 36 as persons sympathetic to the labor movement.

[41]Early in 1928 the Workers' party began to sponsor the erection of dual unions such, for example, as the National Miners' Union, National Textile Workers' Union, and the Needle Trades' Workers' Union. These unions and others were brought together in the Trade Union Unity League in September 1929, when the Trade Union Educational League was abolished and "boring from within" AFL unions was officially abandoned in favor of dual unionism. Louis Stanley, "Communist Dual Unionism," *Labor Age,* Vol. 18, October 1929, p. 9.

and conquer all obstacles which the subtle new capitalism raises." "There is no question," Muste asserted, "of our loyalty to the American Federation of Labor. We are more loyal to the A. F of L. than many of those who attack us. We will show our loyalty to the A. F. of L. by fighting for the principles of progressive trade unionism."[42]

The meeting then proceeded to designate itself the Conference for Progressive Labor Action, adopt *Labor Age* as its official journal, elect a twenty-six member executive committee, and draft a policy statement. With respect to the latter action, the CPLA affirmed the major ideas of the February challenge to progressives and declared further that the object of the CPLA was "to carry on research, educational work and agitation among the workers, both organized and unorganized in industry and agriculture, in order to stimulate in the existing and potential labor organizations a progressive, realistic, militant labor spirit and activity in all its phases—trade union, political, cooperative and educational."[43] Membership in the CPLA was opened to all labor and farm organizations of a trade union, educational, cooperative, or political nature and to the individual members of such organizations as well.[44]

Those elected to the executive committee were A. J. Muste (chairman); James Maurer (first vice-president); Carl Holderman (second vice-president), a member of the UTW's executive council and first vice-president of the Full-Fashioned Hosiery Workers; A. J. Kennedy (treasurer); Louis Budenz (executive secretary); Leonard Bright (secretary), a member of the Bookkeepers' and Stenographers' Union; Justus Ebert, editor of the *Lithographers' Journal;* Abraham Lefkowitz; Israel Mufson; Clinton S. Golden; J. B. S. Hardman; Leonard Craig, a Brookwood graduate who was education director of the Pennsylvania Federation of Labor; Joseph Schwartz, a member of the Jewelry Workers and, in 1930, secretary of Philadelphia Labor College; Charles V. Maute, a Brookwood graduate and president of a New York City local of the

[42]Quoted in Bright, "C.P.L.A. Organizes," *ibid.,* Vol. 18, June 1929, p. 3.
[43]*Ibid.,* p. 4; "Statement of Policy of the C.P.L.A.," *ibid.,* Vol. 18, June 1929, pp. 6–7. See also Muste, "Progressives on the March," *ibid.,* Vol. 18, June 1929, p. 8.
[44]Bright, "C.P.L.A. Organizes," *ibid.,* Vol. 18, June 1929, p. 4.

128

Railway Clerks; Nathaniel Spector, a member of the general executive board of the Cloth Hat and Cap Makers; Frank Crosswaith, a founder of the Brotherhood of Sleeping Car Porters; Henry R. Linville; Frank Manning of the UTW; Winston Dancis, a postal clerk; Walter Wilson, a left-wing Brookwood student; James Oneal, editor of the Socialist *New Leader;* Norman Thomas, head of the Socialist party; and the following, unidentified persons: Andrew Vance, Frank Morris, Carl Johanntges, and Nellie Lithgow.[45] The CPLA opened its national headquarters in New York City on June 10, 1929, and during the following two or three years at least seventeen branch organizations were opened in such strategic industrial cities as Philadelphia, Pittsburgh, Youngstown, Cleveland, Detroit, and Chicago.[46]

The CPLA did not escape the attention of the AFL Executive Council which, in a broadside printed in the *American Labor World,* labeled the CPLA a "dual or dissenting" organization and advised trade unionists to boycott it financially:

There is... [an] organization recently formed, [the Council declared in July 1929] called the Conference for Progressive Labor Action. Its avowed purpose is to "bore from within" the American Federation of Labor. It declares that it intends to use every effort at its command to remake the American Federation of Labor.... The Executive Council warns the membership of the American Federation of Labor against this organization.... Do not make any financial contribution in response to any appeal this organization may make for help... dissenting or dual groups are not clothed with authority to speak for Labor or to act for Labor.[47]

[45]*Ibid.*, pp. 5–6; Justus Ebert, "What Have the Progressives Done?", *ibid.*, Vol. 18, July 1929, pp. 6–8.

[46]"C.P.L.A. on the Job," *ibid.*, Vol. 18, July 1929, p. 20; "Progressives Forge Ahead," *ibid.*, Vol. 18, October 1929, p. 21; "C.P.L.A. Wins Warm Approval," *ibid.*, Vol. 18, December 1929, pp. 10–12; "C.P.L.A. Activities Extended," *ibid.*, Vol. 19, January 1930, p. 20; "C.P.L.A. Covers Wide Area," *ibid.*, Vol. 19, March 1930, p. 23; "C.P.L.A. Potent Force in Labor World," *ibid.*, Vol. 19, April 1930, p. 23; "Across the Continent," *ibid.*, Vol. 20, February 1931, p. 21; "C.P.L.A. 'Goes to the Country,'" *ibid.*, Vol. 20, March 1931, p. 21; "Wider Fields Open for C.P.L.A.," *ibid.*, Vol. 20, April 1931, p. 21; "The Active Workers Conference, A Report," *ibid.*, Vol. 21, April 1932, p. 6; Joseph Brooks, "Silk Workers March," *ibid.*, Vol. 21, June 1932, p. 10; Louis Budenz, "Ohio Jobless Take State Action," *ibid.*, Vol. 21, November 1932, p. 4.

[47]*American Labor World,* Vol. 30, July 1929, pp. 10–11. See also Green to Margaret Wall (a Brookwood graduate), June 17, 1929, PCB #6, Book 402, NYSSILR Library.

The AFL's *Weekly News Service* remarked that the CPLA was "blessed by those who believe they have a divine commission to lead the workers" and that AFL history was "replete with similar whoopee." CPLA leaders were a "group of professional tingling souls who dream of a Labor Party."[48] William Green declared that an insignificant number of persons, the "disguised proponents of another philosophy" who failed to grasp the voluntary nature of the labor movement, had performed the mistaken but familiar tactic of formulating a socialist program which had little hope of ever being realized.[49] Without mentioning the CPLA by name, the IAM remarked that some persons were criticizing the AFL "with fiendish delight" because the organization did not organize the unorganized; the union concluded that the unorganized "decline to be organized" and that AFL leaders could not simply wave their hands and change the situation.[50]

On the other hand, Benjamin Stolberg hoped that the CPLA would "set out vigorously to accomplish its announced aims." He prophesied, and with marked accuracy, that if the CPLA failed in this respect, "the work will be done by another movement which will inevitably follow it." Stuart Chase, who served on the CPLA's committee on research and publications, felt the CPLA represented "the most definite start made lately in the direction of progressive unionism." He did not think that the AFL was "getting anywhere at all" and that it needed a more comprehensive program such as the CPLA had formulated.[51]

It can hardly be doubted, however, that the CPLA's initial failure to win the cooperation of the more moderate progressives and, concurrently, its enlistment of rather large nonunion and Socialist party elements severely limited its appeal to trade unionists. In addition, before CPLA activities could get well under way the nation was plunged into the Great Depression, which threw millions of men and women out of work and temporarily submerged

[48]AFL., *Weekly News Service,* June 15, 22, 1929.
[49]*American Federationist,* Vol. 36, July 1929, pp. 788-790. John Spargo and the *New York Times* also deprecated the founding of the CPLA. *New York Times,* May 28, June 13, 1929.
[50]*Machinists' Monthly Journal,* Vol. 43, September 1931, p. 540.
[51]*New York Times,* June 9, 1929.

trade union reform sentiment, in whatever degree it existed in the labor movement, beneath a welter of demands for food, clothing, shelter, and jobs. Even in the absence of such checks as these, the CPLA would probably not have gone far, because there was still little rank-and-file interest in unionism in the mass-production industries.

The depression, which handicapped CPLA efforts on the industrial front, stimulated, with the help of the victory of the Labor party in the British election of 1929, the CPLA's interest in radical, independent political action and caused this interest eventually to take precedence over all other aspects of the CPLA program.[52] Thus, William Z. Foster has characterized CPLA people as the "little brothers of the big labor fakirs" and as " 'left' Social-Democrats" who wanted to form a political organization as a rival to the Communist party.[53]

Despite the CPLA's eventual preoccupation with politics, a few of its activities are of some relevance to the central theme of this study. For example, CPLA leaders and members encouraged and participated in the several attempts made between 1930 and 1933 to replace the UMW with what they hoped would become a "clean, fighting, intelligent" coal miners' union. They believed that a strong miners' union would invigorate the entire labor movement

[52]As early as March 1930, independent political action was reported to be the primary interest of most CPLA branches, and in November, 1931, *Labor Age* announced that the CPLA was transforming itself into "a militant left-wing political organization." "C.P.L.A. Potent Force in Labor World," *Labor Age*, Vol. 19, April 1930, pp. 23–24; "A Challenge to Militants," *ibid.*, Vol. 20, November 1931, pp. 4–5.

The CPLA's growing concern for political action brought on a bitter struggle between the followers of Muste and the Socialist party representatives for control of the CPLA political program. The Musteites, who wanted the projected party to advocate violence, if necessary, to overthrow capitalism, were able to oust the Socialist party element from CPLA councils in September 1932. In December 1933 the CPLA began to form the American Workers party, and in December 1934, this party absorbed the Trotskyite Communist League of America. Muste, "Independent Political Action—Yes, but What Kind?", *ibid.*, Vol. 19, June 1930, pp. 6–8; Muste, "Do We Need a New Political Party in the United States?", *ibid.*, Vol. 20, April 1931, pp. 10–13, 29; "Report on Political Organization," *ibid.*, Vol. 20, August 1931, pp. 6–7; "Norman Thomas, the Communists and Our Political Discussion," *ibid.*, Vol. 20, September 1931, pp. 3–4; "The National Executive Committee and Officers," *ibid.*, Vol. 21, September 1932, p. 5; *Labor Action*, Dec. 20, 1933, Dec. 15, 1934.

[53]Foster, *History of the Communist Party of the United States*, p. 249.

and greatly increase the chances of extending organization to the steel, automobile, and other industries.[54] Events have proved, of course, that the CPLA was correct in the latter analysis, but they have also proved that John L. Lewis himself was capable of building a strong miners' union when the time became propitious and of championing, thereafter, the cause of industrial unionism.

The CPLA often reasserted the progressive demand for organizing campaigns in the industries largely untouched by unionism and vowed that the workers in these industries would never be divided, with its consent, among the craft unions. Muste wisely guessed in 1931 that, should the AFL discountenance the affiliation of future industrial unions formed in the basic industries, a new federation of industrial unions would be formed and would become "a new powerful force in American life."[55]

The CPLA made frequent appeals for "agitators" to work in the basic industries and reported in May 1930 that its representatives were "busy at several points in the steel industry lining up the more advanced workers, organizing study groups, analyzing the steel industry for the problems involved in its unionization and thus laying the ground work for future concerted action against the open shop practices which now confront the workers."[56] Subsequently, the CPLA explained that its work in the steel industry had a two-fold aspect:

> On the one hand, it has aimed at putting new spirit into the Amalgamated Association of Iron, Steel and Tin Workers and bringing a new leadership to the front in that organization, using that organization insofar as possible for more aggressive work among the unorganized than it has engaged in for a good many years. On the other hand, our

[54]Muste, "The Crisis in the Miners' Union," *Labor Age,* Vol. 19, March 1930, p. 8; "The Miners' Crisis...and Progress," *ibid.,* Vol. 20, April 1931, p. 3; "Wider Fields Open for C.P.L.A.", *ibid.,* Vol. 20, April 1931, p. 21; "The Future in the Miners' Union," *ibid.,* Vol. 20, May 1931, p. 3; Israel Mufson, "The Rank and File Convention at St. Louis," *ibid.,* Vol. 20, May 1931, pp. 12–13; William Stoffels, "Revolt of Illinois Miners," *ibid.,* Vol. 21, September 1932, pp. 6–7; Tom Tippett, "A New Miners' Union in Illinois," *ibid.,* Vol. 21, October 1932, pp. 4–5. In 1933 Tom Tippett became educational director of the Progressive Miners of America which had been formed with CPLA assistance in September 1932. *Labor Action,* June 15, 1933.

[55]Quoted in *New York Times,* March 7, 1931. For a similar statement, see Muste, "The C.P.L.A. Policy in Unions," *Labor Age,* Vol. 20, July 1931, p. 10.

[56]"One Year and After," *Labor Age,* Vol. 19, May 1930, p. 22.

workers recognize that it may in the end prove impossible really to revive the Amalgamated, and that in any case for the present it touches only the smallest portion of the steel workers. Therefore the work of building up groups who will serve as organizing centers among their fellow-workers in places absolutely untouched now by the Amalgamated is also going on.[57]

In the spring of 1931 the *Mahoning Valley Steel Worker,* published clandestinely by the CPLA members, began to circulate among steel workers in eastern Ohio, and in June 1932 the CPLA announced the formation of a secret steel workers' union called the Brotherhood of the Mills with contacts in "more than 100 key centers and mills in the steel district."[58] The Brotherhood was still in existence in January 1933 and, according to the CPLA, was laying "secure foundations for an organization campaign one of these days in steel."[59] There is no trace of the Brotherhood after the passage of the NIRA and the subsequent, successful but short-lived, organizing campaign undertaken by the Amalgamated. CPLA agitation among the steel workers may have contributed in a small way, however, to the dissatisfaction with Amalgamated leadership which burst into internal revolt in 1934.[60]

The outstanding concern of the CPLA during 1930–1931 was for the adoption of a program of government-sponsored unemployment insurance. The organization announced the beginning of a national campaign for unemployment insurance in June 1930, under the direction of Louis Budenz. Although Muste and Mufson made separate and extensive tours of the country to promote the cause of unemployment insurance, and although many CPLA branches did important work for the principle, the campaign was

[57]"The Active Workers Conference, A Report," *ibid.,* Vol. 21, April 1932, p. 5.
[58]"The Fight Grows Hotter," *ibid.,* Vol. 20, June 1931, p. 22; "News Notes About Our Branches," *ibid.,* Vol. 21, June 1932, p. 18.
[59]*Labor Action,* Jan. 21, 1933.
[60]CPLA representatives established a weak opposition within the Amalgamated and introduced into the union's 1932 convention a resolution which sought to place more emphasis upon organizing in the steel industry by creating the office of general organizer. The proposition was defeated by a vote of 28 to 8. Horace B. Davis, *Labor and Steel,* pp. 256–257. In addition, Elmer Cope, perhaps the leading CPLA "agitator" in the steel industry and a member of the Warren, Ohio, lodge of the Amalgamated, played a prominent role in the "rank-and-file" movement within the Amalgamated between 1934 and 1936. *Labor Action,* April 2, 1934; Robert R. R. Brooks, *As Steel Goes,* p. 68.

confined largely to the East and particularly to New York City, where frequent street meetings, a series of mass demonstrations, and constant lectures helped keep the insurance issue before the public and especially before organized labor.[61] With the help of several economists and scholars the CPLA also drafted model state and federal unemployment insurance bills. The state bill was introduced into a number of state legislatures, and the federal bill, one of the first of its kind, was introduced into the Senate by Senator Robert F. Wagner of New York in January 1931. Many of the features of these bills, including merit rating, employer financing, and a federal subsidy for state administration, were also to be features of the unemployment-insurance provisions of the federal Social Security Act of 1935.[62] The ILGWU supported the Wagner bill, and the IAM wrote approvingly of both CPLA-drafted bills.[63]

In 1932 the CPLA campaigned against racketeering in AFL unions, focusing its attention upon such racketeers, or alleged racketeers, as Howell H. "Little Caesar" Broach, Theodore M. "Czar" Brandle, Sam Kaplan, and Joseph Fay. In January 1933 the CPLA participated in the founding of a National Committee against Labor Racketeering and Allied Evils. Among the twenty-five members of this committee were A. J. Muste; Paul Brissen-

[61]"Unemployment Insurance—The Next Step," *Labor Age*, Vol. 19, June 1930, pp. 21–22; "All Hands on Deck," *ibid.*, Vol. 19, November 1930, p. 19; "Unemployment Insurance," *ibid.*, Vol. 20, January 1931, p. 23; "Across the Continent," *ibid.*, Vol. 20, February 1931, pp. 21–22; A. J. Muste, "Where Do American Workers Stand Today?", *ibid.*, Vol. 20, March 1931, pp. 14–15, 29; Israel Mufson, "The Story of the Stuffed Shirt," *ibid.*, Vol. 20, March 1931, pp. 10–11, "C.P.L.A. 'Goes to the Country'", Vol. 20, March 1931, p. 21; "Wider Fields Open for C.P.L.A.," *ibid.*, Vol. 20, April 1931, p. 21; "C.P.L.A. Widens Its Action," *ibid.*, Vol. 20, May 1931, p. 20; Israel Mufson, "The Depression Hits the Southwest," *ibid.*, Vol. 20, June 1931, pp. 23, 29.

[62]"Healthy Response to Latest C.P.L.A. Campaign," Vol. 19, July 1930, p. 22; "Our Unemployment Insurance Bills," *ibid.*, Vol. 19, October 1930, pp. 22–23; "Unemployment Insurance," *ibid.*, Vol. 20, January 1931, p. 22; *Congressional Record*, 71 Cong., 3 Sess., Vol. 74, p. 1753. The persons who helped draft the CPLA bills were Paul Brissenden, John A. Fitch, Harry W. Laidler, Alfred L. Bernheim of the Labor Bureau, Inc., Murray W. Lattimer of the Industrial Relations Counselors, and Nathan Fine from the Research Department of the Rand School. The two bills are printed in "C.P.L.A. Unemployment Insurance Bills," *Labor Age*, Vol. 19, December 1930, pp. 21–23.

[63]ILGWU, *Proceedings, 1932*, p. 89. P. J. Conlon, "Unemployment Insurance Legislation," *Machinists' Monthly Journal*, Vol. 43, February 1931, pp. 70–74.

den; Paul Douglas; Robert Morss Lovett of the University of Chicago; George Soule, associate editor of the *New Republic;* Freda Kirchwey, associate editor of the *Nation;* and Roger N. Baldwin, director of the American Civil Liberties Union.[64]

Despite these activities, the CPLA's influence among trade unionists steadily waned, largely as the result of the organization's increasing involvement in revolutionary politics. Perhaps the culminating blow to CPLA prestige was struck by the directors of Brookwood Labor College in March 1933 when they indicated that they could no longer support CPLA policies. The rift had been coming for more than two years. The directors declared that the CPLA's political sectarianism, its encouragement of independent dual unions, and its attacks upon union bureaucracy and racketeering were injecting Brookwood into internal union disputes and sowing dissension in the labor movement. As a result, Muste and two other faculty members and nineteen of Brookwood's twenty-eight students left the college.[65] Within eight months Muste and his followers established the left-wing, anticapitalist American Workers party. The CPLA was disbanded shortly thereafter, and thus took no part in the progressive labor movement of the New Deal period.[66]

[64]" 'Little Caesar' Broach and Local 3," *Labor Age,* Vol. 21, April 1932, pp. 15–16; Louis F. Budenz, " 'Czar' Brandle: A Study in Success," *ibid.,* Vol. 21, June 1932, pp. 15–17, 28; *ibid.,* Vol. 21, August 1932, pp. 1–2; *ibid.,* Vol. 21, October 1932, p. 1; *Labor Action,* Jan. 21, Feb. 25, 1933.

[65]"Muste Quits in Rift over CPLA," *Brookwood Review,* Vol. 11, May 1933, pp. 1, 3; *Labor Age,* Vol. 22, February-March 1933, p. 1; "Whither Brookwood," *Labor Age,* Vol. 22, February-March 1933, pp. 14–15; "The Statement of Purpose Which Brookwood Repudiated," *Labor Age,* Vol. 22, February-March 1933, pp. 16–17; "Brookwood Turned Right and We Left," *Labor Age,* Vol. 22, February-March 1933, p. 17.

[66]The American Workers party was not, as originally formed, a Communist organization. However, the party drifted rapidly to the left and adopted Trotzkyism in December 1934. James P. Cannon, *The History of American Trotzkyism,* pp. 169–188.

⊹ CHAPTER VI ⊹

Depression, New Deal, and Labor Organizing

BETWEEN 1929 and 1935 there developed in the economy and in the labor movement the final basic conditions which were to lead to the formation and success of the CIO. Thus the depression eventually created great unrest among working people, and early New Deal measures caused this unrest to be expressed in desires for unions and collective bargaining. Also, while the molders of AFL policy were driven by the depression to add, in their official statements if not always in their actions, the first significant amendments to voluntary principles, they did not change their attitude toward industrial unionism, nor did they mount vigorous organizing drives. This chapter is, therefore, a summary and analysis of three major matters: (1) the AFL's reaction to the depression; (2) the New Deal collective bargaining policy; and (3) the strategies and results of labor organizing in the mass-production industries during 1933–1935.

I

According to statistics compiled by the AFL, the number of persons unemployed in the United States increased by roughly 10,500,-000 between January 1930 and March 1933, when an all-time high of some 13,700,000 was reached.[1] Like many other observers of the depression, AFL leaders were rather slow to appreciate its severity

[1]AFL, *Proceedings, 1933,* p. 85.

136

and to recommend ways of meeting the unemployment situation. By October 1931, however, when unemployment according to the AFL's figures stood at nearly 7,800,000, the leaders of the AFL had become fully aware of the crisis proportions of the depression. In its report to the Vancouver convention of that year, the Executive Council analyzed in detail the causes of the depression. It contended that in the 1920's employers, in response to technological innovations, had simply cut down their work forces rather than reduce the hours of labor. Consequently, unemployment increased by 1,000,000 during that decade, and employers, who through technical advances derived a greater product from fewer and fewer workers, realized a disproportionate financial reward as compared with the gains made by laboring men and women. The unequal distribution of wealth resulted in underconsumption, an unbalanced economy, and depression. Since the failure to shorten hours and increase wages in proportion to increases in productivity had brought on the depression, the correction of these errors was the principal, if not the only, method by which a balanced economy could be restored and recovery effected.[2]

For a time the officers of the AFL assumed that employers were willing and financially able voluntarily to reduce hours and increase wages and that to bring about this result all that was necessary was the publication by federal fact-finding agencies of statistics covering wages, hours, unemployment, and the distribution of the national income. For example, in advocating in 1931 the formation of a federal labor board, the Executive Council indicated that the board should simply compile periodic indexes of the need for shorter hours and higher wages and that "it need have only the authority to make facts public in order to render service and have effective influence."[3] Finally despairing of industry's ability or desire to introduce a shorter work week on its own initiative, however, the AFL on January 5, 1933 endorsed the

[2]Ibid., 1931, pp. 61–67. See aso ibid., 1932, pp. 22–28; American Federationist, Vol. 39, September 1932, p. 986. The AFL's analysis of the causes of the depression is oversimplified and incomplete. For a more rounded treatment of the subject, see George Henry Soule, Prosperity Decade, pp. 275–335.

[3]AFL, Proceedings, 1931, p. 62.

Black Thirty-Hour bill which had been introduced into the Senate the previous December by Senator Hugo L. Black of Alabama.[4]

The AFL hesitated many months before it reluctantly endorsed unemployment insurance as a solution to the immediate subsistence problem of the jobless. As late as July 11, 1932 the AFL Executive Council, according to a *New York Times* report, preferred a plan for the provision of a five hundred dollar loan by the federal government to each unemployed person.[5] Opposition to a government insurance scheme was grounded partly in the conviction that such a device would indirectly weaken unions by transferring the loyalty of workers to the government (because the government would administer the insurance program) and to employers (who woud finance the program through a payroll tax). AFL leaders also feared that union members would be denied unemployment compensation if they refused to accept nonunion jobs and that this situation would directly weaken trade unions and spur the development of company unions.[6]

Statements by William Green and Victor Olander are pertinent to the above points. Addressing the ILGWU convention in May 1932, Green said that upon "the question of unemployment insurance, the A. F. of L. is not so much opposed to the principle as it is jealous of its own protection and its own life. We don't want to exchange our birthright for a mess of pottage. If we can develop some unemployment insurance plan that would guarantee the perpetuation of our movement, in my judgment the A. F. of L. would support it."[7] On another occasion, Green complained that government-sponsored unemployment insurance was an unsafe pol-

---

[4]United States Congress, Senate, *Thirty-Hour Work Week, Hearings before a Subcommittee of the Committee on the Judiciary on S. 5267,* 72 Cong., 2 Sess., pp. 1–23. Perhaps with greater bluff than sincerity, Green told the subcommittee that the AFL might resort to a general strike to secure the universal adoption of the thirty-hour week. *Ibid.,* pp. 21–22.

[5]*New York Times,* July 11, 1932.

[6]See William Green to John B. Andrews (of the American Association for Labor Legislation), Aug. 12, 1932, Box 47, Ms., John B. Andrews Papers, New York State School of Industrial and Labor Relations; Victor Olander to Andrews, Feb. 23, 1933, Box 50, *ibid.;* Andrews to George Meany, Jan. 19, 1934, Box 54, *ibid.;* "Summary of a Conference between Andrews and Gerard Swope, June 14, 1932," Box 47, *ibid.;* "Minutes of an American Association for Labor Legislation Meeting, June 29, 1932," Box 47, *ibid.*

[7]ILGWU, *Proceedings, 1932,* p. 159.

icy which would "pull at our vitals and destroy our trade union structure."[8] Victor Olander also cried out against unemployment insurance claiming that it would foster paternalism and the enslavement of the workers; insurance ought not to be promoted, he advised, merely "with the cry, 'There are hungry men, there are hungry women, they must be fed.' Good God, that is the excuse for the oldest profession the world knows. Have we so far lost our virtue that we think of nothing else except bread...[and] employment?"[9] Abruptly, however, on July 22, 1932, the Executive Council endorsed a federal compulsory unemployment insurance law,[10] and so also did the Cincinnati convention of the AFL later that year.

The explanation for this reversal of AFL policy is to be found not in the propaganda of the labor progressives but in the growing acuteness of unemployment itself which, between 1930 and 1932, served to swing the balance in the labor movement in favor of an insurance program. Some of the unions which joined the movement for unemployment insurance during these years were the UMW, ILGWU, ACW, UTW, AFT, IAM, Wood Carvers, Lithographers, Railway Clerks, Pocket Book Workers, Flint Glass Workers, and the Amalgamated Association of Iron, Steel and Tin Workers.[11]

Some of the Council members, however, continued after the Cincinnati convention to entertain serious doubts as to the propriety of a government-sponsored insurance scheme. Less than two weeks after that conclave, John P. Frey informed Colonel Ross that "a number of the members of the Executive Council were in rather strong opposition personally [to unemployment insurance] but did not care to state their position because of the popular move-

---

[8]AFL, *Proceedings, 1931*, pp. 397–398.

[9]*Ibid.*, pp. 392–393. For the antiunemployment insurance opinions of other AFL leaders, see *ibid.*, pp. 375, 378–379, 382, 390.

[10]*New York Times*, July 23, 1932.

[11]AFL, *Proceedings, 1930*, pp. 309–310, *1931*, p. 371; AFT, *Proceedings, 1930*, p. 119; IAM, *Proceedings, 1928*, pp. 43, 49–51; ILGWU, *Proceedings, 1932*, p. 207; Amalgamated Association of Iron, Steel and Tin Workers of North America, *Proceedings, 1932*, pp. 1900–1901; *Labor Age*, Vol. 19, October 1930, pp. 2, 18, Vol. 19, December 1930, pp. 2, 16, Vol. 21, March 1932, p. 1; "The Balance Sheet of Labor," *World Tomorrow*, Vol. 13, October 1930, p. 391.

ment which has developed in favor of this utterly impossible and visionary program."[12]

A factor which assumed increasing importance in the AFL's recovery program—as a stimulus to the raising of wages and shortening of hours—was the organization of the unorganized workers. The Executive Council argued that the enrollment of workers in trade unions would increase labor's bargaining power and thus offer some assurance that the proceeds from industrial output would be distributed equitably and that "periodic breakdowns" would, therefore, be avoided.[13] In fact, feeling that rising unemployment had aroused (among those unorganized workers who were still employed) the desire to join unions, a special conference of AFL leaders recommended in February 1932 that, finances permitting, individual unions ought to initiate organizing campaigns.[14] Nothing came of the proposal, however, and the explanation given by Arthur Wharton of the IAM's inability to cooperate certainly must also have applied with equal force to other unions. Wharton remarked that the IAM was preoccupied with maintaining a minimum loss of membership and that it would be unable to do any real organizing until there was evidence of the return of prosperity.[15]

At the same time, sentiment favoring the legislative enforcement of the right to organize began to develop within the AFL and was nurtured especially by the UMW. The UMW-sponsored Watson-Rathbone bill of 1928 urged the establishment of collective bargaining as a partial remedy for the ills of the coal industry, and this idea was repeated in the Davis-Kelly mining bill of 1932.[16] The Executive Council declared in 1931 that the organization of workers into trade unions was essential and should be accepted as "public policy,"[17] and, of course, the AFL supported the Norris-LaGuardia Act of 1932 which declared in a policy statement that the worker shall

[12]Frey to Ross, Dec. 12, 1932, Container 13, Frey Papers.
[13]AFL, *Proceedings, 1931,* pp. 45, 63, *1932,* p. 31.
[14]William Green to the Presidents of National Unions, Feb. 12, 1932 (NUF #1).
[15]Wharton to Green, Feb. 16, 1932, NUF #1, *ibid.*
[16]Irving Bernstein, *The New Deal Collective Bargaining Policy,* pp. 23–24.
[17]AFL, *Proceedings, 1931,* p. 63.

have full freedom of association, self-organization, and designation of representatives of his own choosing, to negotiate the terms...of his employment, and that he shall be free from the interference, restraint, or coercion of employers of labor, or their agents, in the designation of such representatives or in self-organization or in other concerted activities for the purpose of collective bargaining or other mutual aid or protection.[18]

On January 19, 1933 Philip Murray, then vice-president of the UMW, appeared before a subcommittee of the Senate Committee on the Judiciary and urged that the Black Thirty-Hour bill be amended so as to guarantee that no workers "shall be denied the right to collectively bargain for their wages through chosen representatives of their own."[19] On February 17 John L. Lewis advised the Senate Committee on Finance, which was investigating current economic problems, that a "board of emergency control" should be established with "plenary emergency power" to enforce the workers' right to bargain collectively. Lewis added that if the workers "in our major industries" were accorded the right to organize, they could "police those industries against Communism, or any other false and destructive philosophy."[20]

The first specific public statement by the AFL national office on this subject was made in April when Green wrote in the *American Federationist* that it was "time to mobilize public opinion in support of the right of workers to organize."[21] Finally, in early May, the AFL secured the adoption of an amendment to the Black bill which provided for the enforcement by the federal government of the workers' right to organize and bargain collectively through their chosen representatives.[22]

[18]*Statutes at Large,* Vol. 47, p. 70.

[19]United States Congress, Senate, *Thirty-Hour Work Week, Hearings before a Subcommittee of the Committee on the Judiciary on S. 5267,* 72 Cong., 2 Sess., p. 288.

[20]United States Congress, Senate, *Investigation of Economic Problems, Hearings before the Committee on Finance Pursuant to S. Res. 315,* 72 Cong., 2 Sess., pp. 300–301.

[21]*American Federationist,* Vol. 41, April 1933, p. 343.

[22]United States Congress, House, *Thirty-Hour Week Bill, Report No. 124,* 73 Cong., 1 Sess., Vol. 1, p. 3; Bernstein, *The New Deal Collective Bargaining Policy,* pp. 25, 30–31.

II

The Black bill was the first recovery measure to gain the support of the Roosevelt administration. The bill was passed by the Senate on April 6 and referred to the House on April 17. Feeling that in the absence of a guaranteed minimum wage a reduction in hours would cause a further drying up of purchasing power, Secretary of Labor Perkins, evidently acting on suggestions previously made by Sidney Hillman[23] and with the full support of President Roosevelt, presented to the House Labor Committee a minimum-wage amendment to the Black bill. The Secretary also proposed a more flexible hours standard which permitted the setting of a work week of up to forty hours. Green, out of the fear that it would tend to reduce the hourly earnings of skilled workers, withheld AFL support of the minimum-wage amendment, but he accepted the hours amendment.[24]

On May 10 the Labor Committee reported the Black bill to the House, incorporating in it Green's amendment, a provision which required industries operating in interstate commerce to pay "a just and reasonable weekly wage sufficient to...maintain standards of living of decency and comfort," and the thirty-hour week, which might under special conditions be increased.[25] The bill, however, never came to a vote in the House largely because President Roosevelt had withdrawn his support from the measure on May 1 on the ground that the widespread opposition to the bill among employers rendered it ineffective as a step in the direction of recovery.[26]

[23]As early as December 1932 Hillman, in a memorandum to Roosevelt, urged the establishment of a legislative minimum wage. Matthew Josephson, *Sidney Hillman,* pp. 357, 361. According to William Green, Hillman was the only unionist among those present at a March 30, 1933, conference with Madame Perkins who favored such a law. Green says that John L. Lewis and all the other labor leaders at the conference, including himself, "expressed our opposition" to the proposal. Green to Lewis, May 17, 1933, NUF #7 (UMW), AFL-CIO Archives.

[24]Frances Perkins, *The Roosevelt I Knew,* pp. 192–196. Matthew Woll declared that Perkins' minimum-wage proposal would place in the Secretary's hands "the authority to socialize all American industries." Quoted in *New York Times,* April 28, 1933.

[25]United States Congress, House, *Thirty-Hour Week Bill, Report No. 124,* 73 Cong., 1 Sess., pp. 2–3. The bill as revised by the House Labor Committee also stipulated that any provisions of the antitrust laws which were inconsistent with the provisions of the bill were to be suspended. *Ibid.,* p. 3.

[26]Bernstein, *The New Deal Collective Bargaining Policy,* p. 31.

By this time the President's own recovery program was beginning to take shape. Shortly after he assumed office in March, Roosevelt had requested Senator Robert Wagner to begin work on a re-employment measure, and the President made a similar request of Raymond Moley, a member of his "brain trust," on April 11.[27] By early May, Wagner and Moley, with the aid of several other persons, had formulated separate recovery measures, and representatives of the two groups were immediately called to the White House by the President to draft a single recovery bill. It is difficult to calculate the degree of on-the-spot influence wielded by labor spokesmen in the drafting of Section 7(a), the bill's right to organize and collective bargaining guarantee.[28] Regardless, however, of

[27]Wagner and Moley were for a time each unaware of the efforts being made by the other with respect to the drafting of recovery proposals. *Ibid.,* p. 32; Moley, *After Seven Years,* pp. 187–189.

[28]Bernstein indicates that both the Wagner and Moley groups had included collective bargaining provisions in their recovery proposals and that W. Jett Lauck, an economist for the UMW, and Donald Richberg had drafted these collective bargaining provisions. He states further that at the White House conferences a committee of seven persons, which did not include a trade unionist, did the actual work of incorporating in the National Industrial Recovery bill the ideas the conferees agreed upon. Bernstein, *The New Deal Collective Bargaining Policy,* pp. 31–33. Charles Frederick Roos says that at first the AFL was ignored at the White House conferences and that it sought to have its views stated by Colonel Malcolm C. Rorty who was "associated with the United States Chamber of Commerce" and was "generally identified with big business." Later, however, at Rorty's suggestion, Secretary Perkins had the AFL send a representative and thereafter "it took an active part in shaping policies." Roos, *NRA Economic Planning,* p. 40 n. In her version of the matter, Secretary Perkins claims that the White House group drafted a bill which contained no collective bargaining provision, that she then called William Green in, and that at Green's suggestion Section 7 (a) was put into the bill by General Hugh S. Johnson, who was to become Administrator of the National Recovery Administration. Miss Perkins adds that Section 7 (a) "was a problem in semantics. It was a set of words to suit labor leaders, William Green in particular." (It seems unlikely, however, that the first draft of the recovery bill did not include a collective bargaining provision, especially since the Wagner and Moley groups had already agreed upon the need for one. Perhaps Secretary Perkins was thinking about the Black bill hearings.) Perkins, *The Roosevelt I Knew,* pp. 199–200. John L. Lewis, after reciting his union's pre-New Deal interest in getting a law on the subject of organizing and bargaining, declares that the UMW knew in detail what was being done during the drafting of the recovery bill, and that the union had Wagner's assurance "that no law would be drawn which did not meet with the approval of organized labor." Lewis, "Labor and the National Recovery Administration," *Annals of the American Academy of Political and Social Science,* Vol. 172, May 1934, p. 58. In 1938 Frey complained to Herbert Hoover that the AFL knew nothing of the recovery bill until the day preceding its introduction into Congress. Frey to Hoover, June 8, 1938, Container 9, Frey Papers. Woll, addressing the ILGWU convention in 1934, boasted that the NIRA "emanated from no brain of labor, nor did it originate in the councils of labor." ILGWU, *Proceedings, 1934,* p. 278.

what one's conclusions on this matter may be, it is still pertinent to recall that the UMW, especially, and also the AFL's president and Executive Council had in several public statements called for such a measure.

In addition to Section 7(a), the bill, which if enacted was to remain in effect for only two years, provided for the suspension of the antitrust laws so as to permit employers to form industry-wide trade associations and to draft codes of fair competition which were to be submitted to the National Recovery Administration for approval. Section 7(a) was the only mandatory code provision. The bill was introduced into Congress on May 17, 1933.

The AFL was not completely satisfied with Section 7(a), and Green persuaded the House Committee on Ways and Means to accept two amendments which he felt made the section more effective in its protection of the right to organize.[29] The bill finally became law when it was signed by Roosevelt on June 16, 1933.

Section 7(a) of the National Industrial Recovery Act declared:

(1) That employees shall have the right to organize and bargain collectively through representatives of their own choosing, and shall be free from the interference, restraint, or coercion of employers of labor, or their agents, in the designation of such representatives or in self-organization or in other concerted activities for the purpose of collective bargaining or other mutual aid or protection; (2) that no employee and no one seeking employment shall be required as a condition of employment to join any company union or to refrain from joining, organizing, or assisting a labor organization of his own choosing; and (3) that employers shall comply with the maximum hours of labor, minimum rates of pay, and other conditions of employment, approved or prescribed by the President.[30]

[29]*American Federationist*, Vol. 40, June 1933, pp. 566–567; Lewis Lorwin and Arthur Wubnig, *Labor Relations Boards*, pp. 28–31; Bernstein, *The New Deal Collective Bargaining Policy*, pp. 33–34.

[30]*Statutes at Large*, Vol. 48, pp. 198–199. On August 1, 1933 Roosevelt prescribed in the President's Reemployment Agreement a maximum work week of between thirty-five and forty hours and a minimum wage of between thirty and forty cents per hour for all factory or mechanical workers and artisans. In accordance with clause three of Section 7 (a), employers generally complied with these standards. Of the more than five hundred basic codes which were approved by the President between 1933 and 1935 the vast majority stipulated a maximum forty-hour week and a minimum wage of between thirty and forty cents per hour. Leverett S. Lyon *et al., The National Recovery Administration*, pp. 318–319, 368, Appendix B, pp.

Although the section did not define collective bargaining and although the NIRA was silent on the role collective bargaining might play in the drafting of codes to be submitted to the NRA, the AFL was hopeful that the labor provisions of the individual codes would jointly be agreed upon by trade unions and trade associations.[31] Such a procedure would obviously have been a boon to labor organizing and might also have been regarded as requiring the immediate recognition of trade unionism in the mass-production industries. On the other hand, many employers in all likelihood would have refused to cooperate with the NRA had they been expected to accede to trade union demands in the drafting of their codes, and in addition, the NRA itself was chiefly interested in expediting the code-making process. Therefore, on June 19, NRA Administrator Hugh S. Johnson announced that code labor provisions did not have to be negotiated by collective bargaining and that it was not the purpose of the NRA to organize the unorganized workers.[32]

Moreover, it is clear that Section 7(a) did not expressly outlaw the company union and that the latter might, therefore, be considered an agency for collective bargaining within the meaning of the NIRA. The AFL fully realized this and admitted that the section did not make the company union as such illegal, but it nevertheless declared that the NIRA withdrew protection from the

---

900–901. The AFL was never satisfied, however, with the code wage-and-hour provisions and argued that the minimum wages were too low to effect any substantial increase in mass-purchasing power and that the hours actually worked were far too high to effect any substantial decrease in unemployment. AFL, *Proceedings, 1933*, pp. 69–70, *1934*, pp. 89–96. In fact, the AFL only reluctantly agreed to the setting of minimum wages in the codes. Matthew Woll, *Labor, Industry and Government*, pp. 65–66; Roos, *NRA, Economic Planning*, p. 45; David A. McCabe, "The American Federation of Labor and the NIRA," *Annals of the American Academy of Political and Social Science*, Vol. 179, May 1935, pp. 144–145.

[31]"Recovery Program," *American Federationist*, Vol. 40, June 1933, p. 629; Vol. 40, July 1933, p. 695.

[32]Lorwin and Wubnig, *Labor Relations Boards*, pp. 54–57; Lyon *et al.*, *The National Recovery Administration*, p. 427; Bernstein, *The New Deal Collective Bargaining Policy*, pp. 57–58. A few of the AFL's stronger unions, primarily those in the needle trades and the UMW, were able to establish a collective bargaining relationship with employers with regard to the code labor provisions. Lyon *et al.*, *The National Recovery Administration*, pp. 430–431, 441 n.; Solomon Barkin, "Collective Bargaining and Section 7 (b) of NIRA," *Annals of the American Academy of Political and Social Science*, Vol. 184, March 1936, p. 171.

company union and that the erection of company unions would be "inconsistent" with the act and would constitute a "violation of the spirit, if not the letter of the Act."[33] On the other hand, the NAM and the Chamber of Commerce believed that Section 7(a) fully safeguarded company unions and, in fact, the open shop.[34] Many industrialists, who had not looked upon the company union as a collective bargaining agency prior to June 1933 and who had, indeed, carefully distinguished between employee representation and collective bargaining,[35] extended the term "collective bargaining" to the activities of their employee representatives after the passage of the recovery act in order "to be on the safe side."[36] In addition, a few employers refused to accept Section 7(a) as compelling them to depart from their long-established practice of bargaining with their employees individually. Other employers, of course, were not unwilling to recognize bona fide trade unions.[37]

Despite the fundamental weaknesses of the NIRA as a protrade-union measure, the spirit of the act provided the stimulus for widespread, aggressive labor organizing and encouraged many unorganized workers to believe that a new deal for labor had dawned; immediately following the act's passage there was a spontaneous uprising of workers to join trade unions.[38] Between July and August 1933 the AFL issued 340 charters to directly affiliated local

[33]*American Federationist*, Vol. 40, July 1933, p. 678; Green, "Labor's Opportunity and Responsibility," *ibid.*, Vol. 40, July 1933, p. 694; *ibid.*, Vol. 40, December 1933, p. 1327.

[34]Lorwin and Wubnig, *Labor Relations Boards*, pp. 50–51; Rinehart J. Swenson, "The Chamber of Commerce and the New Deal," *Annals of the American Academy of Political and Social Science*, Vol. 179, May 1935, p. 141.

[35]McCabe, "American Federation of Labor and the NIRA," *Annals of the American Academy of Political and Social Science*, Vol. 179, May 1935, pp. 149–150.

[36]Henry C. Metcalf, "Employee Representation," *ibid.*, Vol. 184, March 1936, p. 187. See also David J. Saposs, "Employee Representation as Labor Organization," *ibid.*, Vol. 184, March 1936, p. 192. Ernest T. Weir, chairman of the board of the Weirton Steel Company, affords a specific example of the manner in which anti-trade-union employers adjusted to Section 7 (a). In July 1933 Weir established company unions in his plants and subsequently declared that he was a staunch advocate of collective bargaining and that his and other company-union plans fully complied with the meaning and the intent of Section 7 (a). Weir, "New Responsibilities of Industry and Labor," *ibid.*, Vol. 172, March 1934, p. 82.

[37]National Industrial Conference Board, *Individual and Collective Bargaining under the N.I.R.A.*, pp. 32–33.

[38]*American Federationist*, Vol. 40, September 1933, p. 908; Vol. 40, November 1933, p. 1175.

trade and federal labor unions, and Green estimated, certainly with more enthusiasm than accuracy however, that during those two months the total membership of the AFL had increased by 1,500,000 to 2,000,000 members. "We are witnessing a sight," Green assured the AFL's 1933 convention, "that even the old, tried veterans of our movement never saw before. From every city and every town and every hamlet...the workers are marching, organizing, keeping step, coming with us into the great American Federation of Labor." They were joining the AFL "because they realize that there is a new day and a new deal," and nothing, Green concluded, "is going to stop them from coming in." Frank Morrison, the AFL secretary, spoke of the inception in July of the greatest wave of organization in the AFL's history; the movement was "sweeping over every city and town in North America," and it would surpass in "numbers, intensity, and duration" the movement of 1916–1920 which, Morrison asserted, had added 2,000,000 members to the AFL.[39]

As the same time, however, antitrade-union employers initiated a drive for the establishment of company unions which by the early fall of 1933 had taken on the proportions of a nationwide counteroffensive against trade unionism.[40] According to the AFL president, the company-union movement had by February 1934 nullified the workers' right and desire to join unions of their own choice.[41] Indeed, an investigation by the National Industrial Conference Board of 3,314 companies, which employed an estimated 27 percent of the workers in the fields of manufacturing and mining, indicated that company-union membership had almost doubled in these concerns between June and November 1933. In these companies alone, as of November, there were 1,164,294 company unionists. They were concentrated in the steel, automobile, rubber, petroleum-refining, and food-products industries.[42]

As a consequence in large part of the divergent interpretations

[39]AFL, *Proceedings, 1933*, pp. 8–9, 33, 38.

[40]*American Federationist*, Vol. 40, July 1933, p. 679; Green, "Labor's Opportunity and Responsibility," *ibid.*, Vol. 40, July 1933, p. 694; Lyon *et al., The National Recovery Administration*, p. 490.

[41]*American Federationist*, Vol. 41, February 1934, p. 132.

[42]National Industrial Conference Board, *Individual and Collective Bargaining under the N.I.R.A.*, Tables 1, 5, and 6, pp. 16, 22, 24.

of Section 7(a) by the representatives of labor and industry and the vigorous competition for members between trade unions and company unions which followed the enactment of the NIRA, a wave of labor disputes began to plague the recovery program. To handle these disputes President Roosevelt on August 5 authorized the establishment of the National Labor Board.[43]

The National Labor Board was unable in the really crucial cases which it handled to force recalcitrant employers to abide by its decisions. Until February 1934, in fact, the Board had no power whatsoever to enforce its decisions, and by that time its prestige had already declined considerably. Beginning in February, the Board was enabled by executive order to request the Compliance Division of the NRA to remove the Blue Eagle held by an employor violator of Section 7(a) or to refer cases of noncompliance to the Attorney General who might prosecute such cases in the federal courts or institute injunction proceedings.[44] Neither of these methods proved sufficient in actual practice to secure compliance with the Board's rulings.[45]

Senator Wagner sought to reshape and strengthen the New Deal collective bargaining policy in the Labor Disputes bill which he introduced into the Senate on March 1, 1934. The bill, which contained many features of the Wagner Act of 1935, was designed to prohibit company unions, and it proposed to give adequate enforcement powers to a federal labor board. The bill gained little support, however, and at Roosevelt's insistence the Congress passed in its stead Public Resolution No. 44 which authorized the President to establish a board or boards to deal with Section 7(a) controversies. FDR signed the resolution on June 19.

[43]The NLB was a joint board which included as representatives of labor Dr. Leo Wolman, William Green, and John L. Lewis, and as representatives of industry Walter C. Teagle, Gerard Swope of General Electric, and Louis E. Kirstein of the Filene Company. Senator Wagner served as impartial chairman of the board.

[44]Lorwin and Wubnig, *Labor Relations Boards,* pp. 227–228; Harry A. Millis and Emily Clark Brown, *From the Wagner Act to Taft-Hartley,* pp. 22–23. The Blue Eagle was the symbol of compliance with the NIRA which the federal government awarded to all employers in codified industries.

[45]Blue Eagles were removed by the NRA in four instances but this action worked little hardship upon employers and did not constitute a significant penalty. Lyon *et al., The National Recovery Administration,* p. 484. The only case referred by the NLB to the Attorney General was the Weirton Steel Company case.

Public Resolution No. 44 was a stopgap measure the primary purpose of which was not to resolve the basic issues raised by the failure of the NLB but rather to provide some method for averting a general strike of steel workers which seemed imminent in the middle of June.[46] The National Labor Relations Board, which was created on June 29 and began to function as the successor to the NLB on July 9, was given only those enforcement powers which the NLB had had.[47] Employer resistance to the NLRB's decisions was, if anything, more general than it had been to the rulings of the earlier board.

By December 1934 William Green had become convinced that Section 7(a) was an inadequate expression of the workers' right to organize and bargain collectively and that the NLRB was valueless as an enforcement agency. He therefore began to urge the enactment of a permanent and more effective labor relations law.[48] In the meantime, in anticipation of the scheduled expiration of the NIRA on June 16, 1935 (the act was actually declared unconstitutional in April) Senator Wagner had begun to revise his Labor Disputes bill. In February 1935 he introduced a slightly altered version of the bill which was adopted by the Senate and the House on June 27 and signed by the President on July 5.

The Wagner Act (National Labor Relations Act) went far beyond Section 7(a) of the NIRA in its effort to promote trade unionism. It not only asserted the right of workers to organize and bargain collectively but surrounded this guarantee with a stipulation of five unfair labor practices which made it virtually impossible for employers to engage in any kind of antiunion activity without subjecting themselves to litigation. Although not speci-

[46]Lorwin and Wubnig, *Labor Relations Boards*, pp. 258–261, 335. In accordance with the authority granted to him by Public Resolution No. 44, Roosevelt established, on June 28, a National Steel Labor Relations Board. This board and other "resolution 44" boards were to operate until June 16, 1935, unless they were abolished sooner by the President or Congress.

[47]The NLRB was a public, rather than a joint, labor-management board. Its members were: Lloyd K. Garrison, Dean of the University of Wisconsin Law School; Harry A. Millis, head of the University of Chicago's Department of Economics; and Edwin S. Smith, the Commissioner of Labor and Industries for Massachusetts.

[48]*American Federationist*, Vol. 40, December 1934, p. 1290. See also *ibid.*, Vol. 41, March 1935, pp. 243–244; Green, "What Labor Wants," *ibid.*, Vol. 41, March 1935, p. 249.

fically outlawing the company union, the law provided for it by denying to employers any part in the formation or operation of a labor organization. As for enforcement power, the new National Labor Relations Board was authorized to issue cease and desist orders and, on its own initiative, to seek the enforcement of such orders in the federal circuit courts. After two years of confusion and experimentation, the federal government provided in this act a positive means of encouraging the development of organized labor in the United States.[49]

III

Unfortunately, by the time the Wagner Act was passed company-union membership had leaped to an estimated total of 2,500,000 to 3,000,000 as compared with the 1,263,194 members reported for 1932.[50] If one assumes the accuracy of these figures, it would seem that company-union membership increased at a much faster rate after the advent of the New Deal than did trade union membership as a whole[51] and certainly far surpassed trade union gains in the basic industries. Company unions were concentrated in such industries as steel, automobiles, and rubber which trade unions had always found difficult or impossible to organize. There was, as a matter of fact, hardly an important establishment in the three industries which in 1935 did not have a company union in operation.[52]

The explanation for the unfavorable membership situation in which the AFL found itself in 1935 lies not only in the ineffectiveness of the labor boards and in employer opposition but also in the nature of AFL leadership itself. Between 1933 and 1935 the AFL national office and the individual craft unions (especially

[49]For a more detailed account of the legislative history of the Wagner Act, see Bernstein, *The New Deal Collective Bargaining Policy*, pp. 84–128.

[50]National Industrial Conference Board, *Collective Bargaining through Employee Representation*, Table 1, p. 16; Lyon *et al.*, *The National Recovery Administration*, p. 524.

[51]A sample survey of company-union membership conducted by the Bureau of Labor Statistics in April 1935 tends to substantiate this conclusion. Department of Labor, Bureau of Labor Statistics, *Characteristics of Company Unions 1935, Bulletin No. 634*, pp. 50–51.

[52]Lyon *et al.*, *The National Recovery Administration*, p. 525. An important exception was the Ford Motor Company, which conducted its bargaining on an individual employee basis.

the metal trades' unions which, of course, had the greatest potential stake in mass-production organizing) did not launch or plan large-scale, cooperative campaigns to establish unionism in the unorganized, basic industries. This omission represented a divergence from the cooperative approach to organizing in the mass-production industries which had been introduced in the steel campaign of 1909–1910 and subsequently followed in the steel, automobile, and textile drives of later years. In these campaigns, organizing had been conducted or at least planned as a joint effort with both AFL headquarters and interested national unions contributing money and organizers and with direction and supervision resting in the hands of the AFL's president. In 1933, however, the AFL's controlling leaders apparently did not consider carefully planned, cooperative campaigns necessary or practicable (although, as will be noted later, some craft unions, acting separately, did send organizers into the basic industries). Yet the AFL often asserted that the amount of benefits working people might derive from the recovery program depended to a large extent upon the growth of trade unionism.[53] All William Green could do, under the circumstances, was to use the AFL's existing resources in money and organizers to further organization and to rely heavily upon the labor boards and local leaders to increase labor's ranks. So Green, reporting in August 1933 that the AFL's national office was being deluged with pleas for organizing assistance from workers throughout the country, advised that the "responsibility for leadership and for initiative must rest with local persons" and that the AFL would "carry them a message of cheer and hope and duty."[54]

Although Green's August statement might give the impression that the AFL did nothing at all to further the movement toward unionism, this was not the case. Green and Morrison did step into the organizing vacuum created by the failure of the unions with claims in the mass-production industries to propose a grand campaign strategy and, with a staff of thirty-three paid organizers, began

[53]See for example Green, "Labor's Opportunity and Responsibility," *American Federationist*, Vol. 40, July 1933, pp. 693–694; *ibid.*, Vol. 40, August 1933, pp. 789–790; *ibid.*, Vol. 40, November 1933, p. 1176; *ibid.*, Vol. 40, December 1933, pp. 1294–1295; and AFL *Proceedings, 1933*, pp. 9, 63, 70–71, 150.

[54]*American Federationist*, Vol. 40, August 1933, pp. 790–791, 794.

to place workers in federal labor unions under the direct control of AFL headquarters. Since the AFL had employed eighteen organizers in 1932, one must conclude that the fifteen-member increase in 1933 represented the total additional effort the organization was able and willing to make in response to the rare opportunity to organize the unorganized. With such a small force at his command, in only five instances could Green assign an organizer to a single industry rather than to an entire region.[55]

Moreover, the policies which guided the modest organizing the AFL national office did undertake were promptly contested by the craft unions, whose position was in turn disputed with equal promptness by a group of reform leaders. The aftermath was a poor membership harvest and, ultimately, a civil war in the labor movement.

As early as June 30, 1933 Green, in the absence of any instructions to the contrary and in fact with the evident approval of James O'Connell (who was still president of the Metal Trades Department), directed AFL organizers to place all workers, regardless of skill, in federal labor unions.[56] In a letter to AFL organizer Coleman Claherty he added that, if at some later date some of these workers were found to come "clearly" under the jurisdiction of an existing international union, "we can arrange for a transfer."[57] There is reason to conclude, however, that Green still believed, as he had in 1928, that jurisdictional lines were not clear in the mass-production industries and that the federal labor unions should therefore serve as the nuclei for new national unions with

[55]These were: the automobile, rubber, aluminum, radio, and gasoline filling-station industries. Marjorie R. Clark, "Recent History of Labor Organization," *Annals of the American Academy of Political and Social Science,* Vol. 184, March 1936, p. 162.

[56]Green to William Collins (AFL organizer), June 30, 1933, PCB #12, Book 460, NYSSILR Library. In a letter to organizer Coleman Claherty in July, Green said that the MTD agreed to placing all workers in federal labor unions. Since the MTD was not to meet in convention until September, and since at that time it overwhelmingly disapproved of Green's organizing policy, the writer assumes that Green was actually referring in July to O'Connell, who for many years had favored an industrial form of organization. See Green to Claherty, July 14, 1933, PCB #12, Book 461, *ibid.*

[57]Green to Claherty, Aug. 23, 1933, PCB #12, Book 465, *ibid.* See also Green to George Hough (unidentified), Sept. 11, 1933, PCB #12, Book 467, *ibid.*

industry-wide jurisdiction. Thus, confiding once again in his old friend Max Hayes, Green said in July 1933:

You know enough about these mass production plants to know and understand that no success can attend any organizing effort unless these workers are organized into Federal Unions. *The craft lines have practically been wiped out because the workers employed specialize and thus the services of the rounded-out skilled machinists and other skilled workers are not required.* We can only succeed in organizing these workers employed in mass production plants by forming Federal Unions, embracing within them, *all* the workers employed in the different industries.[58]

If Green's policy did not postulate the eventual establishment of new, and completely industrial, national unions in the basic industries, it at least did not promise the crafts a very bright future in these areas.

Had there been no interference with the modest organizing effort, of the type described, which the AFL initiated in 1933, the effort might have produced a greater membership dividend than it did and might have grown in proportions. For, as will be revealed in succeeding pages, the unorganized workers did want industrial unions.

Several craft unions, however, the IAM, the Boilermakers, and the Metal Polishers especially, began early to protest the inclusion of skilled workers in federal labor unions and also to try themselves to organize basic-industry workers whom they claimed were within their charter jurisdictions.[59] The IAM appears to have been the most active, most consistent, and most militant defender of traditional craft organizing and continued in this role until 1937, when it made a complete about-face and became a chief promoter, among the anti-CIO unions, of industrial organizing where necessary to meet the competition of the CIO.

Concerned primarily about the nature of the AFL campaign in the automobile industry, IAM president Arthur Wharton wrote

[58]Green to Hayes, July 28, 1933, PCB #12, Book 462, *ibid.*, italics added.
[59]For early criticism by the Boilermakers and Metal Polishers of AFL organizing methods, see Harry Nicholas (vice-president of the Boilermakers) to Green and Morrison, Sept. 13, Nov. 21, 1933, NUF #1 (Boilermakers); W. W. Britton (president of the Metal Polishers) to Morrison, Aug. 10, 1933, NUF #7 (Metal Polishers), AFL-CIO Archives.

to Green on July 29, 1933 calling attention to various complaints he had received about machinists being placed in federal labor unions. "I trust," he counseled firmly and with seeming forbearance, "that you will see the importance of getting out a circular letter which will remove this misunderstanding."[60] Two days later, not waiting for Green's reply, Wharton communicated with Frank Morrison and now anxiously explained that reports were increasing with regard to "this interference" and that something had to be done to correct the situation:

Representatives of the A. F. of L., through central bodies and volunteer organizers, as well as some salaried representatives, are [Wharton continued] attending meetings arranged for by officers of our organization and are urging all of the mechanics to join the Federal Labor Union at a $2.00 initiation fee, whereas our organization's minimum fee is $5.00. This is absolutely destructive to our organizing work.

I urged...President Green in my letter of July 29, to send out an official circular to all concerned correcting the misrepresentations which have been published in the press and which are being...used by Communists to the effect that the A. F. of L. has forsaken craft unionism and [has] taken up industrial organization. It is imperative that some action be taken immediately.[61]

About dues and fees, Wharton later admitted that IAM people were being called grafters and racketeers because they were asking for initiation fees of $5.00, $7.00, $8.00, $10.00, or $20.00, "as the case may be in the various communities" and for dues of $1.75 per month, whereas the AFL's federal unions charged a flat $2.00 fee and only $1.00 monthly dues.[62]

In defense of his leadership, Green shortly replied that the AFL was not inclined purposely to disregard the rights of national unions but that in some instances in the automobile campaign it was "for the moment" impossible to respect these rights. "Ultimately," however, proper jurisdiction would be established, and in the meantime he advised Wharton to have IAM organizers take up their problems with AFL organizers in the field.[63] Wharton

[60]Wharton to Green, July 29, 1933, NUF #6 (IAM), *ibid*.

[61]Wharton to Morrison, July 31, 1933, NUF #6 (IAM), *ibid*.

[62]Wharton to Green, Aug. 8, 1933, NUF #6 (IAM), *ibid*. See also Harvey W. Brown, "Initiation Fees and the July Referendum," *Machinists' Monthly Journal*, Vol. 47, July 1935, p. 400.

[63]Green to Wharton, Aug. 2, 1933, NUF #6 (IAM), AFL-CIO Archives.

was not to be put off so easily. The IAM had already suffered great damage in its organizing work, he said, and nothing would suffice to correct matters except the prompt dispatch of a circular letter to the state federations, city centrals, and the AFL's organizers advising them that henceforth machinists were not to be included in federal labor unions. Wharton did not think that Green really appreciated "just what we are facing when we go into a mass meeting outlining our program and then have a representative of the A. F. of L. get up and tell the mass meeting that they can all join the Federal Labor Union for $2.00."[64]

At the same time that Wharton began to question the nature and results of AFL organizing, he also sensed, in a campaign begun by the Amalgamated Association of Iron, Steel and Tin Workers, a threat to IAM claims in the steel industry. He complained to Morrison that the Amalgamated was in fact, and without warrant, exercising industrial jurisdiction.[65] Informed of Wharton's attitude, Michael Tighe, certainly with more candor than diplomacy, exclaimed that he was "getting damned tired of these complaints from parties who are ignorant of the situation they complain about" and that as he had stated

...to you [Morrison] over the telephone we do not want anyone to join our organization that does not legally belong to it. Neither are we going to throw them out of the organization if they won't join... their craft.... [I trust] that I have made the position of our Association clear and that we won't hear so much about this one or that one claiming jurisdiction until at least we know whether any of us will have jurisdiction, which is at present a very disputable question as the Corporate powers are [not] going to loosen their hold without showing their teeth, and they can show them.[66]

The IAM continued to lodge protests against the tactics of the Amalgamated,[67] and finally an exasperated Tighe, writing directly to Wharton, declared:

[64]Wharton to Green, Aug. 8, 1933, NUF #6 (IAM), *ibid.*
[65]Wharton to Morrison, July 19, 1933, NUF #6 (IAM), *ibid.*
[66]Tighe to Morrison, July 22, 1933, NUF #6 (IAM), *ibid.*
[67]For example, see H. J. Carr (vice-president of the IAM) to Morrison, Aug. 17, 1933, NUF #6 (IAM); Wharton to Morrison, Aug. 31, 1933, NUF #5 (Amalgamated Association of Iron, Steel and Tin Workers); Wharton to Tighe, Oct. 23, 1933, NUF #6 (IAM), *ibid.*

I will now state it to you [that] our organizers have been instructed that when a worker signs the pledge card of our Association and his occupation is not in consonance with our jurisdiction, the organizer is to tell the applicant that his place is with the organization of his craft and advise him to join it. But if the applicant will not join, for reasons that he thinks sufficient . . , then before having such person stay outside as a menace to the movement, our organization will take him in.

Now the question might be asked, Does the trade union movement want to keep men out and by so doing make them go into company unions and defeat the very purpose of the Movement? If that is going to be the policy of the movement in general, then I say the movement is doomed.[68]

Unimpressed, Wharton's quick rejoinder was that the Amalgamated was not collecting initiation fees (the intimation being that this explained the machinists' preference for the Amalgamated) and that the IAM's officers would "determine upon a policy to meet the cut-rate tactics of organizations who disregard our jurisdiction." He was sorry that a joint steel campaign could not be worked out.[69]

The IAM also failed to get any satisfactory action from Green on federal labor union organizing. Green did not issue the requested circular letter despite continuing IAM protests.[70] Such a letter was discussed by the AFL Executive Council at its September 6–15 meeting,[71] and the IAM, claiming that at that time the Council authorized Green to send one, tried repeatedly, and for several months fruitlessly, to get Green's cooperation.[72]

Toward the end of September at the annual convention of the Metal Trades Department the developing struggle, destined to stall the forward march of labor for months to come, erupted into the open. Undoubtedly at the prompting of the IAM, the MTD

---

[68]Tighe to Wharton, Oct. 30, 1933, NUF #6 (IAM), *ibid.*

[69]Wharton to Tighe, Nov. 1, 1933, NUF #6 (IAM), *ibid.*

[70]H. J. Carr to Morrison, Aug. 25, 28, 1933, NUF #6 (IAM), *ibid.*

[71]H. J. Carr to Edward Keenan (recording secretary of an IAM local lodge), Sept. 16, 1933, NUF #6 (IAM), *ibid.*

[72]H. J. Carr to Morrison, Sept. 16, 1933; Wharton to Green, Sept. 20, 1933, NUF #6 (IAM), *ibid.* In response partly to the IAM's persistence in the matter, Green finally on February 19, 1934, sent out the kind of letter the IAM had been requesting since the previous July. Discussion of this topic is resumed in Chapter VII.

charged that the AFL (through its federal unions) and "certain International Unions calling themselves 'basic trades' " were violating the charter rights of the craft unions by accepting everybody, without regard to their special skills, into membership. As for the AFL, it had chartered over five hundred federal labor unions since July, the Department asserted, and most of them were unnecessary because their members "should have been placed in the proper existing trade union." The practice, if unchecked, would completely demoralize, if not destroy, the craft unions. The Department was determined, therefore, to petition the forthcoming AFL convention for "executive action at once that will stop this detrimental practice."

At this point in the MTD proceedings, Green appeared and explained that in the rush of organization many persons were being improperly placed. He gave his assurances, however, that the Executive Council was "determined to respect and observe the jurisdictional rights of all International unions"; questions of jurisdiction would eventually be adjusted "and men placed in their appropriate organizations." When the *New York Times* announced, incorrectly, that the MTD officers favored industrial unionism, the convention hastily declared against "any form of organization, vertical, industrial, or otherwise, except the form of organization now existing for each International Union."[73]

There is reason to believe that Green actually had little heart for trying to comply to the fullest with the views he expressed before the metal tradesmen. Shortly after the MTD convention he wrote to William Collins, the AFL representative in the automobile industry, and in language reminiscent of that used earlier by Michael Tighe, explained that if machinists in the automobile industry could be persuaded to join the IAM, "it is perfectly all right for them to do so." On the other hand, if they and other skilled workers could not be persuaded to join craft unions, "then it is the duty of all concerned to strengthen and establish the Federal Labor Union."[74] As a matter of fact, with an expression of discouragement that was perhaps as much feigned as real, he

[73]MTD, *Proceedings, 1933*, pp. 42–44, 45, 55. See also *New York Times*, Sept. 28, 1933.
[74]Green to Collins, Oct. 18, 1933, PCB #13, Book 471, NYSSILR Library.

confessed to Wharton himself that in the mass-production industries AFL organizers were often faced with the alternative of setting up a federal labor union or no union at all.[75]

As it promised, the MTD brought before the AFL convention in October the matter of preserving craft jurisdictions in the mass-production industries. However, the MTD's position, unrealistic to be sure but with the strength of tradition and charter grants behind it, was openly challenged at the convention by those who believed that organization ought to proceed along a new, industrial union basis.

It is apparent, therefore, that within four months after the enactment of NIRA, the three fundamental elements in the AFL's internal struggle had already come to the surface. That is, the mass-production workers had, with unprecedented spontaneity, demonstrated an enthusiasm for organization but were at the same time unwilling to be divided among the crafts, wanting to remain together in the same union; on the other hand, some of the AFL's craft leaders had invoked their legal claims to these workers; and finally, one or two AFL leaders had indicated a willingness to push for the adoption of an industrial union policy. With the issue thus squarely joined, organizing, inseparably entangled in the structural dispute, slowly ground to a halt; and the great debate, which began at the AFL's 1933 convention and which will be related in later pages, grew in magnitude until the rupture came and organizing began again in 1936.

It would seem useful, before going on to the great debate, to describe and then try to evaluate the results of labor organizing in the basic industries through the years 1933–1935. As for the AFL national office, Green and Morrison issued 1804 charters to directly affiliated federal labor unions during this period. The greatest number of charters were granted to lumbermen and to automobile and rubber workers. A considerable number of unions were also established among the gasoline filling-station employees and the gas and by-product coke, cement, aluminum, and radio workers.[76] The average annual membership of directly affiliated

[75]Green to Wharton, Nov. 14, 1933, PCB #13, Book 474, *ibid.*
[76]AFL, *Proceedings, 1935,* p. 95.

unions increased by 78,700 between 1933 and 1934 but only by 22,400 between 1934 and 1935. In 1935 membership in these unions stood at 111,500, which was only a small portion of the millions of workers in the mass-production industries, although it was the highest enrollment ever reported for directly affiliated unions. The membership of 111,500 would undoubtedly have been considerably higher had not 620 directly affiliated unions, more than a third of all those established between 1933 and 1935, surrendered their charters to the AFL in 1935. During that year the AFL suffered a net loss of 314 of these unions, excluding those that joined internationals.[77] There is reason to believe, moreover, that most of the loss of directly affiliated unions occurred during the late months of the AFL's 1935 fiscal year and, therefore, that the membership of directly affiliated unions was substantially below 111,500 as of August 1935. In November 1934, for example, the Executive Council of the AFL estimated that there were 60,000 to 70,000 unionists in Akron and that the vast majority were rubber workers. However, when Green conferred an international charter upon the rubber workers in September 1935, he placed their membership at between 15,000 and 30,000.[78] Also, the number of automobile unionists may have declined by as much as 50 percent between the end of 1933 and August 1935[79] and, at any rate, stood at only 25,788 at the latter date.[80] It would seem, therefore, that the wave of enthusiasm for bona fide trade unionism which was generated by the NIRA had begun to subside drastically by 1935. At

[77]*Ibid., 1933,* pp. 31, 33, *1934,* p. 30, *1935,* p. 29. The 1935 membership of federal labor unions was probably not reduced to any great extent by the transfer of about 7,000 lumbermen and 26,000 automobile workers to the international unions. The lumbermen were not turned over to the Carpenters until April 1935, and the automobile workers did not form their international union until August 26. Since the AFL's fiscal year ended on August 31, and since the figure of 111,500 is an average of monthly membership statistics, the transfer of 33,000 members in April and August could not have appreciably altered the annual average. In 1933 and 1934 only thirteen directly affiliated unions joined parent organizations.

[78]*Ibid., 1934,* p. 44; United Rubber Workers of America, *Proceedings, 1935,* p. 16. Julius Hochman of the ILGWU estimated that the membership of rubber workers' unions declined from 40,000 in 1934 to 4,500 by the middle of 1935. Hochman, "High Tide at Atlantic City," *Nation,* Vol. 141, Nov. 6, 1935, p. 540.

[79]Clark, "Recent History of Labor Organization," *Annals of the American Academy of Political and Social Science,* Vol. 184, March 1936, pp. 161, 166.

[80]See a tabulation titled "Automobile Workers Unions Affiliated with the AFL" and dated Aug. 23, 1935, CIO #1.

the same time, company unionism was growing, and as of April 1935, there were at least 97,400 company unionists in 985 establishments in the steel, automobile, and rubber industries alone.[81]

It is impossible to count with any assurance of accuracy the number of basic industry workers who joined craft unions during the first two years of the New Deal. However, even if one were to include in this category the entire net increase in membership registered by all fourteen of the MTD's affiliates, the total would be but 68,300. The memberships of five of these unions actually decreased or remained the same, and of the nine unions which registered increases, the IBEW (certainly in the 1930's more a building trades than a metal trades union) and the IAM accounted for a total increase of 63,400 members.

Indeed it is significant to note that all AFL unions, exclusive of the direct affiliates, recorded a total net membership increase of 817,462 between 1933 and 1935. Although this represented a relatively sharp increase, the gain was by no means evenly distributed among the roster of 108 unions. Twenty-five of the latter actually experienced membership declines; 21 remained stationary in strength; and 62 were able to enlarge their memberships. Of the latter number, however, only 16 added 10,000 or more members and they accounted for a total increase of 714,900. Moreover, 11 of the 16 unions were industrial or semi-industrial in structure and they added 554,100 members.[82] Among the 11 industrial or semi-industrial unions were the 6 founding members of the Committee for Industrial Organization and they alone expanded by 455,000 members. The membership advances of the 11 industrial or semi-industrial unions combined with the increase in federal labor union strength come to a total of 655,189 members, which

[81]Department of Labor, Bureau of Labor Statistics, *Characteristics of Company Unions 1935, Bulletin No. 634,* Table 1, p. 35, Table 2, p. 37. There were undoubtedly more than 97,400 company unionists in these establishments. A number dealt with their employees through both trade unions and company unions, but the BLS did not determine the number of employees involved in each type of bargaining. The total number of employees in the latter sort of establishment was 61,900.

[82]These 11 unions were the UMW, UTW, ILGWU, ACW, Oil Workers, Brewery Workers, Mine, Mill and Smelter Workers, Boot and Shoe Workers, Hotel and Restaurant Employees, Longshoremen, and the Flat Glass Workers. The remaining 5 craft-type unions were: the IBEW, IAM, Teamsters, Bricklayers, and Railway Clerks.

obviously goes a long way toward explaining the AFL's 1933–1935 net membership growth (918,551 members). With a few important exceptions the craft unions, including those that were not MTD affiliates, did not enlarge their memberships.[83]

On the basis of this general appraisal, and not counting the gains made by national unions which already enjoyed broad jurisdictions in the basic industries (such, for example, as the UMW, UTW, Oil Workers, Amalgamated Association of Iron, Steel and Tin Workers, and the Mine, Mill and Smelter Workers), it would appear that organized labor (meaning AFL headquarters and the craft unions) probably did not have in 1935 more than 150,000 dues-paying members in the giant industries.

The moderate, if not weak, effort made by the AFL and the crafts to organize the basic industries is in itself an important factor which must be considered in any critique of the meager results of such organizing. In response to criticism on this point, the AFL contended prior to 1937 that because the depression had severely taxed its financial resources, it was simply unable to supply the organizers needed and requested by local leaders.[84] The organization did increase its staff of paid organizers from 33 in 1933 to 55 in 1934. Thereafter, however, the staff dropped to 50 in 1935 and fell to 38 in 1936.[85] The AFL's financial argument has the appearance of validity as an aid to a better understanding of the organizing problem. That is, although the AFL never operated in the red during these years, its general fund balance fluctuated between only $35,000 and $100,000.[86] Nevertheless, the controlling AFL leaders did not exhaust all the possibilities for raising additional funds. For example, they could have used the defense fund, main-

[83]The above data are taken or computed from the annual, dues-paying membership figures reported by the AFL. See AFL, *Proceedings, 1935*, pp. 29, 32–33. The figures are not so reliable as those presented by Wolman in his *Ebb and Flow in Trade Unionism*, but since Wolman's study ends with 1934, it has been necessary to use the AFL data.

[84]PCB #16, Book 505, Document Numbers 422–427, PCB #20, Book 548, Document Numbers 77–82, 193–199, and 427, NYSSILR Library; AFL, *Proceedings, 1934*, p. 324, *1935*, pp. 366–372; *American Federationist*, Vol. 40, August 1933, pp. 790–791.

[85]AFL, *Proceedings, 1933*, p. 31, *1934*, p. 30, *1935*, p. 29, *1936*, p. 41.

[86]*Ibid., 1933*, pp. 29–30, *1934*, pp. 28–29, *1935*, pp. 25–26. An example of extremely bold financial risk-taking was furnished by the UMW which in 1933 gambled its last $75,000 on the organizing campaign which brought the union nearly 200,000 members in a single year. Cecil Carnes, *John L. Lewis, Leader of Labor*, pp. 240–241.

tained for direct affiliates, to finance general organizing work. Between 1933 and 1935 this fund grew by more than $250,000; in 1935 it totaled almost $590,000.[87] As an even more lucrative fundraising measure, an AFL convention could have imposed a monthly assessment upon the affiliated national and international unions. In 1934 the organization explicitly withheld approval of such procedure upon the recommendation of its Committee on Organization, which expressed satisfaction with the existing scope of the AFL's organizing activity and called attention to a gain of hundreds of thousands of members since the preceding year.[88]

In contrast to the AFL's pre-1937 attitude, it must be noted that in 1937 when the old-line leaders finally awoke to the fact that the AFL would have to organize (along industrial as well as craft lines) or surrender the leadership of the labor movement to the CIO, they voted unanimously for an assessment and saw to it that the national office of the AFL hired a total of 229 organizers.[89] In the four-year period following 1937, the AFL employed an average of 150 organizers per year.[90] Finally, the AFL more than tripled its organizing expenditures during 1937–1939 as compared with the similar three-year period 1933–1935.[91] When the chips were really down, the AFL found a way to organize.

The AFL's initial failure to mount more extensive campaigning lies in the psychology and craft outlook of its controlling leaders, a number of whom were plainly indifferent to any organizing at all. Small to begin with, their unions had weathered the depression

[87]AFL, *Proceedings, 1933,* pp. 29–30, *1934,* pp. 28–29, *1935,* pp. 25–26. Between 1933 and 1935 the AFL spent only $48,309 from the defense fund and all but $2,659 of this amount was spent in 1935. Use of the fund for general organizing would have required the transfer of money from it to the AFL's general fund. Actually, $15,000 was so transferred in 1933. At the AFL's 1935 convention, a delegate suggested that as much as $100,000 might be taken from the defense fund to enable the AFL to hire additional organizers. *Ibid., 1935,* p. 370. Between 1936 and 1941 the AFL transferred $225,000 from the defense fund to the general fund.

[88]*Ibid., 1934,* pp. 345–346.

[89]*Ibid., 1937,* pp. 75, 106–107, 633–634. Prior to 1937 the most recent assessment authorized by the AFL was in 1918. Between 1889 and 1918 the AFL levied fifteen assessments. "List of Assessments Levied by the American Federation of Labor," CIO #2, AFL-CIO Archives.

[90]AFL *Proceedings, 1938,* p. 71, *1939,* p. 38, *1940,* p. 43, *1941,* p. 43.

[91]*Ibid., 1933,* pp. 29–30, *1934,* pp. 28–29, *1935,* pp. 25–26, *1937,* pp. 71–72, *1938,* pp. 67–68; *1939,* pp. 34–35.

in fair style, and the leaders therefore felt no need to organize when Section 7(a) became law. Others, while willing to organize, had never considered the mass-production industries a major source of new members. The IBEW leaders provide a case in point. They could have immediately laid claim to the skilled electrical workers enrolled in federal labor unions but, contrarily, waived jurisdiction over them—with the comment that at some later date they might want to reconsider the decision.[92] Although the IBEW was increasing its own membership in areas outside the mass-production industries, the union remarked in March 1934 that organizing within these industries should "not proceed too rapidly, for new men must be absorbed wisely, and must receive proper education in union principles. Workers governed for years by the propaganda of big corporations are not ready for participation in the democracy of labor."[93]

It is also certain that in 1933 the thinking of some craft leaders was still affected by the record of past failures in organizing campaigns which involved big employers. Advance planning and cooperative drives had not paid off, and consequently the leaders came to believe that mass-industry workers were unorganizable and that big employers were unbeatable. Defeatism worked against any great release of organizing energy. The very muteness of many of the craft unions on this vital subject of organizing the unorganized is in itself ample testimony to their apathy. One combs their convention proceedings, journals, and correspondence with AFL leaders in vain to discover evidence of organizing interest.

A second factor accountable for the small membership return from organizing during 1933–1935 is that despite Green's initial moves in the direction of encouraging industrial unionism, campaigning was, at least officially, conducted along craft lines. Craft leaders who were interested in organizing in the basic industries expected to divide the federal labor union membership among their unions, and some of them also tried to attract skilled workers directly into their own organizations. Organizing with these ends in view will necessarily be narrower in scope than organizing

[92]G. M. Bugniazet to Morrison, Aug. 28, 1933, NUF #4 (IBEW), AFL-CIO Archives.
[93]*Journal of Electrical Workers and Operators*, Vol. 33, March 1934, p. 116.

which also includes the enrollment of the vast groups of lower-skilled workers.

A final, most important matter to be mentioned in reviewing the poor results of union drives is the great debate itself. In actual practice, the moderate organizing which was launched never proceeded smoothly even along craft lines. At the beginning, unorganized workers of all skills rushed into federal unions in large numbers and this response alone created problems which the old-line leaders neither anticipated nor desired and which they could not solve. Moreover, as the Wharton-Green-Tighe correspondence shows, even the highly skilled members refused to join the craft unions when asked to do so. Edward Kaiser, a staunch craft unionist and the president of the Stove Mounters, admitted in 1936 that it was impossible to dissolve the federal labor unions "as that has been tried and [it has been] found [that] the membership would not stay when they were told to join with a craft organization."[94] Evidence on this point is not, however, restricted to these second-hand accounts but is also supplied by the workers themselves and is scattered throughout succeeding pages. The upshot of the matter was the structural controversy and an organizing standstill.

Part of the explanation for the anticraft-union bias of the mass-production workers does lie in the fact, duly noted by Wharton and others, that the crafts generally levied much higher fees and dues than did the federal labor unions (and higher also, one must add, than were levied by company unions). In fact, despite the deflationary effect of the depression, the crafts did not reduce membership costs. For example, the Boilermakers were still charging a $10.00 minimum initiation fee and $1.50 minimum monthly dues; the Pattern Makers were charging similar minimums of $5.00 and $2.35. Some of the crafts even raised these charges. Thus, the IAM increased its minimum dues in 1929 from $1.50 to $1.75; the IBEW in 1930 raised its initiation fee to a minimum of $10.00 and its dues to a minimum of $3.00; the Metal Polishers raised its minimum fee to $10.00 in 1929; in 1935 the Sheet Metal Workers voted to raise its initiation fee to a $15.00 minimum and its dues

[94]Kaiser to Frey, July 13, 1936, Container 5, Frey Papers.

to a minimum of $2.50; and the Bridge, Structural, and Ornamental Iron Workers upped the initiation fee in 1932 to a range of $100.00 to $200.00.[95]

Under the circumstances, it is easy to see that once even the skilled mass-production workers became accustomed to $2.00 fees and $1.00 dues (or perhaps no charges at all in a company union), they found it difficult to see any reason for spending two or three or fifty times those sums in order to join a craft union.[96] When the AFL insisted that they make such a transfer, they often abandoned the organized labor movement. As an illustration, after the boilermakers in two federal locals in Denver, Colorado, had refused to join the Boilermakers' Union, the union president confessed to Morrison:

This is another instance of...the impossibility of un-scrambling the egg....In other words it is impossible to divide up men after they have been taken into one of these Federal Labor Mulligan Unions where they are admitted for...[$2.00] and about $1.00 per month dues, and the thing that seems so strange to me, Brother Morrison, is that after all the complaints filed...the A. F. of L. continues to issue such charters, and then when an effort is made to correct the damage that has been done, the result is a thoroughly disorganized shop or plant with a body of men sore and disgusted because they have been misled; and it is no wonder then that you have been served with notice that they have decided to sever relations with all things connected with the American Federation of Labor.[97]

In response to this snag in recruiting, and in most cases also after

[95]Constitution and By-Laws of the International Brotherhood of Boilermakers, Iron Ship Builders and Helpers of Amerca, 1920, pp. 60–61, 1934, pp. 67–68; Laws of the Pattern Makers' League of North America, 1926, pp. 39–41, 1938, pp. 40–41; Constitution of the Grand Lodge, District and Local Lodges, International Association of Machinists, 1929, p. 86; Constitution of the International Brotherhood of Electrical Workers, 1930, pp. 15, 32; International and Local Laws Governing the Metal Polishers, Buffers, Platers, and Helpers International Union, 1929, p. 19; Constitution and Ritual of the Sheet Metal Workers' International Association, 1935, pp. 40–42; Constitution of the International Association of Bridge, Structural, and Ornamental Iron Workers, 1932, p. 41.

[96]As a matter of fact, a surprisingly large number of mass-production workers believed that the $1.00 dues prescribed by the AFL for federal labor union members was too high. They complained that many federal labor unionists had returned their charters for this reason and had joined company or independent unions. See AFL, Proceedings, 1934, pp. 609–610, 612, 668–672, 1935, pp. 688–689.

[97]Franklin to Morrison, Aug. 7, 1934, NUF #1 (Boilermakers), AFL-CIO Archives.

the passage of the Social Security Act in 1935 (which made provision for benefits that some unions traditionally paid out of dues), a number of the craft unions belatedly began to reduce their charges. Thus, in the summer of 1935, the IBEW, having finally decided that it would like to enroll the radio and electrical appliance workers and admitting that its costs had theretofore repelled these people, authorized lower fees (only $1.50 minimum) and dues for "non-beneficial" members.[98] The Carpenters, who wanted the loggers and lumbermen, reduced their dues by two thirds in August 1934 and explained that "in this way we can hold these members, otherwise they would drop out quickly."[99] The IAM "sensed the danger" in lowering its dues and therefore would not consider this step, but late in 1935 the union did authorize a reduction of the initiation fee to $3.00 for an emergency period of ninety days during an organizing drive in a totally nonunion area.[100] The Molders and the Metal Polishers also dropped both their fees and dues.[101]

Nevertheless, as events have proved, remedial measures along the lines suggested above were not devised quickly enough, were not adopted generally by the crafts, and what is more important, were not directed at the heart of the organizing problem. Regardless of their differences in skill, the mass-production workers in a single plant all wanted to be members of the same local union— and craft organizing did not permit recognition of this simple truth. Besides, the only union experience these workers had was as members of company unions and federal labor unions, both of which were industrial in the membership sense of the term. It was only natural, therefore, that they should have demanded new, national unions in the basic industries.

[98]"Busy March Meeting of Council," *Journal of Electrical Workers and Operators,* Vol. 34, April 1935, p. 185; "Detailed and Tabulated Vote of Local Unions upon Referendum Propositions I, II, and III," *ibid.,* Vol. 34, August 1935, p. 334. *Constitution of the IBEW, 1941,* pp. 20–22.

[99]Frank Duffy to Frank Morrison, Aug. 29, 1934, NUF #3 (Carpenters), AFL-CIO Archives.

[100]Brown, "Initiation Fees and the July Referendum," *Machinists' Monthly Journal,* Vol. 47, July 1935, pp. 400–401; "Result of July 1935, Referendum," *ibid.,* Vol. 47, September 1935, p. 511; *ibid.,* Vol. 47, October 1935, p. 612.

[101]*Constitution and Rules of Order of the International Molders' Union of North America, 1938,* pp. 26–28; *International and Local Laws Governing the Metal Polishers, Buffers, Platers, and Helpers International Union, 1935,* pp. 18–19.

Green realized well indeed that the industrial union orientation of these workers was the fundamental obstacle which craft organizing could not hurdle. In response to Wharton's continuing complaints in 1935 that the AFL was not enforcing the craft organizing policy, Green declared that the AFL was not to blame if "those employed in automobile, aluminum, rubber, cement, and other mass production industries have developed mass thinking and have become mass minded. It is these workers who present very grave difficulties." He told Wharton that if the Executive Council wanted AFL headquarters to stop organizing because of these difficulties, it ought to be frank enough to say so.[102]

The initial demand for new industrial unions came from the federal labor unionists themselves, and it was they who at all times provided the fundamental support for the success of the industrial union movement of the 1930's. Denied the right, which they felt Section 7(a) gave them, to have their own autonomous, industry-wide unions, the federal labor unionists began as early as January 1934 to erect national councils of federal labor unions in particular industries. Against the advice of Green (whose private opinions and official actions often seemed to clash during these years), James B. Carey set up a Radio and Allied Trades National Labor Council.[103] Late in January a conference of almost one hundred federal unions was held in Washington, D. C.; it announced that the radio workers had formed a national council and that the workers in the aluminum, food, metal-products, and electrical equipment industries were planning to organize similar coordinating agencies.[104] As a means of circumventing the ever more insistent demand for national unions, the AFL began in June 1934 to approve and to aid in the establishment of the national councils.[105] By mid-1935 at least eight national councils were functioning.[106]

[102]Green to Wharton, April 9, 1935, PCB #18, Book 527, NYSSILR Library.

[103]Green to Carey, Dec. 21, 1933, PCB #13, Book 478; Green to Carey, Jan. 29, 1934, PCB #14, Book 482, *ibid.*

[104]*Labor Action*, Feb. 1, 1934.

[105]For example, see Green to Collins, May 29, 1934, PCB #15, Book 495; Green to Phil Hannah (secretary of a federal union of gasoline filling-station operators), April 16, 1934, PCB #15, Book 490; Green to Lewis G. Hines (AFL organizer), Aug. 8, 1934, PCB #16, Book 502, NYSSILR Library.

[106]William Green, "Lumber Workers Organize," *American Federationist*, Vol. 41, September 1934, p. 965; *ibid.*, Vol. 42, February 1935, p. 184; Vol. 42, March 1935, pp. 299, 304; Vol. 42, May 1935, p. 496; Vol. 42, August 1935, pp. 859–860; "Coun-

The national councils had no autonomous authority, however, nor did they offer to federal labor unionists any assurance that they would not still be parceled out among the crafts. Another complication was that federal labor unions, much to their chagrin, were not eligible to receive strike aid from the AFL defense fund until a full year after their charter date.[107] The wholesale disintegration of these unions in late 1934 and in 1935 is to be explained in large part, therefore, by the AFL's procrastination on their demand for new national unions with industry-wide jurisdiction, by craft union efforts to take over all or some of their members, and by the competition and attraction of company unions.[108] The same factors caused those federal labor unionists who remained in the AFL to back wholeheartedly the rising protests of insurgent leaders.

As already intimated, by 1935 some of the craft unions, notably the IBEW, Carpenters, and IAM, had taken their first halting steps toward organizing on an industrial basis in certain areas. This tendency, however, had not yet become general among the crafts and was initiated in an atmosphere of minority labor opinion which was becoming increasingly hostile toward leaders with conservative reputations. Moreover, as will be clarified later, the willingness of some craft unions to take in lower-skilled workers

cil of Gas and By-Product Coke Workers," *ibid.*, Vol. 42, December 1935, p. 1328; Clark, "Recent History of Labor Organization," *Annals of the American Academy of Political and Social Science,* Vol. 184, March 1936, p. 164. The most important of these councils were in the rubber, automobile, aluminum, lumber, and gas and by-product coke industries.

[107]There is much correspondence between Green and federal labor union officers on this point. As a small sample, see Green to Harry Davis, April 30, 1934, PCB #15, Book 492; Green to Thomas A. Maneron, May 9, 1934, PCB #15, Book 493; Green to Arthur J. Sumner, May 23, 1934, PCB #15, Book 494, NYSSILR Library.

[108]As an indication of the growing dissatisfaction of mass-production workers with their status as federal labor union members, see Arthur E. Greer (president of the Hudson local of automobile workers) to Green, July 28, 1934, PCB #16, Book 502, *ibid.* This large local voted 987 to 5 to return its federal labor union charter to the AFL. See also, Green to Raymond Miller (president of an automobile federal), Aug. 2, 1934, PCB #16, Book 502, *ibid.*; Green to Philip Johns (president of an automobile federal), Aug. 9, 1934, PCB #16, Book 503, *ibid.*; Green to Carl J. Shipley (president of an automobile federal), Nov. 26, 1934, PCB #17, Book 513, *ibid.*; John Hall (corresponding secretary of a federal union of chemical workers) to Green, March 20, 1935, PCB #18, Book 526, *ibid.*; L. A. Polmanteer (recording secretary of an automobile federal) to Green, July 30, 1935, NUF #7 (Pattern Makers) AFL-CIO Archives.

was conditioned upon the acceptance by the latter of inferior voting privileges. Had the key craft unions broadened their membership bases and lowered their dues in 1933, it is certain that by 1935 more workers would have been union members. Even such progressive strides as these would not, it seems, have obviated the need for new national unions in some industries—unless one assumes that a number of the crafts would have become mammoth "general" trade unions as the Teamsters is now becoming. At any rate, it is something of an exaggeration to say, as Frey and Wharton have said, that the crafts would have made much more impressive membership gains during 1933–1935 if AFL organizers and the federal labor unions had not competed with them for the loyalty of the skilled workers.[109]

To recapitulate, it would seem that there were three major obstacles to successful organizing in the basic industries during the first years of the New Deal. Leadership and policy problems within the labor movement itself operated as both cause and effect in vastly complicating organizing prospects. In a spirit of hostility to "outside" trade unions, many employers quickly and with telling effect built strong company-union barricades against labor's advance. Likewise, the labor boards which functioned between 1933 and 1935 were unable to play the positive role in promoting trade unionism that the NLRB was able to play after 1935. To these principal points, one might add that several AFL and individual national-union leaders were burdened with time-consuming responsibilities in their wholehearted cooperation with the NRA. Continuing, sharp unemployment after 1933 also operated as an impediment to successful organizing, although one must remember that this obstacle was still present in the latter 1930's and that in spite of it both the AFL and the CIO recruited hundreds of thousands of new members.

There were additional drawbacks to organizing which were peculiar to the steel and automobile industries. In the steel industry, the Amalgamated became crippled by a rank-and-file revolt against the leadership of Michael Tighe and his associates. On

[109]For Frey's and Wharton's views, see AFL, *Proceedings, 1934,* p. 582, *1935,* p. 558; IAM, *Proceedings, 1936,* pp. 41–42.

February 5, 1935 Tighe revoked the charters of twenty rebellious lodges, and although the lodges were reinstated on October 1, 1935, the move did not bring harmony to the steel union. The prospects for successful organizing in the automobile industry received a definite setback by the terms of the agreement signed on March 25, 1934 by President Roosevelt, William Green, and representatives of automobile employers and federal labor unions. The agreement created a tripartite Automobile Labor Board which conducted elections on the basis of proportional representation rather than majority rule. Under this type of arrangement, any group of employees (organized or unorganized) and any union (company union or trade union, AFL affiliate or independent) was allowed to seek representation on the basis of its membership strength. From the trade union standpoint, the experiment added untold confusion and turmoil to the organizing problem in the automobile industry.

CHAPTER VII

Labor's Great Debate

BECAUSE the American Federation of Labor did not make greater progress in organizing the unorganized between 1933 and 1935, there occurred during these years a rebirth of the labor reform movement, but this time on a much larger scale than ever before. The movement, however, remained primarily ideological in character until after the AFL's Atlantic City convention (1935) voted against unrestricted industrial unionism in the mass-production industries. The Committee for Industrial Organization, formed in November 1935 as a result of this decision, rapidly became an organizing center and directed successful campaigns among the steel, automobile, rubber, and other workers. Finally, in November 1938 the Committee became the Congress of Industrial Organizations, thus formalizing the split which, practically speaking, had already existed for more than two years. This chapter carries the story of conflict over union structure through the Atlantic City convention.

I

The labor progressives of the 1930's fought for industrial unionism for much the same reasons as had their predecessors, especially those of the 1920's. While it would not be useful, therefore, to state their full argument for a change in union structure, that part which was new or was re-expressed in a more effective way can be profitably set down. They contended, for example, that the mass-production industries had created the "composite mechanic" who

171

might, in the course of a single day, be called upon to do work coming under the jurisdiction of several craft organizations; therefore, even if these mechanics were successfully placed in craft unions, they would be a source of constant jurisdictional controversy and work stoppage. Marking out craft jurisdictions in the unorganized industries would also, if successfully implemented, deny the workers a united front in collective bargaining and strike action. Their contracts would be negotiated and would expire at different times, thus allowing the employer to go "round and round the circle, cutting everybody at will." A variety of crafts would have difficulty in agreeing upon strike demands and when to strike, and all unions would be affected by the strike call of any single union. Industrial unions would not only dispose of these problems, but they were, in the last analysis, the only organizations strong enough to bring industrial giants such as General Motors and United States Steel to terms. Before the NIRA was invalidated the progressives also argued that industrial unionism would permit labor to speak with one voice, rather than many voices, on the various code authorities which operated on an industry-wide basis.[1]

The advocates of structural change were convinced that industrial unions would not only win millions of mass-production workers to unionism, but that these unions would, in other ways, increase the power and prestige of the labor movement. They would arouse interest in unionism among workers generally, would stimulate within their own memberships a greater demand for union label goods and, in these ways, would serve even to increase craft union memberships. A growing labor movement would, in turn, be better equipped to cope with big business and finance as represented by the National Association of Manufacturers and the United States Chamber of Commerce, would enjoy a more prominent role in the nation's political life, and would be better

[1]Committee for Industrial Organization, *Case for Industrial Organization*, pp. 11–12, 27–28, 42; AFL, *Proceedings, 1933*, p. 190, *1934*, pp. 581–586, *1935*, pp. 523, 525–526; UMW, *Proceedings, 1934*, Vol. 1, p. 160; "What is Industrial Unionism?", *Advance*, Vol. 20, January 1934, p. 19; George L. Berry, "Industrial Versus Craft Unions," *American Pressmen*, Vol. 45, August 1935, p. 15; Sidney Hillman, "The NRA, Labor, and Recovery," *Annals of the American Academy of Political and Social Science*, Vol. 172, March 1934, p. 75; Hillman to William Green, Dec. 12, 1935, PCB #20, Book 547, NYSSILR Library.

able to advance purchasing power so that the mass of people could purchase and consume industrial output. Increasing union membership would improve the AFL's financial condition and permit the Executive Council, which was handicapped in its work by a lack of funds, to execute its duties more effectively and make a greater contribution to the welfare of organized labor.[2]

Also it is not surprising that a number of employers at this time preferred to deal with a single, industrial union rather than with an array of craft unions. Indeed, according to one account, Gerard Swope contacted the AFL shortly after the passage of the NIRA and expressed a willingness to permit all General Electric employees to become members of an industrial union. After consulting with the Executive Council, Green informed Swope that the AFL could not undertake to organize GE employees on such a basis.[3] In October 1934 the Council admitted that some employers whose employees were not organized had claimed that they would be willing to deal with industrial unions.[4]

Public defenses of craft unionism were not made so frequently, nor were they so consistent, as the arguments for industrial unionism. Craft unionists apparently believed, to begin with, that the charters which were granted by the AFL to international unions and which recognized specific craft jurisdictions were contracts which could not legally be altered by a "mere vote."[5] In addition,

[2]CIO, *Case for Industrial Organization*, pp. 5, 26; AFL, *Proceedings, 1935*, pp. 542–550, 736, 740; *Typographical Journal*, Vol. 84, February 1934, p. 108; Hillman to Green, Dec. 12, 1935, PCB #20, Book 547, NYSSILR Library.

[3]Benjamin Stolberg, "A Government in Search of a Labor Movement," *Scribner's Magazine*, Vol. 94, December 1933, p. 349. Frances Perkins indicates that FDR was impressed by Swope's preference for industrial unionism and even talked to John Sullivan of the New York State Federation of Labor "about the possibility of industrial unions being organized in plants like General Electric. Sullivan, a conservative fellow, gave no encouragement, and the matter was dropped." Perkins, *The Roosevelt I Knew*, p. 309.

[4]AFL, *Proceedings, 1934*, p. 43. Evidence from a later period that employers were more amenable to bargaining with industrial than craft unions can be found in a study of NLRB election results for the years 1943 and 1944 which indicated that employers approved industrial unions in 70 percent of the instances in which they expressed a preference. Millis and Brown, *From the Wagner Act to Taft-Hartley*, p. 143.

[5]MTD, *Proceedings, 1935*, pp. 42, 98–99; AFL *Proceedings, 1935*, p. 558. The industrial unionists replied to this constitutional defense of craft unionism by contending that the mass-production industries did not exist and were not anticipated at the time most craft unions were chartered and, therefore, that no craft

173

they argued that craft unionism had made the AFL the only great and enduring labor federation, whereas federations of industrial unions such as the Knights of Labor, the American Railway Union, the Western Labor Union, the Socialist Trade and Labor Alliance, and the Industrial Workers of the World had, without exception, disintegrated.[6]

Because the policy of segregating workers into crafts had been successful in the past, use of this policy did not, craft unionists insisted, explain the lack of progress in organizing the basic industries during 1933–1935. On the contrary, craft organizing was still valid. The trouble was that many, perhaps most, mass-production workers simply were unorganizable. They would not join any type of trade union, craft or industrial, either because they feared their employers would discharge them for so doing or, more commonly, because they were basically indifferent to unionism. Matthew Woll's speech before the AFL's San Francisco convention in 1934 illustrates this attitude. Woll declared that the subject of organization in the basic industries "deals more with the unorganized, and perhaps unorganizable, than it deals with questions of craft or industrial organizations."[7] In March of the same year, the IBEW opined that American workers were not clamoring for entrance into unions and that criticism of the labor movement for failing to unionize them was misdirected.[8] The IAM often stated pointedly that the AFL's organizing policy had not failed but that antiunion employers kept workers from joining unions and that the workers themselves blocked the further extension of unionism because they had neither the will nor the desire to organize.[9] On the very eve

unions had been granted jurisdiction in these industries. CIO, *Case for Industrial Organization*, p. 30; *AFL Proceedings, 1935*, p. 523.

[6]MTD, *Proceedings, 1935*, pp. 41–42; AFL, *Proceedings, 1935*, pp. 556–557; *Official Magazine* (of the Teamsters), Vol. 31, February 1934, p. 12; Vol. 31, March 1934, p. 11. As to this argument, the industrial unionists pointed out that the Knights of Labor did not represent industrial unonism and that the other federations were small sects working outside the AFL with philosophical and doctrinal considerations dominating their policies. The present industrial union movement was, they declared, completely practical, and it enjoyed the full support of many of the largest AFL unions. CIO, *Case for Industrial Organization*, pp. 36–38.

[7]AFL, *Proceedings, 1934*, p. 593.

[8]*Journal of Electrical Workers and Operators*, Vol. 33, March 1934, p. 116.

[9]*Machinists' Monthly Journal*, Vol. 47, December 1935, p. 728; *ibid.*, Vol. 48, January 1936, p. 38; H. W. Brown, "The Uninformed Critics of Craft Unionism,"

of the CIO's birth, Arthur Wharton was still asking "Who are these people on the outside who want to come in? Haven't they had the same opportunity to join a labor organization that we [oldtimers] had?.... Just what is the different situation in the old days and now...? If you ask me...I will say it is a lack of a will to organize."[10] Another IAM spokesman declared that the notion that mass-production workers were eager to join industrial unions was "pure bunk"; they would not join any union voluntarily and in fact could not even be driven into one.[11] Similarly, John P. Frey maintained that a large number of workers had "no irresistible desire to join a union."[12] Still, as already noted, both Frey and Wharton also claimed that workers would have joined the crafts in larger numbers than they did had the federal labor unions not interfered with craft campaigning.

Craft unionists had a variety of motives for invoking this explanation of the unorganizability of mass-production workers. For some of them, the explanation served as a cloak for their defeatist attitude or for their selfish desire to prevent any organizing at all. Others, who wanted to organize and had full faith in craft methods, genuinely wished to clear the crafts of the obstructionist charges hurled by the industrial unionists. A few, who had lowered their costs and invited some unskilled workers to join but still made little organizing headway, sincerely believed that mass-production employees were not union material. In 1937, after the rough-and-tumble CIO had conclusively and often dramatically proved that these workers were organizable, craft leaders abandoned the contrary notion and adjusted their policies accordingly.

While defending the historic legality and the propriety of maintaining their own unions' jurisdictions in the basic industries, craft leaders also assailed the concept of industrial unionism.

---

ibid., Vol. 48, January 1936, pp. 47–48; Charles Sehl, "An Analysis of 'Lewis' Brand of Industrial Unionism,'" ibid., Vol. 48, February 1936, pp. 74–75, 124; IAM, Proceedings, 1936, p. 17.

[10]AFL, Proceedings, 1935, p. 570.

[11]Machinists' Monthly Journal, Vol. 48, August 1936, p. 481.

[12]Frey to Thomas J. Donnelly, Nov. 16, 1935, Container 8, Frey Papers. For additional comments on this subject of the unorganizability of the workers, see "Government Must Step in When Industry Fails, Green Declares," Machinists' Monthly Journal, Vol. 48, May 1936, p. 275; William D. Mahon to William Green, July 7, 1936, CIO #1, AFL-CIO Archives.

Workers of all skills and trades should not be placed in the same union, they argued, because they would not "mix" any more than oil and water nor nest together any better than the sparrow and the hawk.[13] Perhaps part of this reasoning derived from a feeling of the social superiority of skilled over unskilled workers. Such an attitude was doubtless held by Daniel Tobin who, referring to the Teamsters, declared in October 1934 that there were 135,000 members in the union and that "they are not the rubbish that have lately come into other organizations."[14] Also, some craft leaders were convinced that the unskilled, by sheer force of numbers, would control the policies of industrial unions and consequently would ignore the well-being of the craftsmen who had "spent a life-time establishing themselves in a trade."[15] Wage policy was their first concern, and they believed that skilled workers would have to accept lower wages in industrial unions than they could obtain through strategic craft organizations.[16] Moreover, craft leaders could not consent to the establishment of new, industrial unions because they felt that the inclusion of skilled tradesmen in such unions would result in the destruction of a number of crafts. Those which would be wiped out, it was thought, were the Draftsmen, Pattern Makers, Molders, IAM, IBEW, Boilermakers, Sheet Metal Workers, Blacksmiths, Plumbers, and the Stationary Engineers.[17]

Some defenders of AFL tradition pictured industrial unionism as a series of separate and apparently unrelated plant unions or

[13]*Machinists' Monthly Journal,* Vol. 49, August 1937, p. 543; "John L. Lewis—Industrial Unionism, Unsound and Destructive," Container 5, Frey Papers.

[14]AFL, *Proceedings, 1934,* p. 453. Almost a year later Tobin found it difficult to understand how his union had increased its membership "while persistently and consistently refusing to charter undesirables or to give a charter of affiliation to a certain riff-raff that seek affiliation...for purposes that are not only selfish but in some instances inexplainable." *Official Magazine* (of the Teamsters), Vol. 32, September 1935, p. 15.

[15]Boilermakers, *Proceedings, 1937,* p. 128.

[16]Brown, "Uninformed Critics of Craft Unionism," *Machinists' Monthly Journal,* Vol. 48, January 1936, pp. 46–47; Frey, "Industrial Unionism, Unsound and Destructive," *ibid.,* Vol. 48, August 1936, p. 492; "Minutes of Meeting of the Executive Council [of the IAM] from February 17 to 26, 1936," *ibid.,* Vol. 48, p. 15 of an appendix; *Official Magazine* (of the Teamsters), Vol. 31, February 1934, p. 12; AFL, *Official Information and Publicity Service,* July 10, 1936, CIO #1, AFL-CIO Archives.

[17]MTD, *Proceedings, 1934,* p. 30. See also IAM, *Proceedings, 1936,* p. 17.

assumed that industrial unionism meant that a separate union would be required for each product that a company turned out. In the latter case, it was suggested that there would be perhaps fifty industrial unions in a single company like General Electric and that "you would still have one union on strike while all the others remained at work."[18] In the former, it was contended that plant unions would be weaker in bargaining power and financial resources than national organizations of skilled tradesmen and that with this type of industrial unionism "there would and could be no labor movement."[19] One craft spokesman was content merely to remark that the problem of delimiting an industry for the purpose of forming an industrial union was so complicated that if pursued it "would throw the trade union movement or even the industrial movement into such confusion that no one would be able to straighten out the tangle."[20]

It is to be noted again at this point that (unlike other craft unions) the IAM, IBEW, and the Carpenters began, even before the CIO proved itself, to think in terms of organizing on an industrial basis in selected areas. During 1934–1936 these three unions reduced their costs of membership and obtained from the AFL permission to take over the federal labor unions of aircraft workers (IAM), radio and electrical appliance workers (IBEW), and loggers and lumbermen (Carpenters). The IAM also claimed in 1934 all workers in independent automotive parts plants.[21] While these unions may have had a positive interest in organizing lower-skilled workers, it also seems certain that their actions were a calculated response to the dilemma in which they found themselves. That is, they had discovered that they could not pluck just

[18]George J. Bowen, "What is Industrial Unionism?", *Machinists' Monthly Journal*, Vol. 48, March 1936, pp. 176–177. Bowen was acting general vice-president of the IAM.

[19]Woll, *Labor, Industry and Government*, pp. 92–93. See also MTD, *Proceedings, 1934*, p. 28.

[20]AFL, *Proceedings, 1935*, p. 554.

[21]H. W. Brown to William Collins, June 22, 1934, NUF #6 (IAM), AFL-CIO Archives; "Extract from AFL Executive Council Minutes, September-October, 1934," NUF #6 (IAM), *ibid.;* Duffy to Morrison, Aug. 29, 1934, NUF #3 (Carpenters), *ibid.;* "Extract from AFL Executive Council Minutes, Jan. 29–Feb. 14, 1935," NUF #3 (Carpenters), *ibid.;* Green to Dillon, May 21, 1935, PCB #19, Book 531, NYSSILR Library; AFL, *Proceedings, 1936*, p. 97.

the skilled workers from the above occupations, and they also realized that the skilled and unskilled alike in these areas were demanding their own international unions. In these circumstances it was considered preferable to take basic industry workers into the craft unions where they could be controlled and subordinated. The broadening of the membership bases of these crafts was to some extent therefore a negative expression of concern for the unskilled and a move taken perhaps with some reluctance—as certainly was the case in 1937 when the old-line unions generally agreed to meet the CIO unions on their own ground.

The above analysis seems to be especially relevant to the IBEW and the Carpenters. In making it possible for lower-skilled electrical workers to join, the IBEW stipulated that local unions of these "non-beneficial" members (so called because they did not participate in the IBEW insurance and pension program) could have only one vote at the national union convention for every one hundred members; on the other hand, the older beneficial locals of skilled electricians were allowed one vote for every member they claimed.[22] In explanation, the IBEW stated that "the skilled workers in a given industry should be weighted with respect to the unskilled," for the skilled workers, although fewer in number, were "more important in negotiation and even in the use of economic pressure upon management." The whole controversy over union structure actually arose, said the IBEW, from this problem of preserving the leadership of skilled workers.[23] The Carpenters did not allow the representatives of local unions of loggers and lumbermen any votes at all in the national convention, conferring upon them the status only of fraternal delegates.[24] Measures such as these, exuding a spirit of craft consciousness, were as far as the crafts would go, on their own initiative and in the absence of the pressure later applied by CIO successes, toward a recognition of the need for industrial unionism. The measures

[22]*Constitution of the International Brotherhood of Electrical Workers, 1941,* pp. 4, 20–22.

[23]"Hitherto Unconsidered Matters in Dispute," *Journal of Electrical Workers and Operators,* Vol. 36, January 1937, p. 4.

[24]Hutcheson to the Officers and Members of All Non-Beneficial Local Unions of the United Brotherhood of Carpenters and Joiners of America, June 4, 1936. NUF #3 (Carpenters), AFL-CIO Archives.

were not sufficient to prevent the rise of international unions of electrical manufacturing and lumber industry workers.

II

The opening skirmish in labor's great debate over organizing and structural policies in the 1930's took place at the AFL's Washington convention of October 1933. Upon MTD instructions John P. Frey introduced into the convention a resolution requesting the Executive Council to cease admitting into federal labor unions "any mechanic or laborer" over whom established international unions had jurisdiction. At the same time, Elisabeth Christman, a representative of the National Women's Trade Union League and the Glove Workers' Union, called for the development of "functional" unions in the rubber, textile, automobile, meat packing, and other industries where the craft form of organization "has obviously not been successful." As a step in this direction, she recommended that a "Strategy Board" be formed to map out general plans for extending organization to unorganized industries and for strengthening "the united action of the regular craft unions." A third resolution, introduced by a federal labor union delegate, requested that the jurisdictional claims of established international unions over members of the federal labor unions in the public utility industry be suspended for one year in order to permit the full organization of the industry.[25]

These three resolutions were referred to the Committee on Resolutions for its recommendations. Failing to reach unanimous agreement, the committee submitted majority and minority reports to the convention. The majority report, signed by all but one member, summarized the AFL's traditional organizing policy and stressed the facts that the AFL was an entirely voluntary organization, that its affiliated unions retained unqualified autonomy, and therefore that no structural changes could be made except by the agreement of these unions. Federal labor unions, the majority report declared, should continue to serve the temporary purpose of bringing organization to the workers in mass-production plants "when the affiliated national and international unions give consent

---

[25]AFL, *Proceedings, 1933*, pp. 500–501.

to the granting of...federal labor union charters." AFL organizers should be instructed to cooperate rather than compete with the organizers of affiliated unions and to turn over to affiliated unions all craft mechanics when there was a sufficient number of them "to maintain their organizations in the plant or to form a local union of their trade."[26]

Charles P. Howard, the Typographers' president, wrote the minority report and before presenting it for the delegates' consideration he stated that "the future of this organization and the degree of its success depend upon molding our policies to fit new conditions, rather than attempting to mold the workers of this country to policies that have been in effect for half a century. I am one of those who believe," he concluded, "[that] the time has arrived when the American labor movement cannot stand still."

Reading from his report, Howard said that changes in production had so altered the nature of the work performed by millions of men that it was "difficult or impossible" to admit them to craft unions. Lines of demarcation between craft jurisdictions were not distinguishable in many industries and in these areas organization should proceed "upon a different basis." However, no federal labor union should be created in a plant where the "preponderant" number of workers came under the jurisdiction of a single national or international union. On the other hand, a federal labor union charter should be granted when craft jurisdictional claims were not clear or when the drawing of jurisdictional lines "would interfere with continuity of employment." Howard added an element of confusion to his proposals by suggesting that federal labor union members "who are engaged upon work coming under the jurisdiction of National and International unions" could be transferred to these unions "if and when it becomes practicable to do so." Although the tenor of his report indicates that he opposed the complete dismemberment of federal unions, Howard did not recommend the formation of new, national, industrial unions in the mass-production industries.[27]

Before these reports could be debated on the convention floor, Frey moved that they be referred to the Council and that that body

[26]*Ibid.*, pp. 501–502.   [27]*Ibid.*, pp. 502–504.

should at the earliest possible moment call a conference of the interested international unions to consider the entire subject. Although some delegates wanted a fuller explanation of the reports, Green complained that "that would bring on a discussion," and the referral motion was then carried.[28] Woll and Howard appear to disagree in their accounts of this convention action. According to Woll, the Committee on Resolutions, apparently including Howard, agreed "that immediately upon presentation of both reports there would be offered a motion that a conference be called of the national and international unions in order to discuss this problem of organization and reach a positive conclusion."[29] Howard, on the other hand, has intimated that he was not a party to such an understanding and that the move was prompted merely by a desire to avoid at the convention any discussion of organizational matters. Rather "than consider the question upon the floor of the convention," he has recounted, "an uncompromising member of the committee on resolutions [Frey] who had refused repeatedly to compromise moved that the matter be referred to a conference."[30]

The *Railway Clerk*, still edited by Phil Ziegler, who also remained a director of Brookwood Labor College, commented that labor progressives "were disappointed to see the convention do the ostrich trick of sticking its head in the sand" when the industrial union issue was raised and that, although the minority report approached the problem haltingly, it would if adopted have been a step in the right direction. Keeping the matter off of the convention floor indicated "some fear that the minority report might. . . [have been] adopted had it been put to a vote."[31]

The conference of national and international unions was duly called and met in Washington on January 24 and 25, 1934. Representatives of seventy-five national and international unions and of the AFL's four departments were in attendance. Because the UMW was meeting in convention in Indianapolis, it sent no dele-

---

[28]*Ibid.*, 504.

[29]ILGWU, *Proceedings, 1940,* p. 251.

[30]International Typographical Union, *Proceedings, 1936,* p. 90.

[31]*Railway Clerk,* Vol. 32, November 1933, pp. 325–326. For somewhat similar opinions, see *New York Times,* Oct. 14, 1933; David J. Saposs, "Industrial Unionism," *Journal of Political Economy,* Vol. 43, February 1935, p. 78.

gates to the Washington conference.[32] In their joint report to the convention, however, the UMW officers indicated, for the first time, that they were ready to further the cause of industrial unionism, which, they argued, was the only force capable of establishing collective bargaining in certain mass-production industries, and they expressed the hope that the Washington conference would authorize industrial unions for such industries as steel, lumber, rubber, textiles, automobiles, and electrical manufacturing. They were particularly anxious to see the steel industry organized, an accomplishment which they felt would weaken the resistance of the steel companies to UMW organizing of the captive mines. The UMW, its officers declared, had no intention of interfering "with the operation of successfully organized trade unions which have demonstrated their worth and real efficiency over a long period of years and are rendering most valued service to their membership." There was, on the other hand, an imperative necessity for the AFL to enunciate a sound and practical organizing policy.

In approval of this policy statement, the UMW's committee on the officers' report emphatically declared that "the attempt to develop craft unionism in great industrial plants...is altogether wrong and at complete variance with the spirit of the times. We note with regret the retarded progress of organization in many of the large industrial plants of the nation, and we know that this has been due in many instances to the injection of the craft unionism issue. An industrial plant should be organized as an industrial plant: all men, whatever their craft, may belong to one union."[33]

On January 23, shortly before the Washington conference assembled, another significant display of industrial union sentiment was evinced by delegates from nearly one hundred federal labor unions who gathered in the nation's capital to discuss the structural issue. These federal labor unionists demanded that the AFL continue to issue federal labor union charters, that a bureau be established to stimulate the formation of federal labor unions,

[32]In 1936, after the structural controversy had caused much bitterness in the labor movement, John L. Lewis accused the Executive Council of arranging the Washington conference for late January purposely to rule out the participation of the UMW. UMW, *Proceedings, 1936*, p. 175.

[33]*Ibid.*, 1934, Vol. 1, pp. 55–56, 160.

whose members would not be partitioned among the crafts, and "that where a reasonable and sufficient number of such Federal unions form a national association and apply for a national or international charter, same shall be immediately granted by the Executive Council of the American Federation of Labor." The delegates tried without success to obtain a hearing before the international union conference.[34]

Despite the absence of UMW and federal labor union representatives, the Washington conference recognized the formation of new unions as an eventual possibility. It is clear, nevertheless, that the unions visualized by the conference could not, in the strict sense, be called industrial unions and that the conference was more concerned with protecting existing jurisdictions than with establishing new ones.

In his opening remarks to the conference, Green was hopeful, in a vague and mild way, that changes would be made in AFL policies. He spoke at length of the NRA and, while he did not know just what part of the NRA program would be permanently retained and what part eventually discarded, he did know that "we will . . . [never] return absolutely to the old order." It was therefore necessary for AFL leaders "in our organizing movement, in our administrative work . . . to adjust ourselves to this changed condition." Taking the floor, Daniel Tobin then announced that it would not take long to decide the matter before the conference, because the delegates were pretty well bound by the principles of their individual unions, and for this reason he suggested that the conference be used to discuss the NRA.

Green proceeded, nevertheless, with the business at hand and appointed a ten-member committee, chaired by Matthew Woll, to bring in a report on the three resolutions referred to the conference. The report acknowledged that the conference had neither the power nor the authority to alter the principle of trades autonomy and that in organizing the unorganized the structure, rights, and interests of the craft unions "must be followed, observed and safeguarded." However, the AFL, it was declared, should take

[34]From the text of a statement released by the federal labor unionists and printed in *Labor Action,* Feb. 1, 1934.

command of organizing work with the "objective in mind" not only of promoting craft unionism but of "encouraging" the formation of new national and international unions "where no such organizations now prevail." The report also recommended a four-point organizing program. In the first place, organization should proceed with increased vigor, the "fullest possible latitude" should be exercised in the granting of federal labor union charters, and the Executive Council should adjust the jurisdictional disputes which were likely to follow "in the spirit of taking full advantage of the immediate situation and with the ultimate recognition of the rights of all concerned." Secondly, the Executive Council was advised to arrange conferences among the organizers of the AFL, the national and international unions, and the local units so as to avoid or lessen conflicts over the "forms and character of organizations being promoted" and the financing of organizing work. Special conferences were suggested for the representatives of the several departments and divisions of the AFL in order to review, and to make further plans for, organization. Finally, the Washington conference recommended that the AFL sponsor and furnish speakers for mass meetings among wage earners throughout the country and that it utilize the press, radio, and every other available means to foster the spirit of organization.

President Franklin of the Boilermakers arose, after Woll had read the committee's report, and said that he feared "the autonomous rights of the National and International Unions were at stake" and that he was unalterably opposed to federal labor unions being erected on an industrial basis—that is, including in their memberships the skilled workers who belonged to the crafts. Woll answered that organizing was imperative, that whatever form was best designed to enroll workers should be used, and that the rights of national unions must be protected. Howard seemed to equivocate less than anyone else when he asserted that he was willing to change AFL policies "to meet the decision of the millions of unorganized workers in the country" and that he would not be supporting the committee's report if he did not think its content embodied such a change.

Green then made another long speech in the course of which

he warned that the workers were going to organize "with or without us" and that prudence dictated welcoming those who were eligible to join federal locals. AFL policy must be flexible enough to organize the unorganized and yet preserve the integrity of existing unions. Upon the conclusion of these speeches, Franklin said that he now understood and agreed with the report. It was adopted by a unanimous vote.[35]

The report's favorable reference to the formation of new unions might lead one to believe that the craft unions were willing to waive permanently their jurisdictional claims over the mass-production workers. Subsequent events were to prove, however, that the craft unionists had surrendered their rights only to those workers whom they did not wish to admit to their own unions and that they were perhaps even more determined, after the Washington conference, to enforce their membership claims in the mass-production industries. If Daniel Tobin, who was a member of the drafting committee of the Washington conference, can, in this instance, be considered their spokesman, the craft unionists believed that the conference dealt a severe blow to industrial unionism. According to Tobin the conference clearly reaffirmed the autonomous rights of each international union; industrial unionism, on the other hand, "was most definitely thrown on the junk pile" and would not, therefore, pose a threat in the immediate future to the successful policy of trades autonomy.[36]

That craft unionism gained the victory was conclusively affirmed by the provisions of a circular letter which Green sent to all AFL organizers on February 19, 1934. Green acted at the behest of Wharton (and perhaps others) who had advised AFL headquarters that "in view of the action taken by the conference," AFL field representatives ought to be told to put this action into effect.[37] The letter instructed AFL organizers not "to persuade and influence workers who are eligible to membership in national or international unions to join federal labor unions. Only those who are

[35]For the above account of the Washington conference, see the "Proceedings of the Conference of Presidents of National and International Unions Held at Washington, D. C., January 24–25, 1934," NUF #1, AFL-CIO Archives.
[36]*Official Magazine* (of the Teamsters), Vol. 31, March 1934, pp. 10–11.
[37]Wharton to Morrison, Jan. 31, 1934, NUF #6 (IAM), AFL-CIO Archives.

ineligible to membership in national and international unions should be organized into federal labor unions."[38] This was precisely the kind of order that Wharton had been demanding since the previous July and for which the MTD had petitioned at the AFL's 1933 convention. Whether or not the craft unionists really intended to encourage the creation of new internationals, it is evident that they would first try to skim the skilled cream from the organizing crop.

Although the letter reflected a significant change in policy, it did not effect a significant change in practice. To be sure, Green and Morrison had been forced, under constant pressure, to revise their original thinking on organizing strategy. But many AFL organizers, who received a commission for each new federal labor union they formed, were still more interested in issuing charters and then moving on than they were in hanging around and trying to decide the often vexatious, if not insoluble, problems of who the skilled workers were and in which craft unions they should be placed. Some of these organizers also doubtless favored industrial unionism solely as a matter of principle. Above all, however, there remained the will of the mass-production workers to stay in the same union. Even when such old and reliable wheel horses among AFL organizers as Coleman Claherty and Hugh Frayne tried to implement Green's orders, their efforts did not meet with any great or lasting success.[39]

It is not at all surprising, therefore, that after February 19 some of the craft unions began to complain very bitterly indeed to Green and Morrison that AFL laws were not being executed. The Boilermakers, who were still trying and failing to detach "their" craftsmen from two Denver federals, threatened that the AFL would probably have "to choose between the membership of these two Federal Unions and our International Brotherhood," for they could not allow their jurisdiction to be destroyed and their rights lost.[40] Thereupon, despite an ultimatum from Green that the fed-

[38]Quoted in Saposs, "Industrial Unionism," *Journal of Political Economy*, Vol. 43, February 1935, pp. 78–79.

[39]*Ibid.*, p. 79; Green to Frayne, March 28, 1934, PCB #14, Book 488, NYSSILR Library.

[40]J. N. Davis (assistant president of the Boilermakers) to Green and Morrison, April 16, 1934, NUF #1 (Boilermakers), AFL-CIO Archives.

eral labor union charters would be revoked if the Boilermakers' claims were not respected, the AFL organizer in charge of the federal locals held an election and the membership voted against segregation.[41] The Metal Polishers' president was also greatly vexed at the organizing situation and indicated that, although in the past he had tried to minimize friction with the AFL, "from now on the men that belong to our trade should be told to get into that trade."[42]

Charging that the federal labor unions had already cost the IAM forty to fifty thousand members and that now even the membership of some of the IAM's own lodges was at the point of disintegration in favor of joining federal locals, the IAM clamored for a crackdown on AFL organizers and for an end to the issuance of charters to federal locals formed on an industrial basis.[43] Although Green repeatedly and faithfully communicated IAM protests to his field staff with the admonition that the February 19 circular had to be enforced and the IAM's jurisdiction had to be respected, his efforts were unavailing. Try as he might and did, Green could not force the newly organized workers to accept a policy they did not want.[44]

The great tragedy of the situation was that the IAM (and the craft unions in general) still could not read or refused to read the

[41]Green to John E. Gross (secretary of the Colorado State Federaton of Labor), April 23, 1934, PCB #15, Book 491, NYSSILR Library; Franklin to Morrison, Aug. 7, 1934, NUF #1 (Boilermakers), AFL-CIO Archives.

[42]Britton to Green, March 28, 1934, NUF #7 (Metal Polishers), AFL-CIO Archives.

[43]See Wharton to Green, March 16, 1934, PCB #14, Book 488, NYSSILR Library; Wharton to Green, April 26, 30, 1934, NUF #6 (IAM), AFL-CIO Archives; Wharton to Green and Morrison, May 1, 1934, NUF #6 (IAM), AFL-CIO Archives; Eric Peterson (IAM grand lodge representative) to Wharton, May 23, 1934, PCB #15, Book 497, NYSSILR Library; Wharton to Green, June 1, 1934, PCB #15, Book 497, NYSSILR Library; H. W. Brown to Green and Morrison, July 17, 19, 1934, NUF #6 (IAM), AFL-CIO Archives.

[44]See Green to Francis P. Fenton (AFL organizer), March 22, 1934, PCB #14, Book 488, NYSSILR Library; Green to Wharton, April 14, 23, 1934, PCB #15, Books 490, 491, ibid.; Green to David Mitchell (AFL organizer), April 14, 1934, PCB #15, Book 490, ibid.; Green to Lester Boone (AFL organizer), April 14, 1934, PCB #15, Book 490, ibid.; Green to Wharton, May 25, 1934, NUF #6 (IAM), AFL-CIO Archives; Green to John A. Lonergan (AFL organizer), June 18, 1934, PCB #16, Book 500, NYSSILR Library; Green to Wharton, July 2, 1934, NUF #6 (IAM), AFL-CIO Archives; James P. McWeeney to Green, July 17, 1934, PCB #16, Book 501, NYSSILR Library.

bold handwriting on the wall. Instead, the IAM continued to aim critical blasts at Green and advised him in mid-July that henceforth no federal labor union should be established in any metal manufacturing plant until the charter application had been approved by the IAM.[45] Although later the IAM momentarily recognized that the real obstacle was not the AFL but the mass-production workers themselves, it nevertheless decided that if machinists would not join IAM locals "then they must remain outside the A. F. of L. until such time as the laws of that organization provide for...Industrial unions."[46]

Stymied in its endeavor to effect craft union claims in the basic industries, the craft-controlled AFL could hardly have been expected at this point to encourage the formation of new international unions, as it had agreed to do in January, because such unions would undoubtedly have attracted the skilled federal labor union members, as well as the unskilled. However, the AFL did begin in June 1934 to approve the formation of national councils. The first council was formed in the rubber industry on June 4; that it was made up of representatives not only of federal labor unions but also of sixteen craft locals is indicative of Claherty's temporary success in enforcing the February 19 order.[47] Federal locals representing about forty thousand rubber workers opposed this type of council,[48] however, and it did not serve as a pattern for the creation of councils in other industries.

Strongly inclined toward industrial unionism, the rank-and-file leaders of the automobile workers gathered in Chicago in May and discussed their interest in having a new international union in the automobile industry.[49] Green and Collins were informed of this development, and Collins thereupon proposed to call a meeting of all automobile federal locals "for the purpose of bringing into the

[45]Brown to Green, July 17, 19, 1934, PCB #16, Book 500, NYSSILR Library. See also Bowen to Wharton, June 3, 1934, PCB #15, Book 497, *ibid.*

[46]*Machinists' Monthly Journal,* Vol. 46, September 1934, p. 428. See also *ibid.,* Vol. 46, October 1934, p. 476.

[47]*American Federationist,* Vol. 41, July 1934, p. 698.

[48]Confidential memorandum, Marjorie Clark (AFL staff employee) to Morrison, May 11, 1934, PCB #15, Book 493, NYSSILR Library.

[49]Carl J. Shipley (president of an antombile federal in South Bend) to All Automobile and Automobile Parts Unions (n.d. but stamped "Rec'd July 3, 1935"), CIO #1, AFL-CIO Archives.

open underground discussion of an international union." In Green's opinion, however, a better plan was "to convince the automobile workers that they are not yet ready for a national organization" by presenting them with facts which would indicate "the size of the organizing work that is not yet completed."[50]

A conference of federal unions of automobile workers was subsequently arranged for June 23. At that time Green urged them to accept a national council and promised that the AFL would grant them an international union as soon as the council became a permanent self-sustaining organization.[51] Accepting this pledge, the automobile unionists formed a council and voted down ten resolutions which demanded the immediate formation of an international union in the automobile industry.[52] The IAM, which had been trying for some time to get automobile organizing established as a joint IAM-AFL affair, was denied admission to the conference. One of its officers disconsolately reported that the federal union make-up of the automobile council "created more than ever the atmosphere for an Industrial Union for the entire automobile industry."[53]

Taking their cue from one of the recommendations of the Washington conference, representatives of the Metal and Building Trades Departments held a number of meetings looking toward the development of a plan which would both preserve the separate existence of their affiliated unions and at the same time meet some of the objections of the industrial unionists to craft union policies. In September 1934 the Metal Trades Department announced that an agreement had been drafted which would permit the departments, acting singly or jointly as the case might demand, to negotiate but one contract for all the metal and building trades unions recognized by a single employer.[54] The plan seems to have envisaged, therefore, a system of plant federations of craft unions coordinated by the Metal and Building Trades

[50]Green to Collins, May 29, 1934, PCB #15, Book 495, NYSSILR Library.
[51]Quoted in *New York Times*, June 24, 1934.
[52]*Ibid.*, June 25, 1934.
[53]H. W. Brown to Collins, Green, Wharton, and McConnell, March 26, 1934, NUF #6 (IAM), AFL-CIO Archives; Brown to Collins, June 22, 1934, NUF #6 (IAM), *ibid.*; Brown to Wharton, June 26, 1934, NUF #6 (IAM), *ibid.*
[54]MTD, *Proceedings, 1934,* pp. 28–31, 89.

Departments. A few contracts of the nature prescribed were actually negotiated, but they did not dispose of the structural issue.

The Washington conference did not cause the AFL to take command of the task of organizing the unorganized nor did it cause the AFL substantially to further the spirit of organization through mass meetings and other media. In March 1934 Green, referring to the accomplishments of the Washington conference, declared that the responsibility for mapping out "labor forward" campaigns rested primarily with central labor bodies and that the AFL would, upon request, supply such bodies with organizing literature and information. He was optimistic as to the success of this type of campaigning and advised the labor movement to "get ready to reach the fifteen million mark in three years."[55]

III

Labor progressives were not at all satisfied with the conclusions and the results of the Washington conference, and before the AFL convention opened in San Francisco in October 1934, many important unions, including most of those which were later to form the Committee for Industrial Organization, had announced their support of industrial unionism. As will presently be noted, however, the pronouncements of several of these unions were flavored with amalgamationist sentiment. Although this sentiment tended to disappear after 1934, it undoubtedly helped to instill among craft unionists the fear that industrial unionism presaged the destruction of certain established crafts.

Between March and October 1934—especially during March, April, and May—the *Brewery Worker,* under the managing-editorship of Israel Mufson who had been a labor progressive in the 1920's, carried stinging attacks upon AFL leadership and the craft form of organization and urged that the mass-production workers be organized along industrial lines. The journal also reprinted criticisms of AFL policies made by the editors of such magazines and newspapers as *Fortune, Scribner's, Nation, Literary Digest, New Republic, St. Louis Post-Dispatch,* and the *Cincinnati Times-Star* and by Walter Lippman, Louis Stark, Reverend Charles E.

[55]*American Federationist,* Vol. 41, March 1934, p. 242.

Coughlin, and General Hugh S. Johnson.[56] On one occasion it declared that the AFL was in national ill-repute and that it comprised many selfish individuals "who are permitted to carry out their narrow, unsocial policies to the detriment of other unions and labor in general." Nonlabor critics might raise a cloud of smoke, the journal continued, but the fire was in the labor movement itself, and labor "must put out that fire, clean out the rubbish of years' accumulation, [and] tear up the underbrush that is feeding the flames and hobbling labor on its road to progress."[57]

In April 1934 the convention of the Amalgamated Association of Iron, Steel and Tin Workers instructed its officers to notify the AFL "that from this date on we are going to have jurisdiction over all people" in the steel industry. At the same time, however, the convention voted against industrial unionism for the automobile, rubber, and other industries.[58]

Charging that the "antiquated craft structure" of many AFL unions was posing a serious obstacle to organizing progress in the mass-production industries, the ILGWU in May 1934 instructed its delegation to the San Francisco convention to propose that all workers in these industries be placed in new industrial unions and that large-scale organizing campaigns be launched in the automobile and steel industries.[59] Early in June the Oil Workers promised that at San Francisco they would "work and vote for the industrial or vertical form of labor organization."[60] During the same month the Teachers indicated that they would ask the forthcoming AFL convention to authorize industrial unions for the mass-production industries and to call a meeting of all AFL unions "to consider ways and means of transferring the craft unions in the American Federation of Labor into industrial unions."[61]

[56]For a small sample of the literature described, see *Brewery Worker*, Vol. 49, March 10, 1934, p. 4; "The Mess Craft Unionism Is In," *ibid.*, Vol. 49, March 24, 1934, p. 5; "A New Federation Needed?", *ibid.*, Vol. 49, April 21, 1934, p. 5; "The American Federation of Labor is Wrong Says All America," *ibid.*, Vol. 49, April 28, 1934, p. 5; "The Road to Ruin," *ibid.*, Vol. 49, May 12, 1934, p. 5.
[57]"We Must Heed Public Opinion," *ibid.*, Vol. 49, March 31, 1934, p. 5.
[58]Amalgamated, *Proceedings, 1934*, pp. 2201–2202, 2210.
[59]ILGWU, *Proceedings, 1934*, pp. 183, 266.
[60]International Association of Oil Field, Gas Well and Refinery Workers of America, *Proceedings, 1934*, pp. 58–59.
[61]AFT, *Proceedings, 1934*, p. 120.

The *Railway Clerk* detected in June a growing sentiment for industrial unionism "that had better not be ignored by the A. F. of L. and the craft unions affiliated with it." The Railway Clerks, the journal affirmed, deplored "the short-sightedness of craft organizations that hold jealously to their jurisdictional rights at the cost of weakening or dismembering existing organizations that technically encroach upon their preserves, and [that] obstruct the organization of unorganized industries where the craft union has obviously become outmoded."[62]

The UTW and the Mine, Mill and Smelter Workers gave the nod to amalgamation in August, the UTW apparently favoring the creation of new industrial unions in the basic industries where no internationals yet existed, as well as the amalgamation of existing craft unions. The UTW also adopted full industrial unionism for itself and called upon the AFL to direct organizing campaigns in the steel, automobile, rubber, metal mining, and other industries.[63] John L. Lewis concluded a Labor Day address with the warning that the time had come "when the employees in mass industries must be permitted and encouraged to organize themselves into industrial unions.... The American Federation of Labor must authorize such a policy."[64] Finally, in October, the Amalgamated Clothing Workers declared that there was no good reason why the San Francisco convention should not adopt industrial unionism "even if speed might snatch a few seats from under those who prefer not to move or move very, very slowly."[65]

On the other hand, the IAM promised plenty of fireworks at San Francisco because it was not ready to dig its own grave; some people might believe that it was more important to get the workers organized than it was to preserve craft unionism, but the IAM could be depended upon to defend to the last ditch its jurisdiction "over the Machinists of this Continent no matter in what industry employed."[66]

[62]*Railway Clerk,* Vol. 33, June 1934, p. 209.

[63]International Union of Mine, Mill and Smelter Workers, *Proceedings, 1934,* pp. 29, 34; UTW, *Proceedings, 1934,* pp. 31–33; Thomas McMahon to Green, June 25, 1936, CIO #1, AFL-CIO Archives.

[64]"Vital Problems Discussed by International Officers in Timely Labor Day Statements," *United Mine Workers' Journal,* Vol. 45, Sept. 1, 1934, p. 3.

[65]"The A. F. of L. in Convention," *Advance,* Vol. 20, October 1934, p. 3.

[66]*Machinists' Monthly Journal,* Vol. 46, October 1934, pp. 476–477.

Twelve resolutions favoring industrial unionism, either in terms of amalgamation, new unions for the unorganized basic industries, or national councils of federal labor unions, were introduced at the AFL convention. Eight were submitted by federal labor unionists; the others by the Teachers, the Mine, Mill and Smelter Workers, the United Hatters, Cap and Millinery Workers, and the Pennsylvania State Federation of Labor. Two additional resolutions introduced by the Metal Trades Department and the Boilermakers requested the AFL to reassert trades autonomy and prohibit the inclusion of skilled workers in federal labor unions.[67]

Plagued for six days by sharp differences of opinion between Lewis and Frey, the Committee on Resolutions finally adopted and presented to the convention a report which originally had been proposed by Howard as a solution to the structural controversy. The report was short, left many questions unanswered, and was later interpreted in conflicting ways both by labor leaders and persons outside the labor movement. The committee declared that mass-production methods, the vast size of industrial and financial organizations which were hostile to labor, and the fact that it had proven "most difficult or impossible" to organize the unorganized into craft unions made it necessary to outline a clear and definite policy to deal effectively with the question of organization. The AFL, the report stated, should formulate policies which would "fully protect" the jurisdictional rights of all craft unions and afford them "every opportunity" to enroll workers coming within their jurisdictions. Craft organization was declared "most effective" in industries where "the lines of demarcation between crafts are distinguishable." However, the report continued, "it is also realized that in many of the industries in which thousands of workers are employed a new condition exists requiring organization upon a different basis to be most effective." To meet this "new condition" the Executive Council was instructed to charter new national or international unions in the automobile, cement, and aluminum industries and in "such other mass production and miscellaneous industries" as the Council felt necessary. The new unions were to be put under the provisional direction and administration of the AFL. The Executive Council was also instructed to inaugurate

[67]AFL, *Proceedings, 1934,* pp. 581–586.

an organizing drive in the iron and steel industry at the earliest possible moment.[68]

The report of the Committee on Resolutions did not state precisely, therefore, whether all workers in the mass-production industries were to be placed in the new unions or whether the skilled workers in these industries were still to be segregated among the crafts. The discussion on the convention floor which followed the reading of the report did not resolve this basic element of confusion. John L. Lewis admitted that there would probably be as many interpretations of the report "as there were conflicting viewpoints" in the Committee on Resolutions. He remarked, however, that there had been a reluctance on the part of certain organizations to concede that skilled workers in the mass-production industries preferred to join industrial unions and that, in accordance with the report, there would be no interference with the "legitimate" work or the "form and structure" of existing unions.

Wharton wanted assurance that the rights of existing unions would be recognized "within reason" and that his union's jurisdiction over garage workers and automobile mechanics who were employed in "that part of the automotive industry, separate and distinct from the manufacturing plants" would not be disturbed. Frey confidently stated that the Machinists would retain its jurisdiction outside the mass-production plants, and he added that new unions would be formed only in "the plants where a large number of workmen who are not craftsmen in the accepted sense of the word are employed on articles produced under mass methods."[69]

In explaining the committee report, Howard asserted that the workers in the giant industries wanted to become members of a single union and that the report did not require a national or international union to surrender any portion of its existing membership. The Boilermakers' president, James Franklin, supported the report with the understanding "that the rights of the craft unions are to be fully protected in all of the plants, *particularly outside of the generally recognized mass production plants.*" Woll assured William Hutcheson of the Carpenters that building trades workers employed in the mass-production industries would not be

[68]*Ibid.*, pp. 586–587.   [69]*Ibid.*, pp. 587–590, 594.

placed in the new unions and that the report did not change the structure of the American labor movement.[70]

Although the convention discussion reveals the existence, or the strong possibility, of disagreement over the meaning of the committee's proposals, industrial and craft union leaders alike appear to have been reluctant during the convention to state their opinions frankly. The differences which existed within the Committee on Resolutions were not thrashed out on the convention floor. With an outward façade of agreement, the convention adopted the committee's report by a unanimous vote,[71] and each side in the structural battle left San Francisco apparently depending upon the Executive Council to vindicate its views when the time came to form new unions and define their jurisdictions.

The United Mine Workers especially seems to have been counting on the Council to foster industrial unionism. The size of the Council was increased from eleven to eighteen members at San Francisco by the creation of seven new vice-presidencies, and Lewis, David Dubinsky of the ILGWU, and George Berry of the Printing Pressmen, all of whom were industrial unionists, won seats on the enlarged Council.[72] Although the craft unions kept control of the Council, the UMW had high hopes that a Council with "new blood" and "more brains" would be responsive to the increasing pressure for policy changes. Knowing that the Council would be enlarged, Lewis informed the San Francisco convention on several occasions during the discussion of the report of the Committee on Resolutions that he had full faith and confidence in the Council's ability to interpret the report.[73] After the convention had adjourned and the new members of the Council had been elected, the UMW declared that the "duty of applying and enforcing the industrial union policy devolves upon the enlarged executive council, and we have every reason to anticipate lively, vigorous action from now on."[74]

After the convention, the UMW also announced in bold language that the program outlined and adopted at San Francisco unequivocally revamped the AFL's traditional organizing policy and that under the new arrangement all workers in the mass-pro-

---

[70]*Ibid.*, pp. 591–594, italics added. [71]*Ibid.*, p. 598.
[72]*Ibid.*, pp. 688–689. [73]*Ibid.*, pp. 589, 590, 594–595.
[74]*United Mine Workers' Journal*, Vol. 45, Nov. 1, 1934, p. 8.

duction industries were to be "organized in One union, regardless of their craft or trade."[75] William Green seems to have reached a similar conclusion while still in San Francisco. "I am happy," he said in his last address to the convention, "over...that wonderful, historic decision authorizing the Executive Council to go out and organize the unorganized. It is but natural to think and understand that where workers are forced to serve in mass production industries they become mass-minded. They think together and they think collectively, and we must pursue such a flexible policy as will enable us to organize them *as solid units* into this great Organized Labor Movement." He promised that the AFL would establish the unions authorized by the convention.[76]

The ILGWU described the San Francisco agreement as clearing "the hurdles which stood in the way of wide organizing drives in several basic industries," and the *Railway Clerk* was of the opinion that, in accordance with the agreement, charters for the workers in mass-production industries "may be issued without regard to the jurisdictional rights of existing craft organizations."[77] Howard said, speaking to the Typographers' convention in 1936, that in drafting the San Francisco agreement he had in mind the issuance of new charters "upon a full industrial basis so that questions of jurisdiction of other organizations would not interfere with organization."[78]

Significantly, the IAM's first published reaction was that the die had been cast and "the Federation is committed to the industrial form of organization"; nevertheless, since self-preservation was the first law of nature, the IAM would not permit the AFL, or any other organization, to violate its jurisdiction "except in a most limited way."[79] Later, however, the IAM contended that the San Francisco convention had refused to sanction industrial unionism, that consequently AFL laws remained unchanged.[80]

[75]*Ibid.*

[76]AFL, *Proceedings, 1934*, p. 683, italics added.

[77]*Justice*, Vol. 16, November 1934, p. 2; *Railway Clerk*, Vol. 33, November 1934, p. 430.

[78]ITU, *Proceedings, 1936*, p. 90. See also Howard to Green, Dec. 2, 1935, PCB #20, Book 547, NYSSILR Library.

[79]*Machinists' Monthly Journal*, Vol. 46, November 1934, p. 523.

[80]Wharton to David Williams (AFL organizer), Feb. 21, 1935, NUF #6 (IAM), AFL-CIO Archives; *Machinists' Monthly Journal*, Vol. 47, November 1935, p. 656; "President's Page," *Machinists' Monthly Journal*, Vol. 47, December 1935, p. 711.

In a rather puzzling editorial, the *Boilermakers' Journal* declared that the craft unions were "fully protected" by the San Francisco agreement, that they were not "very materially" affected by it, and that they were assured protection "in their own sphere."[81] The IBEW believed that the decision guarded the craft unions against the rise of "ephemeral overnight organizations."[82] Frey's personal correspondence indicates an understanding on his part that organization in the mass-production industries was to include the placing of skilled mechanics in their respective craft unions as well as the formation of new unions.[83] Frey reveals, however, that after the convention he was criticized by the presidents of some of the international unions "on the ground that I had given way a great deal more than I had authority to do; that I had gone too far in endeavoring to meet the views of Lewis, Howard, and some of the others."[84]

The *New York Times* editor and Louis Stark, its labor reporter, regarded the decision as an unqualified victory for industrial unionism; craft unions were to be protected "in their own sphere" but all workers in the mass-production industries would be organized into industrial unions.[85] The historian Charles A. Beard thought that the AFL "took certain steps away from historic craft unionism in the direction of organizing workers in great industries into 'vertical unions.' "[86]

Between January 29 and February 14, 1935 the enlarged Executive Council of the AFL met in Washington to grapple with the vitally important issues raised at San Francisco. The election of Lewis, Dubinsky, and Berry to the Council, together with the fact that the convention's pronouncements on organizing policy were, to say the least, cryptically worded, served to transfer to the Council the policy struggle which had theretofore been waged outside that body. At this session of the Council its members therefore

[81]*Boilermakers' Journal,* Vol. 46, November 1934, p. 291.
[82]"A. F. of L. Adopts Flexible Policy," *Journal of Electrical Workers and Operators,* Vol. 33, February 1935, pp. 56, 96.
[83]Frey to Lawrence O'Keefe, July 15, 1936, Container 5; Frey to Walter A. Draper, July 8, 1938, Container 8, Frey Papers. See also MTD, *Proceedings, 1935,* pp. 11–12.
[84]Frey to O'Keefe, July 15, 1936, Container 5, Frey Papers.
[85]*New York Times,* Oct. 12, 13, 21, 1934.
[86]Beard, "Confusion Rules in Washington," *Current History,* Vol. 41, December 1934, p. 337.

clashed over the proper interpretation of the San Francisco declaration. Finally, by a majority vote, the Council decided that, except with the specific consent of the craft unions concerned, no new internationals would be formed which disturbed craft rights in any way.[87] The Council was not united in this interpretation, and it is, therefore, not surprising that it did not, either at the February or later meetings in 1935, carry out all of the instructions of the San Francisco convention and that the actions it did take increased rather than lessened the possibility of an open breach in the labor movement.

As to a steel campaign, Michael Tighe presented the Council with a plan which stipulated that steel plants had to be organized industrially and the steel workers placed directly in Amalgamated lodges rather than in federal labor unions.[88] In complete disagreement with Tighe, the Council directed Green to inaugurate a cooperative campaign of all unions with claims in the steel industry; recruits would be put in federal locals and later divided among the claimants.[89] Green promptly appointed Lewis, Wharton, and Tobin to confer with Tighe on February 13. The quartet met but Tighe, with Lewis's backing, adamantly opposed the Council's plan.[90] Besides, the Amalgamated's internal strife had just come to a climax with the expulsion of the insurgent lodges on February 5, and they were not fully reinstated until October. Because of this situation and the structural impasse, a steel campaign was not undertaken in 1935.[91] Early in 1936 the AFL and the CIO were to fight their first major battle over the steel workers, and in the aftermath the CIO was, practically if not officially, to bypass the Amalgamated and erect the United Steelworkers of America.

At its February 1935 session the Executive Council, which had the previous year awarded aircraft industry federal locals to the IAM, granted the Carpenters' request for jurisdiction over 118 fed-

[87]Wharton to Williams, Feb. 21, 1935, NUF #6 (IAM), AFL-CIO Archives; AFL, *Proceedings, 1935,* p. 537.
[88]Tighe to Green, Jan. 15, 1935, NUF #5 (Amalgamated), AFL-CIO Archives.
[89]"Extract from AFL Executive Council Minutes, Jan. 29–Feb. 14, 1935," CIO #1, *ibid.*
[90]*New York Times,* Feb. 13, 16, July 28, 1935.
[91]AFL, *Proceedings, 1935,* p. 97; Charles P. Howard to Green, March 10, 1936, CIO #1, AFL-CIO Archives.

eral locals of some seven thousand loggers, lumbermen, timber workers, shingle weavers, and sawmill workers. Among the several unexplained bits of AFL politics is the fact that John L. Lewis seconded this move.[92] Although most of these federal locals at first balked at the prospect of having to join the Carpenters, they eventually went along with the Council's decision.[93] In mid-1937, however, a decided majority of them withdrew from the Carpenters, founded the International Woodworkers of America, and affiliated with the CIO, thus unleashing one of the hardest fought engagements of labor's entire civil war.[94]

On February 12, 1935 the Executive Council gave notice that it would create an international union of automobile workers in the near future, that the charter for such a union was being drafted.[95] The IAM had decided scarcely before the echoes had died from the San Francisco convention hall, however, that if and when an automobile union was chartered the IAM would not be agreeable "to have such union include workers in automobile and automobile body building plants, such as machinists, tool makers, die sinkers,

[92]"Extract from AFL Executive Council Minutes, Jan. 29–Feb. 14, 1935," CIO #1, AFL-CIO Archives. The Carpenters originally "directed" Morrison to transfer these federal unions to the Carpenters on August 27, 1934, indicating at the time that "our label is the only one that can be recognized on woodwork." Green answered his order by stating that the AFL Executive Council had the right to decide at its next meeting whether to honor the Carpenters' demand or create a new international union of lumber industry workers. The Carpenters' retort was that "the question of jurisdiction you mention came to us as a surprise. No question of jurisdiction is involved. No other national or international union is involved. No other organization claims them. So where does the question of jurisdiction arise?" The Carpenters could not see "where the Executive Council has anything to do in matters of this kind." At the February Council meeting, Green supported the Carpenters' request. Duffy to Morrison, Aug. 29, 1934; Green to Duffy, Nov. 13, Dec. 18, 1934; Duffy to Green, Nov. 20, 1934, NUF #3 (Carpenters), *ibid.*

[93]The Northwest Council of Loggers, Sawmill and Woodworkers, which represented 99 of the federal unions, originally indicated that it was opposed to the transfer of its members into the Carpenters' organization. Edgar S. Hall (secretary of the Northwest Council) to Green, Dec. 26, 1934, Jan. 8, 1935, NUF #3 (Carpenters), *ibid;* Memo to R. Lee Guard (Green's secretary) from the AFL Bookkeeping Department, Dec. 18, 1934, NUF #3 (Carpenters), *ibid.* Of the 32 individual federal unions which indicated a position with regard to the Council's decision, 21 opposed joining the Carpenters, 2 favored the move, and 9 asked for additional information. See letters in NUF #3 (Carpenters), *ibid.*

[94]For an account of the events leading to the birth of the IWA and the subsequent interunion rivalry over the lumber workers, see Vernon H. Jensen, *Lumber and Labor*, pp. 203–224.

[95]*New York Times*, Feb. 13, 1935.

and maintenance men engaged in the building, repairing, assembling and servicing of tools, dies, and equipment, and those engaged upon experimental work and the operators of all machines in connection with this work."[96] In April 1935 the IAM revealed that the AFL had already tried to charter an automobile union but that the IAM had objected that its rights would not have been protected "if this charter was issued to men, many of whom were eligible to membership in the I. A. of M."[97]

The AFL Council held its second and third quarterly sessions in May and August 1935 and during these sessions evidently revised the automobile charter to meet the Machinists' objections and also drafted a charter for the rubber workers.[98] In a curious move, which may have been prompted by those Council members who believed the mass-production workers were not too enthusiastic about unionism, Green sent a questionnaire to all the rubber and automobile federal locals in June asking whether and when their members wanted an international union.[99] The response from the automobile group was 98.3 percent in favor of the immediate establishment of a union.[100]

At no time between February and late August did the Council draft charters for the cement and aluminum workers; the charters that were drafted protected craft union jurisdictions in the rubber and automobile industries and created international unions of "production" workers rather than industrial unions. It was with this situation in mind that the UMW charged on May 3 that the Council had repudiated the San Francisco agreement which, the miners asserted, required the establishment of industrial unions in the basic industries. Louis Stark, who reported the miners' vexation, also indicated that rumors were being bandied about that

[96]"Minutes of Meeting of the [IAM] Executive Council from November 12 to 17, 1934," *Machinists' Monthly Journal,* Vol. 46, p. 2 of an appendix.

[97]"Minutes of Meeting of the [IAM] Executive Council from April 8 to 17, 1935," *ibid.,* Vol. 47, p. 3 of an appendix.

[98]The Council first declared its intention to form an international union of rubber workers on May 8, 1935. *New York Times,* May 9, 1935.

[99]Green to Rubber Workers Unions, June 10, 1935, PCB #19, Book 533, NYSSILR Library; Green to All Auto Workers Federal Labor Unions, June 19, 1935, CIO #1, AFL-CIO Archives.

[100]Statement dated July 12, 1935, CIO #1, AFL-CIO Archives. The results of the rubber workers' questionnaire are not known to the writer.

John L. Lewis would assume leadership of a movement to erect a rival federation of industrial unions were the AFL to continue to stand in the way of progressive labor policies.[101] Speaking before the Tamiment Economic and Social Institute at Camp Tamiment, Pennsylvania, on June 29, 1935, Sidney Hillman, president of the Amalgamated Clothing Workers, Francis Gorman, a UTW vice-president, Emil Rieve, president of the Hosiery Workers, and Julius Hochman called for more energetic action on the AFL's part in organizing the unorganized and in developing industrial unions.[102]

In a letter to Hillman written early in July, Frey expressed an anxiety lest the personal considerations of certain individuals split the AFL. In response, Hillman, surmising that Frey had reference "to the different points of view as to the best method of organizing the mass production industries," suggested that he and Frey meet in the near future "to discuss these matters objectively." Frey acknowledged that such a meeting would be "advantageous," but his correspondence does not indicate that a meeting ever took place.[103]

On July 19, Frey confided to Victor Olander, who was then secretary of the Illinois Federation of Labor, that he had been gathering material "for what apparently will be one of the principal questions at the coming A. F. of L. Convention—the effort to force the industrial form of union upon a majority of our Internationals." He acknowledged that the industrial union movement had considerable support and he alleged that the movement's supporters apparently did not intend to abide by an adverse majority decision. "There are hotel lobby rumors," Frey said, "that unless they can have their way we may be faced with a secession movement."[104]

Lewis appears to have confirmed these rumors during an interview with Louis Stark late in July. On July 28 Stark reported

[101]*New York Times,* May 4, 1935.

[102]*Ibid.,* June 30, 1935; "Labor Leaders Criticize A. F. of L. Stand on Industrial Unionism," *Brewery Worker,* Vol. 50, July 13, 1935, p. 1.

[103]Hillman to Frey, July 12, 1935; Frey to Hillman, July 15, 1935, Container 5, Frey Papers.

[104]Frey to Olander, July 19, 1935, Container 5, *ibid.*

in the *New York Times* that the outcome of the controversy over union structure was unpredictable but that if the controversy "eventually leads Mr. Lewis and his union out of the A. F. of L., by voluntary choice or through defeat at some future federation convention, the miners will be prepared for that step even if it means the setting up of another and rival labor federation comprising the industrial unions."[105]

After the August meeting of the Executive Council, Green issued a call for a founding convention of the automobile workers to be held in Detroit. On August 26 Green appeared before the convention and presented the charter which created the International Union United Automobile Workers of America. The jurisdiction of the new union within automobile production plants covered only those employees "directly engaged" in the actual assemblying of parts into completed automobiles. All "other employe[s] engaged in said automobile production plants" were to be surrendered to the craft unions. As for the automobile-parts manufacturing industry, the grant of jurisdiction to the new union did not extend to any independent parts companies; and within those parts-manufacturing companies controlled by automobile producers, jurisdiction did not include tool, die, and machinery makers or any employee who was not "directly engaged" in the manufacture of automobile parts.[106] The automobile unionists were not in the least satisfied with the jurisdictional provisions of their charter and they resolved, therefore, that "unless these jurisdictional limitations are removed by the fifty-fifth [1935] convention [of the AFL] the international officers of the United Automobile Workers be, and are hereby instructed to formulate such plans and take such action as in their opinion may seem advisable."[107]

In accordance with the San Francisco agreement, Green appointed, for a probationary period, the president (Francis J. Dillon) and the entire executive board of the UAW. However, the delegates wished to elect their officers, and by a vote of 164 to 112

[105]*New York Times*, July 28, 1935.

[106]The full text of the jurisdictional grant is printed in AFL, *Proceedings, 1935,* pp. 95–96.

[107]Quoted in John A. Fitch, "The Clash over Industrial Unionism," *Survey Graphic,* Vol. 25, January 1936, p. 41.

defeated a resolution which sought approval of the Green appointments. Nevertheless, Green stood his ground, and the delegates then elected a committee to protest the action at the Atlantic City convention.[108]

Before the UAW was a month old, Morrison advised one local to turn over part of its membership to the Pattern Makers. He was unceremoniously informed that the UAW claimed everybody in the industry and that "What we have, we hold, relinquishing no one and with this as a very definite statement, we beg to remain, Fraternally yours,. . . ."[109]

From Detroit Green traveled to Akron to preside, on September 12, over the founding convention of the United Rubber Workers of America. In Akron he encountered even more determined opposition than he had in Detroit. Green informed the delegates that their union's jurisdiction covered all workers in the rubber industry "who are engaged in the mass production of rubber products, same not to include such workers who construct buildings, . . [manufacture or install] machinery, or engage in maintenance work or in work outside of the plants or factories." Immediately, a delegate posed the question as to whether the rubber workers ought to accept the charter. Green's tart reply was that they had no right to decide whether they wanted it or not. The charter was "conferred" upon them and it could neither be amended, accepted, nor rejected.[110]

As a consequence of his experience in Detroit, Green sought to appoint only the president of the URW, leaving the other officers to be elected by the convention. This compromise failed, however, to satisfy the rubber workers, who felt they were fully competent to choose their own chief executive. Therefore, when Green

[108]B. J. Widick, "Two Defeats for William Green," *Nation,* Vol. 141, Oct. 9, 1935, p. 412. See also *New York Times,* Sept. 1, 1935. After the founding convention adjourned, Homer Martin, who had been appointed a vice-president of the UAW, told Green he believed "that your appointment of the officers is going to work out much more successfully than any of us dreamed." Martin to Green, Sept. 4, 1935, CIO #1, AFL-CIO Archives. The UAW established a $2.00 initiation fee and dues of $1.00 a month. Dillon to UAW Locals, Oct. 1, 1935, CIO #1, AFL-CIO Archives.

[109]Harry Marlett (recording secretary of a UAW local) to Morrison, Oct. 30, 1935, NUF #7 (Pattern Makers), AFL-CIO Archives.

[110]URW, *Proceedings, 1935,* pp. 18, 20.

attempted to install Coleman Claherty as president, the delegates voted overwhelmingly (46 to 9) against the move. At that point Green turned the convention over to the delegates saying that he was glad to give them what they wanted. They proceeded to elect Sherman H. Dalrymple as the first URW president, and after Green had left the convention hall, they unanimously adopted a constitution which declared that the union's jurisdictional objective was "to unite in one Organization all men and women eligible for membership, employed in and around factories engaged in the manufacturing of rubber products."[111]

While the leading progressives, warmly supported by the mass-production workers themselves, appear to have been unalterably opposed to the extension of craft union alignments into the basic industries, many of the more important and more conservative craft unions were equally unwilling to sanction any infringement upon trades autonomy. For example, at the September 1935 convention of the Metal Trades Department, the fourteen unions affiliated with the Department pledged their unanimous and uncompromising support of craft unionism and agreed that they would vote as a solid unit to uphold the principle at the AFL's Atlantic City convention.[112]

IV

There was ample indication beforehand, therefore, that decisions of great importance would be made at Atlantic City. In its report to the convention, which was attended by the largest number of delegates in the AFL's history up to that time, the Executive Council explained in a rather conciliatory spirit that it had not chartered new unions in the cement and aluminum industries, as it had been instructed to do at San Francisco, because unionism was too weak in those industries to support stable and self-sustaining internationals.[113] A similar situation prevailed in the radio

[111]*Ibid.*, pp. 31–40, 46–47, 90.

[112]MTD, *Proceedings, 1935*, pp. 11–12, 15–17, 40–42, 45–46, 78, 97–102. Some of the more important unions attached to the MTD at this time were the IAM, IBEW, Boilermakers, Metal Polishers, Plumbers, Operating Engineers, Firemen and Oilers, Pattern Makers, Molders, and the Sheet Metal Workers.

[113]While this explanation appears valid for the cement industry (there were only 1,317 members enrolled in the federal labor unions of cement workers), it is likely

and the gas, coke and by-products industries, the Council declared. Nevertheless, the Council advised that the policy of issuing charters to new international unions should be continued and that their jurisdictions should be determined "in accordance with the circumstances and the requirements of each individual case." The Council was aware that differences of opinion existed in the labor movement with regard to the form new unions should take, but it declared that in "true democratic fashion...a majority of the delegates at a convention...must decide the organization policies of the American Federation of Labor" and that "no man can expect to impose his own will upon the majority against their judgment and matured opinion." The Council urged the city centrals to initiate "labor forward" campaigns with the objective of organizing all of the unorganized workers who came within their jurisdictions and, in addition, declared that it was determined to launch and conduct an organizing campaign in the steel industry.[114]

Sentiment for industrial unionism had become too strong, however, to rely on the Council's promises or to be satisfied with the manner in which the Council had implemented the San Francisco agreement. As a result, 22 industrial union resolutions were introduced into the convention. Fourteen of them called generally for the establishment of industrial unions in the mass-production industries, and some of the same resolutions demanded, in addition, the amalgamation of the craft unions. Each of the 8 remaining resolutions requested an industrial union for a specific industry. The general resolutions, which were considered and reported upon in a body by the Committee on Resolutions, were not printed in the convention proceedings, but Frey has disclosed that 2 of them were submitted by the UTW and the Mine, Mill and Smelter

---

that the IAM's claims in the aluminum industry were very important in preventing the chartering of an international union of aluminum workers. It is even possible that these claims encompassed all of the aluminum workers. The Aluminum Workers Council tried without success to persuade the IAM to relinquish its claims in the industry. Wharton to Green, Dec. 3, 1934, Green to Wharton, Dec. 6, 1934, CIO #1, AFL-CIO Archives; Green to Wharton, March 11, 1935, PCB #18, Book 524, NYSSILR Library; "Minutes of Meeting of the [IAM] Executive Council from April 8 to 17, 1935," *Machinists' Monthly Journal*, Vol. 47, p. 3 of an appendix. For the cement industry membership figure, see Green to R. J. Textor (secretary of a cement federal union), Jan. 25, 1935, PCB #17, Book 519, NYSSILR Library.

[114]AFL, *Proceedings, 1935*, pp. 96–98.

Workers, 2 by the Wisconsin and California federations of labor, and the remaining 10 by federal labor unions, 1 of which was signed by 42 of these unions.[115]

The first and the major debate of the convention came when the Committee on Resolutions reported on the general resolutions favoring industrial unionism. Once again, as in 1933, the committee failed to reach a unanimous agreement. The contest within the committee was, in Frey's words, as "vigorous" as was the later debate on the convention floor,[116] and it ended in the submission to the convention of majority and minority reports. The minority report was signed by six committee members including John L. Lewis, J. C. Lewis of the Iowa Federation of Labor, Howard, Dubinsky, Frank B. Powers of the Commercial Telegraphers, and A. A. Myrup of the Bakery Workers. The majority report was not signed, but it was probably approved by nine committeemen.[117]

The majority of the Committee on Resolutions argued that the industrial unionists either misunderstood the San Francisco declaration or wished to change it. That declaration, said the majority, gave complete protection to craft unions and guaranteed to them all workers coming within their charter jurisdictions. The declaration provided that only "mass production employes," and not the skilled craftsmen or other workers in the mass-production industries, were to be included in the contemplated new international unions. The demands of the industrial unionists would, if acceded to, destroy the craft unions and result in the assimilation of their membership into industrial organizations. The majority report recommended nonconcurrence, therefore, with the fourteen industrial union resolutions.[118]

[115]*Ibid.*, pp. 521, 721, 729–730.
[116]Frey to Donnelly, Nov. 16, 1935, Container 8, Frey Papers.
[117]Nine members of the Committee on Resolutions were among those delegates who later voted against the minority report. They were Woll, Frey, Franklin, Thomas L. Hughes of the Teamsters, P. J. Morrin of the Structural Iron Workers, M. J. Colleran of the Plasterers, John J. Mara of the Boot and Shoe Workers, Fred Baer of the Fire Fighters, and Olander. There were seventeen persons on the committee and two of them, therefore, are not accounted for in the voting. These men are John Possehl of the Operating Engineers and Clarence E. Swick of the Painters. AFL, *Proceedings, 1935,* pp. 206, 523–524, 574–575. Howard contends that before the majority report was presented to the convention only eight members of the committee approved of it and that another member would have signed the minority report had he not been intimidated by the majority. ITU, *Proceedings, 1936,* p. 91.
[118]AFL, *Proceedings, 1935,* pp. 521–522.

The minority of the committee interpreted the San Francisco declaration as requiring that all workers in each mass-production industry be organized into a single, industrial union. It was not their intention, the signers of the minority report assured, to take away from the craft unions any part of their present or potential membership in establishments where skilled craftsmen, "coming under a proper definition of the jurisdiction" of such unions, "predominated." The minority report directed the Executive Council to initiate aggressive organizing campaigns in the industries which were still largely unorganized, to draft unrestricted charters for national and international unions in the basic industries, and to issue similar charters to independent and company-dominated unions that wanted to affiliate with the AFL and to "those organizations now affiliated with associations not recognized by the American Federation of Labor as bona-fide labor organizations."[119]

The convention debate, which lasted for seven-and-a-half hours, turned upon the adoption or rejection of the minority report and bristled with charges and countercharges of broken pledges, personal ambitions, and impending destruction of the labor movement. Lewis and Howard were the chief protagonists on the industrial union side; Woll and Frey led the craft union debaters. Lewis, employing some of his most famous oratory and also some of his finest sarcasm, berated craft unionism and craft unionists and avowed that a change in structural policy was a condition precedent to the future success of the AFL. At San Francisco, he declared, "I was beguiled into believing that an enlarged Executive Council would honestly interpret and administer" the report of the Committee on Resolutions. He had been seduced with fair words and "having learned that I was seduced, I am enraged and I am ready to rend my seducers limb from limb." He was no longer so young nor so gullible as he had been at San Francisco, and he was convinced that the Executive Council was "not going to issue any charter for industrial unions in any industry." Limiting the membership of the automobile and rubber unions to those workers engaged in the assembling processes was "a breach of faith and a travesty upon good conscience." Organization had, during the past year, been a colossal failure; 314 federal labor unions had vanished

[119]*Ibid.*, pp. 523–524.

and they were still "dying like the grass withering before the Autumn sun." If the AFL voted down the minority report "the enemies of labor...will be encouraged and high wassail will prevail at the banquet tables of the mighty." Howard added that the workers of the country were going to organize, and if they were not permitted to organize under the AFL's banners, they would organize "under some other leadership" or without leadership.[120]

Frey contributed a lengthy defense of the historic policy of craft unionism. Woll contended, quoting from the report of the Washington conference, the proceedings of the San Francisco convention, and the AFL's constitution, that craft unionism had not been amended nor compromised in any way. Both men agreed that the minority report would deprive the Executive Council of discretionary judgment in the issuance of charters and that such a "strait-jacket" policy would spell "ruination for the Labor movement." Frey was especially irked by Stark's report that Lewis might set up a rival federation of industrial unions. "Never before," Frey complained, "have I been called upon in this convention to discuss a question which was accompanied by a threat, where the public statement has been made that unless we do what somebody wants us to do, there might be secession and the organization of another Federation of Labor. I am not accustomed to giving any consideration to the man who strives to secure his end by making threats." Frey also charged that during the past year two members of the Executive Council had aided an independent, dual union of shipbuilding workers, and he indicated that their action in this respect had served further to cloud the structural controversy.[121]

Victor Olander was the only convention speaker who seemed willing to seek a compromise settlement. He stated that he preferred to handle the question before the convention "a little differ-

---

[120]*Ibid.*, 524–528, 534–542.

[121]*Ibid.*, pp. 528–534, 552–559. In July 1936 Frey elaborated the latter charge, declaring in a letter to Lawrence O'Keefe of the Molders that John L. Lewis had violated the San Francisco declaration in becoming "the chief adviser and counsellor for the Industrial Union of Marine and Shipbuilding Workers of America" and in helping other dual unions of metal trades' workers. This action, in addition to Lewis's threat to erect a rival federation, had forced the showdown on structural policy at Atlantic City, Frey contended. Frey to O'Keefe, July 15, 1936, Container 5, Frey Papers.

208

ently" than the majority report proposed and that this might involve "a sacrifice here and there of our jurisdictional rights." He believed, however, that the debating had reached the point of no return and that the whole question ought to be referred to the Executive Council for later disposition.[122]

Olander's suggestion elicited no response from the convention, which proceeded to defeat the minority report by a roll-call vote of 18,024 to 10,933 and to adopt the majority report by a voice vote. Approximately 38 percent of the roll-call vote was cast in favor of the industrial union policy, and included in this percentage were the votes of 21 of the AFL's 94 national and international unions.[123] Two additional unions divided their votes; 11 unions abstained from voting.[124]

Of the state federations of labor, city centrals, and federal labor unions which voted, a majority in each instance favored industrial unionism. The state federations voted 14 to 9 for the minority report with 12 of them abstaining; the city centrals' vote was 22 to 19 with 47 organizations, however, declining to vote; and 75 federal labor unions, representing 335 votes, favored the minority report while 8 of them, representing 16 votes, opposed it and 29 of them, representing 58 votes, did not indicate a choice.[125] Judging from the federal labor union vote, there is no doubt but that the mass-production workers overwhelmingly supported industrial unionism.

On the last day of the convention, after most of the delegates had gone home, debate recurred on the structural issue when the convention considered the eight resolutions requesting industrial

[122]AFL, *Proceedings, 1935*, p. 569.

[123]These unions, which included a number of distinctly craft organizations, were Air Line Pilots, Bakery and Confectionary Workers, Brewery Workers, Elevator Constructors, Fur Workers, ILGWU, Flat Glass Workers, Glove Workers, Hat, Cap and Millinery Workers, Jewelry Workers, Mine, Mill and Smelter Workers, UMW, Oil Workers, Paper Makers, Printing Pressmen, Pulp, Sulphite and Paper Mill Workers, Quarry Workers, Teachers, Commercial Telegraphers, and the UTW.

[124]The Meat Cutters cast 149 votes for and 49 votes against the minority report. The Typographers' vote was 611 to 123 in favor of the minority report. The 11 unions which did not vote were Wall Paper Crafts, Upholsterers, Tobacco Workers, Journeymen Tailors, Stove Mounters, Sheep Shearers, Master Mechanics and Foremen of Navy Yards, Iron, Steel and Tin Workers, Foundry Employees, Masters, Mates and Pilots, and the Building Service Employees.

[125]AFL, *Proceedings, 1935*, pp. iii–xx, 574–575.

unions for specific industries. Six of these resolutions were referred to the Executive Council with little objection from the delegates. The remaining two, however, which demanded an extension of jurisdiction for the international unions created in the rubber and automobile industries, were not concurred in by the Committee on Resolutions, and this action brought on the final round of verbal battle at the convention and the first and only round of physical combat between representatives (Lewis and Hutcheson) of the opposing factions.

M. E. Shacklette, a rubber worker, introduced the resolution asking that the jurisdiction of the URW be enlarged to include "all employees in and around the respective factories without segregation of the employees in the industry." A federal labor union delegate took the floor in support of the resolution and informed the convention that the URW had, in accordance with its charter, surrendered its skilled members to the craft unions but that these men had failed to maintain their craft union membership and wanted to join a single union of rubber workers. The URW, the delegate warned, did not propose to organize the craftsmen a second time and again turn them over to other unions.

At this point, the speaker was interrupted by Hutcheson who called for a point of order, asserting that the resolution merely reopened the industrial union proposition which had already been settled. Green was inclined to sustain the point of order, whereupon Lewis took the floor in opposition to it. The UMW president concluded his remarks with a verbal jab at Hutcheson to the effect that the raising of points of order on minor delegates was "rather small potatoes." Hutcheson, a bulky-framed man who weighed over three hundred pounds, jumped to his feet and announced that he was raised on small potatoes and that that was why he was "so small." If Lewis, Hutcheson remarked, had given more consideration to the questions before the convention and less "to attempting, in a dramatic way to impress the delegates with his sincerity, we would not have had to raise the point of order at this late date, we would have had more time to devote to the questions before the convention."[126] Allegedly, Hutcheson also called Lewis a "foul" name, and the two men then fell scuffling to the floor.[127]

[126]*Ibid.*, pp. 725–727.   [127]*New York Times*, Oct. 20, 1935.

When order was restored, several delegates wanted to know why the committee was reporting on the resolution if the question it posed had already been settled and whether the chair meant to forbid discussion. Green answered, "This is Saturday, and the convention does not want to go into a discussion of the subject again, in my opinion, and that is the reason the point of order was sustained." Green's decision was appealed to the convention but was sustained by a show of hands by the narrow margin of 108 to 104.[128]

Despite this ruling, the convention proceeded to debate for more than two hours over the UAW request that it be allowed to enroll "all employes in or around plants engaged in the manufacture of automobile parts and the assembling of such parts into completed automobiles." The resolution was lost, 125 to 104.[129]

As in many previous years, Green was again nominated for re-election to the AFL presidency by John L. Lewis. In his speech of acceptance Green made some comments pertinent to the internal conflict: "This is an historic convention. I think I can declare that no more historic convention of the American Federation of Labor was ever held. During its deliberations...we have been torn by conflicting emotions; we realize, after all, that we have come through with colors flying and our ranks indissoluble and intact... So it becomes our duty now to forget. The debate is over. The problems have been solved. A settlement has been made, and from this convention we must go out united."[130] Less than three weeks later the Committee for Industrial Organization was formed.

[128]AFL, *Proceedings, 1935,* pp. 727–729.

[129]*Ibid.,* pp. 729–750. Several UAW members also submitted a resolution which asked the AFL to call a special convention of the UAW for not later than March 1, 1936, to allow the automobile workers to elect their officers. The resolution was one of sixteen which the convention did not have time to consider and which were referred to the Executive Council. The Council ruled that the question raised by the UAW resolution had been properly decided at San Francisco and, therefore, that no further action was necessary. *Ibid.,* pp. 824–825.

[130]*Ibid.,* pp. 698–699. Woll's vice-presidency was contested by Emil Costello, a federal labor union delegate, but Woll won an overwhelming victory. A closer contest, and one which had important bearing on the internal struggle, was staged between William D. Mahon (president, Street and Electric Railway Employees) and Charles P. Howard for the eleventh vice-presidency, which was vacated on Oct. 7, 1935, by the resignation of George L. Berry. The craft unionists won another victory when Mahon was elected by a roll-call vote of 17,370 to 11,693. *Ibid.,* pp. 702–704, 708–712.

CHAPTER VIII

Toward Civil War

I

ACCORDING to Harvey Fremming, the Oil Workers' president, the Committee for Industrial Organization "was born over a steak at Harvey's Restaurant in Washington" before the Atlantic City convention had adjourned and shortly after the defeat of the minority report of the Committee on Resolutions. Those present, according to Fremming, were Lewis, Murray, and Fremming himself. "The whole idea [of forming a committee] was born there," Fremming has declared. "We suggested the idea [that] since there had been manifested a strong minority, that that minority be perpetuated and more added to that group for the purpose of being prepared for the next convention [of the AFL] to be held at Tampa. That was the reason for it."[1]

On the other hand the general executive board of the ILGWU stated in 1937 that the preliminary decision of the industrial union bloc to remain in close contact and cement its forces for action at future AFL conventions was made at an informal meeting among Lewis, Howard, Hillman, and Dubinsky during the last days of the Atlantic City convention.[2] Perhaps there is some accuracy in both accounts, and at any rate it is clear that before the convention closed on October 19, 1935 some of the leading proponents of industrial unionism had already decided to organize a central, coordinating body.

[1]International Association of Oil Field, Gas Well and Refinery Workers of America, *Proceedings, 1937,* p. 7.
[2]ILGWU, *Proceedings, 1937,* p. 195.

Three weeks after the convention, on November 9, 1935, officers from eight AFL unions met in the UMW building in Washington and set up the Committee for Industrial Organization. John L. Lewis was elected chairman, John Brophy director, and Charles P. Howard secretary of the CIO. The other original members of the organization were Hillman, Dubinsky, McMahon, Fremming, Thomas H. Brown, president of the Mine, Mill and Smelter Workers, and Max Zaritsky, president of the United Hatters, Cap and Millinery Workers.[3] With the exception of Howard and Zaritsky, the committee members had, or were shortly granted, the support of their respective unions. Until his death in the late summer of 1938 Howard served the CIO selflessly, out of his personal concern for the establishment of industrial unionism; he never asked for, nor did he obtain, the backing of his union. Zaritsky enjoyed the support of the Cap and Millinery Department of his union, but the craft-minded hatters did not waver in their allegiance to the AFL, and the union as a consequence never joined the CIO.[4]

The CIO announced that it would operate within the framework of the principles and policies enunciated by its component unions at Atlantic City, that its functions would be "educational and advisory," and that it would seek through these means to "encourage and promote" the organization of the unorganized and the establishment of collective bargaining in the mass-production industries. Other unions would be asked to join the committee and to appoint representatives to meet with it.[5] The CIO set up its offices in the UMW building, hired one or two staff members, and started its own news service. It also began to send literature to state federations of labor and city centrals proclaiming its existence and its objectives.

The official AFL reaction to the formation of the CIO was decidedly unfavorable and made obvious its anxiety for the future

[3] *New York Times*, Nov. 10, 1935.

[4] The Brewery Workers, whom one might expect to have become an early member of the CIO, did not join that body until 1946. Although the American Federation of Teachers strongly supported the CIO program, contributed financially to the Steel Workers' Organizing Committee, and seemed willing in 1938 to consider affiliating with the CIO, the union did not leave the AFL.

[5] *New York Times*, Nov. 10, 1935.

213

of organized labor. William Green addressed letters to each of the CIO leaders on November 23, and although he did not definitely label the CIO a dual organization, he declared that some officers and members of the AFL and its constituent unions "regard separate movements formed within the main organization structure as dual in character and as decidedly menacing to its success and welfare." Experience had shown, he said, that minority movements were "fraught with serious consequences." The CIO might create "a line of cleavage" in the AFL and might definitely widen the "breach" over union structure. A majority decision should be respected by all AFL members until that decision was reversed at a succeeding convention. His conscience and judgment, Green concluded, led him to advise against the formation of the CIO and to "emphasize most vigorously the danger of division and of discord which may follow."[6]

Lewis, who obtained advance knowledge of the letters' contents, immediately resigned his AFL vice-presidency[7] and announced at a press conference on November 25 that Green's advice "won't change our plans at all" and that the CIO leaders were determined to wage as bitter a fight as was necessary for the principle of industrial unionism.[8] Three days later in a nationwide radio address, Lewis outlined the "tragic failure" of the AFL craft unions to organize the mass-production industries, explained the purposes of the CIO, and insisted upon the need for industrial unionism.[9]

As secretary of the CIO, Howard on December 2 officially responded to Green's communications of November 23. He explained that he considered the organization of the unorganized "as being so essential that it overshadows almost every other consideration." He did not agree that the minority was bound in any way to confine its reform activities to the annual convention: it was both ethical and proper for the minority to disseminate its views and to try to convert the rank and file to them in the interim

[6]For example, see Green to Lewis, Nov. 23, 1935, CIO #1, AFL-CIO Archives.
[7]Lewis to Green, Nov. 23, 1935, CIO #1, *ibid.*
[8]Quoted in *New York Times,* Nov. 26, 1935.
[9]"President Lewis Delivers Radio Address on the 'Future of Organized Labor,'" *United Mine Workers' Journal,* Vol. 46, Dec. 15, 1935, pp. 20–21. See also John L. Lewis, *Future of Organized Labor.*

between the annual meetings. What is more, the rank and file itself had the right to be consulted and to help formulate basic union policies. He assured Green that the CIO had no intention of raiding the membership, infringing the "rightful" jurisdiction, or changing the structure of any existing craft union, or of doing anything that would invite or promote dualism. The Council's failure to charter industrial unions in the industries specified at San Francisco was, he declared, the only reason why the CIO had been formed.[10] The replies of other CIO leaders added little to Howard's analysis, except that Zaritsky indicated the CIO would "cooperate with all existing unions in any effort they are willing to undertake to organize the mass production industries" and that the ACW thought the CIO would "render all possible assistance" to the mass-production workers in their attempts to form strong AFL unions.[11]

Stating that it was being "bruited about" that Green personally sympathized with the industrial union policy, Lewis tried to convince Green by letter that he would be happier and of greater service to labor were he to resign the AFL presidency and assume leadership of the CIO. Green's position, Lewis contended, of privately favoring industrial unionism and at the same time officially opposing it was vulnerable to criticism, and in addition, the craft unionists might rightfully desire more than his perfunctory support. Why not "return to your father's house?" Lewis asked, "You will be welcome."[12] Green replied indignantly that he and thousands of other people regarded the CIO as a dual organization and that never in his life had he supported a dual or secession move-

[10]Howard to Green, Dec. 2, 1935, CIO #1, AFL-CIO Archives. Green later acknowledged, in a speech before the 1936 convention of the UMW, that a union had the right to advocate reforms between the annual conventions of the AFL, but he insisted that there was an unbridgeable difference between this type of activity and "the setting up of an organization within an organization for the purpose of carrying on...educational...or organization work." *UMW, Proceedings, 1936,* pp. 303–304.

[11]Zaritsky to Green, Dec. 6, 1935; Hillman to Green, Dec. 12, 1935, CIO #1, AFL-CIO Archives.

[12]Lewis to Green, Dec. 7, 1935, CIO #1, *ibid.* Roy Horn, president of the Blacksmiths, believed that Lewis offered Green the headship of the CIO because he (Lewis) already realized the CIO was going to fail and he wanted to "unload" it on Green. Horn to Green, Dec. 9, 1935, CIO #1, *ibid.*

ment. He was already in his "father's house," and he intended to execute AFL policies at any cost.[13]

Before the CIO was a month old there was some indication that the ILGWU (which, in contrast with such unions as the UMW and the ACW, had long maintained close ties with the AFL) was not enthusiastic about the CIO's existence and would support it only with reservations. David Dubinsky informed the general executive board of the ILGWU on December 7 that he did not fully agree "with the tone and approach" of certain CIO leaders. He affirmed, however, that the union's profound sympathy for the objectives of the CIO could not be altered. Thereupon the board decided by the close vote of 12 to 10 that the ILGWU would support the CIO "so long as it adheres to the purposes originally outlined by it. Our International Union...would strenuously oppose any movement which has for its purpose to act as an opposition to the American Federation of Labor or to promote any dualism."[14]

Some of the more conservative AFL leaders and unions took a disparaging and critical view of the CIO. Tobin, for example, presumed that the "industrial bug" would blow up in time as it had always done in the past. Industrial unionism was merely a "foolish phantom held out to the unthinking workers." He advised his teamsters to aid wherever possible in stamping out "the awful serpent of industrial trade unionism that would destroy this International and weaken the entire structure of the Labor Movement."[15] At Green's suggestion, Tobin contacted President Roosevelt (through Postmaster General James A. Farley), and assuring him that the labor split would eventually heal and all labor would

[13]Green to Lewis, Dec. 9, 1935, CIO #1, *ibid.*

[14]ILGWU, *Proceedings, 1937,* pp. 197–198. Not until 1956 did the ILGWU reveal the closeness of the vote. See *Report of the General Executive Board* [of the ILGWU] *to the 29th Convention, 1956,* p. 27. After unity talks between CIO and AFL representatives in the early winter of 1937 failed to bring results, the ILGWU became increasingly less active in CIO affairs and never joined the Congress of Industrial Organizations. According to Fremming, Dubinsky was from the start a "most uncertain quantity. He was never definite upon any subject. He was never certain upon any program of the Committee for Industrial Organization." Oil Workers, *Proceedings, 1938,* p. 262.

[15]*Official Magazine,* (of the Teamsters), Vol. 33, March 1936, pp. 9–13. See also *ibid.,* Vol. 33, January 1936, pp. 4–7; "Report of the Meeting of the General Executive Board in Miami, Florida, Beginning January 23, 1936," *ibid.,* Vol. 33, March 1936, pp. 7–8.

return to the AFL's "conservative, law-abiding, progressive method of organization," suggested that in the meantime the friends of the President should "refrain from expressing an opinion in this controversy." After a few days delay FDR answered that he was acting on Tobin's advice.[16]

The IAM, which was sure that the "misguided" CIO would eventually fall to pieces, nevertheless resolved against allowing the organization to "ride roughshod over the will of the majority."[17] *The Boilermakers' Journal,* while not mentioning the CIO by name, said that certain labor leaders who would "destroy CRAFT organizations" were out to make "everything mass organization."[18] Frank Duffy, editor of the *Carpenter,* commented lightly that industrial unionism "has been tried and found wanting. Why, then, should be pay any more attention to it."[19] The IBEW declared that British trade union experience had proved that organization by industry was "impossible without strong centralized authority verging on dictatorship."[20]

In a lengthy communication addressed to the local councils of the MTD, John P. Frey stated that it was the evident intention of the CIO to give "militant assistance" to the establishment of industrial unions; furthermore, the CIO was trying to develop "a nation-wide organization" and as a consequence it was the responsibility of the councils openly to condemn and actively to resist any propaganda favorable to the CIO which might arrive at their offices.[21] Green likewise exhorted all state and local bodies under direct control of the AFL and all AFL organizers to conform to the organizing policy enunciated at Atlantic City.[22]

The formation of the CIO in a labor atmosphere predominantly

[16]Tobin to Farley, Dec. 10, 1936; FDR to Tobin, Dec. 21, 1935; Tobin to Green, Jan. 3, 1936, NUF #4 (Teamsters), AFL-CIO Archives.

[17]*Machinists' Monthly Journal,* Vol. 47, December 1935, p. 728; *ibid.,* Vol. 48, January 1936, pp. 38–39; "President's Page," *ibid.,* Vol. 48, January 1936, p. 28.

[18]*Boilermakers' Journal,* Vol. 48, January 1936, p. 5.

[19]Duffy, "Industrial Unionism a Failure," *Carpenter,* Vol. 56, February 1936, p. 5.

[20]"British Evaluate Industrial Unionism," *Journal of Electrical Workers and Operators,* Vol. 35, March 1936, p. 134.

[21]Frey to the Officers and Members of the Affiliated Metal Trades Councils, Dec. 17, 1935, CIO #1, AFL-CIO Archives.

[22]Green to the Officers and Members of State Federations of Labor, City Central Labor Unions, and Directly Affiliated Local Trade and Federal Labor Unions, Dec. 4, 1935; Green to All Organizers of the AFL, Dec. 11, 1935, CIO #1, *ibid.*

hostile to industrial unionism indeed presented a delicate situation and one which was not improved by Lewis' departure from the Executive Council. Since Berry also left the Council in October 1935 to accept the position of federal Coordinator of Industrial Cooperation, the only outspoken advocate of industrial unionism who remained on the Council was David Dubinsky.[23] The Council was likely, therefore, to take prompt and decisive action with regard to the CIO.

Realizing that the Council would meet in Miami, Florida during the last two weeks of January 1936, CIO Director Brophy forewarned Green that if the Council did not quickly remove the barriers to organizing and to forming industrial unions in the mass-production industries, "serious consequences" might result.[24] Howard and Zaritsky, who wanted to defend the CIO and create a more conciliatory attitude toward it, were permitted to attend the Council meeting.[25] From the extremists on the craft union side, however, came the demand, presented to the Council by the MTD officers, that the Council suspend all unions which did not abandon the CIO within thirty days.[26]

The Council's decision on the CIO issue, while not conciliatory, was indicative of some restraint. The Council perceived a growing conviction among persons within and outside of the labor movement that the CIO constituted a challenge to the AFL and would ultimately become a dual labor federation. For this reason the Council advised, but did not order, the CIO to dissolve immediately. To help achieve this result the Council appointed a three-member committee (George M. Harrison of the Railway Clerks, Joseph N. Weber of the Musicians, and G. M. Bugniazet of the IBEW) to confer with the CIO leaders "at the earliest date possible." The committee was instructed to submit a report of the

[23]Mahon, who was elected at Atlantic City to fill the vacancy created by Berry's resignation, favored "a certain amount" of industrial unionism in the great industries. Mahon to Green, July 7, 1936, CIO #1, *ibid.* The Council appointed Felix H. Knight, president of the Railway Carmen, to fill the vacancy created by Lewis' resignation.

[24]Brophy to Green, Jan. 10, 1936, CIO # 1, *ibid.*

[25]Zaritsky to Green, Dec. 30, 1935, Green to Zaritsky, Jan. 6, 7, 1936, CIO #1, *ibid.*; ITU, *Proceedings, 1936,* p. 92.

[26]MTD, *Proceedings, 1936,* pp. 15, 42.

218

conference results to the May session of the Council. Also the Council prepared and sent instructions to all state, city, and federal labor bodies and to AFL organizers to the effect that these groups, being subordinate to the AFL's supreme authority, could not give "allegiance, assistance or support" to the CIO.[27]

Upon learning of this decision, the UMW, in convention at Constitution Hall in Washington, authorized its executive board to withhold the payment of per capita taxes to the AFL whenever "conditions and circumstances may warrant." Lewis bellowed that the Council members would "be wearing asbestos suits in hell" before the CIO dissolved. Several days later William Green appeared before the miners and in a long and emotional address he pronounced the CIO unions to be in open rebellion against the AFL. He regretted exceedingly that the miners were "near the point where they will step out of affiliation" with the AFL, and he pleaded with them to remain loyal "to your father, your parent, the great organization that chartered you and that has fathered you and protected you."

When Green had completed his remarks Lewis instantly called for a vote of confidence, asking all those delegates to stand who had been persuaded to change their attitude toward the CIO. Two delegates stood up. Lewis then labeled the Council's recent decision an ultimatum which demanded that he and his associates "like quarry slaves at night, scared to their dungeon, dissolve, disband, cease and desist." All those who favored compliance with this ultimatum were asked to stand. A single delegate stood up. Then in a final dramatic act Lewis asked that all delegates who desired that the UMW's convention policies be executed rise to their feet. The delegates rose in a body and applauded for some time. Turning to Green, Lewis triumphantly announced: "President Green, you have received the answer of the United Mine Workers of

[27]"Extract from the [AFL] Executive Council Minutes, Miami, Florida, Jan. 15–29, 1936," CIO #1, AFL-CIO Archives. Dubinsky was absent when this decision was reached. It is not clear whether he did or did not attend any part of the January 1936 session of the Council. The instructions for the subordinate groups of the AFL were mailed on February 7 and 10. See Green to the Secretaries of State Federations of Labor, City Central Unions and Directly Affiliated Local and Federal Unions, Feb. 7, 1936; Green to All Volunteer and Paid Organizers, Feb. 10, 1936, CIO #1, ibid.

America to your ultimatum. . . . you may carry back to your organization the answer. . . that has just been given by this Convention."[28]

A copy of the Council's January decision was sent to each of the CIO leaders on February 7. Lewis, whose actions have not always been predictable, gladly accepted the bid to meet with the AFL committee and wondered whether the meeting could be arranged for February 19, 20, or 21. He was advised that Harrison, chairman of the AFL committee, had sailed for Europe and would not seek a meeting until sometime after he returned in March.[29] The CIO leaders thereupon gathered in Washington on February 21 and drafted a full reply to the Council's decision. They stated that the continued functioning of the CIO was not only justifiable but was also essential. The Council had found nothing in their actions which violated the AFL constitution, and the charge of incipient dualism was not supported with evidence. In regard to the instructions the Council had sent to subordinate groups, the CIO leaders denied that they were trying to secure the "allegiance, assistance or support" of these groups, and moreover, it was their understanding that the instructions did not in any way affect the rights of "these directly affiliated bodies to go on record for industrial unionism. . . [and] to seek aid from or spread the literature of our Committee." In fact, it would be completely undemocratic and irregular for the Council to try to interfere with these rights.[30]

Apart from the merits of the last-mentioned dispute, Green reports that state and city labor organizations "fought and fought" over industrial versus craft unionism in 1936. Of the state federations, ten endorsed the CIO and thirteen adopted pro-AFL resolutions or tabled, voted against, or otherwise prevented action on pro-CIO resolutions. It was Green's guess that many of the mem-

[28]UMW, *Proceedings, 1936,* pp. 172, 176, 297–309. See also "A. F of L. Ultimatum Rejected by International Convention," *United Mine Workers' Journal,* Vol. 47, Feb. 15, 1936, p. 10.

[29]Lewis to Green, Feb. 13, 1936; Green to Lewis, Feb. 14, 1936, CIO #1, AFL-CIO Archives.

[30]CIO Members (with the exception of Brown) to Green, Feb. 21, 1936, CIO #1, *ibid.* The president of the Meat Cutters, Patrick Gorman, also was critical of the Council's decision. He said that he knew of no dual unions set up by the CIO and that it was no great crime "for a national committee to tell the workers that industrial organization is best for them." If the Council enforced its decision, a split would occur and the Council would be more responsible for such a split than would the CIO. Gorman to Green, Feb. 26, 1936, PCB #20, Book 552, NYSSILR Library.

bers of state and city bodies who were sympathetic to the CIO were under the impression that the CIO represented a new labor movement which had been created as a rival to the AFL.[31]

Before considering the Council's post-Atlantic City dealings with the UAW and the URW, it is necessary to recall that these unions, in defiance of their charters and by separate and unilateral acts, had adopted industrial jurisdictions. Since their will to have such jurisdictions was irrevocably firm, the already difficult situation was not improved at Atlantic City. There the AFL with equal resolve had voted its disapproval of their bids for industrial unionism. As a result of the latter development, however, the Council could now, upon the highest authority, insist that the UAW and URW rescind their amendatory acts and revert to their original charter jurisdictions. At its post-convention meeting in 1935, the Council did in fact decide that it would not approve the constitutions of these unions until they were amended in accordance with Council recommendations. The language of the changes which the Council proposed and sent to the unions for their action was almost precisely the language of their original charter grants.[32] Neither of the unions appears to have accepted, nor even to have acknowledged receipt of, the Council's amendments.

At Miami the Council ordered the UAW to withdraw the charters from forty-three of its automotive parts' locals (which Green had just turned over to the UAW the previous November) and to instruct their members to join craft unions (primarily the IAM). On the other hand, the Council did promise the UAW a convention no later than April 30, 1936 at which time it could elect its own officers.[33] The convention was duly held, the automobile workers elected Homer Martin their president and resolved that the UAW would permit no other organization to effectuate

---

[31]IAM, *Proceedings, 1936,* p. 242; Green to 31 National and International Unions, March 20, 1936, PCB #21, Book 553, NYSSILR Library; "State Federation of Labor Conventions' Action on Industrial Unionism, 1936," CIO #1, AFL-CIO Archives; Green to Mahon, July 22, 1936, PCB #21, Book 562, NYSSILR Library.

[32]See Green to Dillon, Nov. 12, 1935; Green to Dalrymple, Nov. 12, 1935, PCB #20, Book 545, NYSSILR Library.

[33]"Extract from the [AFL] Executive Council Minutes, Miami, Florida, Jan. 15–29, 1936," printed in *Machinists' Monthly Journal,* Vol. 48, p. 12 of an appendix; Wharton to Green, Dec. 20, 1935, printed in *ibid.,* Vol. 48, pp. 11–12 of an appendix; "Minutes of Meeting of the [IAM] Executive Council from February 17 to 26, 1936," *ibid.,* Vol. 48, pp. 9–11 of an appendix.

claims in the automobile industry.[34] In July both the UAW and the URW joined the CIO.[35] Green thought the UAW's action, at least, was "an exhibition of the basest ingratitude that man could show to a parent organization."[36]

At its January 1936 meeting the Council also denied a request by the National Radio and Allied Trades Council for a national union charter and instead awarded the federal unions of radio workers to the IBEW.[37] The IAM began immediately to negotiate with the IBEW for the transfer to the IAM of all radio workers who "properly belonged" to it.[38] Perhaps unaware of the latter maneuver, James Carey of the NRAT met with IBEW President Daniel W. Tracy and inquired as to the terms on which the radio workers were to join his union. Tracy explained that they would not have to pay initiation fees and that they could choose between "beneficial" and "non-beneficial" membership, the latter permitting lower dues payments than the former and consequently having a diminished voting strength. The NRAT promptly (February 8–10) held council in Washington and agreed not to affiliate with the IBEW.[39] Wasting little time Tracy then filed a formal protest with Green in which he charged that the CIO had "abetted and unduly influenced" the radio workers in their rejection of the IBEW affiliation proposal and that the CIO, in so doing, had unmistakably set up a dual union in the electrical industry.[40]

It was not until March 21 and 22, however, that the NRAT

[34]UAW, *Proceedings, 1936,* pp. 159–160.

[35]Green to Homer Martin, July 13, 1936, PCB #21, Book 561, NYSSILR Library; J. Raymond Walsh, *C. I. O.,* p. 156.

[36]IAM, *Proceedings, 1936,* p. 244. Green also contended, however, that the AFL had given the UAW unqualified industrial jurisdiction in the automobile assembly plants (as distinct from the automotive parts branch of the industry) and that there was nothing the UAW could do which would add to this grant of jurisdiction. Green to Martin, Aug. 3, 1936, PCB #21, Book 563, NYSSILR Library. Such a contention does not seem justifiable on the basis of a study of the proposed amendments to the UAW constitution which the Council drafted in November 1935.

[37]Green to James B. Carey, Jan. 21, 27, 1936, PCB #20, Books 549, 550, NYSSILR Library.

[38]"Minutes of Meeting of the [IAM] Executive Council from February 17 to 26, 1936," *Machinists' Monthly Journal,* Vol. 48, pp. 12–13 of an appendix.

[39]"I. B. E. W. States Position on Radio Workers," *Journal of Electrical Workers and Operators,* Vol. 35, March 1936, pp. 100, 134.

[40]Tracy to Green, Feb. 27, 1936, CIO #1, AFL-CIO Archives. Green assented to Tracy's analysis. Green to Tracy, March 9, 1936, PCB #20, Book 552, NYSSILR Library.

held a founding convention in Buffalo and formed the United Electrical and Radio Workers of America. The UERWA tried but failed to get an AFL charter[41] and Green immediately ordered all state and city bodies of the AFL to bar UERWA locals from membership.[42] In September the fledgling union recorded its intention to seek affiliation with the CIO and in November the CIO, having by that time clearly become a dual body, accepted the UERWA as its eleventh member union.[43]

Next to the challenge of the CIO itself, organizing the steel industry was certainly the gravest problem the Council faced after Atlantic City. The problem was grave not only because of the strategic importance of steel unionism to the scheme of organizing the mass-production industries but also because Lewis, for reasons of internal UMW policy, assigned the highest priority to a successful steel campaign. He and other CIO leaders as well, during this climactic moment in labor history, must surely have been watching the Council's moves with a jaundiced eye. For its part, the Council did not foresee that if it would have the steel workers organized under its own auspices, it had to move along industrial lines. Considering all the circumstances (the Amalgamated's and the unorganized steel workers' preference for industrial unionism, the outcome of the great debate, and the determination of the CIO), a contrary course could only alienate the Amalgamated and provoke an overt act of organizing on the part of the CIO. A majority of the Council members, however, still believed sincerely that the craft policy would be as successful as any other in the steel industry and that the industry was, after all, not ripe for unionism.

Declining a Council proposal that the Amalgamated step aside temporarily and let the AFL enroll the steel workers in federal labor unions,[44] Michael Tighe submitted his own plan to the Council's Miami session. The plan stipulated that all steel workers be enrolled in Amalgamated lodges, suggested lodge charter fees

[41]Carey to Green, April 13, 1936; Green to Carey, April 14, 1936, PCB #21, Book 555, NYSSILR Library.

[42]Green to State Federations of Labor, City Centrals, and Directly Affiliated Local and Federal Labor Unions, June 23, 1936, PCB #21, Book 560, *ibid.*

[43]UERWA, *Proceedings, 1936*, p. 71; Walsh, *C. I. O.*, p. 156.

[44]"Extract from Minutes of the [AFL] Executive Council Meeting, Atlantic City, October 1935," CIO #1, AFL-CIO Archives.

of twenty-five dollars, and outlined a complicated and relatively high dues system. The Council judged the plan to be neither "satisfactory nor practical" and then directed Green to formulate a substitute program which would include the following terms and conditions: an estimate of the amount of funds needed; a one year campaign, subject to extension for an additional year if necessary; supervision by Green; initiation fees which would not exceed three dollars; and recognition of the jurisdictions of all interested organizations.[45]

Eager to block such a campaign, the CIO on February 22 promised the AFL that it would contribute trained organizers and $500,000 toward a $1,500,000 organizing fund, if a "responsible, energetic person" were placed in charge of the drive and if the steel workers would be placed in a single union.[46] Council opinion, canvassed by Green, was uniformly unfavorable to the offer. Among the comments made were these: the CIO could not raise $500,000; the AFL could not raise $1,000,000; Green, and not a CIO man, would have to head a steel drive; the AFL opposed industrial unionism; it was impossible to organize the steel industry.[47] Green was advised not to answer the CIO message, lest an answer be construed as recognition of the CIO.

In a countermove on March 2, the AFL invited its affiliated unions (which still included the CIO group) to cooperate in raising a $750,000 fund and to assign organizers for a steel campaign.[48] Of about 46 unions which responded, 29 indicated that the matter would be referred to their conventions or executive boards, 12 were unwilling or unable to support a steel drive, and 5 pledged a total of $8,625 and 4 or 5 organizers. The IAM, a key union in this kind

[45]"Extract from Minutes of the [AFL] Executive Council Meeting, Miami, Florida, Jan. 15–29, 1936," CIO #1, *ibid.*; Tighe to Green, Jan. 8, 1936, CIO #1, *ibid.*; Mahon to Green, Nov. 25, 1935, PCB #20, Book 548, NYSSILR Library.

[46]Lewis and Howard to Green, Feb. 22, 1936, CIO #1, AFL-CIO Archives.

[47]See Harry Bates (president of the Bricklayers) to Green, Feb. 25, 1936; Tobin to Green, Feb. 26, 1936; Joseph N. Weber (president of the Musicians) to Green, Feb. 27, 1936; Wharton to Green, Feb. 28, 1936; Bugniazet to Green, Feb. 28, 1936; Edward Gainor (president of the Letter Carriers) to Green, Feb. 29, 1936; Mahon to Green, Feb. 29, 1936; Woll to Green, Feb. 29, 1936; Felix Knight to Green, March 6, 1936, CIO #1, *ibid.*

[48]Green to the Presidents of National and International Unions, March 2, 1936, CIO #1, *ibid.*

of campaign, refused to pledge anything, because it did not wish to encourage a move which lacked the support of all affiliated unions —presumably the IAM had reference to the CIO unions which ignored the March 2 letter.[49]

In the meantime, the rank-and-file leaders of the Amalgamated, still at odds with the Tighe machine, had established regular contacts with Lewis, and early in April they met with the CIO and pleaded with it to lead a steel organizing drive. They estimated that they would be strong enough to control the decisions of the forthcoming convention of the Amalgamated, and they therefore suggested that the CIO present to that convention an offer to organize the steel industry. The rank-and-file spokesmen were assured by the CIO that this would be done.[50]

Accordingly Lewis and Howard wrote to Michael Tighe and proposed the establishment of a joint organizing committee on which the CIO, the Amalgamated, "and other unions willing to contribute to a joint campaign" would be represented. The joint committee would then select responsible organizers and all steel workers could join the same union. Tighe was asked to submit this proposal to the convention of the Amalgamated which was scheduled to begin its sessions at Canonsburg, Pennsylvania, in May.[51] This was the first organizing offer by the CIO which it was prepared to carry through itself, without the cooperation or approval of the Executive Council. It was a token of the CIO's willingness at this point to depart from its "educational and advisory" functions and, if given the opportunity, actually to engage in organizing work.

Contrary to its hopes and expectations, the insurgent group did not hold the reins at Canonsburg, and the Amalgamated officers, who controlled the convention, sent a special committee to Washington on May 5 to confer with the AFL Executive Council in

[49]"Replies to Letter of March 2, 1936," CIO #1, *ibid.;* E. J. Manion (Telegraphers) to Green, April 23, 1936, CIO #1, *ibid.;* Clarence E. Swick (Painters) to Green, April 29, 1936, CIO #1, *ibid.*
[50]Robert R. R. Brooks, *As Steel Goes,* pp. 71–72.
[51]Lewis and Howard to Tighe, April 15, 1936, CIO #1, AFL-CIO Archives. The CIO paid the expenses of some of the delegates who attended the Canonsburg convention. Brooks, *As Steel Goes,* p. 72.

225

regard to a steel campaign.[52] The committee elicited from the Council a new proposal which differed from the Council's January plan only to the extent that the Council, not Green, was to supervise organizing.[53] Learning of the proposal the same day Green sent it to Canonsburg, Lewis thereupon wired the Amalgamated and declared sardonically that Green had merely restated the ancient and futile position of the AFL with regard to organizing in the steel industry and that his letter was filled with "venom and malice" toward the CIO. Green's plan, Lewis charged, would bring a horde of craft organizers into the steel districts. He reaffirmed the CIO proposal and added that the CIO was willing to contribute $500,-000 to an organizing fund.[54] Dubinksy, on the other hand, favored the Council's plan on the ground that the AFL was the only agency with authority to conduct an organizing campaign.[55]

Faced with two clearly competitive bids, the Amalgamated accepted neither. Perhaps feeling that a vote for the CIO offer would be a vote for their own early retirement, and holding in scorn the craft nature of the Council's plan, the Amalgamated's officers prevailed upon the convention to draft and adopt a third plan. This stipulated that all recruits were to be placed in the Amalgamated, although all AFL unions would be asked to help direct and finance the campaign.[56] According to Tighe, this action meant that the Amalgamated had decided "that as a Sovereign organization in itself, it intended to conduct its own business and affairs without interference or dictation from any source."[57] Circumstances would not have it so.

[52]Tighe to Green, May 1, 1936, Green to Tighe, May 2, 1936, CIO #1, AFL-CIO Archives.

[53]"Extract from Minutes of the [AFL] Executive Council Meeting, Washington, D. C., May 5–20, 1936," CIO #1, ibid.; Green to the Officers and Delegates in Attendance at the Convention of the Amalgamated Association of Iron, Steel and Tin Workers, May 8, 1936, CIO #1, ibid.

[54]Lewis to the Amalgamated Association of Iron, Steel and Tin Workers, May 8, 1936, Amalgamated Proceedings, 1936, pp. 2752–2753.

[55]"Extract from Minutes of the [AFL] Executive Council Meeting, Washington, D. C., May 5–20, 1936," CIO #1, AFL-CIO Archives; ILGWU, Proceedings, 1937, p. 200.

[56]Amalgamated, Proceedings, 1936, pp. 2778–2779; Tighe to Green, May 15, 1936, CIO #1, AFL-CIO Archives.

[57]Tighe to Green, May 15, 1936, CIO #1, AFL-CIO Archives.

The Amalgamated sent requests to national unions for financial assistance but the response was "slow and not satisfactory,"[58] and in addition rank-and-file pressure mounted within the union for action favorable to the CIO.[59] Finally Tighe and his fellow officers realized that the Amalgamated could hold out no longer and so they wired Lewis that they were ready to negotiate with him on June 3 in Washington. Lewis brusquely advised Tighe that the steel industry was going to be organized with or without his organization's help and that Tighe and his men would have to decide whether to cooperate or obstruct. "If you do not yet know your own mind," said Lewis, "please stay at home." Tighe's "fluttering procrastination" had already caused serious delay and "must be abandoned."[60] The meeting was held as scheduled and an agreement was drafted which finally made possible the organization of the steel industry. In accordance with its terms the Amalgamated joined the CIO and the Steel Workers' Organizing Committee was created, with full authority to direct an organizing campaign.[61] When Green hinted to the nation's press that an industrial union policy would probably fail in the steel industry and remarked with an air of condescension that he and others would therefore follow the CIO drive with interest,[62] Lewis pretended to be incredulous. He could not believe, he protested to Green, "that you intend doing what your statement implies, i.e., to sit with the women, under an awning on the hilltop, while the steel workers in the valley struggle in the dust and agony of industrial warfare."[63] Actually Green also began at this time to repeat the craft union argument that the unorganized were to a large extent unorganizable.[64]

[58]"Statement by International Executive Board, Amalgamated Association of Iron, Steel and Tin Workers, June 4, 1936," CIO #1, *ibid.*

[59]Brooks, *As Steel Goes,* pp. 72–74.

[60]Lewis to Tighe, June 1, 1936, AFL, *Proceedings, 1936,* p. 91.

[61]The Amalgamated was to have two representatives on the SWOC, the CIO was to contribute up to $500,000 toward the campaign, and the SWOC was to dispense with initiation fees, if advisable, and to fix dues at one dollar a month. The full text of the agreement is printed in *ibid.,* pp. 92–93.

[62]AFL, Information and Publicity Service, June 5, 1936, CIO #1, AFL-CIO Archives.

[63]Lewis to Green, June 6, 1936, CIO #1, *ibid.*

[64]Green to R. E. Zela (unidentified), July 23, 1936, PCB #21, Book 562, NYSSILR Library; Green to J. F. Houchins (editor of *The News Review* of Beckley, W. Va.), Aug. 15, 1936, PCB #22, Book 564, *ibid.*

II

The CIO's overtures to the Amalgamated offered the first substantial evidence that the CIO, goaded by the Council's craft plan for organizing the steel industry, intended to operate as a dual organizing center within the AFL for the establishment of industrial unionism. Thoroughly alarmed, the Executive Council at its May 5–20 meeting prepared hastily for a showdown; it had already determined to suspend or expel the CIO unions and wanted to do so with at least the appearance of legality.[65] According to the AFL's constitution, the Council, acting on its own initiative, could suspend an affiliated union for failure to pay per capita taxes but could revoke the charter of a national or international union only when ordered to do so by a two-thirds majority of a regular convention. Section 8 of Article IX of the constitution, however, authorized the Council *"to make the rules* to govern matters not in conflict with this Constitution,"[66] and the Council, upon the advice of its attorney, Charlton Ogburn, seized upon this general grant of administrative authority to formulate a "rule" giving to itself much broader and more specific punitive powers over AFL unions. Adopted by the Council on May 18, the rule declared that any affiliated national or international union could, between AFL conventions, file charges with the Executive Council against any other affiliated national or international union which allegedly had violated the constitution or the laws of the AFL or any legal order of the Council. The Council was empowered to hold a formal hearing to consider the evidence presented by the accusing and the accused parties. (Ogburn had pointed out that to make a suspension process legal, charges had to be filed and accused unions allowed a hearing.) If the Council found the accused union "guilty," it could take the alternative steps of forgiving the violation of AFL laws, suspending the union, penalizing the union "in any other way," or revoking its charter if such action was ordered or "approved" by a two-thirds convention majority.[67]

[65]See Charlton Ogburn (AFL attorney) to Green, May 1, 1936, CIO #1, AFL-CIO Archives.

[66]"Constitution of the American Federation of Labor," Art. IX, Secs. 8, 12, Art. X, Sec. 3, AFL, *Proceedings, 1936,* pp. xxvi-xxvii, italics added.

[67]*Ibid.,* pp. 121–122.

In listing these penalties, the Council did not precisely follow Ogburn's advice. The attorney accepted at face value the AFL constitution on the point that expulsion had to be ordered by a regular convention, and he believed that a new rule could do no more than enlarge the Council's power to suspend. It was the Council itself which added the word "approved" to the more severe penalty, thus leading one to suspect that some of its members wanted to expel the CIO unions without first taking the intermediate step of suspending them.

At any rate, even if expulsion was only the ultimate goal of the Council, and it certainly was at least that, then the Council had first to amend the AFL's constitution and take action itself rather than refer the matter anew to an AFL convention. For otherwise, assuming that the same percentage of votes would be cast against expulsion as was cast in favor of the minority report at Atlantic City (about 38 percent), an AFL convention could not muster a two-thirds vote for expulsion. On the other hand if the Council could expel the CIO unions prior to the convention, its action would be certain to win convention approval because the ousted unions would not and could not be in attendance to block the move. Even if the unions could be only suspended by the Council, they would, in accordance with the AFL constitution, lose their voting privileges at the convention, and expulsion thus could still be accomplished with ease. The rule of May 18 was, therefore, the Council's answer to a constitutional and political dilemma which could hardly have been approached in any other way, assuming, as the Council majority did, that the CIO unions could no longer be tolerated as full-fledged members of the AFL. Although the rule clearly was questionable from the legal point of view, it was a realistic, though not necessarily honorable, solution to the problem as the Council saw it; without the rule, the Council would have been in the position, perilous and also embarrassing, of being unable to cope with dualism in its own ranks.

Now that the Council believed that events had propelled the crisis far beyond the stage of peaceful negotiation, it hurriedly pushed the Harrison committee, inactive until this time, through its final paces. The objectives in so doing were to give the committee as blameless a burial as possible and to clear the decks so the Council could get on with the disciplinary process.[68] On only one day's notice the CIO leaders were asked to meet with the committee on May 19 in Washington. The meeting, poorly attended, was short and fruitless.[69] On the following day the Harrison committee sent circulars to the unions identified with the CIO, and charging for the first time that the CIO was definitely "a rival and dual organization," demanded that they immediately terminate their relationship with it. The unions were asked to reply within two weeks and were told that the nature of any future action taken by the Council depended upon the character of their replies.[70]

None of the unions complied with the demand that they leave the CIO, variously indicating that the procedure or the charges of the Council were undemocratic, unconstitutional, or unjustifiable. Howard contended, interestingly, that the CIO was not a dual body and would not become one unless it formed a local, national, or other kind of union "outside and beyond the control and jurisdiction of the A. F. of L." He believed apparently that the CIO had a right actually to organize industrial unions as well as to "educate" for them so long as this service was performed for such existing AFL nationals, presumably, as the Amalgamated, the UAW, and the URW. More importantly, Howard also expressed the hope that the Council would "not attempt to exercise authority not delegated to it by the Constitution." He directed Harrison's attention to the fact, as he put it, that the AFL constitution did not permit the Council to "penalize" an affiliated national or inter-

[68]The accuracy of this statement is very clearly revealed in the following excerpt from the Council minutes: "President Green outlined the procedure again as follows: This committee will complete its work at the earliest possible date and file its report with me. I will furnish the Council with copies of it together with complaints that may have been made against the Committee for Industrial Organization by other organizations affiliated with the American Federation of Labor. Then I will ask 'do you authorize me to summon these organizations to appear before the Council to answer the complaints on July 8th?' If authorized I will notify each International union that is affiliated with the Committee for Industrial Organization." "Extract from Minutes of the [AFL] Executive Council Meeting, Washington, D. C., May 5–20, 1936," CIO #1, AFL-CIO Archives.

[69]Harrison Committee to Lewis, May 16, 1936, CIO #1, *ibid*. On the CIO side, representatives of only three unions attended. These unions were the UMW, UTW, and Flat Glass Workers. "Extract from Minutes of the [AFL] Executive Council Meeting, Washington, D. C., May 5–20, 1936," CIO #1, *ibid*.

[70]For example, see Harrison Committee to Howard, May 20, 1936, CIO #1, *ibid*.

national union unless such action was authorized first by an AFL convention.[71]

The Harrison committee letter, along with press reports which were predicting that the Council would suspend the CIO unions, encouraged an anxiously sober exchange of letters (by special messenger) between Lewis and Green—perhaps their last more or less friendly correspondence of this period. Lewis, sensing with deep resentment that Green would hold to his position even in the face of a showdown between industrial and craft unionism, tried to shame and frighten Green into deserting the AFL. It was inconceivable, Lewis moralized, that Green would be a party to the "Brutus blow" planned by the Council. He told Green, moreover, that if he continued to support the Council rather than the UMW and the CIO, he would destroy himself, for his shipmates were even then scheming "to slit your political throat and scuttle your official ship. They are caviling among themselves over the naming of your successor when the perfidious act of separation is accomplished. Why not forego such company," Lewis asked for the second time, "and return home to the union that suckled you. . . ? An honored seat at the Council table awaits you, if you elect to return."[72] Without a moment's hesitation, Green replied that the AFL had created the UMW and by extending it financial aid in 1927 had "made it strong when it was weak," the implication being that Lewis, out of gratitude, ought to accept the AFL's policies and respect its authority. Then, with words that betray no little anguish, Green asserted his legal obligation to remain at the AFL's helm and enforce its laws:

I am President of the American Federation of Labor. I took a solemn obligation to uphold its laws, to be governed by its decisions and to be loyal to its principles and policies. . . . Nothing can be offered as a justification for the sacrifice of honor and a solemn obligation. The mandate of the American Federation of Labor Convention [Atlantic City] became law to me. There will be no resort to subterfuge or expediency in order to evade the discharge of this solemn obligation. The members of the International Union, United Mine Workers of America, would

[71]Howard to Harrison, June 1, 1936, CIO #1, *ibid.* The replies of the other CIO leaders are also here.

[72]Lewis to Green, June 6, 1936, CIO #1, *ibid.*

231

hold me in utter contempt, and rightly so, if I pursued any other course.[73]

In a final rejoinder addressed to "Dear Bill," Lewis, in one of the most quotable and perhaps also one of the most fateful messages he ever sent to anyone, rendered an ethical indictment of Green's position and intimated that they had finally come to a parting of the ways. First denying Green's statement that the AFL had fathered the UMW and proclaiming the AFL's financial aid in 1927 a bagatelle, Lewis then continued:

All this is beside the question. I am not concerned with history. Rather I am concerned with the problems of today and tomorrow. You do not deny that the American Federation of Labor has frittered away two years of valuable time without effectuating the organization of a single worker in the steel industry. You do not deny that your Executive Council is even now scheming to eject your union from the house of labor. You do not deny that the crime for which such ejection will be punishment is the crime of lending aid to the unorganized workers and seeking an expansion of the numerical strength of the American Federation of Labor. Your lament is that I will not join you in a policy of anxious inertia. Candidly, I am temperamentally incapable of sitting with you in sackcloth and ashes, endlessly intoning "O tempora! O mores!"

It is of course needless to discuss further the points of honor involved. You will make your own decisions. For myself, I prefer to err on the side of America's underprivileged and exploited millions, if erring it be.[74]

On June 20, having been advised by the Harrison committee that the CIO had no intention of dissolving, Green, under Council instructions, summoned the CIO leaders to appear singly at varying times between July 9 and 13 before an emergency meeting of the Council in Washington. The purpose of these private meetings was to allow the Council "to learn from you the reasons for your refusal to comply with the request of the committee...and to then consider and determine what further action it should take in the premises."[75] Zaritsky and Howard explained that their unions were

[73]Green to Lewis, June 6, 1936, CIO #1, *ibid.*
[74]Lewis to Green, June 7, 1936, CIO #1, *ibid.*
[75]All the letters were sent out on June 20. For example, see Green to Lewis, June 20, 1936, CIO #1, *ibid.*

not members of the CIO and that there was, therefore, no practicable reason why they, as individuals, should attend. The other CIO leaders also rejected their summonses, the grounds being (in the significant replies) that the Council had not filed charges against them or submitted evidence in support of these charges or indicated what provisions, if any, of the AFL constitution they had violated.[76] Dubinsky also indicated that he would be in Europe throughout the month of July.

It is quite clear that the Executive Council originally planned to suspend the CIO unions (probably including the ITU and the Hatters, Cap and Millinery Workers) at about the end of the July 8–15 emergency session. On behalf of the MTD, Frey on July 9 filed with the Council formal charges against the CIO and the twelve unions which he contended were affiliated with it: the UMW, ACW, ILGWU, UTW, Mine, Mill and Smelter Workers, Oil Workers, Amalgamated Association of Iron, Steel and Tin Workers, UAW, URW, Federation of Flat Glass Workers,[77] ITU, and the Hatters, Cap and Millinery Workers. He declared that the CIO was a dual organization and that its member unions were fostering the dual movement and "fomenting insurrection" within the AFL. Each of these unions, he alleged, had violated that part of the AFL's constitution which required conformity to the AFL's laws, rules, and regulations. Finally, Frey charged that the CIO had taken actions contrary to the majority decision of the Atlantic City convention and that this constituted rebellion against the organizing policies of the AFL. Frey asked the Council in view of these charges to suspend the disobedient unions and advised it that suspension could legally be executed under Article IX, Section 8 which gave the Council "unlimited power."[78]

[76]Zaritsky to Green, June 23, July 28, 1936; Howard to Green, July 1, 1936; Brophy to Green, June 23, 1936; Hillman to Green, July 6, 1936; Dubinsky to Green, June 30, 1936. All letters in CIO #1, *ibid.*

[77]The Federation of Flat Glass Workers had joined the CIO in April, after it had declared in favor of an expansion of its jurisdiction. The union later asked the Executive Council to approve its expansion plans, but the Council declined to do so. If it had acted otherwise, the Flat Glass Workers would have had a jurisdiction at least partly in conflict with the jurisdictions of the Window Glass Cutters League and the Glass Bottle Blowers. *New York Times*, Feb. 21, 1936; Walsh, *C. I. O.*, p. 156; Green to Glen McCabe (president of the Flat Glass Workers), May 21, June 10, July 6, 1936, PCB #21, Books 558, 560, 561, NYSSILR Library.

[78]"Statement of Charges Against C. I. O., July 9, 1936," Container 5, Frey Papers. See also Frey to the Executive Council, July 9, 1936, CIO #1, AFL-CIO Archives.

That the Council waited until August to proceed according to the line suggested by Frey was due to the counsel of Charlton Ogburn. After receiving a copy of Green's June 20 letter to the CIO leaders, Ogburn sent Green in quick succession three warnings that the letter did not satisfy the legal requirements of suspension procedure. For *in advance of the hearings* the Council had to provide the accused unions with a detailed statement of the charges against them and with the May 18 rule which would inform them of the alternative penalties they might suffer if found guilty. Ogburn further counseled that hearings ought to be held and that evidence in support of the charges ought to be taken even though the CIO leaders were not in attendance. In his third warning Ogburn noted a rumor that the Council was going to suspend the unions on July 14 and he accordingly reemphasized his conviction that if the Council did so and if the CIO unions tested the legality of the action, the unions would gain a court victory which "naturally would be a severe blow to the prestige of the Executive Council."[79]

Ogburn's persistence led the Council to decide to initiate the proceedings anew, and on July 16 Green again "requested and invited" the twelve CIO leaders to attend (this time as a group rather than singly) a hearing "on the third day of August, 1936, beginning at 2:30 P. M. in the Executive Council Chamber at the headquarters of the American Federation of Labor." Included in the "invitation" was the list of charges the MTD had brought against the CIO and also the May 18 rule.[80]

In answer, Howard and Zaritsky reiterated the position they had taken toward the earlier summons and added their names to the official CIO response which Lewis forwarded to Green. Lewis' reaction was that the Council contemplated suspending the CIO unions only because it knew that otherwise it could not muster the two-thirds majority required for expulsion at an AFL convention. Yet, he elaborated, suspension by the Council in August would be tantamount to expulsion because it would deprive the affected unions of the right to vote at the Tampa convention and would thus render their expulsion a foregone conclusion. Such a

[79]Ogburn to Green, July 8, 9, 13, 1936, CIO #1, AFL-CIO Archives. Ogburn did not receive a copy of the June 20 letter until July 7.

[80]For example, see Green to Lewis, July 16, 1936, CIO #1, *ibid.*

subterfuge was without warrant in the AFL's constitution, the Council had no right to dismember the AFL, and therefore the "Committee for Industrial Organization declines to submit to its jurisdiction."[81]

In the absence of CIO defenders, the scheduled hearing was held and the Council listened to Frey and Green detail the evidence against the CIO. Their testimony consisted of the relevant portions of the San Francisco and Atlantic City convention proceedings, Stark's report of his 1935 interview with Lewis, all correspondence which had passed between AFL and CIO leaders, the CIO's negotiations with the Amalgamated Association of Iron, Steel and Tin Workers, and other less significant materials.[82] Finally on August 5 the Council judged that the evidence supported conclusively the MTD's charges, the essence of which was that the CIO represented a dual labor movement within the AFL. With the exception of the ITU and the Hatters, Cap and Millinery Workers, the Council ordered the unions identified with the CIO to sever their connections with that body on or before September 5, 1936 or be suspended from the AFL. Against the wishes of Wharton who wanted to include the ITU in the suspended list, the Council directed Green to ask the ITU whether it was a CIO member and if not, whether it intended to require its president to dissociate himself from the CIO. Green was also to inquire of the Hatters, Cap and Millinery Workers whether its laws permitted the Cap and Millinery Department to belong to the CIO, whether that department intended to remain in the CIO, and, if the latter were the case, whether the Hatters' Department intended to dissociate itself from the Cap and Millinery Department.[83]

Howard obliged Green with the information that the ITU would

[81]Howard to Green, July 25, 1936; Zaritsky to Green, July 22, 1936, Lewis to Green, July 21, 1936, CIO #1, *ibid.*

[82]The hearing record is a voluminous one. See "Proceedings of the Executive Council of the American Federation of Labor in the Matter of Charges Filed by the Metal Trades Department against the Committee for Industrial Organization and the National and International Unions Holding Membership Therein, Washington, D. C., August 3, 1936," CIO #1, *ibid.*

[83]"Extract from Minutes of the [AFL] Executive Council Meeting, Washington, D. C., August 3–5, 1936," CIO #1, *ibid.*; Green to Michael Greene (head of the Hatters' Department), Aug. 7, 1936, PCB #21, Book 563, NYSSILR Library; Green to Howard, Aug. 7, 1936, PCB #21, Book 563, NYSSILR Library. Green's letters to the ten unions slated for suspension are also in PCB #21, Book 563, NYSSILR Library.

face the CIO issue for the first time at its September convention and that the ITU's executive council had no authority to require him to leave the CIO. Zaritsky and Michael Greene, head of the Hatters' Department, told the AFL president that the two departments of the Hatters, Cap and Millinery Workers were entirely autonomous, that the Cap and Millinery Department was acting entirely within its rights in supporting the CIO, and that the union as a whole would make its position clear at its October convention.[84] Accepting these explanations as satisfactory, the Council did not suspend the ITU and the Hatters, Cap and Millinery Workers. The ten unions that had endorsed the CIO, however, having disregarded the Council's order, were automatically suspended on September 5.

Sentiment in favor of suspension was not unanimous either within the Executive Council or among the non-CIO unions not represented on the Executive Council. Although Dubinsky was the lone dissenter in the Council's August 5 vote for suspension, Harrison, who was not present at the meeting, also opposed the move. He favored "developing some mutually satisfactory basis of disposing of the...controversy," and besides he doubted "the authority of the Executive Council to suspend an affiliated union without a direct mandate from the convention."[85] William D. Mahon likewise indicated in July that he was against suspension and believed the matter should be handled by the Tampa convention. While agreeing with the Council that the CIO had violated AFL laws, Mahon also contended that the Council was not blameless and that it had not fully executed the instructions of the San Francisco convention. He thought there were splendid men and others who "are as hypocritical as hell," on both sides of the structural question.[86] Dubinsky pleaded with the Council to let the Tampa convention settle the matter and he promised that if this were done he would endeavor to have the CIO leaders accept a simple majority decision of that body.[87] This would seem to sug-

---

[84]Howard to Green, Aug. 18, 1936; Greene and Zaritsky to Green, Aug. 20, 1936, PCB #22, Book 564, NYSSILR Library.

[85]Harrison to Green, July 31, 1936, CIO #1, AFL-CIO Archives.

[86]Mahon to Green, July 7, 1936, CIO #1, *ibid.*

[87]ILGWU, *Proceedings, 1937*, p. 208. According to the UMW, the vote was 13 to 1 for suspension with Dubinsky casting the negative vote, Green not voting, and Harrison and Joseph N. Weber being absent. "Executive Council Vote Will Not

gest that Dubinsky was willing to agree to the CIO's dissolution, if such was ordered in a more democratic way than the Council was planning—for in August there was no reason to believe that a simple majority convention vote could have been other than favorable to dissolution.

From outside the Council came additional expressions of disagreement with the course charted by the MTD and the Council apropos the CIO unions. The Molders, Hotel and Restaurant Employees, Sleeping Car Porters, Barbers, Maintenance-of-Way Employees, Teachers, Brewery Workers, ITU, and the Hatters, Cap and Millinery Workers all expressed concern over the Council's procedure, and most of them also preferred that the CIO matter be handled by the AFL convention.[88] The ITU resolved that the Council had usurped the authority which properly belonged to the annual convention and asserted its right, either alone or in concert with other unions, to engage in educational and organizing activities among the unorganized. Although the union did decline to pledge "faith in and allegiance to" the AFL, it took no steps toward joining the CIO.[89]

The Council's action brought an outburst of stormy protests from the CIO camp. The normally even-tempered Dubinsky charged angrily that the rule devised by the Council in May was

Affect C. I. O. Activities," *United Mine Workers' Journal*, Vol. 47, Aug. 15, 1936, p. 4. However, this tabulation leaves 1 of the 18 Council members unaccounted for. It is possible that this member was Mahon. On the other hand, it may have been Morrison, who along with Green customarily did not vote on Council matters except to break a tie. If it was Morrison, then perhaps Mahon did vote with the majority in order to avoid associating himself with the CIO cause.

[88]Lawrence O'Keefe (president of the Molders) to Frey, July 10, 14, 1936, Container 5, Frey Papers; Untitled statements dated July 27, Sept. 2, 1936, CIO #1, AFL-CIO Archives; W. C. Birthright (general secretary-treasurer of the Barbers) to Green, Sept. 18, 1936, CIO #1, AFL-CIO Archives; F. H. Fijozdal (president of the Maintenance-of-Way Employees) to Green Sept. 15, 1936, CIO #1, AFL-CIO Archives; AFT, *Proceedings, 1936*, pp. 77–78; Brewery Workers, *Proceedings, 1936*, pp. 56, 102. O'Keefe went so far as to charge that Frey had no authority to place charges against the CIO because the MTD had not passed upon the CIO at its 1935 convention and could not have because the CIO was not in existence at that time. He warned Frey that suspension of the CIO unions might increase rather than diminish sentiment for industrial unionism.

[89]In Howard's opinion, the precedent established by the Council in suspending the CIO unions far surpassed the structural controversy in importance because, he said, no union could now remain safely affiliated with the AFL. ITU, *Proceedings, 1936*, pp. 93, 97–109; Howard to Morrison, Aug. 26, 1936, NUF #9 (ITU), AFL-CIO Archives.

a "deplorable subterfuge" which would convince no fair-minded person that the subsequent tragic proceedings were justified. The August 5 decision was, Dubinsky added, "a blow to unity" and an illegal, punitive act which was deliberately calculated to disfranchise the CIO unions at the 1936 convention and which would bring "grave consequences of division and ruin" to all AFL unions. On September 1 Dubinsky notified Green that he was resigning as an AFL vice-president effective immediately.[90] The Council's procedure definitely strengthened rather than strained the ILGWU's loyalty to the CIO.

Lewis raged at the "incredible and crass stupidity" of the Council members who could not trust the judgment of an AFL convention and were led by "personal selfishness and frantic fear" to strip the defendant unions of their voting privileges.[91] Thomas McMahon asserted that if there were any stronger language than Lewis had used to describe the "unbelievably narrow and bigoted" action of the Council, he (McMahon) would have used it.[92] The UTW, meeting in convention in September, called upon all AFL unions to repudiate the "high-handed" action of the Council and to restore at Tampa the unity of the labor movement.[93] The Mine, Mill and Smelter Workers condemned the Council for illegally "splitting the Labor movement" and reaffirmed its trust in the CIO.[94]

III

The Executive Council considered the willingness of the CIO unions to stand suspended as evidence that they were determined to "leave" the American Federation of Labor and maintain their dual organization. Nevertheless, the Council advised the AFL's state and city bodies to take no action for the present time against those member locals whose parent nationals belonged to the

[90]"Suspension Order of CIO Unions Effective September 5," *Justice*, Vol. 18, Aug. 15, 1936, p. 3; Dubinsky to Green, Aug. 28, Sept. 1, 1936, PCB #22, Book 565, NYSSILR Library.

[91]Quoted in "Executive Council Vote Will Not Affect C. I. O. Activities," *United Mine Workers' Journal*, Vol. 47, Aug. 15, 1936, p. 4.

[92]*Textile Worker*, Vol. 2, Aug. 15, 1936, p. 4.

[93]UTW, *Proceedings, 1936*, p. 66.

[94]Mine, Mill and Smelter Workers, *Proceedings, 1936*, pp. 109, 132, 193–194.

CIO.[95] Between June and October the ten CIO unions stopped paying per capita taxes to the AFL,[96] and in early November the MTD instructed its Tampa convention delegate to introduce a resolution calling for the revocation of the charters and thus the expulsion of all the CIO unions which were also affiliated with the AFL.[97] The IAM officers were probably partly responsible for the MTD move, yet the IAM convention, meeting for the first time in eight years, instructed the IAM's Tampa delegates to oppose the suspension or expulsion of the CIO unions.[98] This was probably a reflection in part of the IAM's growing membership in the mass-production industries.

For a few days immediately prior to the Tampa convention, the CIO considered and finally rejected a Hatters, Cap and Millinery Workers' peace proposal which the Executive Council seemed willing to discuss. The United Hatters, Cap and Millinery Workers, meeting in convention in early October, resolved that the Executive Council should refer the matter of suspension to the AFL's November convention in which all CIO unions should have their appropriate representation. In the interval prior to the convention meeting, the AFL and the CIO, it was suggested, should set up special committees to explore the possibility of restoring unity and to plan for the organization of mass-production workers.[99]

Zaritsky dispatched the proposal to Green on October 9 and Green replied that the Council sincerely desired to heal the breach "for which it is in no way responsible" and that an AFL committee was prepared to meet a CIO committee for this purpose.[100] Green appointed Woll, Harrison, and Felix H. Knight of the Railway Carmen as the AFL conference committee, and on the fifteenth the committee informed Zaritsky that it was ready to confer with CIO representatives. The committee, Zaritsky was told, was authorized to discuss all differences "including the restoration of the former

[95]Green to All Affiliated Organizations, Sept. 5, 1936, PCB #22, Book 565, NYSSILR Library.

[96]Green to Henry Ohl, Jr. (president of the Wisconsin Federation of Labor), May 24, 1937, PCB #23, Book 582, *ibid.*

[97]MTD, *Proceedings, 1936,* p. 95. In November, the UERMA, an independent union over which the AFL had no authority, joined the CIO.

[98]IAM, *Proceedings, 1936,* p. 393.

[99]United Hatters, Cap, and Millinery Workers, *Proceedings,* 1936, p. 88.

[100]Green to Zaritsky, Oct. 13, 1936, PCB #22, Book 567, NYSSILR Library.

status of the organizations associated with the Committee for Industrial Organization."[101]

Zaritsky relayed the committee's letter to John L. Lewis and remarked that the committee had "opened wide" the door to negotiation.[102] After the CIO studied the matter in early November, Howard wired Green that negotiation through committees had proved ineffectual and that the CIO had, therefore, authorized its chairman to confer with the AFL president.[103] Green answered that the Council had approved the committee method of negotiation, that he had no authority to change this policy, but that he would gladly meet with Lewis.[104] Lewis retorted that under the circumstances a talk with Green would be futile and that the appropriate time to discuss unity would come after the Council rectified its "outrageous act of suspension" and endorsed unrestricted industrial unionism in the unorganized industries.[105] Thus ended the first attempt to reestablish a unified labor movement.

Excluding Dubinsky, who favored meeting with the AFL,[106] the leaders of the CIO were quite clearly responsible for squelching the proposed peace talks. This is not to say that if they had acted otherwise unity would have resulted, for although the AFL was willing to talk, there is no way of knowing whether its agenda would have included anything other than the abolition of the CIO. Assuming, however, that the AFL was prepared to make substantial concessions to industrial unionism, and positing unity as a desirable goal, then the CIO's conduct is open to greater censure. Lewis, of course, was eager to get on with the SWOC's steel campaign, but he might at least have stopped long enough to sound out the AFL negotiating committee.

In mid-November 1936 the AFL, with almost a million members unrepresented, met in convention at Tampa, Florida. Zaritsky was

[101]AFL Committee to Zaritsky, Oct. 15, 1936, PCB #22, Book 569, *ibid.*

[102]Zaritsky to Lewis, Oct. 19, 1936, United Hatters, Cap and Millinery Workers, *Proceedings, 1939*, pp. 203–204.

[103]Howard to Green, Nov. 7, 1936, AFL, *Proceedings, 1937*, p. 98.

[104]Green to Howard, Nov. 7, 1936, PCB #22, Book 568, NYSSILR Library.

[105]Lewis to Green, Nov. 8, 1936, AFL, *Proceedings, 1937*, pp. 99–100.

[106]*Report of the General Executive Board* [of the ILGWU] *to the 29th Convention, 1956*, p. 28.

the only prominent CIO leader in attendance.[107] Twenty resolutions dealing with the CIO were referred to the Committee on Resolutions. Eighteen of these either asked that the suspensions be lifted, recommended unity plans, or favored the encouragement of CIO organizing efforts. The Structural Iron Workers wanted a ruling on an alleged invasion of its jurisdiction by the CIO, and the MTD peremptorily urged the immediate revocation of the charters of the suspended CIO unions.[108]

It seems almost certain that if Ogburn had not counseled a contrary course, the AFL would have taken the MTD's advice and ousted the CIO unions at Tampa. Shortly after the Executive Council's second suspension plan had begun to unfold in July and Lewis had tagged this plan as a subterfuge which concealed the objective of expulsion, Ogburn had again cautioned the Council against taking precipitate action. Agreeing with Lewis, Ogburn advised that the Council could not suspend the CIO unions as a means of guaranteeing a two-thirds convention vote for their expulsion. A two-thirds vote, said Ogburn, meant two thirds of a full convention and not two thirds of a convention in which the CIO unions were not represented; the latter had the right to vote on a question of their own expulsion. "Suspension for a time from enjoying the privileges of membership in the American Federation of Labor can be imposed on these unions as a penalty for violation of their contracts," he concluded, "but not as a means of obtaining a two-thirds majority for expulsion."[109] Later, after suspension had become a fact, Ogburn added that the Tampa convention ought only to ratify the action the Council had already taken against the CIO; by so doing, it would force the CIO either to disband or to secede from the AFL, and Ogburn thought the CIO might well choose the former course.[110]

[107]The Hatters, Cap and Millinery Workers sent a full delegation to Tampa. Howard chose to boycott the convention, whereas the other five ITU delegates attended it. The AFL constitution did not permit the ten suspended unions either representation or recognition at the annual convention.

[108]AFL, *Proceedings, 1936*, pp. 207, 208–211, 225–226, 231, 237–238, 272, 278, 279, 291, 301, 305, 306, 309, 311–312, 318, 321, 328. Of the 18 pro-CIO resolutions, 3 were introduced by state federations of labor, 9 by city centrals, 5 by federal labor unions (1 of which was signed by 29 such unions), and 1 by the Sleeping Car Porters.

[109]Ogburn to Green, July 22, 1936, CIO #1, AFL-CIO Archives.

[110]Ogburn to Green, Sept. 30, 1936, CIO #1, *ibid.*

After the Tampa convention had begun, Ogburn, worried over an Associated Press report that nine Council members still favored revoking the charters of the CIO unions, sent Green two more anti-expulsion letters. He now indicated that expulsion would be a tactical as well as a legal blunder because expulsion was just what "Mr. Lewis" wanted. In fact he had heard, third hand, that Lewis "was absolutely jittery" for fear the convention would not expel the CIO unions.[111]

It can scarcely be denied that Ogburn's legal argument must have changed some Executive Council minds and thus influenced the Committee on Resolutions (which worked in the shadow of the Council) in its decision to recommend that the convention merely approve the actions already taken by the Council rather than expel the CIO unions. The warning posted by the IAM convention (that IAM delegates to the Tampa conclave would not vote to suspend or expel the CIO unions) was probably the strongest straw in the tactical wind which blew against the Council's expulsion course. At any rate the Committee on Resolutions recommended, in addition to the endorsement of the Council's actions, that the suspension of the CIO unions "remain in effect until the present breach be healed and adjusted," that the special negotiating committee be continued, and, significantly, that the Executive Council be authorized to call a special convention if the suspended unions should create a situation that demands "a more drastic procedure."[112] After a debate of nine-and-a-half-hours, the convention approved the recommendations by a roll-call vote of 21,679 to 2,043.[113] Since the CIO unions could have added only about 10,000

---

[111]Ogburn to Green, Nov. 13, 20, 1936, CIO #1, *ibid.*

[112]Myrup and J. C. Lewis opposed these recommendations but they did not submit a minority report.

[113]AFL, *Proceedings, 1936,* pp. 496–553. Ten unions voted against the report of the Committee on Resolutions. These unions were: the Bakery Workers, Brewery Workers, Brick and Clay Workers, Elevator Constructors, Hatters, Cap and Millinery Workers, American Newspaper Guild, Paper Makers, Sleeping Car Porters, Pulp, Sulphite, and Paper Mill Workers, and the AFT. Also, five sixths of the ITU's vote and one fifth of the Printing Pressmen's vote were cast against the report. The IAM delegates supported the report, thus violating the spirit if not the letter of their instructions to oppose the suspension or the expulsion of the CIO unions.

negative votes,[114] they could not have blocked the action. Had the convention been voting on suspension itself rather than on the recommendations, it is likely that the negative vote would have been greater (the IAM, at least, might have voted negatively), but suspension would still have been easily voted by a simple majority.

[114]Frank Morrison figured that 982,343 members were suspended in 1936. Morrison to Duffy, Oct. 1, 1937, NUF #3 (Carpenters), AFL-CIO Archives. On the constitutional basis of one vote for every one hundred members or major fraction thereof, these members would yield 9,823 votes.

CHAPTER IX

Labor's House Divides

THE difficulties in the way of the reestablishment of labor unity mounted rapidly during the opening months of 1937 when the CIO enjoyed its first great organizing and bargaining successes. These difficulties marked the beginning of a new exchange of fire between the CIO and AFL which resulted in the extension of dualism from the national level to the state and city levels and finally provoked the AFL openly to declare war in May. A truce was called in the closing weeks of 1937 and during this period unity talks were held. It need scarcely be affirmed that the talks failed and that the birth of the Congress of Industrial Organizations came about a year later as the culminating event in the division of labor's house.

I

The first great crack in the antiunion barricade which rimmed the mass-production industries occurred on February 11, 1937 when General Motors, subjected to the novel weapon of the sit-down strike, very strong governmental pressures, and the deft maneuvering of John L. Lewis, signed its first contract with the UAW.[1] Since the agreement did not include a union shop provision, the reaction—very prompt indeed—of William Green and the presidents of the Metal and Building Trades Departments was to send a letter to GM president William S. Knudsen and ask for a conference which would make clear the status of AFL craft unions

[1] For further details, see Levinson, *Labor on the March*, pp. 149–168.

in GM plants.[2] It seems they believed that GM would now be inclined positively toward dealing with the conservative crafts, perhaps as a means of limiting the influence of the new and untried UAW. On the contrary, the GM contract was the first real stimulus to the expansion of organizing, primarily on an industrial union basis, in the automobile and virtually all other mass-production industries.

Another, perhaps even more historic, milestone in the growth of the CIO and the development of American economic life was marked on March 3, 1937 when United States Steel suddenly abandoned its long opposition to trade unionism and recognized the Steel Workers' Organizing Committee as a collective bargaining agency. Although the leadership of Lewis and the limited organizing success of SWOC certainly help explain United States Steel's turnabout, the company could easily have fought off the CIO in early 1937 had it chosen to summon the necessary resources for such a move. Precisely why U.S. Steel did not elect this course is unknown at present, although it has been suggested that cost in itself was a deterrent to battle and that the company was reacting to the current political atmosphere which was scarcely tolerant of industrial violence.[3] In any case, the Lewis-Taylor agreement was a second great victory for the CIO and industrial unionism. After the steel and automobile victories, the CIO in March set up organizing committees for the textile and petroleum industries.[4]

Just as the CIO's creation of SWOC had been a strong stimulus to the Executive Council's suspension action in 1936, so now the CIO's organizing and bargaining successes caused the Council to take further retaliatory measures against the CIO and also to change its attitude toward industrial unionism in certain areas.

[2]Green, Frey, and J. W. Williams to Knudsen, Feb. 12, 1937, PCB #22, Book 574, NYSSILR Library.

[3]Walter Galenson, "The Unionization of the American Steel Industry," *International Review of Social History*, Vol. 1, Part 1, 1956, pp. 23–26. Galenson also suggests that Myron Taylor, chairman of the board of U.S. Steel, "was cut from quite a different stripe than his predecessor, Judge Elbert Gary" (and presumably was therefore less antagonistic toward trade unionism). The CIO's campaign in the steel industry is discussed at length in Levinson, *Labor on the March*, pp. 149–168.

[4]"Red Purge Due in Labor Ranks," *Machinists' Monthly Journal*, Vol. 49, May 1937, p. 316; Matthew Josephson, *Sidney Hillman*, pp. 412–413; Levinson, *Labor on the March*, pp. 238–241, 253–254.

Before these developments are outlined, however, it ought to be stated that the Wagner Act apparently did not contribute importantly to the rapid deterioration of AFL-CIO relations in the early months of 1937. The triumph of industrial unionism in the automobile and steel industries was not the result of a National Labor Relations Board ruling that bargaining units in these industries should be figured on an industrial rather than a craft basis. The NLRB had nothing to do with the signing of the GM and U.S. Steel contracts. In fact the NLRB did not begin to intervene in disputes between AFL and CIO unions until mid-1937, its first decision being handed down in June,[5] a month after key AFL craft unions had decided to organize workers from all skill levels.

This is not to deny, however, that some AFL leaders fully realized, even in 1935, that the NLRB might eventually have an important effect upon the structural question. The Wagner Act gave the NLRB discretionary authority to decide, in those instances in which it was asked to conduct representation elections, whether the appropriate bargaining unit should be "the employer unit, craft unit, plant unit, or subdivision thereof."[6] Matthew Woll rightly concluded shortly after the Wagner Act became law that labor leaders would not unilaterally decide "the form and character of organization that shall hereafter prevail in the labor movement," because "that power, to a large degree, has now been lodged in a Federal government agency." Woll feared that the NLRB would favor the employer or plant unit.[7]

It is also to be recognized that the validation of the Wagner Act in April 1937 greatly increased the prestige and activities of the NLRB. Nevertheless at that date there was not yet evidence that the Board would tend to favor industrial unionism in its determination of bargaining units. The sharp controversy between AFL and CIO leaders over the administration of the Wagner Act was reserved for later months and years.[8] It was primarily because of the

[5]Ben Stephansky, "The Structure of the American Labor Movement," in Industrial Relations Research Association, *Interpreting the Labor Movement,* pp. 55–57.
[6]See Sec. 9 (b) of the Wagner Act as printed in Herbert O. Eby, *The Labor Relations Act in the Courts,* p. 233.
[7]AFL, *Proceedings, 1935,* pp. 529–530.
[8]In the late 1930's and until the passage of the Taft-Hartley Act, one member of the NLRB decided *a priori* in favor of industrial unionism and one of the remain-

246

CIO's organizing and bargaining successes, therefore, that the AFL began early in 1937 a series of crucial moves involving the CIO.

At the Executive Council's mid-February 1937 conclave, Green announced that he had revoked the credentials of a number of AFL organizers who were sympathetic to the CIO. The Council, in turn, authorized Green to issue federal charters to workers coming under the jurisdictions of the ten suspended unions "without jeopardy to any of the rights of these organizations" and to expel locals of CIO unions from state and city bodies "where circumstances and conditions" seemed to require such action.[9] As a result of the latter directive, Green pointedly advised the state and city bodies that the AFL could not and would not tolerate any longer their extending support to CIO unions. During 1937 the AFL effected the reorganization of many such bodies by having the locals of CIO unions ousted and pro-CIO officers defeated for reelection.[10]

The AFL's stiffening policy toward subordinate bodies was clearly harmful to the CIO cause. The policy left the locals of CIO unions without state and city parent bodies, thus weakening their organizing power and exposing them to possible membership raids by AFL unions. As a counterstroke to the policy, the CIO announced on March 9 that it would begin to issue its own certificates of affiliation to national, state, and city labor organizations. The CIO would also, the announcement said, issue such certificates to national and international unions and to directly affiliated local unions. The UMW indicated that this step put the CIO on a permanent operating basis.[11]

---

ing two members "seemed to be similarly disposed." Stephansky, "The Structure of the American Labor Movement," p. 56.

[9]Extracts from the Minutes of the [AFL] Executive Council meeting, Washington, D. C., Feb. 8–19, 1937," CIO #1, AFL-CIO Archives. See also Green to Hutcheson, Feb. 20, 1937, PCB #22, Book 574, NYSSILR Library.

[10]Green to the Officers and Members of All Organizations Affiliated with the American Federation of Labor, Feb. 24, 1937, CIO #1, AFL-CIO Archives. For voluminous correspondence concerning the reorganization of state and city bodies, see CIO #1, *ibid.*

[11]"C. I. O. Makes Plans for Progress and Wide Organization," *United Mine Workers' Journal*, Vol. 48, March 15, 1937, p. 3.

II

Only at this very advanced stage of the split, after the CIO had conclusively shown that the mass-industry workers were organizable and that industrial unionism was not a "phantom" policy, did a number of AFL leaders fully realize that twentieth-century economic developments required a twentieth-century brand of unionism. Now with their backs to the craft union wall, they discovered that this wall was a fragile antique, no longer sheltering them against the incursions of the CIO nor lending them an offensive wedge behind which they could mount a counterattack. Even though they did not all agree that craft unionism had to be, or indeed should be, entirely abandoned in the mass-production industries, they did agree that the movement they represented had to start moving—in some direction— to avoid atrophy.

March, April, and May evidently were the crucial months which saw an amazing rebirth of spirit and reorientation of view in the craft ranks. On March 2 the Boilermakers' president wrote Green that the AFL should cease merely complaining about the CIO unions and should "aggressively carry the fight to them."[12] President Britton of the Metal Polishers became gravely concerned over the UAW threat to AFL men (who did not want to be mowed down "like so much grass") in Detroit, Cleveland, and especially Toledo. One AFL organizer in Toledo was not enough, he told Green; quick, militant aid, in the form of one more organizer, was needed. "We can't stand away and send letters," he continued, "We've got to be on the ground leading our men. . . . I am hoping no time will be wasted and that we will immediately establish a movement capable of protecting our men in the manner in which they should be protected." "You ought to get in this game," he admonished Green, "and fight to the very last. By fighting, I mean send capable men on the ground. Let's do it in the manner in which it should be done."[13]

Perhaps the most significant evidence of an AFL awakening, evidence which also beautifully documents from the the craft side

[12]Franklin to Green, March 2, 1937, CIO #1, AFL-CIO Archives. See also Franklin to Green, March 16, 1937, CIO #1, *ibid.*

[13]Britton to Green, March 10, 1937, NUF #7 (Metal Polishers), *ibid.*

the validity of the progressive movement, comes from the IAM. Arthur W. Wharton on March 10, 1937 wrote to the presidents of the Blacksmiths, Boilermakers, IBEW, Molders, Pattern Makers' League, and Sheet Metal Workers, outlined the serious predicament of the crafts relative to the success of the CIO and industrial unionism, and proposed a remedy. He told them that the IAM had just investigated the possibility of organizing the machinists who were among the 2,500 workers at the American Locomotive Plant, Schenectady, New York, and that "as usual" the IAM found that the workers wanted an industrial union, would absolutely refuse to join the several craft unions whose jurisdictions were involved (even if a metal trades council were formed), and therefore would "join up with the C. I. O. unless the A. F. of L. Organizations are willing that they should become members of one organization." Wharton felt that since a "substantial majority" of the workers in question were eligible to join the IAM that the other crafts might be willing to forego their claims and let the IAM place all the workers in an industrial lodge. "I will be glad indeed," he concluded, "to have you advise me just what you think we should do under these circumstances. We are evidently going into a most serious struggle arising out of the unwarranted conduct and actions of the C. I. O. group *and in self defense many of our organizations are going to be forced to meet those situations in a manner contrary to their desire or be forced to step aside and allow the C. I. O. full sway.*"[14]

Unfortunately, George Q. Lynch of the Pattern Makers made the only written response to Wharton's inquiry. Lynch's reply is, however, a most interesting one. It reveals that the Pattern Makers opposed the IAM formula, had no desire itself to enroll unskilled and semiskilled workers, but was in favor of another plan which would guarantee it perhaps a trickle of skilled pattern makers from the mass-production industries. It is obvious, of course, that under the "substantial majority" formula proposed by the IAM, the smaller and more specialized crafts stood to lose to the larger

[14]Wharton to Horn, Franklin, Tracy, O'Keefe, George Q. Lynch (Pattern Makers' League), and J. J. Hynes (Sheet Metal Workers), March 10, 1937, NUF #6, (IAM), *ibid.,* italics added.

crafts many potential skilled recruits. It was for this reason, one may properly infer, that Lynch informed Wharton that he believed the craft unions should remain craft unions and should not accept into membership workers of different kinds and degrees of skill. He rationalized the point, however, by contending that the workers themselves would not join on an industrial basis any national union which had traditionally operated on the craft principle. "Unless I completely misunderstand the psychology of the situation," he reasoned, "these workers seek not only the possibility to join one union but that such a union be divorced from craft principles. No existing Metal Trades International can therefore meet the requirements." Lynch's counterproposal was to allow the unorganized to decide for themselves whether they wanted to join the craft unions or become members of new local unions chartered and controlled by the MTD. While this might enhance the role of the MTD at the expense of some nationals, it would be preferable to subordinating the latter to "the arbitrary and undemocratic policies of the C. I. O. or leaving workers entirely without organization." He could see no other realistic alternative to his suggestion, and certainly, he advised, "we can not longer defend a 'dog in the manger' attitude. . . . If workers want a broader basis of organization, we must supply it or die. We hold no patent rights on the idea or privilege to organize."[15]

The Lynch plan, which permitted both craft organizing and the transformation of the MTD into a catch-all organization for the metal-working industries, probably had support only among the smaller crafts, if indeed it had any support at all outside the Pattern Makers' League. Under this plan the smaller crafts would lose members in proportion as the workers chose to join MTD locals, but the membership risk was not so certain as under the IAM plan. The IAM's position, in essence if not in specific terms, was shortly to become the official new position of the AFL regarding organizing policy.

The first step toward the achievement of the last-named result was taken on April 8. On that day the metal trades' unions met at the Washington headquarters of the AFL and urged the Executive

[15]Lynch to Wharton, March 20, 1937, NUF #6 (IAM), *ibid.*

Council to call a special convention "to consider decisions of the Tampa Convention relative to the C. I. O."[16] Green promptly scheduled an emergency meeting of the Council to begin on April 19.[17] The Council wanted to call a special convention of AFL organizations partly for the purpose of revoking the CIO union charters, but counseled by Ogburn that the AFL constitution did not provide for a special convention and that only a regular convention was cloaked with such punitive authority, decided to hold just a conference of the national and international unions.[18] The latter were to be invited to meet at Cincinnati, Ohio, on May 24. The reason for calling such a conference was indicated in this important policy statement adopted by the Council on April 22:

The Executive Council heretofore hopeful and patient that a more moderate and conciliatory spirit might result in effecting a readjustment [as regards the CIO] now finds it impossible to continue in that spirit if it is to be true to the best interests of all our affiliated unions. *The Executive Council hereafter proposes to pursue a policy and procedure that will not only advance and safeguard the interests of all affiliated unions but . . . will likewise make it possible for all workers heretofore not affiliated to come within the democratic and constructive fold of the American Federation of Labor.* It is to give effect to this *new* policy. . . [that the conference will be called].[19]

In the conference invitations which he mailed on April 30, Green stated that the meeting would "develop plans for carrying on a

[16]MTD, *Proceedings, 1937,* p. 9.

[17]Green to Executive Council Members, April 9, 1937, PCB #23, Book 578, NYSSILR Library.

[18]"Extract from the Minutes of the [AFL] Executive Council Meeting, Washington, D. C., April 19–22, 1937," CIO #1, AFL-CIO Archives; Ogburn to Green, April 16, 21, 1937, CIO #1, *ibid.* According to the Council, the expulsion of the CIO unions was made necessary by the CIO announcement of March 9 that it intended to issue certificates of affiliation to member organizations. This, said the Council, meant that the CIO was no longer a "conference" but was "in substance and in fact. . .a body dual to and destructive of the American Federation of Labor." "Extract from the Minutes of the [AFL] Executive Council Meeting, Washington, D. C., April 19–22, 1937," CIO #1, *ibid.* The Council's choice of language raises the question as to whether the Council now felt that the CIO had not been a dual organization in August 1936. At its convention in late 1937, the AFL amended its constitution to permit the calling of a special convention. AFL, *Proceedings, 1937,* pp. 113–114, 553–554.

[19]"Extracts from the Minutes of the [AFL] Executive Council Meeting, Washington, D. C., April 19–22, 1937," CIO #1, AFL-CIO Archives, italics added.

definite and coordinated plan of organization" and that it would also consider what financial support was needed to execute an "accelerated" organizing program.[20]

At the Cincinnati conference, which was well-attended, the Executive Council indicated that it wished to give effect to its new policy by levying on each member of the AFL's affiliated unions a special monthly assessment of one cent to finance organizing work. The unions present at the conference agreed to consider such an assessment at the next AFL convention and promised, meanwhile, to remit the tax voluntarily beginning June 1, 1937. Thus for the first time in nineteen years the AFL assented, for all practical purposes, to a special assessment. The unions also agreed to initiate aggressive organizing campaigns "within their respective jurisdictions" and to require those of their locals which had not previously done so to join the state and city bodies chartered by the AFL.[21] The latter move was obviously intended to strengthen the finances and thus the organizing power of state and city organizations. To help put into effect the organizing program, Green appointed Lewis G. Hines as his special assistant responsible for "directing, advising, and communicating" with a vastly augmented staff of organizers. Hines was expected "to systemize the organizing work of the American Federation of Labor, to develop the highest degree of teamwork possible, to coordinate our organizing efforts and to promote and advance the organizing campaign of the American Federation of Labor in a highly successful way."[22] While at Cincinnati, the Council issued a charter to the Progressive Miners of America, the small but bitter rival of the UMW.[23]

[20]Green to the National and International Unions, April 30, 1937, PCB #23, Book 580, NYSSILR Library.

[21]AFL, *Proceedings, 1937*, pp. 105–106. The 1937 convention of the AFL made the assessment binding upon all affiliated unions. The ITU refused to pay the tax and was therefore suspended in 1939. The union did not return to the AFL until 1944. AFL, *Proceedings, 1937*, pp. 633–634, *1939*, pp. 345–356, *1944*, pp. 124–125; ITU, *Proceedings, 1938*, pp. 77–91, *1939*, p. 84.

[22]Green to Salaried and Special Organizers, June 14, 1937, PCB #23, Book 584, NYSSILR Library.

[23]Green to Frey, May 28, 1937, PCB #23, Book 582, *ibid*. The Carpenters wanted the Council to suspend the ITU, but the Council decided against taking such action. "Extract from the Minutes of the [AFL] Executive Council Meeting, Cincinnati, Ohio, May 23–30, 1937," CIO #1, AFL-CIO Archives; Duffy to Green, May 11, 1937, CIO #1, AFL-CIO Archives.

In effect, if not in precise language, the new Cincinnati policy significantly amended the Scranton declaration. It marked the end of the broad-scale doctrinal quarrel the craft unionists had cultivated over the years with industrial unionism. At Cincinnati the AFL determined to compete vigorously with the CIO for the allegiance of the unorganized workers, from fear, perhaps, that the CIO might otherwise surpass it in membership strength. In the ensuing frenzied scramble for membership, both the AFL and the CIO chartered craft and industrial unions alike, with at best only fleeting twinges of conscience. Thus in a very real sense, the Cincinnati conference also heralded the beginning of "labor's civil war." In the aftermath, some AFL unions, such as the Teamsters, Carpenters, IAM, and IBEW, emerged with jurisdictions as broad or broader than those claimed by some CIO unions.

The IAM, among the first of the craft unions to move, in philosophy if not in fact, away from the dead center of craft unionism, stood to gain handsomely in membership in the carrying out of the AFL's new policy. Sensing this fact, and buoyed with the knowledge that it would now have the firm support of AFL headquarters (which Wharton certainly felt Green had withheld during 1933–1935), the IAM announced that it was now "prepared for battle" against anyone who trespassed "upon its domain."[24] Ceasing altogether to speak of mass-production workers as being unorganizable, the IAM's most cherished thought now was to get its share of these workers. It therefore began to belittle the CIO, and on one occasion made this clean breast of its feelings:

What a wonderful group of supermen these leaders of the C. I. O. have turned out to be. . . . Well may we place our chins in our cupped hands and ponder over the mysteries of this new cult, which is to be the salvation of the workers. Well may we ask ourselves the question, "Upon what meat have these men fed that they have become so great?" Truly, they must go about all day long singing, "Ah, Sweet Mystery of Life, At Last I've Found Thee." On the other hand, can it be just possible that they are numbered among those of whom it is said, "Whom the Gods would destroy, they first make mad?" Time alone will tell.

[24]*Machinists' Monthly Journal,* Vol. 49, August 1937, p. 542.

Meanwhile...we are confident that our members, everywhere...will
...be found joining with the other loyal Craft Unions singing "Who's
Afraid of the Big Bad Wolf?" Not us. Oo! la! la! la! le![25]

Pep talks were probably common in the summer of 1937 in the
activated AFL camp, but they surely were not of the same quality
as the one just quoted.

The CIO, whether eagerly or not, accepted the AFL challenge
laid down at Cincinnati and established in June a system of per
capita taxes for its own affiliated unions.[26] During the same month,
the Oil Workers removed the words "American Federation of
Labor" from that section of its constitution which dealt with the
sending of delegates to the AFL convention and substituted for
them "any national labor group to which we may be affiliated."[27]
In August the Mine, Mill and Smelter Workers struck out all
reference to the AFL in its constitution and inserted instead the
"Committee for Industrial Organization." The latter union also
suggested that the CIO hold a founding convention immediately
following the October convention of the AFL.[28]

By the end of August the AFL's new organizing policy had
already begun to show a profit in the membership column. The
Executive Council reported an August enrollment of 3,271,726,
which represented an increase of 831,671 members over the AFL's
average membership for 1936.[29] At the same time, however, the
CIO had registered far more impressive membership gains.
Between November 1936 and September 1937 the CIO, according
to its own figures, added more than two million members to its
rolls and for the latter month it claimed a total of 3,718,000 members.[30] This figure included, however, some 45,000 typographers

[25]*Ibid.*, Vol. 49, July 1937, p. 469.

[26]Previous to June the CIO had depended entirely upon voluntary contributions
to finance its activities. In June the CIO levied upon its national and international
unions a tax of five cents per member per month. In contrast, the AFL was charging a regular tax of only one cent per member per month. Levinson, *Labor on the
March*, p. 136; Harris, *Labor's Civil War*, pp. 60–61.

[27]Oil Workers, *Proceedings, 1937*, p. 143.

[28]Mine, Mill and Smelter Workers, *Proceedings, 1937*, pp. 52, 116, 189–190.

[29]On the other hand, the AFL's average membership for 1937 was reported at
2,860,933. AFL, *Proceedings, 1937*, p. 76.

[30]This figure included the memberships of 32 national and international unions
and 525 directly affiliated local unions. Two unions, the Fur Workers and the
American Newspaper Guild, withdrew from the AFL and joined the CIO in 1937,

and hatters, cap and millinery workers who had not joined and did not join the CIO. Also, several CIO unions appear to have grossly exaggerated their memberships. Benjamin Stolberg has estimated that the actual strength of the CIO in September 1937 was nearer 3,300,000 members.[31] If one accepts as accurate Stolberg's figure for the CIO and the AFL's reported membership, then the two organizations were approximately equal in strength in the early fall of 1937.

When the AFL delegates gathered at Denver, Colorado, in October 1937 for their annual meeting, they were faced with a request from the Executive Council for authority to revoke the charters of the suspended CIO unions.[32] The convention approved the Council's request but also sanctioned the continued existence of the special negotiating committee.[33]

While the AFL was deliberating in Denver, more than two hundred CIO representatives gathered in conference at Atlantic City. They authorized the national officers of the CIO to call a founding convention of CIO unions whenever the officers deemed such action advisable. Philip Murray, chairman of the resolutions committee which introduced the proposal, declared that CIO leaders had been considering a convention call for several months and that there were two developments which made "a cohesive movement" necessary. In the first place, it was clear that no CIO union could find protection in the AFL because that organization prohibited from membership "any union, any member of any union, that swears allegiance to the policies of the CIO." Second, all CIO units had to be affiliated under one great banner if the yet unorganized workers were to be given the kind of organization they wanted. The Atlantic City conference agreed, in addition to

and 18 newly formed or previously independent unions became CIO affiliates during that year. The CIO also claimed 50 industrial union councils on the city level and 4 on the state level. Walsh, *C. I. O.,* p. 156.

[31]Stolberg, *Story of the CIO,* p. 28 n. In arriving at this figure, Stolberg suggests, for example, that the UTW claimed 200,000 more members than it actually had and that the Agricultural, Canning, and Packing Workers overestimated its strength by 80,000 members.

[32]The AFT and the Sleeping Car Porters petitioned the convention in favor of the initiation of unity negotiations with the CIO. The AFT included the railroad brotherhoods and all other bona fide independent unions in its unity proposal.

[33]AFL, *Proceedings, 1937,* pp. 377–417.

authorizing a founding convention, to set up state and city coordinating bodies as fast as possible.[34]

III

The drift toward a bifurcated labor movement was unexpectedly interrupted by a second and more serious attempt to reestablish harmony between the rival organizations. On October 12, 1937 just a day after the AFL Executive Council had been empowered to revoke the charters of the suspended CIO unions, the CIO unanimously adopted and sent to the AFL's Denver convention an invitation to inaugurate unity conferences.[35] In contrast with the situation in October 1936 at which time it had refused to negotiate by the committee method, the CIO now suggested that committees of one hundred members each be selected for the unity talks. Accompanying the peace offer were expansive praise of CIO achievements and an accusation that in the past AFL leadership had been content "to keep labor shackled to decrepit policies and puny in its numbers." The CIO also indicated that it would not barter away any of its "basic" policies.[36]

The AFL reply of October 14 declared that the CIO was responsible for the confusion, division, and conflict in the labor movement and that the CIO had previously spurned every honorable effort to restore unity. Although the AFL felt that the language of the CIO's invitation was "designed more for propaganda than expressive of a real desire for peace and unity," it informed the CIO that its special committee stood ready to meet "a like committee representative of any or all" of the CIO organizations and was "clothed with full authority" to negotiate a unity agreement.[37] After a further exchange of telegrams it was decided that a unity

[34]CIO, *The Program of the C. I. O.,* pp. 8–11.

[35]The invitation was drafted by the CIO Committee on Resolutions as a substitute for the peace proposals which were submitted to the CIO conference by several unidentified national unions. *Ibid.,* pp. 18–19.

[36]Fremming to Frank Morrison, Oct. 12, 1937, ILGWU, *The Position of the International Ladies' Garment Workers' Union in Relation to CIO and AFL, 1934–1938,* pp. 38–40. See also "C. I. O. Challenges A. F. of L. to Cooperate for Unity," *United Mine Workers' Journal,* Vol. 48, Oct. 15, 1937, pp. 3–4.

[37]Morrison to Fremming, Oct. 14, 1937, ILGWU, *Position of the International Ladies' Garment Workers' Union in Relation to CIO and AFL,* pp. 40–42; AFL, *Proceedings, 1937,* pp. 580–581.

conference would begin on October 25 in Washington and that the CIO would send ten committeemen while the AFL would retain its three-member committee.[38]

There was little basis for agreement in the proposals submitted by each committee at the start of the conference, and although negotiations continued for several weeks, the conference adjourned in failure on December 21, 1937. The CIO initially suggested that all of its national and local unions should be accepted into the AFL at the same time; that an autonomous department, to be known as the Committee for Industrial Organization, should be formed with undivided control over its affiliated organizations and their members and with sole jurisdiction over organizing, on an industrial basis, the workers in the mass-production, marine, public utility, service, and basic fabricating industries; and that a joint convention should be held to approve and effectuate its plan. As a counter proposition the AFL demanded the immediate dissolution of the CIO and agreed to accept immediately into membership only the ten CIO unions which had been suspended. All other CIO unions should then confer with the AFL unions which contested their jurisdictions and all conflicts not solved by October 1938 should receive final disposition at the AFL convention scheduled to meet in that month. The AFL proposed also that aggressive organizing should proceed along both craft and industrial lines "as circumstances and conditions may warrant."[39]

Murray, who was chairman of the CIO committee, immediately declared that acceptance of the AFL proposal by the CIO would amount to an abject surrender. If the suspended unions were to return to the AFL, they would betray the remaining twenty CIO

[38]Fremming to Morrison, Oct. 15, 1937, Morrison to Fremming, Oct. 15, 1937, Murray to Morrison, Oct. 16, 1937, and Morrison to Murray, Oct. 17, 1937, AFL, *Proceedings, 1938*, pp. 87–89. Woll, Harrison, and Bugniazet spoke for the AFL. The CIO was represented by Murray, Hillman, Dubinsky, Fremming, Carey, Dalrymple, Homer Martin, Michael Quill, president of the Transport Workers, Joseph Curran, president of the National Maritime Union, and Abram Flaxer, president of the State, County, and Municipal Workers. "Peace Conference Takes a Recess After Three Days Session," *United Mine Workers' Journal*, Vol. 48, Nov. 1, 1937, pp. 4, 23. Hillman became ill during the first day of the conference and he did not thereafter participate in its sessions. ACW, *Proceedings, 1938*, p. 53.

[39]The full texts of the CIO and AFL proposals are printed in "Peace Conference Takes a Recess After Three Days Session," *United Mine Workers' Journal*, Vol. 48, Nov. 1, 1937, p. 3–4.

unions by leaving them without a parent organization and exposing them to craft union raids. His committee therefore understood
the AFL offer as a "rejection of the principle of industrial organization in mass production and other basic industries."[40] In regard
to the CIO plan, the IAM thought it "bordered on brazen effront-
ery" and amounted to an attempt on the part of the "Big Bad
Wolf" to devour the "Meek Little Lamb."[41]

What took place at the conference thereafter has been sharply
disputed between the AFL and the CIO. The AFL committee,
whose interpretation was reported to the Executive Council in
February 1938 and later was made public, contended that after the
initial proposals were rejected a "basis for agreement" was formulated and accepted by both committees but was later vetoed by
John L. Lewis. This "basis for agreement," the AFL committee
reported, stipulated that all CIO unions would be admitted
together into the AFL after joint conference committees had
adjusted the conflicts with the twenty CIO unions which did not
hold AFL charters. Furthermore within sixty to ninety days after
all disputes were adjusted, a special convention would be held in
which the CIO unions would have full membership rights. The
agreement pledged the AFL to specify certain industries in which
the industrial form of organization should prevail and to consider amending its constitution to prohibit the Executive Council
from suspending or revoking the charter of a national or international union without direct instructions from an AFL convention.

The AFL committee stated further that Murray was absent when
the agreement was reached—an important factor in considering
whether a valid agreement was made—and that when he learned of
it and consulted with Lewis about it, he "refused to carry out the
understanding" and proposed instead that a subcommittee take up
the entire subject anew. The AFL insisted that the CIO honor the
agreement but assented, nevertheless, to the subcommittee idea.
Lewis and Murray for the CIO and Green and Harrison for the
AFL then met. Lewis demanded that the discussion of jurisdic-

[40]Quoted in *ibid.*, p. 4.
[41]*Machinists' Monthly Journal*, Vol. 49, November 1937, p. 749.

tional matters be deferred until after all the CIO unions had obtained AFL charters and that no CIO unions should be suspended in the event their jurisdictional conflicts with AFL unions were not adjusted. Green and Harrison asserted that such a procedure would establish dualism within the AFL, and on this note the conference abruptly ended.[42]

Lewis and Murray denied that an agreement had been reached and that the AFL committee had made any substantial concessions to CIO proposals. Specifically they declared that the position of the AFL committee throughout the negotiations called first for the return to the AFL of the suspended unions and only later for the chartering of other CIO affiliates. Lewis and Murray also contended that the AFL committee, unlike the CIO negotiators, had no power to negotiate a binding settlement and for this reason was unable to make definite policy commitments on any issue.[43]

Daniel Tobin, who was a member of the AFL Executive Council at the time, agreed with Lewis and Murray that the AFL was prepared to take back immediately only those CIO unions which had left the AFL and that the remaining CIO unions were to be chartered by the AFL after the jurisdictional problems in which they were involved with the craft unions were solved. Tobin also stated that the AFL committee "had no power to make any kind of agreement without reporting back to the Executive Council."[44] At the very beginning of the conference the Carpenters also made clear its position that the AFL committee had no final bargaining authority and that it had to consult with the Executive Council upon possible settlement terms.[45] Moreover, it will be noted shortly that the AFL committee did, in fact, consult with the Council in

[42]"A Report Submitted by Woll, Bugniazet, and Harrison to the Executive Council of the American Federation of Labor, Miami, Florida, Feb. 3, 1938," CIO #2, AFL-CIO Archives. See also AFL, *Proceedings, 1938*, pp. 89–91.

[43]"C. I. O.-A. F. of L. Peace Parley Is in Recess Again," *United Mine Workers' Journal*, Vol. 48, Nov. 15, 1937, p. 4; UMW, *Proceedings, 1938*, pp. 67–68, 102–106. The Lewis-Murray interpretation became the official position of the CIO with regard to the failure of the conference. See CIO, *Program of the C. I. O.*, p. 35; CIO, *Proceedings, 1938*, p. 34. The ACW and the Mine, Mill and Smelter Workers, neither of which was represented at the conference, supported this position. See *Advance*, Vol. 24, January 1938, p. 2; ACW, *Proceedings, 1938*, pp. 51–52; Mine, Mill and Smelter Workers, *Proceedings, 1938*, p. 77.

[44]*Official Magazine* (of the Teamsters), Vol. 35, January 1938, p. 10.

[45]Hutcheson and Duffy to Green, Oct. 26, 1937, CIO #2, AFL-CIO Archives.

December. This issue is not important in itself, however, and one can even question whether the CIO committee, despite Murray's statements to the contrary, could have concluded an agreement without securing the prior approval of John L. Lewis. Such a technical issue begs the more profound question whether either side, or both sides, possessed a sincere and abiding will to reestablish peace and unity in the labor movement.

As for the CIO committeemen, five of them (in addition to Lewis and Murray) supported the Lewis-Murray account of the AFL's admissions proposal, but Dubinsky and Abram Flaxer, president of the State, County, and Municipal Workers, supported the AFL committee's point of view. Howard, who was secretary to the conference group, concluded after perusing the unofficial minutes of the conference that the record was confused with regard to the position of the AFL committee on this matter.[46]

The closest scrutiny of additional, previously unpublished evidence does not yield an understanding of exactly what happened at the conference. There is proof, however, that by November 29, the apparent date of the first meeting of the subcommittees, jurisdictional problems had been discussed in detail and considerable progress had been made. The AFL committee had pledged important concessions to some of the larger CIO organizations and had suggested that some of the smaller ones merge with their AFL counterparts. In the former category are, for example, the UAW, URW, the Textile Workers' Organizing Committee, and the National Maritime Union, to each of which the AFL committee conceded a virtually unqualified industrial union status. The committee also agreed that industrial unionism should prevail in the cement, aluminum, flat glass, and agricultural and food-processing industries. Notwithstanding these and other indications of progress, there were a number of extremely serious jurisdictional problems which had not been resolved by November 29. Perhaps the most

[46]"Just What Was What in the CIO-AFL Unity Negotiations, Statements by the Participants," *Advance,* Vol. 24, February 1938, pp. 16–17. For Dubinsky's opinion, see *Justice,* Vol. 20, Jan. 1, 1938, p. 16. Fremming did not publicly reveal his position. As previously indicated, Hillman supported the Lewis-Murray interpretation, but it must be remembered that he did not attend the conference after its first session.

troublesome of these involved the Carpenters and the International Woodworkers of America, and the IBEW and the UERMWA (whose title now read "United Electrical, Radio, and Machine Workers of America"). Also although the AFL committee was willing to grant the SWOC uncontested jurisdiction in steel production mills, it declined to extend the grant to steel fabricating plants. The Oil Workers' jurisdiction was challenged by four metal-trades unions, and the Industrial Union of Marine and Shipbuilding Workers also had serious membership conflicts with several AFL unions.[47]

Without minimizing the gravity of the jurisdictional problems not resolved by November 29, it is logical to believe that the switch to smaller committees which took place about November 29 was a reflection of the progress that had been made and an indication of some confidence that an early reunion of labor's ranks might be achieved.[48] It is also logical to assume that the full AFL committee had amended its original proposal so as to permit the CIO unions to enter (or reenter as the case might be) the AFL in a body after all jurisdictional disputes were settled. In the absence of such an amendment it is difficult to believe that the peace talks would have continued so long after their October inaugural and that subcommittees would have begun to function. Although it does not seem plausible that the full CIO committee formally accepted the new AFL plan, the plan did narrow the differences

[47]A complete resume of the AFL committee's suggestions regarding the settlement of jurisdictional issues was prepared by Murray and submitted to the conference on November 29. The document contains thirty-four entries, each of which deals with a separate CIO union or with an industry. See "Copy of Memorandum presented by Philip Murray, Chairman C. I. O. Committee, to Special Committee A. F. of L. while in conference November 29, 1937," CIO #2, AFL-CIO Archives. See also "Just What Was What in the CIO-AFL Unity Negotiations, Statements by the Participants," *Advance*, Vol. 24, February 1938, pp. 16–17.

[48]Tobin and Duffy became alarmed when the "super" committees, as they called them, were set up, and they wired Green posthaste as follows: "Noticing that entire committee now is composed of Green, Harrison, Lewis, and Murray, we are anxious that no promises or commitments of any kind be made until Executive Council is informed of everything transpiring. International Brotherhood of Teamsters and United Brotherhood of Carpenters...will not be bound by any promises made in behalf of said organizations until they are fully consulted and have given their consent. Frank Duffy present here listening to dictation of this telegram." Tobin to Green, Dec. 1, 1937, CIO #2, *ibid.* As will be noted shortly, Green had already, on November 29, sent the Council members notices of a special meeting.

between the two organizations, so conspicuous in their opening proposals.

Moreover, in the course of the three meetings which the subcommittees held, the CIO also made a significant concession. Lewis and Murray agreed to drop the CIO demand for an autonomous department with exclusive authority over organizing in mass-production and other industries—certainly the most unreasonable aspect of the CIO's original proposition.[49] Since both sides probably were agreed that the CIO unions should join the AFL at one time, the only remaining obstacle so far as procedure is concerned was whether membership conflicts should be settled before or after the merger. On the surface this might appear to have been no obstacle at all, and one might easily conclude that the CIO's rejection of the AFL formula was therefore a confession of hypocrisy and a sign that some CIO leaders, especially Lewis, rated personal ambition, prestige, and the emoluments of office above a united labor movement.[50] In reality, however, the obstacle was a most important one for both sides. By backing its formula and opposing that of the CIO, the AFL purposed to force a solution, favorable to itself, of the several extremely serious jurisdictional conflicts. It was determined, for example, to secure, as a condition precedent to the chartering of any CIO unions, the dissolution of the IWA and the UERMWA and the inclusion of their memberships in the ranks of the Carpenters and the IBEW.[51] Thus the AFL hoped that its

[49]Unsigned, untitled, and undated four-page typewritten statement, CIO #2, *ibid.* The statement reads as though it were written by Green. See also *Official Magazine* (of the Teamsters), Vol. 35, January 1938, p. 10.

[50]This was the interpretation placed on the CIO's action by the AFL committee and by individual AFL leaders and unions. Labor historians have come to similar conclusions. Thus Harris has stated: "In labor circles the consensus of informed opinion, even among certain CIO leaders, is that Lewis himself was primarily responsible for breaking off the 1937 negotiations, and that in doing so he missed the opportunity of a lifetime." Harris, *Labor's Civil War*, p. 228. Matthew Josephson has charged that Lewis "was less than serious about reunion with the AFL." Josephson, *Sidney Hillman*, p. 429. Joel Seidman only recently remarked that the "CIO's rejection of the compromise offer, in advance of specific negotiations on jurisdiction [but of course such negotiations did take place before the conference rupture], suggests that union structure was now secondary to considerations of office, power, and prestige in the eyes of some leaders." Seidman, "Efforts Toward Merger, 1935–1955," *Industrial and Labor Relations Review*, Vol. 9, April 1956, p. 358.

[51]Green very definitely promised Hutcheson that no agreement would be made which did not provide for the return of the loggers and lumbermen (who had left the Carpenters and formed the IWA) to the Carpenters and for the absorption of

plan would press the CIO to sacrifice some of its larger affiliates in order that those remaining could gain entry into the AFL. On the other hand, by deferring jurisdictional conferences until after each CIO union had received an AFL charter and by stipulating that unresolved conflicts should not result in the suspension of any CIO unions, the CIO sought to guarantee the continued existence of certain of its unions.

It is especially relevant at this point to indicate that the agreement which produced the merger of the AFL and CIO in 1955 was a vindication of the position taken by the CIO in 1937. In accordance with the terms of the 1955 concord, each one of the CIO unions was to be permitted to join the AFL-CIO and thereafter the merger of dual unions was to be encouraged (but not required). The agreement therefore explicitly recognized dualism as a legitimate and possibly permanent condition within the merged labor movement. Nor was this all. The 1955 merger agreement provided for the creation of an autonomous Industrial Union Department with the old CIO unions as its core (but with no organizing power such as the CIO had demanded for such a department in October 1937).[52] Since during the 1937 negotiations the CIO finally withdrew its demand for a department, it appears that in so far as the two matters just discussed are concerned, a settlement on the CIO's terms in 1937 would have been more favorable to the AFL than was the 1955 accord. In any case it seems unjustifiable to label the CIO of 1937 as insincere about unity when the very terms it proposed then became the basis for unity eighteen years later—an event universally applauded as an exhibition of labor statesmenship. As for the AFL, it was not yet ready in 1937 to put its stamp of approval on dualism. As soon as the talks moved into the subcommittee stage, Green convoked a special meeting of the Execu-

the UERMWA by the IBEW. Green to Hutcheson, Nov. 12, 1937, CIO #2, AFL-CIO Archives. Frey was firmly opposed to any settlement with the CIO which did not "preclude the existence of dual International Unions within the A. F. of L." "Memorandum on Essential Conditions for Unity," submitted by Frey to Green on Oct. 21, 1937, CIO #2, AFL-CIO Archives. For evidence as to the date and the authorship of this memorandum, see Frey to Green, Dec. 13, 1937, CIO #2, *ibid.*

[52]"AFL-CIO Merger Agreement" [a reproduction of the document itself], *Industrial and Labor Relations Review*, Vol. 9, October 1955, pp. 122–123.

tive Council, and on December 3 and 4 the Council considered and finally rejected the CIO offer.[53]

A reluctance to tolerate dualism may, in itself, explain the AFL's contribution to the conference breakdown, but there were additional matters of a non-jurisdictional and non-organizational nature which likely influenced the AFL decision. The CIO had by this time demonstrated a much greater interest in political action than the AFL had shown, and moreover, a few CIO unions had fallen prey to Communist leadership. Even before the peace talks had begun, John P. Frey charged, in a memorandum for internal AFL consumption, that members of the Central Executive Committee of the Communist party were working "actively" with the CIO and that a unity agreement would have to provide for the removal from CIO unions of all known Communists. "There is," he added, "another angle to the problem which must not be overlooked. The C. I. O. has definitely entered the political field and if it were re-united with the A. F. of L. [it] would probably endeavor to force a political commitment." At bottom, however, Frey did not want unity because he felt that the AFL was besting the CIO and that Lewis, shrewdly and with malice aforethought, had devised the peace conference for the sole purpose of unloading the CIO on the AFL and "then charging the A. F. of L. with incompetency."[54]

On December 13, just eight days before the peace talks officially ended, Frey sent Green, Woll, Bugniazet, and Harrison a "strictly confidential" letter in which he again analyzed the CIO's internal situation and concluded that nothing had happened since he filed the October memorandum "which would lead me to in any way modify the views I expressed in the memorandum." The content of this letter surely indicates that Frey, at least, was disturbed, not by any lack of desire on Lewis' part to return to the AFL but, on the contrary, by his excessive desire to return. The letter also

[53]Green to members of the Executive Council, Nov. 29, 1937, PCB #24, Book 596, NYSSILR Library; *Official Magazine* (of the Teamsters), Vol. 35, January 1938, p. 10. It is also a possibility, remote or real, that the Council disapproved the AFL committee's concessions to individual CIO unions.

[54]"Memorandum on Essential Conditions for Unity," submitted by Frey to Green on Oct. 21, 1937, CIO #2, AFL-CIO Archives.

encourages the assumption that even after the Executive Council meeting of December 3–4 some AFL leaders favored the continuation of talks with CIO spokesmen:

Since the first meeting of the two committees [Frey began] there have been certain changes taking place within the C. I. O. itself which lead me to feel justified in again submitting for your consideration and possible assistance, facts and opinions which may be helpful in protecting the interests of the legitimate trade union movement.

Immediately upon returning to Washington December 6th [after attending the Council meeting?], I sought out certain sources of information which I had found in the past to be reliable, so that I might have some knowledge of what had been taking place within the C. I. O.

From the information I secured, which I have every reason to believe is reliable, it appears that the internal situation in the C. I. O., and John L. Lewis' position in that organization, has become much more serious.

Aside from the leading personalities in the C. I. O., between [sic] whom there has been developing increasing personal friction, there appears to be a financial condition making it impossible to continue financing the C. I. O. program as it has been carried out during the year; an impossibility of prevailing upon the great majority of newly organized within the C. I. O. to pay dues; a growing difference of opinion as to what the political policy of the C. I. O. should be; and a growing dread of the stronger and stronger hold within the C. I. O. which is being secured by the Communist Party as a part of its program in the United States.

* * *

Apparently Lewis is aware of the desperate situation in which the C. I. O. now finds itself, and is concerned in finding some policy which would enable him to save his face and maintain his prestige in the trade union movement, and as a political influence in the country.

I am of the opinion that because of conditions referred to in this memorandum, John L. Lewis will use his skill and make every effort to create a situation through propositions made to the A. F. of L. Committee, the purpose of which would not be so much unity within the A. F. of L. as saving his own face, and placing himself in a position where he could unload many of his present problems upon the A. F. of L.

265

Unquestionably the C. I. O. is much weaker internally than it was a few months ago. Its feeling of confidence early this year has been replaced by one of grave doubt . . . [The AFL, on the other hand, had regained its confidence and this] confidence is our great strength. . . . I am thoroughly convinced that any agreement with the C. I. O. reached by the representatives of the A. F. of L. which weakened this confidence or opened the way for internal dissensions within the A. F. of L. would do far more damage than good.[55]

To a degree, Frey's thoughts may have been an expression of wishful thinking, but the information he gathered does strongly intimate that Lewis was not unwilling even in December to make peace with the AFL. Frey's information cannot, of course, be accepted as proof that Lewis was so motivated. Evidence from the CIO side, and preferably from Lewis himself, is needed before definite conclusions can be drawn.

There is some evidence from CIO files to indicate that due to the recession of 1937, the CIO was, as Frey had been informed, faced with a financial problem. In December the CIO requested its regional offices to eliminate all but the most necessary expenditures.[56] Replying to a request for organizers, Walter Smethurst, executive assistant to John L. Lewis, explained that "it is necessary for us to bide our time until we can get a break in this recession and an upswing at which time it . . . [will be our intention] to again expand our organizational activities."[57] There is still no proof here, however, that the financial problem was severe enough to encourage, and that it did in fact encourage, Lewis to seek unity with the AFL.

The readily accessible evidence relative to the 1937 unity talks is not, therefore, conclusive concerning either the depth of detail reached, the point or points which induced failure, or the allocation of responsibility for failure. It is doubtful, however, that Lewis alone, or the CIO alone, forced the conference rupture, as

[55]Frey to Green, Woll, Bugniazet, and Harrison, Dec. 13, 1937, CIO #2, *ibid.*

[56]Harry Bridges (president of the International Longshoremen's and Warehousemen's Union) to Walter Smethurst, Dec. 18, 1937, Ms., Files of the Congress of Industrial Organizations.

[57]Smethurst to Miles Sweeney (a CIO regional director), Feb. 3, 1938, *ibid.* As late as September 1938 the CIO was unable to compete with the AFL in the number of organizers it could put in the field. Smethurst to William Dalrymple (SWOC field director in California), Sept. 1, 1938, *ibid.*

the AFL has charged and others have believed. Risking a conclusion based on evidence primarily from the AFL side, it would seem that the CIO was equally, if not more, desirous of unity than was the AFL. On one point, however, the record is rather convincing—by 1937 craft versus industrial unionism no longer totally eclipsed all other issues as a barrier to peace and unity in the labor movement. Indeed it should be emphasized that as soon as the AFL revamped its structural outlook at Cincinnati, unity became a more feasible goal, and immediately the CIO (taking the initiative itself) entertained returning to the AFL. That a merger was not effected in 1937 is explained primarily, it would seem, by the existence of several difficult jurisdictional problems (which were not, to be sure, entirely bereft of structural significance) and the AFL's opposition to dualism. Failure was also a reflection of the fact that the differences between the AFL and the CIO extended beyond organizational matters and included, for example, communism and political action.[58] The full breadth of the labor conflict of the 1930's is set forth in the following chapter.

IV

Following the failure of the conference, events moved rapidly toward a definitive break between the AFL and the CIO. The AFL, proclaiming that it was now time to "meet the challenge of the C. I. O. in a militant, determined and uncompromising way," terminated the services of an additional thirty-eight pro-CIO organizers, began systematically to purge its state and city bodies of CIO influence, and between February and May 1938 revoked the charters of all the suspended unions with the exception of the ILGWU.[59] While expelling the Federation of Flat Glass Workers, the AFL also organized and chartered a rival National Flat Glass

[58]It is to be noted that by 1955, when merger was finally consummated, the CIO had ousted its allegedly Communist-dominated unions and that the AFL had copied the CIO's political program. Thus in 1955 these two matters were not the impediments to merger that they probably were in 1937. The political interests of the CIO are discussed in some detail in the following chapter.

[59]Green to National and International Unions, State Federations of Labor, City Central Bodies, and Directly Affiliated Unions, Dec. 29, 1937, CIO #2, AFL-CIO Archives; Green to AFL Organizers, Jan. 24, Feb. 23, 1938, PCB #25, Books 599, 601, NYSSILR Library; Green to Presidents of Nationals and Internationals with Locals in Pennsylvania, Feb. 28, 1938, PCB #25, Book 602, NYSSILR Library; AFL, *Proceedings, 1938*, pp. 102–103.

Workers Union.[60] In a necessary but incidental legal move, Green resigned from the UMW.[61] He had since late 1936 successfully evaded UMW efforts to try him on charges of conspiracy to suspend the UMW and promoting a dual union (PMA) in the coal fields.[62]

During a two-day conference in April 1938 the CIO decided that in the immediate future it would call a convention of its affiliated unions in order to form a permanent federation of labor. Julius Hochman, representing the ILGWU at the conference, abstained from voting on this decision, and his action aroused suspicion within the CIO that the ILGWU was ready to leave the organization. From the very beginning the ILGWU had not supported the CIO in an unqualified way, and when in 1937 some of its knit-goods' members in Cleveland began to join AFL federal unions, the ILGWU lent its eager support to a rapprochement with the AFL. The peace talks having failed, Dubinsky broke publicly with the other CIO leaders, and according to Woll, was only awaiting "some provocation upon the part of the leaders of the C. I. O." as an excuse to rejoin the AFL. Nevertheless, in April 1937 Dubinsky gave his assurances that the ILGWU had no plans at that time for withdrawing from the CIO.[63] Howard, on the other hand, declared that the ITU had always been intent only upon reforming the AFL from within and that although the establishment of the CIO as a rival federation was inevitable, he would not

[60]The new AFL union was directed by Glen McCabe who had been president of the Federation of Flat Glass Workers. Green to McCabe, Jan. 22, 1938, PCB #25, Book 599, NYSSILR Library; Green to Harvey Brannon (president of a local union of the new NFGWU), June 2, 1938, PCB #26, Book 609, *ibid.*

[61]AFL, Information and Publicity Service, Feb. 11, 1938, CIO #2, AFL-CIO Archives.

[62]For further information on this subject, see "President Green Summoned Before International Board," *United Mine Workers' Journal*, Vol. 47, Nov. 15, 1936, p. 4; "Board Members Resent Green's Slap at Their Integrity," *ibid.*, Vol. 47, Dec. 1, 1936, pp. 3–4; "William Green is Ousted from the Union by the Board," *ibid.*, Vol. 49, June 1, 1938, p. 5; UMW, *Proceedings, 1938*, pp. 69–71, 413; Green to Lewis, Nov. 19, 1936, PCB #22, Book 569, NYSSILR Library; Frank Morrison to All Organized Labor, Feb. 25, 1937, PCB #23, Book 575. NYSSILR Library.

[63]Dubinsky to Green, June 9, 1937, CIO #2, AFL-CIO Archives; Green to Dubinsky, June 14, 1937, CIO #2, *ibid.*; Green to Dubinsky, June 18, 1937, PCB #23, Book 584, NYSSILR Library; *Justice*, Vol. 20, Jan. 1, 1938, pp. 16–17; Woll to Green, Dec. 29, 1937, CIO #2, AFL-CIO Archives; "C. I. O. Leaders Decide to Set Up Permanent Organization," *United Mine Workers' Journal*, Vol. 49, May 1, 1938, p. 3.

ask his union to leave the AFL and join the CIO. In May Howard was defeated for reelection to the office of ITU president, partly because of his profound sympathy for the CIO, and in July he died, never witnessing the founding of the Congress of Industrial Organizations.[64]

In October Lewis issued the call for a convention to meet in Pittsburgh on November 14, 1938.[65] Thirty-four national and international unions, 8 organizing committees, 23 state councils, 116 city and county councils, and 137 directly affiliated local industrial unions responded to the convention call.[66] The general executive board of the ILGWU, however, voted unanimously against participating in the convention; in 1940 the ILGWU reaffiliated with the AFL.[67]

The delegates to the Pittsburgh convention adopted a constitution which designated the new labor federation the "Congress of Industrial Organizations" and elected the following slate of officers: John L. Lewis, president; Philip Murray and Sidney Hillman, vice-presidents; and James Carey, secretary. An Executive Board composed of one representative from each affiliated national union, international union, and organizing committee was also created as the inter-convention governing body.[68] After five days of deliberation the Congress of Industrial Organizations was successfully launched—the climax of almost four decades of structural conflict within the labor movement.[69]

[64]*Typographical Journal*, Vol. 92, May 1938, pp. 548–550; ITU, *Proceedings, 1938*, p. 8; Green to Hutcheson, June 8, 1938, CIO #2, AFL-CIO Archives.

[65]For the full text of the convention call, see "CIO to Hold Convention to Form Permanent Organization," *United Mine Workers' Journal*, Vol. 49, Oct. 15, 1938, p. 6.

[66]John L. Lewis reported a total CIO membership of 3,787,877. CIO, *Proceedings, 1938*, pp. 36–37.

[67]ILGWU, *Position of the International Ladies' Garment Workers' Union in Relation to CIO and AFL*, pp. 77–78; ILGWU, *Proceedings, 1940*, pp. 450–453.

[68]CIO, *Proceedings, 1938*, pp. 15–26, 36–37, 132–154, 264–275.

[69]Little more than a month after the founding convention, a split occurred in the ranks of the UTW. Part of its membership, including President Francis J. Gorman (McMahon had resigned in January 1937 to become Director of Labor in Rhode Island), returned to the AFL, taking with it the title of the organization. The CIO textile workers then adopted the new title of "Textile Workers Union of America." "Minutes of the 1938 Biennial Convention of the UTW" reported in UTW (AFL), *Proceedings, 1939*, p. 7.

CHAPTER X

The Breadth of Conflict

ORGANIZING the unorganized into industrial unions was the outstanding plank in the progressive labor platform of the 1930's. So important was this plank that without it a rival house of labor neither would nor could have been built. Yet, as intimated, there were other planks in the progressive program which, in combination with the organizational and structural one, pointed to a rather thorough reformation of labor's traditional outlook.

It is thus possible to explain the progressive movement as a broad, more or less formalized, and certainly well articulated, reform program. On the other hand, the movement was to a certain extent, and especially in its later years, also a power struggle. Whether the movement's objective be considered to have been primarily reform or primarily power, one finds among its supporting unions and personalities motives both selfish and altruistic. It is the purpose of this chapter first to indicate the nonstructural planks in the reform program of the 1930's; second, to render an opinion on the reform versus power question and to point out some of the selfish and selfless motives peculiar to some of the leaders and unions of the progressive movement. The writer does not pretend, however, that his discussion of the very complex problem of the scope and motivation of the progressive movement is at all points either definitive or incontrovertible; a more thorough treatment of the matter must await a more comprehensive study of the early years of the CIO, particularly with regard to its financial and organizing history.

I

Foremost among the nonstructural planks of the labor reform program of the thirties was the demand that AFL conservatives make a definitive break with antistatism and champion a comprehensive legislative platform. Although, as already recounted, the AFL was on record by the early 1930's as favoring unemployment and old-age insurance, there was a feeling among some union leaders that the Executive Council was making too little effort toward the legislative fulfillment of these goals and that labor ought also to broaden its social reform program to include the provision at the federal level of sickness, disability, and maternity benefit programs. Many urgent appeals along this line were directed to the AFL in 1934.[1] Former Secretary of Labor Perkins has recalled that in 1934 when her Department began to hammer out a federal social security measure it was "something of a problem to secure the wholehearted support of the A. F. of L., which held fast to the old Gompers' position that every gain made by working people should be won in collective bargaining."[2] Green, who surely reflected Council opinion on the matter, was still fearful lest government aid to working people cause them to desert the labor unions to which they had traditionally looked for protection. He asked Frey, who planned a trip to England in the fall of 1933, to try to bring back an answer to the question "as to whether unemployment insurance and relief measures employed by the State have retarded or accelerated the growth of Trade-Unionism." An answer based on British experience would, he thought, "help us . . . to understand the real effect that social justice legislation might have upon the future growth and development of our Trade-Union movement in the United States."[3]

The AFL does not seem to have played a vital, leading role in this country's adoption of a social security program in 1935,[4] for

[1] AFT, *Proceedings, 1934*, p. 127; UTW, *Proceedings, 1934*, pp. 44–45; AFL, *Proceedings, 1934*, pp. 598–608. Ten resolutions advocating AFL support for social insurance measures were introduced into the San Francisco convention. Among the introducers were the ILGWU, AFT, Hotel and Restaurant Employees, and the Amalgamated Association of Iron, Steel and Tin Workers.

[2] Perkins, *The Roosevelt I Knew*, p. 288.

[3] Green to Frey, Oct. 24, 1933, PCB #13, Book 472, NYSSILR Library.

[4] See Boxes 52–56, Andrews Papers, NYSSILR Library.

although the organization endorsed the Social Security Act, it was anxious lest the act might "vitally affect" the benefit programs long maintained by some of its affiliates.[5] The Committee for Industrial Organization, on the other hand, considered itself more aware of and more responsive to the broader social needs of the workers than the AFL and announced in October 1937 that it favored "a complete health program" at the federal level, a vast increase in the coverage of the Social Security Act, and the encouragement of low-cost federal housing projects.[6]

With regard to a minimum-wage law, both Hillman and Dubinsky resented the AFL's opposition to the inclusion of a minimum-wage provision in the Black Thirty-Hour bill (1933). First denying the validity of the AFL's argument that a minimum wage tended to reduce the income of the skilled worker, Dubinsky added that he wanted "the unskilled worker, who has been exploited most, [to] get protection, *particularly when he is not organized.*"[7] When the AFL objected to the Fair Labor Standards bill in 1937 on the ground that the minimum wage was too low,[8] the CIO charged that the AFL had joined hands with sweat-shop politicians to kill the bill.[9] The AFL supported the bill in 1938, but the CIO's approval of it has been described as more enthusiastic and forthright,[10] and President Roosevelt gave Hillman much credit for the bill's enactment.[11]

To further the accomplishment of broad legislative aims, the progressives placed much emphasis upon political action and the need for elevating its importance in the labor movement. Between 1933 and 1936 an independent labor party was urged upon the American Federation of Labor by the ILGWU, UTW, ACW,

---

[5]AFL, *Proceedings, 1935,* p. 493.

[6]CIO, *Program of the C. I. O.,* pp. 12–14.

[7]United States Congress, Senate, Committee on Finance, *Investigation of Economic Problems, Hearings before the Committee on Finance Pursuant to S. Res. 315,* 72 Cong., 2 Sess., p. 875; ILGWU, *Proceedings, 1934,* p. 395, italics added.

[8]AFL, *Proceedings, 1937,* pp. 164–167.

[9]"A. F. of L., Sweat Shops and Slave Drivers Kill Wages-Hours Bill," *United Mine Workers' Journal,* Vol. 49, Jan. 1, 1938, p. 15; "C. I. O. Leaders Decide to Set Up Permanent Organization," *ibid.,* Vol. 49, May 1, 1938, p. 4.

[10]George Gilmary Higgins, *Voluntarism in Organized Labor in the United States, 1930–1940,* p. 116.

[11]Josephson, *Sidney Hillman,* p. 447.

UAW, Amalgamated Association of Iron, Steel and Tin Workers, Teachers, and the Hatters, Cap and Millinery Workers. In 1932 the UMW turned down a third-party resolution but declared itself in favor of "a more cohesive political movement on the part of organized labor." In 1934 the union instructed its delegates to the AFL convention to vote on the labor party issue "as they deem advisable." Eighteen resolutions favoring a labor party were introduced into the 1936 convention of the UMW, but the union finally endorsed the re-election of Franklin D. Roosevelt. Labor party resolutions were also defeated at the AFL's conventions of 1933, 1934, and 1935.[12]

On April 2, 1936, just a few months after the establishment of the Committee for Industrial Organization, the CIO executive officers announced the formation of Labor's Non-Partisan League as an agency for the coordinated expression of the CIO's political program.[13] In July of the same year, the American Labor party was founded in New York by the ILGWU, ACW, and the Hatters, Cap and Millinery Workers as a state affiliate of Labor's Non-Partisan League.[14] There was strong sentiment in the ILGWU, ACW, and UTW for using the American Labor party or Labor's Non-Partisan League as the base upon which to erect a national labor party, but the Congress of Industrial Organizations finally indicated in 1938 that Labor's Non-Partisan League would continue to function within the existing political framework and would adequately afford to organized labor the opportunity to participate

[12]ILGWU, *Proceedings, 1934,* pp. 167–169; Joseph Schlossberg, "An Object Lesson," *Advance,* Vol. 20, March 1934, p. 19; "The A. F. of L. in Convention," *Advance,* Vol. 20, October 1934, p. 3; UTW, *Proceedings, 1934,* p. 34; *Textile Worker,* Vol. 1, Oct. 19, 1935, p. 4; UAW, *Proceedings, 1936,* p. 162; Amalgamated Association of Iron, Steel and Tin Workers, *Proceedings, 1933,* p. 2042; "Convention Summary," *American Teacher,* Vol. 20, September–October 1935, p. 34; UMW, *Proceedings, 1932,* p. 453, *1934,* pp. 350–356, *1936,* pp. 214–216; AFL, *Proceedings, 1933,* pp. 452–453, *1934,* pp. 556–557, *1935,* pp. 293, 758–776. The Hotel and Restaurant Employees, which was not identified with the industrial union bloc, also favored a labor party. AFL, *Proceedings, 1934,* p. 556, *1935,* p. 202.

[13]ACW, *Proceedings, 1934,* p. 65; Josephson, *Sidney Hillman,* pp. 394–395.

[14]ILGWU, *Proceedings, 1937,* pp. 7, 189; ACW, *Proceedings, 1938,* pp. 68–69; "American Labor Party Launched in New York State," *Advance,* Vol. 22, August 1936, p. 14. Upon the establishment of the American Labor party Dubinsky resigned from the Socialist party, to which he had belonged for many years. Shannon, *The Socialist Party of America,* p. 256.

vigorously in the political life of the nation.[15] In 1943 Labor's Non-Partisan League was replaced by the Political Action Committee which, until the labor merger in 1955, served as the political wing of the CIO.[16]

A few of the less tradition-bound and more liberal-minded AFL leaders, such as George Berry and George Meany (then president of the New York State Federation of Labor) supported Labor's Non-Partisan League and the ALP,[17] but officially the AFL disapproved of this new political machinery. When LNPL was but three weeks old, Green spread the word that LNPL was a deviation from the time-honored nonpartisan policy. He counseled labor to "avoid division even in the pursuit of its political policies" and to maintain, therefore, a "strict and close" adherence to nonpartisanship.[18] Berry, a founder of LNPL, asked Green to become a member of the organization but Green politely declined saying that he intended "in the future as in the past to subscribe to the nonpartisan political policy of the American Federation of Labor."[19]

In 1937 when Berry left the League to become a United States Senator from Tennessee and John L. Lewis became the League's chairman, its AFL supporters began to dwindle. In the fall of that year LNPL nominated a few CIO leaders for local public office. According to Green, AFL unionists bitterly opposed the CIO candidacies, and the local elections "became a vital factor in the struggle between the Federation and the CIO." The following spring the AFL exhorted its subordinate bodies to stop providing membership and financial support to LNPL.[20]

Within a decade, however, the AFL had followed CIO prece-

[15]ILGWU, *Proceedings, 1937,* pp. 319–323; ACW, *Proceedings, 1938,* p. 73; UTW, *Proceedings, 1936,* pp. 28, 51–52, 54–55; CIO, *Proceedings, 1938,* pp. 230–231.

[16]For an account of the establishment of the PAC, see Joseph Gaer, *First Round.*

[17]See "American Labor Party Launched in New York State," *Advance,* Vol. 22, August 1936, p. 14; Josephson, *Sidney Hillman,* pp. 394–395, 400.

[18]Green to All Affiliated Organizations, April 23, 1936, PCB #21, Book 556, NYSSILR Library.

[19]Green to Berry, April 27, 1936, PCB #21, Book 556, *ibid.*

[20]Green to the Officers of National and International Unions, State Federations of Labor, and City Central Labor Unions, March 21, 1938, PCB #25, Book 603, *ibid.* Green did not ask the national and international unions to stop supporting LNPL, but such a request was implicit in the mere fact that he sent them the letter.

dent and had set up Labor's League for Political Education.[21] Agreement on the political-action front helped smooth the road to merger in 1955, which led, in turn, to the erection of the Committee on Political Education as the political voice of the united labor movement. These various political committees and leagues of the post-New Deal period admittedly have not amended the basic, nonpartisan nature of labor's political action. Yet it would be erroneous to assume that labor's political action of the pre-New Deal and post-New Deal periods has been identical. For the last twenty years (ten in the case of the AFL) labor has maintained permanent (rather than temporary, election-year) political machinery and has committed a far greater proportion of its time, personnel, and money to politics than it formerly did.

Discrimination against Negro workers, still practised by a sizeable number of AFL unions, also served to alienate some of the labor progressives of the 1930's. Between 1932 and 1936 the UMW, ILGWU, and the AFT joined with the Sleeping Car Porters in demanding that the AFL take positive action toward eliminating anti-Negro practices (whether based on custom or constitutional and ritual clauses) in the labor movement.[22]

The San Francisco convention authorized Green to appoint a five-member committee to investigate thoroughly the status of the Negro in the labor movement and to report its findings and policy recommendations to the Atlantic City convention. The committee, of which John Brophy was a member, made an extensive study and then filed with the Council a majority report (signed by four members including Brophy) and a minority report. The majority report suggested that all AFL unions barring or otherwise discriminating against Negroes should immediately undertake to conform to the AFL's often-announced policy of equalitarianism, that the AFL should henceforth refuse to charter discriminatory unions, and that the AFL should conduct a continuing educational

[21]John L. Lewis, who had brought his miners back into the AFL in 1946 and had taken a seat on the Executive Council, was partly responsible for the AFL's decision to establish LLPE. See *Report of the General Executive Board* [of the ILGWU] *to the 29th Convention, 1956,* p. 33.

[22]UMW, *Proceedings, 1932,* pp. 405–406, *1936,* pp. 218–219; ILGWU, *Proceedings, 1934,* p. 166; AFL, *Proceedings, 1934,* pp. 325–326, 330–334.

campaign on the subject of race discrimination. Rather than submit both reports to the Atlantic City convention, the Council turned the matter over to George Harrison who, in the spirit of the minority report, concluded that while a few nationals excluded colored workers, they had the right, as autonomous affiliates, to do so and the AFL could resort only to education to remedy the situation.[23] Brophy believed that the "maneuvering" of the Council was evidence that it had from the start looked upon the investigation as a face-saving device for the AFL rather than "an honest attempt to find a solution of the Negro Problem in the American labor movement."[24]

The Executive Council also declined in 1935 to endorse the Negro Labor Committee which had been formed by representatives of 110 New York City unions in July 1935 to fight discrimination against Negroes in the labor movement and to act as the rallying center for organizing Negroes into AFL unions.[25]

The Congress of Industrial Organizations declared in its constitution, adopted in 1938, that its first objective was "to bring about the effective organization of the working men and women of America regardless of race, creed, color, or nationality."[26] Commenting on this provision, the CIO explained that many of the "old-line craft unions" discriminated against Negroes and "failed to do anything for women workers and young people." The aim of the CIO was "to organize all workers, Negro or white, skilled or unskilled, men or women, American or foreign-born."[27] The CIO also organized a National Committee to Abolish Racial Discrimination, which by the end of 1944 had eighty-five local branches.[28] On the other hand, eighteen AFL unions in 1945 still excluded Negroes or treated them unequally. Since that date, however, considerable progress has been registered by these unions in providing equal treatment for colored workers. By 1951 seven of the eighteen unions had removed all discriminatory clauses from their consti-

[23]AFL, *Proceedings, 1934*, pp. 330–334, *1935*, pp. 808–819.
[24]Brophy to Green, Nov. 6, 1935, PCB #20, Book 545, NYSSILR Library.
[25]*New York Times*, July 21, 1935; AFL, *Proceedings, 1935*, p. 827.
[26]CIO, *Proceedings, 1938*, p. 126.
[27]CIO, *The CIO, What It Is and How It Came to Be*, pp. 57–58.
[28]Robert Clifton Weaver, *Negro Labor, A National Problem*, p. 220.

tutions; five others had made such clauses inoperative in all states and cities having fair employment practices acts.[29]

Matthew Woll continued in the 1930's to serve as acting president of the National Civic Federation. Other labor leaders, however, were and had long been disturbed over the AFL-NCF entente, and finally at Atlantic City the UMW sponsored a resolution to the effect that "no officer of the American Federation of Labor shall act as an officer of the National Civic Federation, or be a member thereof." The move was obviously aimed at Matthew Woll. Upon learning of it, Woll sent a telegram to Ralph M. Easely insisting that his resignation as acting president be accepted. Woll informed the convention of his action and explained apologetically that he had been trying to resign the office for the past two years but that "on each occasion I was prevailed upon to continue for a while longer."[30] At the same convention the UMW introduced, and the delegates affirmed, a resolution which prohibited the *American Federationist* from accepting "advertisements or paid printing of any character from concerns which do not generally recognize and practice collective bargaining with legitimate organizations of labor," thus ending the purchase of space in that journal by company-union and open-shop employers.[31]

A reversal of an AFL policy long criticized by labor progressives was actually effected in 1934 when, at the instigation of the ILGWU, the AFL once again interested itself in the International Federation of Trade Unions and initiated the negotiations which led to reaffiliation in 1937. The ILGWU took the initiative in the matter because it believed that American labor ought to assist

[29]Lloyd H. Bailer, "Organized Labor and Racial Minorities," *Annals of the American Academy of Political and Social Science*, Vol. 241, March 1951, pp. 101–107. The Committee for Industrial Organization also took a special interest in the white-collar worker. See CIO, *The C. I. O. and the White Collar Worker*.

[30]Woll later seconded the motion to adopt the anti-NCF resolution. The resolution passed with no objections. AFL, *Proceedings, 1935*, pp. 439, 474–475, 794. Lewis is reported to have remarked with regard to this resolution that he was "sick of looking at newspapers on Monday morning and trying to find out whether Mr. Woll's statements were made in behalf of the National Civic Federation or the American Federation of Labor." Quoted in "Five Rounds," *Time*, Vol. 26, Oct. 28, 1935, p. 12. Throughout the 1920's and early 1930's the ILGWU had adopted anti-NCF resolutions. See ILGWU, *Proceedings, 1922*, pp. 115–116, *1924*, p. 238, *1925*, p. 153, *1932*, p. 194, *1934*, pp. 98, 320.

[31]AFL, *Proceedings, 1935*, pp. 793–794.

those democratic trade union movements in Europe which had not yet been crushed by the twin boots of Fascism and Nazism.[32] Interestingly enough, Matthew Woll represented the AFL in the reaffiliation negotiations.[33] He had kicked off the traces of isolationism and had begun to travel a generally broader road in the labor movement than he had traveled in many a year.

Evidently there was also some feeling in the CIO camp that the AFL had not done enough to combat racketeering in the labor movement.[34]

II

In the opinion of this writer the progressive labor movement of the 1930's was, until 1937, more a crusade to modernize the foundations of unionism than primarily a power struggle. This interpretation is certainly arguable, but not any more so, for example, than the proposition that the American Civil War was primarily a moral crusade against slavery rather than primarily an effort on the part of the industrial North to break the power of the agricultural South. The writer chooses to believe that great movements which advance the interests of an institution or a nation often have their origins in ideals, in man's ultimate sense of moral purpose; that these movements often necessarily involve a power struggle if ideals are to be carried into effect; and that the rewards which come to the crusaders are the inevitable and merited by-products of their success. This is not to say, therefore, that the progressive laborites of the 1930's did not covet positions of greater security, power, and status; indeed some of them saw such positions as ends in themselves. In fact it would appear that in 1937 the struggle as a whole became primarily a selfish one for power supremacy between two organizations that had attained a rough similarity in their ideals and principles.

[32]ILGWU, *Proceedings, 1934,* pp. 320–321; AFL, *Proceedings, 1934,* pp. 573–574, *1937,* pp. 195–197. The AFL began to participate in the affairs of the International Labor Organization in 1934, and the ILO was not therefore an issue between the progressives and conservatives. John L. Lewis was the first AFL representative at an ILO conference. AFL, *Proceedings, 1934,* p. 85.

[33]Green to Woll, May 27, 1937, PCB #23, Book 581, NYSSILR Library.

[34]See ILGWU, *Proceedings, 1934,* p. 409, *1940,* pp. 450–451, 456–457; AFL, *Proceedings, 1935,* p. 589.

Certain it seems, however, that prior to 1937 the basic impulse to conflict sprung from the progressives' desire, for the good of the labor movement and society at large, to rebuild and rededicate to new and grander purposes the cause of unionism. The establishment and growth of the CIO, as a Committee at least, are factors which can be explained primarily in terms of the desire of a few farsighted men to do more for American labor than some of the old-line leaders were able or willing to do. It is doubtful that the Committee would ever have taken a first breath had not Lewis, Hillman, Howard, Dubinsky, and Zaritsky felt an obligation to convert the temporary decline of organized labor into a speedy forward march along many paths. These five men were the statesmen architects of the CIO, for they had no expectation of a direct membership return or other direct reward for their own unions from the investment of their time and money in the mass-production industries. Even Lewis, who as will be noted later had exceptionally strong personal reasons for heading the progressive movement, gave fully of his own time and talent and of his union's money in that most celebrated cause of the CIO—organizing the unorganized wherever they were to be found.

As the great debate itself amply testifies, the progressives did not have the fixed intention, from the start, of launching a rival labor movement. Contrarily, they first tried to persuade other AFL leaders to support their cause. In addition, however, the progressives opened in 1932 a drive to place their representatives on the Executive Council where they would be in a position, it was surely hoped, to effectuate their reform ideas. Presumably, one can speak of the campaign to enlarge the Council as a bid for greater power on the part of the progressives.

The enlargement campaign was spearheaded by the UMW and the Typographers, and was actively supported by the ILGWU, UTW, and the Hotel and Restaurant Employees. Although many unions encouraged the campaign solely out of concern for making the Council more representative of the AFL's membership, the sponsors of the measure were quite distinctly motivated by the feeling that the Council, as constituted, was behind the times and too often remiss in its duties. They wanted to "pack" the Council, just

279

as Roosevelt later wanted to "pack" the Supreme Court. For example, in urging the 1932 convention to sanction an enlargement of the Council from eleven to twenty-eight members, John L. Lewis admitted that he was "one of those who is now dissatisfied . . . with some of the official acts of the Executive Council and with some of the failures of the Executive Council to act under certain circumstances." On the basis of allegations made by Daniel Tobin, it would seem that Lewis was also dissatisfied with William Green's leadership, was regretful of the fact that he had helped boost Green into the AFL presidency, and was hoping to place on the Council another UMW member who would speak vigorously for the progressive bloc.[35] Green knew only too well that he was one of Lewis's targets, for he opposed enlargement of the Council and voted for it only because the UMW's unit rule forced him to do so.[36] Frank X. Martel of the Typographers also scored the Council for not concerning itself "with those things that beset the trade-unionist and the worker of this country until after the thing is passed"; he charged that this policy was followed "because the Executive Council, instead of being an Executive Council, is a council of elders." Howard added that there was "too much harmony" in the American Federation of Labor and that the Council, if enlarged, would make wiser decisions than it had in the past.[37]

When the resolution to enlarge the Council was again considered at the 1933 convention, the supporting arguments were more tempered than in the previous year, although Thomas Kennedy of the UMW referred to a need for "new blood" and "more intelligence" on the Council and for a Council "that will be responsive to the will of the vast army of members in the American labor movement, a Council that will be constructive in every particular." Also, Howard acknowledged that new leadership was required if the problems confronting the labor movement were to be solved.[38] The proposed enlargement of the Council received only modest support in 1932 and 1933, but in 1934, after the progressives had

[35]Tobin made his allegations in 1933. He went so far as to charge that certain language in the enlargement resolution indicated that Lewis was actually scheming for the removal of Green from the Executive Council. AFL, *Proceedings, 1933*, p. 394.

[36]*Ibid.* This information also comes from Tobin.

[37]*Ibid., 1932*, pp. 425–437.   [38]*Ibid., 1933*, pp. 387–388, 392.

agreed to cut the number of new vice-presidencies from seventeen to seven (thus making a Council of eighteen members), the measure passed with little opposition. It passed primarily because it no longer posed such a major threat to the control of the conservatives. It was easy to find four stalwarts on the tory side (Daniel Tobin, William Hutcheson, Harry C. Bates of the Bricklayers, and Edward Gainor of the Letter Carriers) to offset the three leading progressives (John L. Lewis, David Dubinsky, and George Berry) who joined the Council.[39]

The enlargement campaign therefore fell short of its original numerical goal, and so far as the balance of power still lay with the conservatives the campaign can be interpreted as a failure. Despite the fact that the insurgents were still outnumbered on the Council they, however, counted on wielding influence in that body out of proportion to their numerical strength. When they failed to do so, and also lost the day at Atlantic City, they created a power center of their own—the Committee for Industrial Organization. The Committee, as founded, sought to accomplish its aims through education and persuasion. Later, however, as a consequence of the Council's attempt to mount a membership drive along craft lines in the steel industry, the Committee struck out on its own as an organizing body. Within a year thereafter, AFL loyalists recognized the need for industrial organizing—not, however, as a bid for the re-establishment of harmony but as preparation for civil war. Although at this point the parties still had some important ideological differences, the struggle became one largely for power in itself, for members, and for dues.

As suggested by Martel's "council of elders" comment, the progressives believed that they were fighting the battle of youth against age. By 1934 the Council enlargement drive had become popularly known as the annual "beard pulling" contest.[40] When the enlarged Council failed to measure up to his expectations, Dubinsky declared that the workers still wanted "younger blood" infused into the leadership veins of the AFL; younger leaders were progressive, older ones were conservative.[41] On the basis of a very small sample, it appears that the top progressives were about ten years

[39]*Ibid.*, *1934*, pp. 686–691.   [40]*Ibid.*, p. 658.
[41]UTW, *Proceedings*, *1936*, pp. 61–62.

younger than the top conservatives.[42] The age gap must surely have been much bigger as between the controlling leaders of the AFL and the officers of the many new national unions which eventually became affiliates of the CIO. Part of the attraction in joining the CIO was undoubtedly the greater opportunity for recognition which it offered to young leaders. Such leaders naturally preferred an early opportunity to test their leadership wings in the CIO rather than face the prospect of wilting on the vine of seniority in the AFL.

While until 1937 the progressives were engaged primarily in a reform movement and were jockeying for power with which to implement their reform notions, a great many individuals and unions in the progressive camp were interested partly, and in some cases largely, in grinding their own axes. In a general way, the entire CIO group stood to gain indirectly from the organizing of the unorganized—to the extent, at least, that organizing would be followed by increases in the purchasing power of the mass-production workers. But of course the non-CIO unions stood to share this gain. The same logic is applicable to a government program of unemployment compensation, old-age benefits, and minimum wages—with the qualification that the CIO unions and the unorganized needed these measures more than did the relatively better paid craftsmen who were so prominent among the conservatives.

The ACW and the ILGWU expected to profit from the expansion of unionism in the textile industry. The substandard wages in textiles tended to depress wages in the men's and women's clothing industries, especially in the South. These two unions, therefore, supplied most of the funds for the Textile Workers Organizing Committee in the hope that organizing would be followed by wage increases. The ACW alone reportedly spent more than a million dollars during two years of TWOC campaigning.[43] In a measure, the ACW and the ILGWU were making investments

---

[42]Thus in 1934 the average age of Dubinsky (42), Hillman (47), Lewis (54), and Howard (55) was 49.5 years, while the average for Woll (54), James Wilson (58), Tobin (59), Hutcheson (60), Wharton (61), and Frey (63) was 59.1 years.

[43]Josephson, *Sidney Hillman,* p. 418. The ACW and the ILGWU made original TWOC contributions of $500,000 and $112,000 respectively.

rather than donations. A minimum-wage law would raise wages particularly in the textile industry, and one can again see, therefore, why Hillman and Dubinsky exerted themselves so vigorously on behalf of such legislation. The UMW also gave bountiful sums to TWOC, but presumably with no hope of or desire for a substantial return of any kind.[44] It scarcely need be mentioned that the UTW stood first in line to receive the benefits of both TWOC organizing and a minimum-wage law.

A number of other unions which helped found or later joined the Committee for Industrial Organization did so because they had become involved in jurisdictional disputes with craft unions. Their action was forced, not initiatory, and was concerned more with their own protection than with reform. They wanted to help themselves, in terms either of retaining industrial jurisdictions they had already been granted or of acquiring industrial jurisdictions to which they believed they had rightful claim (because the crafts had never organized in the industries concerned). In other words, the industrial union movement of the 1930's was directed not alone at organizing the unorganized into new industrial unions; it was aimed also at protecting or adding to the jurisdictions of national unions that had been in existence for many years. Thus, during 1934–1935, the Mine, Mill and Smelter Workers, one of but two unions to which the AFL had explicitly granted full industrial jurisdiction, was attacked by thirteen craft unions. The Executive Council and the Atlantic City convention upheld the craft claims.[45] The Oil Workers, which grew very rapidly after 1933 and eagerly sought an industrial jurisdiction, reluctantly agreed in 1934 to surrender to the Boilermakers all employees in the petroleum industry who came within the Boilermakers' claimed jurisdiction.[46] Unfortunately for the Oil Workers, however, several more craft unions began to claim skilled oil workers. At the Atlantic City convention, ten unions affiliated with the Metal and Building Trades Departments charged that the Oil Field, Gas Well and Refinery Workers had invaded their juris-

[44]*Ibid.* The UMW's original contribution was $100,000.
[45]"Agreement, Anaconda Copper Mining Company," Container 1, Frey Papers; AFL, *Proceedings, 1935*, pp. 615–665; *New York Times*, May 4, 1935.
[46]AFL, *Proceedings, 1934*, p. 598.

dictions and demanded that the union either hand over to them all disputed members within thirty days or forfeit its charter. Reason prevailed in the Committee on Resolutions to the extent that the time limit was discarded, and in this revised form the resolution was referred to the Executive Council for further action.[47] One need scarcely look beyond this telling sequence of events for an explanation of why the Oil Workers became a charter member of the CIO.

The record, as detailed in previous chapters, clearly shows that the Amalgamated Association of Iron, Steel and Tin Workers, the UAW, and the URW were also unable, because of the invocation of craft claims, to establish themselves as industrial unions. It is extremely doubtful that Michael Tighe, at least, would ever have surrendered to Lewis in 1936 had the AFL granted the Amalgamated an industrial jurisdiction. A few AFL unions never joined the CIO, notwithstanding the fact that they had jurisdictional disputes with the crafts and that they gave their vote to the industrial bloc at Atlantic City.[48] The Brewery Workers, whose membership future looked bright indeed after the repeal of prohibition in 1933, also became involved in jurisdictional disputes with the crafts, but the union did not join the CIO until 1946—evidently because it believed until then that it would be worse off outside than within the AFL.[49]

It would seem, therefore, that some unions saw the CIO as a bastion for the direct and immediate protection of their own members. What these smaller, less powerful, and (in some cases) less experienced unions would have done had not Lewis, Hillman, and the others championed their cause and provided them refuge makes for interesting speculation. Perhaps they would

[47]*Ibid., 1935,* pp. 825–827.

[48]Two such unions were the Meat Cutters and the Pulp, Sulphite and Paper Mill Workers. The latter's jurisdiction was challenged by seven unions, especially the Carpenters. See PCB #15, Book 491, Document Numbers 473–478, Book 492, Document Numbers 131, 133, NYSSILR Library; A. W. Muir (Carpenters' representative) to Hutcheson, Oct. 3, 1935, Gust Anderson (Central Labor Union of Seattle, Washington) to Hutcheson, Nov. 5, 1935, John P. Burke (Pulp, Sulphite and Paper Mill Workers) to Green, Dec. 4, 1935, PCB #20, Book 546, *ibid.,* Green to Hutcheson, Dec. 17, 1935, PCB #20, Book 547, *ibid.,* Burke to Green, Feb. 20, 1936, PCB #20, Book 552, *ibid.*

[49]AFL, *Proceedings, 1933,* pp. 114–115, 317–353, *1934,* pp. 144–152, 446–459, *1935,* p. 684. See also "Organized Labor Movement, 1929 to 1937," *Monthly Labor Review,* Vol. 45, February 1937, p. 300.

eventually have fashioned their own CIO. Perhaps they would have survived as independent unions or as wards of the state. Perhaps jurisdictional disputes with craft unions would have destroyed or weakened them.

As a matter of fact, eleven craft unions tried, but of course failed, to amend the jurisdiction of the UMW, then the king and long the symbol of industrial unionism. The action of these craft unions probably bore no important relationship to the UMW's insurgency. Nevertheless the episode deserves telling, because it illustrates so well the extremity of craft action and the breadth of conflict over the structural question.

On June 28, 1935 Victor S. Gauthier, the grand lodge representative of the IAM, appeared before the House Committee on Ways and Means, which was considering the Snyder bill, the House version of what ultimately became the Bituminous Coal Conservation Act, and offered a long list of amendments to the bill which, he said, were intended to "guarantee the opportunity of self determination for any craft or class of workers, employed by the operators of bituminous-coal mines." Gauthier declared that such a guarantee was included in the Wagner Act and the Railway Labor Act and that failure to include it in the Snyder bill "may very well lead to the denial of the right of self-organization and collective bargaining to crafts or classes of employees not part of that group of employees who constitute the majority of workers employed by bituminous-coal operators."[50]

Practically the entire MTD and other unions as well were behind this legislative thrust at the UMW's long-recognized industrial jurisdiction, for when the House committee declined to accept the IAM's amendments, ten additional craft unions began to petition individual members of Congress to alter the bill. There were, they said, thirty-five thousand craftsmen and professional workers in the coal industry who were eligible, and ought to be allowed, to join unions other than the UMW.[51] Lewis has asserted that the AFL

[50]United States Congress, House, Committee on Ways and Means, *Stabilization of Bituminous Coal Mining Industry, Hearings before a Subcommittee of the Committee on Ways and Means on H. R. 8479,* 74 Cong., 1 Sess., pp. 563–564.

[51]This petition is reproduced in the "Minutes of Meeting of the [IAM] Executive Council from September 9 to 14, 1935," *Machinists' Monthly Journal,* Vol. 47, pp. 4–6 of an appendix. In addition to the IAM, the petitioning unions were: the

Executive Council also favored the IAM-sponsored amendments and that the Council called him to Washington and offered to endorse the proposed coal legislation if he would accept the amendments. Lewis rejected the offer and, according to his own account, he was then "summoned almost by subpoena" to attend a meeting of the Metal Trades Department officers and asked "to show cause why the United Mine Workers of America should not accept those amendments."[52]

The craft effort to detach skilled workers from the UMW was a failure,[53] and although it surely aggravated the UMW, that union was in no sense forced out of the AFL by the crafts. When the UMW left the AFL it was not walking the plank. Rather the union was abandoning what it took to be a sinking ship, and it had ripe plans for a more powerful and more modern vessel than it thought the AFL then represented.

The UMW was particularly anxious to see the steel workers organized and their wages and other conditions improved, because this would make it easier for the captive miners (coal miners employed in mines owned by the steel companies) to improve and to stabilize their own conditions. The size of the UMW's financial contribution to steel organizing is a revelation, in part, of this interest. Of $1,500,00 spent by the Steel Workers' Organizing Committee, $1,078,000 came from the coffers of the UMW.[54] The union also furnished some of the top SWOC leaders—for example, Philip Murray, Van Bittner, William Mitch, and John Brophy.[55] For the same reason that the ACW and ILGWU were interested in organizing the textile industry, so also was the UMW interested in organizing the oil, gas, coke, and chemical industries.

IBEW, Boilersmakers, Molders, Operating Engineers, Firemen and Oilers, Technical Engineers, Hod Carriers, Carpenters, Blacksmiths, and Railway Clerks.

[52]UMW, *Proceedings, 1936,* pp. 177–178. See also AFL, *Proceedings, 1935,* pp. 642–643.

[53]It should be noted, however, that the same principle for which the crafts contended in 1935 was incorporated in the Taft-Hartley Act twelve years later. Taft-Hartley permits any craft group in an established bargaining unit to withdraw from that unit, through the so-called "Globe" election process, and function independently. The extent to which this process has disturbed industrial bargaining units and the degree of its importance in encouraging the merger of the AFL and CIO are subjects worthy of research.

[54]Harris, *Labor's Civil War,* p. 125.

[55]*Ibid.;* Levinson, *Labor on the March,* p. 189.

The UMW gave the Petroleum Workers' Organizing Committee its chairman, Thomas Kennedy. Twenty CIO organizers were assigned to the UMW for work among the gas, coke, and chemical workers.[56]

It is possible to impute to Lewis the lust for power in itself as a motive in his seeking and winning a seat on the Executive Council, his headship of the CIO, and his direction of Labor's Non-Partisan League. In the latter instance his objective may have been the Vice-Presidency of the United States.[57] At any rate, it does appear that many of the AFL faithful found greater strength with which to fight the CIO in their conviction that Lewis was obsessed with an unreasoning rule-or-ruin attitude.[58]

Even though Lewis may have had an inordinate craving for power, it flies in the face of the whole progressive movement to assert that the CIO was an unnecessary accident committed by Lewis and that it had no nobler claim to life than his machinations for personal power gave it.[59] The CIO was a logical outcome of a broadly conceived and broadly supported reform movement, and, further, Lewis himself surely saw the CIO as something more than a vehicle for his own greater glory. And while admitting that Lewis was easily the brightest star in the CIO firmament,[60] one can still believe that he would not have twinkled at all without the support he received from other capable leaders. Actually it is possible to contend that unions were more important than particular individuals in the rearing of the CIO and that in the absence of Lewis, Hillman, and associates, other leaders of their unions would sooner or later have headed a reform movement. Of course, the bedrock of the progressive movement was economic change, particularly the

[56]Levinson, *Labor on the March*, pp. 253–254, 275.

[57]Josephson, *Sidney Hillman*, p. 474.

[58]For example, see IAM, *Proceedings, 1936*, p. 130; Bridge, Structural and Ornamental Iron Workers, *Proceedings, 1936*, pp. 215–220; Boilermakers, *Proceedings, 1937*, pp. 328–329; *Journal of Electrical Workers and Operators*, Vol. 35, March 1936, pp. 114–115, Vol. 35, April 1936, p. 160, Vol. 37, February 1938, pp. 67, 106; *Boilermakers' Journal*, Vol. 49, December 1937, pp. 317–318.

[59]See IAM, *Proceedings, 1936*, p. 130; Bridge, Structural and Ornamental Iron Workers, *Proceedings, 1936*, pp. 215–220.

[60]Lewis himself is quoted as having boasted that he "conceived and built the CIO." Saul Alinsky, *An Unauthorized Biography*, p. 237.

rise of the mass-production industries. Without that development, the AFL could have continued serenely in the Gompersian mold.

As for the expectations of individuals other than Lewis, it seems plausible that Hillman, although a dedicated progressive, also calculated that the value of his personal stock would rise quicker and to a higher peak if transferred to the CIO. He had brought his union into the AFL only in 1933, and he had therefore developed little loyalty to that body. In terms of seniority, he was far from being the most eligible candidate for a position on the AFL Executive Council. As a member of the CIO, on the other hand, he stood only a rung or two below the leadership summit. Dubinsky, Zaritsky, and particularly Howard seem not to have regarded the progressive movement as a recipe for their personal success. Hoping to convince others of the purity of his purpose in advocating an increase in the size of the Executive Council, Howard vowed in 1932 that he sought no position for himself, and recalling this statement, he turned down a vice-presidential nomination tendered him at San Francisco.[61] So strong was Howard's liberal spirit that he even risked (and lost) the leadership of his own union on the question of his CIO partisanship.

In summary, it can be stated that in its origins the CIO was truly a progressive reform movement which sought an adjustment of labor's policies all along the line. And although the leading progressives were out to clip the wings of the leading conservatives, their impulse to action was born more of altruism than of egoism. The conflict was between the industrial unionists and the craft unionists, the lesser skilled and the higher skilled, the mass-production workers and the building and metal tradesmen, the "politicals" and those who thought almost exclusively in terms of collective bargaining, those who wanted to assure minimum standards even to the unorganized and those who thought in terms of particular union groups, those who eschewed bias toward Negro and women workers and those who practiced it, young leaders and old leaders, those who favored low dues and those who favored high dues, idealists who took in all society at a glance and business unionists who specialized in advancing the interests of a craft at a

[61]AFL, *Proceedings, 1934*, pp. 689–691.

time. In the last analysis, the conflict was between the progressives and the conservatives.

III

It is, of course, true that even before the establishment of the Congress of Industrial Organizations in 1938 the AFL leadership had, in words if not always in deeds, regretfully if not enthusiastically, begun to alter and to broaden traditional policies. Economic progress created a need for such policy changes, but in the absence of voluntary action by the AFL leadership, the phenomena which actually forced the changes were the progressive movement, the Great Depression, and the New Deal recovery and reform program. As early as 1932, for example, the Executive Council, under pressure created by disastrous unemployment and the unrest of many AFL unions, officially blessed the idea of a government-sponsored program of unemployment insurance; in 1933 the Council supported and advocated legal enforcement of organizing and bargaining rights; in 1934 craftsmen approved for the first time the creation of new unions in the mass-production industries; and in 1937 they unequivocally committed the AFL to organizing on a full industrial as well as a craft basis.

Perhaps it was the success of the CIO, after as well as before 1938, which was more important than anything else in awakening the conservative leaders of the labor movement to a full sense of their duties and to a genuine appreciation of the urgent need for revising traditional principles. AFL-CIO President George Meany has himself testified that the "great departure of the organizations from the AFL to form the CIO did one thing. . . . I can assure you it woke up some people in the AFL—and that's a matter of record, not just talk. From that point of view, it was good."[62] As a consequence of the AFL's awakening, there were by the early 1950's no longer any really fundamental policy differences between that organization and the CIO, and this fact greatly facilitated the reunification of the labor movement in 1955. One can see in the program and in the activities of the AFL-CIO the fruition of the

[62]Quoted in John Herling, "Where Does Big Labor Go from Here?", *Collier's,* Vol. 137, Jan. 20, 1956, p. 54.

goals announced and championed by the labor progressives twenty and even thirty years ago. Although they cannot be given full credit for the changes wrought, their contribution was indeed momentous.

Whether the new progressive unionism can be explained in terms of the pure and simple unionism of the Gompers' tradition is perhaps an academic question (involving the matter of how far a point can be stretched without making it invisible). One can easily maintain that modern unionism is still moored to "job-conscious" principles;[63] on the other hand, Gompers himself would probably be a stranger in the union halls of today. Perhaps the term "social unionism" would therefore more appropriately describe the present labor movement.[64] Regardless of the label one prefers, however, the fact remains that today organized labor is doing different things in different ways than it was in the pre-New Deal era. And not all of the old-timers have in fact been able to keep the pace. John P. Frey, who learned more than a little bit from Samuel Gompers, wrote with dismay in 1952 that the "American labor movement has wandered far afield from some of the basic principles which Gompers taught.... Under Mr. Gompers' régime, the trade union movement stood upon its own feet; now it must depend, to a large extent, upon the support of State and Federal administration."[65] These echoes from the past reach only a tiny audience in today's house of labor. Progressivism is now master of labor's estate.

[63]Selig Perlman, "The Basic Philosophy of the American Labor Movement," *Annals of the American Academy of Political and Social Science,* Vol. 241, March 1951, pp. 59–63.

[64]Joseph Shister, "Unresolved Problems and New Paths for American Labor," *Industrial and Labor Relations Review,* Vol. 9, April 1956, pp. 453–456.

[65]Frey was not sure what the results of this change would be, but he was sure that "those who place over-much dependence upon the existence of Federal agencies are without the inherent strength upon which...a trade union movement" must be built. Frey to Scott Bartlett (unidentified), April 28, 1952, Container 2, Frey Papers.

Bibliography

MANUSCRIPT SOURCES

CIO File. Microfilm, AFL-CIO Archives.
Convention Files of the AFL. Microfilm, AFL-CIO Archives.
Copy Books of William Green. Microfilm, NYSSILR Library.
Files of the Congress of Industrial Organizations.
Henry and Edsel Ford Papers. Ford Motor Company Archives.
John B. Andrews Papers. NYSSILR Library.
John P. Frey Papers. Library of Congress.
National Union Files. Microfilm, AFL-CIO Archives.
Notes on Brookwood Labor College supplied to the writer by Helen Norton Starr.
Saposs, David J. Notes on "Trade Union Organization Work," Brookwood Labor College, 1929–1930. Typed copy in the writer's possession.

GOVERNMENT DOCUMENTS

Congressional Record. 66 Cong., 2 Sess. to 73 Cong., 2 Sess.
Department of Labor, Bureau of Labor Statistics. Characteristics of Company Unions 1935, Bulletin No. 634. Washington, 1938.
Department of Labor. Proceedings of the First Industrial Conference (Called by the President), October 6 to 23, 1919. Washington, 1920.
House Committee on Ways and Means. Stabilization of Bituminous Coal Mining Industry, Hearings before a Subcommittee of the Committee on Ways and Means on H. R. 8479. 74 Cong., 1 Sess. Washington, 1935.
House Committee on Ways and Means. Tariff Readjustment—1929, Hearings before the Committee on Ways and Means. 18 vols. 70 Cong., 2 Sess. Washington, 1929.
Saposs, David J., and Sol Davison. Structure of AFL Unions. Research

Memorandum No. 8. Washington: National Labor Relations Board, Division of Economic Research, 1939.

Senate Committee on Finance. *Investigation of Economic Problems, Hearings before the Committee on Finance Pursuant to S. Res. 315.* 72 Cong., 2 Sess. Washington, 1933.

Senate Committee on Finance. *Tariff Act of 1929, Hearings before a Subcommittee of the Committee on Finance on H. R. 2667.* 18 vols. 71 Cong., 1 Sess. Washington, 1929.

Senate Committee on the Judiciary. *Thirty-Hour Work Week, Hearings before a Subcommittee of the Committee on the Judiciary on S. 5267.* Washington, 1933.

Statutes at Large of the United States of America. Vols. XLIV–XLVIII. Washington, 1927–1934.

Thirty-Hour Week Bill. House Report No. 124. 73 Cong., 1 Sess. Washington, 1934.

NEWSPAPERS

AFL-CIO News. 1957.
Daily Worker. 1928.
Labor Action. 1933–1934.
New Leader. 1929.
New York Times. 1919–1938.
Washington Daily News. 1931.

CONVENTION PROCEEDINGS OF TRADE UNIONS AND OTHER LABOR GROUPS

Amalgamated Association of Iron, Steel and Tin Workers of North America. *Proceedings, 1932–1936.*

Amalgamated Association of Street and Electric Railway Employees of America. *Proceedings, 1929.*

Amalgamated Clothing Workers of America. *Proceedings, 1922–1938.*

American Federation of Full Fashioned Hosiery Workers. *Proceedings, 1920–1928.*

American Federation of Labor. *Proceedings, 1886–1947.*

American Federation of Teachers. *Proceedings, 1923–1938.*

Annual Conference of Teachers in Workers' Education. *Proceedings, 1924–1930.*

Brotherhood of Maintenance of Way Employees. *Proceedings, 1925.*

Brotherhood of Painters, Decorators and Paperhangers of America. *Proceedings, 1925–1929.*

Brotherhood of Railway Carmen of America. *Proceedings, 1925, 1929.*

Brotherhood of Railway and Steamship Clerks, Freight Handlers, Express and Station Employees. *Proceedings, 1922–1935.*

International Association of Bridge, Structural and Ornamental Iron Workers. *Proceedings, 1924–1940.*

International Association of Machinists. *Proceedings, 1920–1936.*

International Association of Oil Field, Gas Well and Refinery Workers of America. *Proceedings, 1934–1938.*

International Brotherhood of Boilermakers, Iron Ship Builders, Welders and Helpers of America. *Proceedings, 1920–1937.*

International Brotherhood of Electrical Workers. *Proceedings, 1919–1929.*

International Brotherhood of Teamsters, Chauffeurs, Stablemen and Helpers of America. *Proceedings, 1925, 1930, 1935.*

International Ladies' Garment Workers' Union. *Proceedings, 1920–1940.*

International Ladies' Garment Workers' Union. *Report of the General Executive Board to the 29th Convention, 1956.* New York: ILGWU, 1956.

International Molders' Union of North America. *Proceedings, 1923 1928, 1934.*

International Typographical Union. *Proceedings, 1920–1940.*

International Union of Mine, Mill and Smelter Workers. *Proceedings, 1928–1938.*

International Union United Automobile Workers of America. *Proceedings, 1936, 1937.*

International Union of United Brewery, Flour, Cereal and Soft Drink Workers of America. *Proceedings, 1920–1939.*

Metal Trades Department. *Proceedings, 1919–1938.*

Order of Railroad Telegraphers. *Proceedings, 1927.*

United Brotherhood of Carpenters and Joiners of America. *Proceedings, 1924, 1928, 1936.*

United Cloth Hat and Cap Makers of North America. *Proceedings, 1921, 1923.* Cloth Hat, Cap and Millinery Workers' International Union. *Proceedings, 1925, 1927, 1929.*

United Electrical and Radio Workers of America. *Proceedings, 1936–1938.*

United Hatters, Cap and Millinery Workers' International Union. *Proceedings, 1934, 1936.*

United Mine Workers of America. *Proceedings, 1921–1938.*

United Rubber Workers of America. *Proceedings, 1935–1938.*

United Textile Workers of America. *Proceedings, 1921–1939.*

Upholsterers' International Union of North America. *Proceedings, 1927.*

Workers' Education Bureau of America. *Proceedings, 1921–1927.*

————. *Outline of the Major Actions Taken by the 6th Annual Convention of the Workers' Education Bureau, 1929.*

293

————. *Report of the Executive Committee, Workers' Education Bureau of America, to the National Convention, 1925, 1927, 1929.*

TRADE UNION CONSTITUTIONS AND LAWS

Constitution and By-Laws of the International Brotherhood of Boilermakers, Iron Ship Builders and Helpers of America, 1920–1944.

Constitution of the Grand Lodge, District and Local Lodges, International Association of Machinists, 1921–1937.

Constitution of the International Association of Bridge, Structural and Ornamental Iron Workers, 1919–1936.

Constitution of the International Brotherhood of Electrical Workers, 1919–1941.

Constitution and Ritual of the Sheet Metal Workers' International Association, 1915–1938.

Constitution and Rules of Order of the International Molders' Union of North America, 1918–1938.

International and Local Laws Governing the Metal Polishers, Buffers, Platers, and Helpers International Union, 1919–1938.

Laws of the Pattern Makers' League of North America, 1926–1938.

BOOKS AND PAMPHLETS

Alinsky, Saul David. *John L. Lewis, An Unauthorized Biography.* New York: Putnam, 1949.

American Labor Year Book, 1921–1922, 1923–1924, 1925, 1926, 1927, 1929, 1930. New York: The Rand School of Social Science, 1922–1931.

Bernstein, Irving. *The New Deal Collective Bargaining Policy.* Berkeley: University of California Press, 1950.

Brooks, Robert R. R. *As Steel Goes...Unionism in a Basic Industry.* New Haven: Yale University Press, 1940.

Brookwood Labor College. *Brookwood, 1927.* [Katonah, New York: Brookwood Labor College, 1927?]

————. *The Only Resident Trade Union Educational Institution in the United States.* [Katonah, New York: Brookwood Labor College, 1927?]

Budenz, Louis Francis. *Men Without Faces, The Communist Conspiracy in the U. S. A.* New York: Harper, 1950.

Cannon, James P. *The History of American Trotskyism: Report of a Participant.* New York: Pioneer, 1944.

Carnes, Cecil. *John L. Lewis, Leader of Labor.* New York: Robert Speller, 1936.

Christie, Robert A. *Empire in Wood: A History of the Carpenters' Union.* Ithaca: New York State School of Industrial and Labor Relations at Cornell University, 1956.

The Commission of Inquiry, The Interchurch World Movement. *Report on the Steel Strike of 1919*. New York: Harcourt, Brace & Howe, 1920.

Committee for Industrial Organization. *The Case for Industrial Organization*. Washington: CIO, 1936.

————. *The C.I.O.; What it is and How it Came to Be*. Washington: CIO. [1941]

————. *The Program of the C.I.O.* Washington: CIO. [1937?]

Commons, John R., ed. *Trade Unionism and Labor Problems*. 2nd series. Boston: Ginn, 1921.

Davis, Horace B. *Labor and Steel*. New York: International, 1933.

Douglas, Paul H. *Real Wages in the United States, 1890–1926*. Boston: Houghton Mifflin, 1930.

Draper, Theodore. *The Roots of American Communism*. New York: Viking, 1957.

Dunn, Robert W. *The Americanization of Labor; The Employer's Offensive Against the Trade Unions*. New York: International, 1927.

Easely, Ralph M. *Proposed Industrial Relations Department, The National Civic Federation*. New York: NCF, 1924.

Eby, Herbert O. *The Labor Relations Act in the Courts*. New York: Harper, 1943.

Faulkner, Harold Underwood. *American Economic History*. 6th ed. New York: Harper, 1949.

Foster, William Z. *History of the Communist Party of the United States*. New York: International, 1952.

Gaer, Joseph. *The First Round; The Story of the CIO Political Action Committee*. New York: Duell, Sloan & Pearce, 1944.

Gitlow, Benjamin. *I Confess; The Truth About American Communism*. New York: E. P. Dutton, 1940.

Gompers, Samuel. *Seventy Years of Life and Labour: An Autobiography*. 2 vols. New York: E. P. Dutton, 1925.

Gray, Justin. *The Inside Story of the Legion*. New York: Boni & Gaer, 1948.

Green, Marguerite. *The National Civic Federation and the American Labor Movement, 1900–1925*. Washington: The Catholic University of America Press, 1956.

Gregory, Charles O. *Labor and the Law*. New York: W. W. Norton, 1946.

Hardman, J. B. S., ed. *American Labor Dynamics in the Light of Post-War Developments*. New York: Harcourt, Brace, 1928.

Harris, Herbert. *Labor's Civil War*. New York: A. A. Knopf, 1940.

Helbing, Albert Theodore. *The Departments of the American Federation of Labor*. Baltimore: Johns Hopkins Univ. Press, 1931.

Higgins, George Gilmary. *Voluntarism in Organized Labor in the United States, 1930–1940*. Washington: The Catholic University of America Press, 1944.

Hoxie, Robert Franklin. *Trade Unionism in the United States*. New York: D. Appleton, 1923.

ILGWU. *The Position of the International Ladies' Garment Workers' Union in Relation to CIO and AFL, 1934–1938*. [New York]: ILGWU. 1938.

Industrial Relations Research Association. *Interpreting the Labor Movement*. Madison: IRRA, 1952.

Jensen, Vernon H. *Lumber and Labor*. New York: Farrar & Rinehart, 1945.

Jones, Richard Seelye. *A History of the American Legion*. Indianapolis: Bobbs-Merrill, 1946.

Josephson, Matthew. *Sidney Hillman, Statesman of American Labor*. New York: Doubleday, 1952.

Levinson, Edward. *Labor on the March*. New York: Harper, 1938.

Lewis, John L. *The Future of Organized Labor*. Washington: CIO. [1935?]

Lorwin, Lewis L. *The American Federation of Labor, History, Policies, and Prospects*. Washington: The Brookings Institution, 1933.

————, and Arthur Wubnig. *Labor Relations Boards: The Regulation of Collective Bargaining under the National Industrial Recovery Act*. Washington: The Brookings Institution, 1935.

Lyon, Leverett S., *et al. The National Recovery Administration, An Analysis and Appraisal*. Washington: The Brookings Institution, 1935.

McKelvey, Jean Trepp. *AFL Attitudes Toward Production, 1900–1932*. Ithaca: New York State School of Industrial and Labor Relations at Cornell University, 1952.

Military Training Camps Association. *The Military Training Camps Association of the United States*. [Chicago: MTCA, 1925?]

Millis, Harry A., and Emily Clark Brown. *From the Wagner Act to Taft-Hartley, A Study of National Labor Policy and Labor Relations*. Chicago: University of Chicago Press, 1950.

Mitchell, John. *Organized Labor: Its Problems, Purposes and Ideals and the Present and Future of American Wage Earners*. Philadelphia: American Book and Bible House, 1903.

Moley, Raymond. *After Seven Years*. New York: Harper, 1939.

Nadworny, Milton J. *Scientific Management and the Unions, 1900–1932*. Cambridge: Harvard University Press, 1955.

National Industrial Conference Board. *Collective Bargaining Through Employee Representation*. New York: NICB, 1933.

O'Neal, James, and G. A. Werner. *American Communism, A Critical*

Analysis of Its Origins, Development and Programs. rev. ed. New York: E. P. Dutton, 1947.

Perkins, Frances. *The Roosevelt I Knew.* New York: Viking, 1946.

Perlman, Selig. *A Theory of the Labor Movement.* New York: Macmillan, 1928.

————, and Philip Taft. *History of Labor in the United States, 1896–1932.* Vol. IV, *Labor Movements.* New York: Macmillan, 1935.

Peterson, Florence. *American Labor Unions: What They are and How They Work.* rev. ed. New York: Harper, 1952.

President's Research Committee. *Recent Social Trends in the United States; Report of the President's Research Committee on Social Trends.* 2 vols. New York: McGraw-Hill, 1933.

Reed, Louis S. *The Labor Philosophy of Samuel Gompers.* New York: Columbia University Press, 1930.

Robinson, Jesse S. *The Amalgamated Association of Iron, Steel and Tin Workers.* Baltimore: Johns Hopkins Press, 1920.

Roos, Charles Frederick. *NRA Economic Planning.* Bloomington, Ind: Principia, 1937.

Saposs, David J. *Left Wing Unionism: A Study of Radical Policies and Tactics.* New York: International, 1926.

Shannon, David A. *The Socialist Party of America.* New York: Macmillan, 1955.

Soule, George Henry. *Prosperity Decade; from War to Depression: 1917–1929.* New York: Rinehart, 1947.

Stolberg, Benjamin. *The Story of the CIO.* New York: Viking, 1938.

Taft, Philip. *The A. F. of L. in the Time of Gompers.* 1st ed. New York: Harper, 1957.

Walsh, J. Raymond. *C.I.O.; Industrial Unionism in Action.* New York: W. W. Norton, 1937.

Weaver, Robert Clifton. *Negro Labor, A National Problem.* New York: Harcourt, Brace, 1946.

Woll, Matthew. *Labor Industry and Government.* New York: D. Appleton-Century, 1935.

Wolman, Leo. *Ebb and Flow in Trade Unionism.* New York: National Bureau of Economic Research, 1936.

ARTICLES

"Academic Labor." *Time:* Vol. 30, Nov. 29, 1937, pp. 66–67.

"Across the Continent." *Labor Age:* Vol. 20, February 1931, pp. 21–22.

"The Active Workers Conference, A Report." *Labor Age:* Vol. 21, April 1932, pp. 4–6.

"AFL-CIO Merger Agreement." *Industrial and Labor Relations Review:* Vol. 9, October 1955, pp. 122–124.

"A. F. of L. Adopts Flexible Policy." *Journal of Electrical Workers and Operators:* Vol. 33, February 1934, pp. 56, 96.

"The A. F. of L. in Convention." *Advance:* Vol. 20, October 1934, p. 3.

"A. F. of L. Sweat Shops and Slave Drivers Kill Wages-Hours Bill." *United Mine Workers' Journal:* Vol. 49, Jan. 1, 1938, p. 15.

"A. F. of L. Ultimatum Rejected by International Convention." *United Mine Workers' Journal:* Vol. 47, Feb. 15, 1936, pp. 10–15.

"All Hands on Deck." *Labor Age:* Vol. 19, November 1930, pp. 19–21.

"The American Federation of Labor is Wrong, Says All America." *Brewery Worker:* Vol. 49, April 28, 1934, pp. 5, 7.

"American Labor Party Launched in New York State." *Advance:* Vol. 22, August 1936, p. 14.

"As Others See Us." *Brookwood Review:* Vol. 5, December–January 1926–1927, p. 2.

Bailer, Lloyd H. "Organized Labor and Racial Minorities." *Annals of the American Academy of Political and Social Science:* Vol. 241, March 1951, pp. 101–107.

"The Balance Sheet of Labor." *World Tomorrow:* Vol. 13, October 1930, p. 391.

Barkin, Solomon. "Collective Bargaining and Section 7(b) of NIRA." *Annals of the American Academy of Political and Social Science:* Vol. 184, March 1936, pp. 169–175.

Barnett, George E. "American Trade Unionism and Social Insurance." *American Economic Review:* Vol. 23, March 1933, pp. 1–15.

Beard, Charles A. "Confusion Rules in Washington." *Current History:* Vol. 41, December 1934, pp. 333–339.

Berry, George L. "Industrial Versus Craft Unions." *American Pressman:* Vol. 45, August 1935, pp. 15–17.

————. "The Legion and Labor." *American Federationist:* Vol. 29, September 1922, pp. 680–681.

"Board Members Resent Green's Slap at Their Integrity." *United Mine Workers' Journal:* Vol. 47, Dec. 1, 1936, pp. 3–4.

Bowen, George J. "What is Industrial Unionism?" *Machinists' Monthly Journal:* Vol. 48, March 1936, pp. 176–177.

Bright, Leonard. "C.P.L.A. Organizes." *Labor Age:* Vol. 18, June 1929, pp. 3–6.

"Bring School to Workers." *Labor Age:* Vol. 17, October 1928, p. 11.

"British Evaluate Industrial Unionism." *Journal of Electrical Workers and Operators:* Vol. 35, March 1936, pp. 95–97, 134.

Brooks, Joseph. "Silk Workers March." *Labor Age:* Vol. 21, June 1932, p. 10.

"The Brookwood Alumni Protest." *Labor Age:* Vol. 18, March 1929, p. 32.

"Brookwood Directors Review Year's Work." *Machinists' Monthly Journal:* Vol. 38, June 1926, pp. 259–260.

"Brookwood Trade Union Summer School." *School and Society:* Vol. 19, June 21, 1924, p. 727.

"Brookwood Turned Right and We Left." *Labor Age:* Vol. 22, February–March 1933, p. 17.

"Brookwood's 'Youth' Institute." *Labor Age:* Vol. 16, December 1927, p. 11.

Brown, Harvey W. "Initiation Fees and the July Referendum." *Machinists' Monthly Journal:* Vol. 47, July 1955, pp. 400–401.

————. "The Uninformed Critics of Craft Unionism." *Machinists' Monthly Journal:* Vol. 48, January 1936, pp. 46–48.

Bruere, Robert W. "Resolution No. 68; the A. F. of L. Goes in For Research." *Survey:* Vol. 57, Dec. 15, 1926, pp. 374–375.

Budenz, Louis F. "'Czar' Brandle: A Study in 'Success.'" *Labor Age:* Vol. 21, June 1932, pp. 15–17.

————. "Industrial Unionism vs. Company Unionism?" *Labor Age:* Vol. 15, October 1926, pp. 5–7.

————. "Ohio Jobless Take State Action." *Labor Age:* Vol. 21, November 1932, pp. 4–5.

————. "Why Industrial Unionism?" *Labor Age:* Vol. 16, June 1927, p. 23.

Budish, J. M. "Breaking the Vicious Circle." *Labor Age:* Vol. 17, May 1928, pp. 2–3.

————. "Selling Unionism—To Whom?" *Labor Age:* Vol. 18, April 1929, pp. 17–19.

————. "Whose Business?" *Labor Age:* Vol. 17, June 1928, pp. 7–8.

"Busy March Meeting of Council." *Journal of Electrical Workers and Operators:* Vol. 34, April 1935, pp. 158, 185.

Calhoun, Arthur W. "Mr. Calhoun and Brookwood." *New Republic:* Vol. 60, Aug. 21, 1929, p. 20.

"A Challenge to Militants." *Labor Age:* Vol. 20, November 1931, pp. 4–5.

"The Challenge to Progressives, An Editorial Statement." *Labor Age:* Vol. 18, February 1929, pp. 3–7.

"C.I.O.-A.F. of L. Peace Parley is in Recess Again." *United Mine Workers' Journal:* Vol. 48, Nov. 15, 1937, p. 4.

"C.I.O. Challenges A.F. of L. to Cooperate for Unity." *United Mine Workers' Journal:* Vol. 48, Oct. 15, 1937, pp. 3–4.

"C.I.O. Leaders Decide to Set Up Permanent Organization." *United Mine Workers' Journal:* Vol. 49, May 1, 1938, pp. 3–4.

"C.I.O. Makes Plans for Progress and Wide Organization." *United Mine Workers' Journal:* Vol. 48, March 15, 1937, p. 3.

"C.I.O. to Hold Convention to Form Permanent Organization." *United Mine Workers' Journal:* Vol. 49, Oct. 15, 1938, p. 6.

Clark, Marjorie R. "Recent History of Labor Organization." *Annals of the American Academy of Political and Social Science:* Vol. 184, March 1936, pp. 161–168.

Cohn, Fannia M. "Are Women Organizable?" *Labor Age:* Vol. 16, March 1927, pp. 18–19.

————. "Company Unions and Workers' Education." *Labor Age:* Vol. 15, October 1926, pp. 2–4.

Commons, John R. "Tendencies in Trade Union Development in the United States." *International Labor Review:* Vol. 5, June 1922, pp. 855–887.

————. "Workers Education and the Universities." *American Federationist:* Vol. 34, April 1927, pp. 424–426.

"A Composite Picture of What American Labor is Thinking and Doing." *Labor Age:* Vol. 10, November 1921, p. ii.

Conlon, Peter J. "Unemployment Insurance Legislation." *Machinists' Monthly Journal:* Vol. 43, February 1931, pp. 70–74.

"Convention Summary." *American Teacher:* Vol. 20, September–October 1935, pp. 20, 34.

Cook, Cara. "Brookwood Stuff That Counts." *Labor Age:* Vol. 16, September 1927, pp. 5–7.

Cooper, Lyle W. "The American Federation of Labor and the Intellectuals." *Political Science Quarterly:* Vol. 43, September 1928, pp. 388–407.

————. "The American Labor Movement in Prosperity and Depression." *American Economic Review:* Vol. 22, December 1932, pp. 641–659.

————. "Organized Labor and the Trust." *Journal of Political Economy:* Vol. 36, December 1928, pp. 720–739.

————. "The Tariff and Organized Labor." *American Economic Review:* Vol. 20, June 1930, pp. 210–225.

"Council of Gas and By-Product Coke Workers." *American Federationist:* Vol. 42, December 1935, pp. 1328–1338.

"C.P.L.A. Activities Extended." *Labor Age:* Vol. 19, January 1930, pp. 19–21.

"C.P.L.A. Covers Wide Area." *Labor Age:* Vol. 19, March 1930, pp. 22–24.

"C.P.L.A. 'Goes to the Country.'" *Labor Age:* Vol. 20, March 1931, pp. 21–22.

"C.P.L.A. on the Job." *Labor Age:* Vol. 18, July 1929, pp. 19–20.

"C.P.L.A. Potent Force in Labor World." *Labor Age:* Vol. 19, April 1930, pp. 21–24.

"C.P.L.A. Unemployment Insurance Bills." *Labor Age:* Vol. 19, December 1930, pp. 21–23.

"C.P.L.A. Wins Warm Approval." *Labor Age:* Vol. 18, December 1929, pp. 11–13.

Craig, Leonard. "Workers' Education in Pennsylvania." *Machinists' Monthly Journal:* Vol. 40, October 1928, p. 667.

Dabney, Thomas L. "Negro Workers at the Crossroads." *Labor Age:* Vol. 16, February 1927, pp. 8–10.

"Detailed and Tabulated Vote of Local Unions Upon Referendum Propositions I, II, III." *Journal of Electrical Workers and Operators:* Vol. 34, August 1935, p. 334.

Dewey, John. "Freedom in Workers Education." *American Teacher:* Vol. 13, January 1929, pp. 1–4.

————. "Labor Politics and Labor Education." *New Republic:* Vol. 57, Jan. 9, 1929, pp. 211–214.

Duffy, Frank. "Industrial Unionism a Failure." *Carpenter:* Vol. 56, February 1936, pp. 2–5.

Dunn, Robert W. "Company Union in Oil." *Labor Age:* Vol. 15, April 1926, pp. 15–18.

Ebert, Justus. "What Have the Progressives Done?" *Labor Age:* Vol. 18, July 1929, pp. 6–8.

"Endowment Campaign Generously Endorsed." *Brookwood Review:* Vol. 5, October–November 1926, p. 1.

Epstein, Abraham. "Pensions for Aged Workers." *Labor Age:* Vol. 16, December 1927, p. 20.

"Establish Scholarship to Honor Jim Maurer." *Brookwood Review:* Vol. 5, February–March 1927, p. 1.

"Executive Council Vote Will Not Affect C.I.O. Activities." *United Mine Workers' Journal:* Vol. 47, Aug. 15, 1936, pp. 3–4.

"$50,050 for Building and Endowment Fund in Sight." *Brookwood Review:* Vol. 6, February–March 1928, p. 1.

"The Fight Grows Hotter." *Labor Age:* Vol. 20, June 1931, pp. 20–22.

Fitch, John A. "The Clash Over Industrial Unionism." *Survey Graphic:* Vol. 25, January 1936, pp. 39–42.

"Five Rounds." *Time:* Vol. 26, Oct. 28, 1935, p. 12.

Flexner, Jean A. "Brookwood." *New Republic:* Vol. 43, Aug. 5, 1925, pp. 287–289.

"Friends Rally to Brookwood." *Labor Age:* Vol. 17, October 1928, p. 21.

"The Future in the Miners' Union." *Labor Age:* Vol. 20, May 1931, pp. 3, 26.

Galenson, Walter. "The Unionization of the American Steel Industry." *International Review of Social History:* Vol. 1, Part 1, 1956, pp. 8–40.

"Government Must Step in When Industry Fails, Green Declares." *Machinists' Monthly Journal:* Vol. 48, May 1936, p. 275.

Green, William. "A Great American Institution." *American Teacher:* Vol. 20, November–December 1935, pp. 3–4.

————. "Labor's Opportunity and Responsibility." *American Federationist:* Vol. 40, July 1933, pp. 692–694.

————. "Lumber Workers Organize." *American Federationist:* Vol. 41, September 1934, pp. 962–966.

————. "What Labor Wants." *American Federationist:* Vol. 42, March 1935, pp. 248–253.

"Green's 'Irrefutable Charges' Answered." *Brookwood Review:* Vol. 7, December–January 1928–1929, pp. 1, 4.

Hardman, J. B. S. "Communism in America." *New Republic:* Vol. 64, Sept. 3, 1930, pp. 63–67.

"Healthy Response to Latest C.P.L.A. Campaign." *Labor Age:* Vol. 19, July 1930, pp. 22–24.

Herling, John. "Where Does Big Labor Go From Here?" *Collier's:* Vol. 137, Jan. 20, 1956, pp. 54–55, 58–61.

Hillman, Sidney. "The NRA, Labor and Recovery." *Annals of the American Academy of Political and Social Science:* Vol. 172, March 1934, pp. 70–75.

"Hitherto Unconsidered Matters in Dispute." *Journal of Electrical Workers and Operators:* Vol. 36, January 1937, pp. 3–5, 37.

Hoagland, Henry E. "Trade Unionism in the Iron Industry: A Decadent Organization." *Quarterly Journal of Economics:* Vol. 31, August 1917, pp. 674–689.

Hochman, Julius. "High Tide at Atlantic City." *Nation:* Vol. 141, Nov. 6, 1935, pp. 539–540.

Holland, Rebecca. "A Brookwood Class in Action." *Brookwood Review:* Vol. 2, April 15, 1924, p. 6.

"How Can We Organize the Big Industries?" *Brookwood Review:* Vol. 6, September 1927, pp. 1, 5.

" 'How to Organize' Conference." *Labor Age:* Vol. 16, November 1927, p. 10.

Hutchinson, Margaret. "Organize the Unorganized." *Labor Age:* Vol. 17, February 1928, pp. 4–5.

"I.B.E.W. States Position on Radio Workers." *Journal of Electrical Workers and Operators:* Vol. 35, March 1936, pp. 100, 134.

"I.L.G.W.U. Builds Body and Brain." *American Teacher:* Vol. 20, September–October 1935, pp. 23–24.

"Industrial Unionism." Samuel Gompers to A. Rosebury, April 2, 1912, *American Federationist:* Vol. 19, May 1912, pp. 371–375.

"International Import of Labor Symbolized." *Brookwood Review:* Vol. 4, May–June 1926, p. 3.

" 'Jim' Maurer's Warning." *Labor Age:* Vol. 18, May 1929, pp. 3–4.

Jenkins, Albert H. "Machinist Makes Good in Man-Sized Job." *Machinists' Monthly Journal:* Vol. 47, February 1935, p. 74.

"Just What Was What in the CIO-AFL Unity Negotiations." *Advance:* Vol. 24, February 1938, pp. 16–17.

Kennedy, Thomas. "Industrial Unionism, Miners' Experience Approves It." *Labor Age:* Vol. 15, September 1926, pp. 2–3.

"Labor Leaders Criticize A. F. of L. Stand on Industrial Unionism." *Brewery Worker:* Vol. 50, July 13, 1935, p. 1.

"Labor Places Ban on Brookwood College and Asks Trade Unions to Sever All Connections With It." *United Mine Workers' Journal:* Vol. 39, Sept. 1, 1928, p. 11.

"Labor Publication Society." *Labor Age:* Vol. 10, November 1921, p. ii.

"Labor Summer School." *Brookwood Review:* Vol. 2, April 15, 1924, p. 8.

Laidler, Harry W. "The Future of the Review." *Socialist Review:* Vol. 10, April–May 1921, pp. 33–35.

"Last Call for the 'How to Organize' Conference." *Labor Age:* Vol. 17, January 1928, p. 5.

"Leader's Mistake." *New Republic:* Vol. 38, March 12, 1924, pp. 60–61.

Lefkowitz, Abraham. "A. F. of L.'s Demands Spurned." *Labor Age:* Vol. 17, August 1928, p. 12.

Lever, E. J. "Labor College of Philadelphia." *Machinists' Monthly Journal:* Vol. 37, April 1925, pp. 203–204.

————. "Shop Economics." *Machinists' Monthly Journal:* Vol. 37, December 1925, pp. 662, 687–688.

————. "What of the Metal Trades?" *Labor Age:* Vol. 15, August 1926, pp. 11–13.

Lewis, John L. "Labor and the National Recovery Administration." *Annals of the American Academy of Political and Social Science:* Vol. 172, March 1934, pp. 58–63.

" 'Little Caesar' Broach and Local 3." *Labor Age:* Vol. 21, April 1932, pp. 15–16.

McCabe, David. "The American Federation of Labor and the NIRA." *Annals of the American Academy of Political and Social Science:* Vol. 179, May 1935, pp. 144–151.

McNamara, Andrew T. "The Baltimore Conference on Unemployment." *Machinists' Monthly Journal:* Vol. 40, June 1928, pp. 354–355.

Maurer, James H. "Autobiography of a Labor Leader." *Atlantic:* Vol. 131, May–June 1923, pp. 577–584, 742–750.

"The Mess Craft Unionism is In." *Brewery Worker:* Vol. 49, March 24, 1934, p. 5.

Metcalf, Henry C. "Employee Representation." *Annals of the Ameri-*

can *Academy of Political and Social Science:* Vol. 184, March 1936, pp. 184–191.

"The Miners' Crisis...And Progress." *Labor Age:* Vol. 20, April 1931, p. 3.

Mittelman, Edward B. "Basis for American Federation of Labor Opposition to Amalgamation and Politics at Portland." *Journal of Political Economy:* Vol. 32, February 1924, pp. 86–100.

Mufson, Israel. "American Supremacy Tested." *Labor Age:* Vol. 17, September 1928, p. 20.

————. "Conference on Hours of Work and Unemployment." *American Federationist:* Vol. 35, September 1928, pp. 1109–1110.

————. "The Depression Hits the Southwest." *Labor Age:* Vol. 20, June 1931, pp. 23, 29.

————. "Machinists, Weeds, and Brookwood Labor College." *Machinists' Monthly Journal:* Vol. 38, May 1926, pp. 202–203, 239.

————. "Organizing the Unorganized." *Survey:* Vol. 59, March 15, 1928, pp. 757–758.

————. "The Rank and File Convention at St. Louis." *Labor Age:* Vol. 20, May 1931, pp. 11–13.

————. "The Story of the Stuffed Shirt." *Labor Age:* Vol. 20, March 1931, pp. 10–11.

————. "What of Union Management Cooperation?" *Labor Age:* Vol. 15, October 1926, pp. 8–10.

Muste, A. J. "Appeal to Youth!" *Labor Age:* Vol. 16, July 1927, pp. 2–4.

————. "Back Up Labor Education! *Labor Age:* Vol. 17, July 1928, pp. 5–6.

————. "Brookwood Labor Institute." *American Federationist:* Vol. 32, October 1925, pp. 939–942.

————. "Brookwood—Labor's Training Camp." *Amalgamated Illustrated Almanac:* 1924, p. 153.

————. "The C.P.L.A. Policy in Unions." *Labor Age:* Vol. 20, July 1931, pp. 8–10.

————. "The Crisis in the Miners' Union." *Labor Age:* Vol. 19, March 1930, pp. 4–8.

————. "Do We Need a New Political Party in the United States?" *Labor Age:* Vol. 20, April 1931, pp. 10–13.

————. "From Dawn to Dusk at Katonah." *Labor Age:* Vol. 14, October 1925, pp. 1–3.

————. "Getting the Most Out of Your Organizer." *Labor Age:* Vol. 16, November 1927, pp. 15–17.

————. "Independent Political Action—Yes, But What Kind?" *Labor Age:* Vol. 19, June 1930, pp. 6–8.

————. "The Kind of Unionism That Will Not Organize the Basic Industries." *Labor Age:* Vol. 16, April 1927, pp. 2–4.

————. "The Kind of Unionism That Will Organize the Basic Industries." *Labor Age:* Vol. 16, May 1927, pp. 7–9.

————. "Mother Throws Out the Baby." *Labor Age:* Vol. 17, October 1928, pp. 20–21.

————. "Nothing to Offer?" *Labor Age:* Vol. 17, March 1928, pp. 2–4.

————. "Organizing and the Organizer." *Brookwood Review:* Vol. 6, September 1927, pp. 3–4.

————. "Peace or Pep?" *Labor Age:* Vol. 17, January 1928, pp. 6–7.

————. "Progressives on the March." *Labor Age:* Vol. 18, June 1929, pp. 7–8.

————. "Where do American Workers Stand Today?" *Labor Age:* Vol. 20, March 1931, pp. 14–15, 29.

————. "Who Closed Door on Negotiations?" *Brookwood Review:* Vol. 7, February–April 1929, p. 2.

————. "Who's Your Organizer?" *Labor Age:* Vol. 16, October 1927, pp. 9–10.

————. "Whose Job?" *Labor Age:* Vol. 17, February 1928, pp. 6–8.

"Muste Quits in Rift Over C.P.L.A." *Brookwood Review:* Vol. 11, May 1933, p. 1, 3.

"The National Executive Committee and Officers." *Labor Age:* Vol. 21, September 1932, p. 5.

National Industrial Conference Board. "Individual and Collective Bargaining Under the N.I.R.A., A Statistical Study of Present Practice." *NICB Bulletin:* November 1933.

"Negroes Can Organize is Conference Feature." *Brookwood Review:* Vol. 5, June–July 1927, pp. 1, 3.

"A New Federation Needed?" *Brewery Worker:* Vol. 49, April 21, 1934, pp. 5, 7.

"News Notes About Our Branches." *Labor Age:* Vol. 21, June 1932, p. 18.

"Norman Thomas, The Communists and Our Political Discussion." *Labor Age:* Vol. 20, September 1931, pp. 3–4.

Norton, Helen G. "Brookwood in Its First Decade." *Labor Age:* Vol. 20, May 1931, pp. 18–19.

————. "Brookwood's Summer Institute, 1927." Survey: Vol. 59, Oct. 15, 1927, pp. 95–96.

————. "Considering the Negro." *Labor Age:* Vol. 16, August 1927, p. 11.

————. "Young Labor Speaks Up." *Survey:* Vol. 60, June 15, 1928, p. 346.

"One Year and After." *Labor Age:* Vol. 19, May 1930, pp. 21–24.

"Organized Labor Movement, 1929 to 1937." *Monthly Labor Review:* Vol. 44, January–February 1937, pp. 1–9, 292–318.

"Our Negro Brothers." *Labor Age:* Vol. 16, June 1927, p. 22.

"Our Unemployment Insurance Bills." *Labor Age:* Vol. 19, October 1930, pp. 22–23.

"Peace Conference Takes a Recess After Three Days Session." *United Mine Workers' Journal:* Vol. 48, Nov. 1, 1937, pp. 3–4, 23.

Perlman, Selig. "The Basic Philosophy of the American Labor Movement." *Annals of the American Academy of Political and Social Science:* Vol. 241, March 1951, pp. 57–63.

"President Green Summoned Before International Board." *United Mine Workers' Journal:* Vol. 47, Nov. 15, 1936, p. 4.

"President Lewis Delivers Radio Address on the 'Future of Organized Labor.'" *United Mine Workers' Journal:* Dec. 15, 1935, pp. 20–21.

"Progressives Forge Ahead." *Labor Age:* Vol. 18, October 1929, pp. 21–23.

"Radicals; Mr. Garland's Million." *Time:* Vol. 37, June 20, 1941, p. 17.

"Recovery Program." *American Federationist:* Vol. 40, June 1933, pp. 627–631.

"Red Purge Due in Labor Ranks." *Machinists' Monthly Journal:* Vol. 49, May 1937, pp. 314–316.

"Report on Political Organization." *Labor Age:* Vol. 20, August 1931, pp. 4–7, 28.

"A Resident Labor College at Katonah, New York." *School and Society:* Vol. 13, April 9, 1921, pp. 436–437.

"Result of July, 1935, Referendum." *Machinists' Monthly Journal,* Vol. 47, September 1935, p. 511.

"The Road to Ruin." *Brewery Worker:* Vol. 49, May 12, 1934, p. 5.

Saposs, David J. "Employee Representation as Labor Organization." *Annals of the American Academy of Political and Social Science:* Vol. 184, March 1936, pp. 192–198.

————. "Industrial Unionism." *Journal of Political Economy:* Vol. 43, February 1935, pp. 69–83.

————. "Labor." *American Journal of Sociology:* Vol. 34, May 1929, pp. 1012–1020.

————. "The Line-Up at Cincinnati." *Labor Age:* Vol. 11, September 1922, pp. 18–20.

Schlossberg, Joseph. "An Object Lesson." *Advance:* Vol. 20, March 1934, pp. 11–19.

"Seaside Subjects." *Time:* Vol. 26, Oct. 21, 1935, p. 11.

Sehl, Charles. "An Analysis of 'Lewis' Brand of Industrial Unionism.'" *Machinists' Monthly Journal:* Vol. 48, February 1936, pp. 74–75, 124.

Seidman, Joel. "Efforts Toward Merger, 1935–1955." *Industrial and Labor Relations Review:* Vol. 9, April 1956, pp. 353–370.

Shafran, Eva. "A Good Beginning—What Next?" *Labor Age:* Vol. 17, March 1928, pp. 4–5.

Shister, Joseph. "Unresolved Problems and New Paths for America Labor." *Industrial and Labor Relations Review:* Vol. 9, April 195(pp. 447–457.

"A Soldier-Labor Alliance." *Literary Digest:* Vol. 75, Nov. 4, 1922, p[12–13.

"Speed Industrial Unionism!" *Labor Age:* Vol. 17, March 1928, p. 24.

Stanley, Louis. "Communist Dual Unionism." *Labor Age:* Vol. 1£ October 1929, pp. 9–11.

"Statement of Policy of the C.P.L.A." *Labor Age:* Vol. 18, June 192♀ pp. 6–7.

"The Statement of Purpose Which Brookwood Repudiated." *Labo Age:* Vol. 22, February–March 1933, pp. 16–17.

Stoffels, William. "Revolt of Illinois Miners." *Labor Age:* Vol. 21, Se[tember 1932, pp. 6–7.

Stolberg, Benjamin. "A Government in Search of a Labor Movement.' *Scribner's Magazine:* Vol. 94, December 1933, pp. 345–350.

————. "Muddled Millions." *Saturday Evening Post:* Vol. 213, Feb 15, 1941, pp. 9–10, 88–90, 92.

"Studies in Curriculum." *Brookwood Review:* Vol. 1, April 15, 192♂ p. 2.

"Suspension Order of CIO Unions Effective September 5." *Justice* Vol. 18, Aug. 15, 1936, p. 3.

Swenson, Rinehart J. "The Chamber of Commerce and the New Deal.' *Annals of the American Academy of Political and Social Science* Vol. 179, May 1935, pp. 136–143.

Tippett, Tom. "A New Miners' Union in Illinois." *Labor Age:* Vol 21, October 1932, pp. 4–5.

"Two Millions for Brookwood is Aim." *Brookwood Review:* Vol. 4 May–June 1926, p. 1.

"Unemployment Insurance." *Labor Age:* Vol. 20, January 1931, pp. 22–23.

"Unemployment Insurance—The Next Step." *Labor Age:* Vol. 19, June 1930, pp. 21–24.

"Vital Problems Discussed by International Officers in Timely Labor Day Statements." *United Mine Workers' Journal:* Vol. 45, Sept. 1, 1934, pp. 3–4.

"We Must Heed Public Opinion." *Brewery Worker:* Vol. 49, March 31, 1934, p. 5.

Weir, Ernest T. "New Responsibilities of Industry and Labor." *Annals of the American Academy of Political and Social Science:* Vol. 172, March 1934, pp. 76–87.

" 'Welfare Capitalism' Conference Subject." *Brookwood Review:* Vol. 6, June–August 1928, pp. 1, 4.

"What is Industrial Unionism?" *Advance:* Vol. 20, January 1934, p. 19.

"Whither Brookwood." *Labor Age:* Vol. 22, February–March 1933, pp. 14–16.

"Who is This A. J. Muste?" *World Tomorrow:* Vol. 12, June 1929, pp. 250–254.

"Wider Fields Open for C.P.L.A." *Labor Age:* Vol. 20, April 1931, pp. 21–22.

Widick, B. J. "Two Defeats for William Green." *Nation:* Vol. 141, Oct. 9, 1935, pp. 412–413.

"William Green is Ousted From the Union by the Board." *United Mine Workers' Journal:* Vol. 49, June 1, 1938, p. 5.

Wilson, Walter. "Labor Fights the American Legion." *American Mercury:* Vol. 34, January 1935, pp. 1–11.

Wolfson, Theresa. "Schools the Miners Keep." *Survey:* Vol. 56, June 1, 1926, pp. 308–310, 332.

Woll, Matthew. "The Economic Policy Proposed by American Labor." *Annals of the American Academy of Political and Social Science:* Vol. 154, March 1931, pp. 85–88.

————. "The International Labor Office: A Criticism." *Current History:* Vol. 31, January 1930, pp. 683–689.

————. "Labor and the Tariff." *Boilermakers' Journal:* Vol. 41, August 1929, pp. 321–324.

————. "Organized Labor Demands Repeal of the Sherman Act." *Annals of the American Academy of Political and Social Science:* Vol. 147, January 1930, pp. 185–188.

————. "Organized Labor's Volteface on the Trusts." *Current History:* Vol. 25, October 1926, pp. 68–71.

" 'Youth' Conference Covers Much Ground." *Brookwood Review:* Vol. 6, December–January 1927–1828, pp. 1, 2.

Ziegler, Phil E. "Why Amalgamation?" *Labor Age:* Vol. 12, August 1923, pp. 1–3.

Index

Absolon, William, 113, 115
Aircraft industry, 34, 177, 198
Alexander, Magnus W., 64
Aluminum industry, 34, 193, 200
Amalgamation, *see* Industrial unionism and American Federation of Labor
American Federation of Labor, founding philosophy, 4–9; Scranton declaration and organizing, 13 ff.; attitude toward legal enforcement of right to organize and bargain collectively, 36–8; attitude toward social insurance legislation, 38–40; national trade departments of, 54; policy of union-management cooperation, 55–67, 78–81; relations with National Civic Federation, 67–71; military alignments of in 1920's, 71–8; isolationist foreign policy of in 1920's, 81–2; attitude toward tariff and government regulation of business in 1920's, 82; appraisal of strategy of defense, 82–5; and Workers' Education Bureau, 88–90; and Brookwood Labor College, 111 ff.; attitude toward workers' education, 121–4; reaction to formation of Conference for Progressive Labor Action, 129–30; reaction to Great Depression, 136–41; and New Deal collective bargaining policy, 142–50; organizing response to Sec. 7(a) of NIRA, 150–8; results of organizing, 1933–1935, 158–64; Washington convention, 179–81; Washington conference, 181–6, 189–90; San Francisco convention, 193–7; Executive Council meetings in 1935, 197 ff.; Atlantic City convention, 204–11; and formation of Committee for Industrial Organization, 213 ff.; suspension of CIO unions by, 228–37; and Hatters' peace plan, 239–40; Tampa convention, 240–3; change of policy in regard to organizing and industrial unionism, 247–50; Cincinnati conference, 250–3; 1937 unity negotiations with CIO, 256–67; definite split with CIO unions, 267–9; and social legislation in 1930's, 271–2; and labor political action in 1930's, 272–5; and Negro workers in 1930's, 275–6; and National Civic Federation in 1930's, 277; and International Federation of Trade Unions, 277
American Federation of Labor-Congress of Industrial Organizations, 74, 263, 289–90
American Federationist, 70–1, 277
American Labor party, 273–4
American Labor Union, 35
American Legion, 72–4
American Railway Union, 174
Army Industrial College, 71
Army War College, 71, 72
Atlantic City convention, Executive Council report to, 204–5; resolutions on structural issue introduced, 205–6; majority report of Committee on Resolutions, 206; minority report, 207; debate on minority report, 207–9; vote on minority report, 209; and United Rubber Workers' request for industrial jurisdiction, 209–10; Lewis-Hutcheson scuffle, 210; and United Automobile Workers' request for industrial jurisdiction, 211; Green's closing remarks to, 211
Automobile, Aircraft and Vehicle Workers, United, 24
Automobile industry, 13, 193; organizing campaign of 1914, 23; campaign of 1926–1928, 57–63; special obstacles to organizing, 170; General Motors-United Automobile Workers' contract, 244–5; *see also* Automobile, Aircraft and Vehicle Workers; Automobile Workers,

Date Due